PERFECTLY FULFILLED
PROPHECIES
AND THE
DESTINY OF MANKIND

DR. PETER ZHAO

Perfectly Fulfilled Prophecies and the Destiny of Mankind
Copyright © 2024 by Dr. Peter Zhao.

All rights reserved. No part of this publication may be reproduced, distributed, or transmitted in any form or by any means, including photocopying, recording, or other electronic or mechanical methods, without the written consent of the publisher. The only exceptions are for brief quotations included in critical reviews and other noncommercial uses permitted by copyright law.

MILTON & HUGO L.L.C.
4407 Park Ave., Suite 5
Union City, NJ 07087, USA

Website: *www. miltonandhugo.com*
Hotline: *1- 888-778-0033*
Email: *info@miltonandhugo.com*

Ordering Information:
Quantity sales. Special discounts are granted to corporations, associations, and other organizations. For more information on these discounts, please reach out to the publisher using the contact information provided above.

Library of Congress Control Number:		2024926651
ISBN-13:	979-8-89285-349-1	[Paperback Edition]
	979-8-89285-348-4	[Digital Edition]

Rev. date: 11/22/2024

CONTENTS

Acknowledgments ix
List of Figures and Tables xi
Preface xiii
Introduction xvii

PART 1	Lunar and Solar Calendars.. 1
Chapter 1	Introduction to Lunar and Solar Calendars 3
Chapter 2	The Hebrew Lunisolar Calendar 5
Chapter 3	Babylonian Lunisolar Calendar 12
Chapter 4	Enoch's Solar Calendar 15
Chapter 5	Chinese Lunisolar Calendar 17

PART 2	World Chronology 19
Chapter 6	Introduction to the World Chronology 21
Chapter 7	The Chronology of the Ancient Near East.................. 24
Chapter 8	Chronology of Babylon and Persia 37
Chapter 9	Chinese Chronology.. 41
Chapter 10	Biblical Chronology.. 64
Chapter 11	Chronology of Judah and Israel's Kings 81
Chapter 12	The Length of Yeshua's Ministry 104
Chapter 13	Herod's Reign 111
Chapter 14	Sabbatical and Jubilee Years 114

PART 3	Biblical Numerical Prophecies....................................123
Chapter 15	Introduction to Biblical Prophecies 125
Chapter 16	Daniel's Prophecy on the 69th Week: Messiah Anointed 130
Chapter 17	Daniel's Prophecy on the First Half of the 70th Week 136
Chapter 18	Daniel's Prophecy on Suspension of 2300 Evening-Morning Burnt Offerings 141
Chapter 19	Daniel's Prophecy on the 1290th Day........................ 145

Chapter 20	Prophetic Dream of Nebuchadnezzar on Seven Times 153
Chapter 21	Daniel's Prophecy on the Period of Shattering the Holy People's Power 162
Chapter 22	Ezekiel's Prophecy on the Population of Israel at its Re-birth 166
Chapter 23	Ezekiel's Prophecy on Two Destructions of Jerusalem 168
Chapter 24	Jeremiah's Prophecy on 17 Shekels of Silver 171
Chapter 25	Jeremiah's Prophecy on 70 Years 176
Chapter 26	Isaiah's Prophecy on the Breaking of Ephraim in 65 Years 182
Chapter 27	Zechariah's Prophecy on Striking down the Little Sheep 186
Chapter 28	Prophecy of Moses on the Ages of the World and the Universe 193

PART 4	Proof for Yeshua Being the Messiah 201
Chapter 29	Introduction to the True Messiah 203
Chapter 30	Yeshua Messiah from Some Descriptive Prophecies ... 207
Chapter 31	Yeshua's Prophecy on His Burial and Resurrection 216
Chapter 32	Yeshua's Prophecy on the Destruction of the Holy Temple 226
Chapter 33	Yeshua's Prophecies on His First Century Return 232
Chapter 34	Birthday of Yeshua Messiah 245

PART 5	End-Time Prophecies: World Destiny 255
Chapter 35	Introduction to the End-Time Prophecies 257
Chapter 36	Daniel's Prophecy on the Last Half of the 70th Week .259
Chapter 37	Daniel's Prophecy on the 1335th Day 262
Chapter 38	Daniel's Prophecy on the Fourth Beast 265
Chapter 39	Possible Interpretation of Chapters 12-13 of Revelation 269
Chapter 40	Possible Sequence of the World Events in Near Future 276

APPENDIXES ... 283

Appendix A   The Delta-T Parameter for Eclipses ... 285
Appendix B   Paper on the Nonconstancy of the Speed of Light .. 287
Appendix C   Paper on Zhao's Modified Cosmological Model 303
Appendix D   Hebrew Lunisolar Calendars of Important Years ... 317

Julian year 3971 BC ... 318
Julian year 3970 BC ... 320
Julian year 2315 BC ... 322
Julian year 2314 BC ... 324
Julian year 1550 BC ... 326
Julian year 1542 BC ... 328
Julian year 1534 BC ... 330
Julian year 1457 BC ... 332
Julian year 977 BC ... 334
Julian year 976 BC ... 336
Julian year 969 BC ... 338
Julian year 605 BC ... 340
Julian year 599 BC ... 342
Julian year 598 BC ... 344
Julian year 597 BC ... 346
Julian year 587 BC ... 348
Julian year 586 BC ... 350
Julian year 573 BC ... 352
Julian year 572 BC ... 354
Julian year 561 BC ... 356
Julian year 457 BC ... 358
Julian year 168 BC ... 360
Julian year 165 BC ... 362
Julian year 38 BC ... 364
Julian year 37 BC ... 366
Julian year 31 BC ... 368
Julian year 6 BC ... 370
Julian year 5 BC ... 372
Julian year 4 BC ... 374
Julian year 26 AD ... 376
Julian year 27 AD ... 378

Julian year 28 AD 380
Julian year 29 AD 382
Julian year 30 AD 384
Julian year 31 AD 386
Julian year 32 AD 388
Julian year 33 AD 390
Julian year 67 AD 392
Julian year 70 AD 394
Julian year 269 AD 396
Julian year 277 AD 398
Julian year 688 AD 400
Julian year 692 AD 402
Julian year 771 AD 404
Julian year 1948 406
Julian year 2019 408
Julian year 2020 410
Julian year 2021 412
Julian year 2022 414
Julian year 2023 416
Julian year 2024 418
Julian year 2025 420
Julian year 2026 422
Julian year 2027 424
Julian year 2028 426
Julian year 2029 428
Julian year 2030 430
Julian year 2031 432
Julian year 3030 434
Julian year 3031 436

Index of Scriptures 439

ACKNOWLEDGMENTS

I acknowledge two special people in the writing of this book. First, I am very grateful to my wife, Grace Chao, who has been my faithful companion physically and spiritually for over 20 years. During the last four years, she has been very patient with me while I spent so many hours in front of my computer. Because of my busy schedule, we have not had much family quality time together. She has fully supported my commitment to writing this book. Second, I would like to thank my son, Joshua who is the first reader of the book. He has carefully copyedited and formatted it even when he was busy with finals.

I would also like to thank my dear friend Pieder Beeli and his wife Emily Beeli for critically reading the first edition of the book. Without their critical eyes, some misprinted numbers would not have been detected. Because of their valuable comments and suggestions, the second edition of the book has been significantly improved. Because Dr. Beeli has a strong background in science, religion, history, and politics, he fully appreciates the value of this book. Here, I quote the introductory part of his comment on the book (with no modification):

This book concerns the
- greatest book ever written: The Bible
- greatest subject for which we can have mathematical and numerical vetting to test hypotheses: Biblical prophecy
- most wonderful conclusion imaginable for this subject (all numerical biblical prophecies have been perfectly fulfilled)

In order to do so, this book makes breakthrough discoveries in
- basic physics (radiation rates, variable speed of light, …)
- cosmology (interpretation of "cold dark matter" to have negative mass, solves the lithium isotope abundance problem…)
- transforming the ancient Chinese documents referencing astronomical phenomena and biblical events like Noah's flood, onto a calendar, a task which a major national effort by the Chinese government involving some 200 experts failed to accomplish (Ch. 9)
- the embedding of God's holy numbers 7, 10 into the astronomical calendar and created the inferred intercalation scheme for Enoch's calendar, the calendar used by Essenes, including Jesus (Ch. 4)
- correcting Israel's calendar and to reveal that Israel's birthday in 1948 occurred on a special feast day and the establishment of an Israeli state fulfills a prophecy of Daniel 12:5-7 "… a time, times and half a time" (1260 years) [chapter 21].

Finally, the content has a sense of urgency (e.g., be prepared for possible cataclysmic events beginning 16 September 2023).

This book may be one of the crowning achievements of human civilization. It is made by someone who was born into a large and poor family in China.

LIST OF FIGURES AND TABLES

Figures:
1. Schematic diagram for the destiny of mankind 23
2. Venus rose on 21 February 1541 BC in Babylon, as predicted from the Stellarium program. 48
3. Predicted solar eclipse on 19 March 1493 BC, observed in Babylon. 52
4. Predicted solar eclipse on 21 September 2666 BC, observed in Xin-Zheng city. 65
5. Predicted solar eclipse on 18 November 2324 BC, observed in Beijing, one of the important cities in Ji-Zhou, the territory of Emperor Yao. 67
6. Venus appeared in the Yi constellation on 18 August 2334 BC (upper panel) and Venus came out of the Yi constellation in the evening from the west on 25 June 2306 BC (lower panel) 68
7. Venus came out of *Fang* (*Scorpius*) on 14 September 2271 BC 69
8. Predicted solar eclipse on 22 November 2167 BC, observed in Zhenxun 71
9. Predicted lunar eclipse on 7 December 1144 BC in Anyang 73
10. Predicted solar eclipse on 15 June 763 BC, observed in Samaria. Jupiter was visible during the eclipse around noontime. 106
11. Schematic diagram of Daniel's numerical prophecies 159
12. A comet-like long-star was like a sword (red), which appeared on 29 July 65 AD and was recorded by the Chinese astronomer. 221
13. Sky view from Baghdad on 9 March 5 BC, as predicted from the Stellarium Program 230
14. Predicted sky view from Xi-An, China on 9 March 5 BC 231
15. Predicted sky view from Jerusalem on April 19 of 5 BC 232

16. Schematic diagram of Daniel's 70 weeks 238
17. The prophetic periods from the books of Revelation and Daniel 240

Tables:
1. The Annual Festivals of Yehowah God 32
2. The Names of Lunar Months in Different Lunisolar Calendars 35
3. The Chronology of the Ancient Near East 44
4. Chronology of Babylon and Persia 54
5. Kings of Tyre 56
6. Chronology of China 60
7. Biblical Chronology 75
8. Relative Chronology of Judah and Israel's Kings 96
9. Absolute Chronology of Judah and Israel's Kings 98
10. Harvest Times in Ancient Israel 113
11. Important Events in Sabbatical Years 122
12. Annihilation of the Jewish Population of Europe in Pre-War Countries, Complied by Lucy S. Dewildowicz 180
13. Annihilation of the Jewish Population of Europe in Pre-War Countries, Complied by the Federal Agency for Civic Education of Germany 181
14. Possible Sequence of the World Events in Near Future 255

PREFACE

People have predicted the end of the world for almost 2,000 years, but none of these predictions has been actualized. Some so-called prophets of God or Biblical scholars in the last twenty years have claimed some specific dates for the end of the world. These claims have circulated on the internet and several social media platforms, such as YouTube and Facebook. Some even prophesied that the world would end on 23 September 2016 or 23 September 2017. While these predicted times have already passed, the end has not yet come. So what is the true destiny of the world? Is there divine influence on the direction of the world and human affairs? Is the end of the world really possible?

Having been a firm atheist before I came to the United States in 1988, I started to believe in the God of Abraham, Isaac, and Jacob, and Yeshua Messiah (Jesus Christ) in 1993 when I was convinced by some Biblical prophecies. I received my Ph.D. in Physics from University of Zürich in 1997 under the supervision of Alex Müller who received the Physics Nobel Prize in 1987. Since 2002, I have been a physics professor in the field of condensed matter physics. I have published over 110 physics papers in highly reputed journals, including two Nature magazine articles (first author) and 12 invited book chapters.

Prior to 2014, I had never seriously tried to write a book outside physics. During my sabbatical leave in that year, I had planned on writing a scientific book on the microscopic mechanism of high-temperature superconductivity, the subject I had studied for many years. But during dinner one day, a few Bible verses I had previously read about the resurrection of Yeshua struck me. I jumped up and told my wife that the Bible was wrong!! I explained to my startled wife that the most important prophecy about the resurrection of Yeshua, which was foretold by Yeshua himself, was not fulfilled at all. I was experiencing **a crisis of faith**!

We have been told that Yeshua was crucified in the afternoon on Friday, buried just before sunset, and rose again before sunrise on Sunday. According to this, from the time of his burial to the time of his resurrection, there would have been only 36 hours at most. This is totally inconsistent with Matthew 12:38-40, "Then certain of the scribes and of the Pharisees answered, saying, master, we would see a sign from you. But he answered and said unto them, 'An evil and adulterous generation seeks after a sign; and there shall no sign be given to it, but the sign of the prophet Jonah: For as Jonah was **three days and three nights** in the whale's belly; so shall the Son of Man be **three days and three nights** in the heart of the earth.'"

Yeshua's own words clearly prophesized that he would be **three days and three nights** (72 hours) in the grave just as Jonah was **three days and three nights** in the fish's belly. If this crucial prophecy were not fulfilled, Yeshua would not be the Messiah and the foundation of Christianity would completely collapse.

My heart for seeking the truth motivated me to investigate this issue thoroughly. I then started to search the Internet for any discussion on this issue. Indeed, I found numerous discussions, and the majority have attempted to maintain the traditional Friday crucifixion and Sunday resurrection. Few have raised objections to the traditional view with the proposition of a Wednesday crucifixion and Saturday resurrection. After I carefully studied the Gospels and the Old Testament Scriptures for many hours, I eventually solved the mystery. I found that this prophecy was in fact fulfilled perfectly, and that the traditional view of Yeshua's crucifixion day was wrong and unbiblical. Since then, I have diligently and critically studied the Scriptures. Instead of writing my book on high-temperature superconductivity, I spent hours upon hours each day studying Biblical prophecies, the world's chronology and history, astronomy, and cosmology.

Perhaps I was moved by the Spirit of God to study numerical prophecies in the Bible. The numerical prophecies are special prophecies with clearly stated numbers, such as prophetic periods. If the numerical prophecies are fulfilled perfectly, the prophecies must come from the true God who is the most powerful and above all things. There are several reasons for the superior credibility of the numerical prophecies. First, no human, under any circumstance, has his own power to predict any future event to happen at an exact time. Only a true and almighty god or deity would have the power to guarantee the perfect fulfillment of his own words foretold by his prophets. A prophecy from a less powerful god would be made void by the most-high God. Second, a numerical prophecy can have only one correct interpretation. Third, the probability for perfect fulfillments of multiple numerical prophecies is nearly zero if these prophecies were not from the most-high God. In contrast, number-free descriptive prophecies are less credible. This is because the interpretations to the descriptive prophecies are quite subjective and could vary significantly with interpreters. These prophecies could even be fulfilled apparently in fabricated stories by someone who would attempt to establish a false religion. For these reasons, only the prophecies containing numerical information can be used to prove or disprove a true religion that comes from the most-high God.

For almost four years, I have diligently studied Biblical prophecies and chronology, as well as the history of the Middle East, of Europe, and of China. I have also investigated the Hebrew, Babylonian, Islamic, and Chinese calendars, as well as Enoch's calendar. I have been able to determine the true Biblical chronology that aligns perfectly with historical records and other secular chronologies such as the Chinese chronology. I have precisely reconstructed the Chinese chronology back to 2716 BC by taking advantage of the astronomical phenomena recorded concurrently with corresponding historical events. With an uncertainty of less than 6 months, the Chinese chronology I have constructed aligns perfectly with all the astronomical phenomena. One remarkable discovery is that the year of Noah's flood in our Biblical chronology is the same as that of China's "great flood," which took place in the 61st year of Emperor Yao, who will be introduced later in this book.

With these accurate chronologies in hand, I can clearly show that all the Biblical numerical prophecies have been perfectly fulfilled. I have also unveiled the prophecies that are yet to be fulfilled by making an end-time chronology. The true destiny of the world can be found from these end-time prophecies that are based solely on the Bible.

The perfect fulfillments of the Biblical numerical prophecies tell us that Yehowah, the most-high God of the Hebrew Bible, is the most-high God of the universe, orchestrating the history of the whole world. The direction of the whole world has been and will continue to be influenced by the most-high God.

INTRODUCTION

Most people are not concerned with the destiny of the world because this issue may be too complex to comprehend, or simply because it seems irrelevant to their daily lives. There are other difficult questions as to the existence of immortal souls and invisible things such as demons, angels, and gods. If they exist, do they influence and direct our visible world? More particularly, if God does exist, what kind of plan does He have for us?

There are essentially three groups of people in the world who have different views on the existence of God or gods and on the origin of the universe and life (in this book the capitalized "God" is used to refer to the most-high God only). The first group believes in the existence of God or gods. For example, the people who place their faith in Christianity, Judaism, or Islam believe that there is only one God who created the heavens, the earth, and life, although some doctrines in these religions are fundamentally repulsive to each other. The second group is made up of atheists who refuse to believe in the existence of supernatural beings. They believe that the universe was generated through natural processes such as the one described by the big-bang cosmology. The third group is composed of agnostics who believe that nothing can be known about the existence and nature of a god or anything beyond the material world.

The atheists argue that they do not believe in God or gods because there is a lack of empirical evidence and because there are inconsistent revelations. They argue that the burden of proof lies not on them to disprove the existence of gods but on the theist to provide rationale for theism.

In this book, we will provide arguments for theism. We hope that our arguments are convincing enough to change the minds of even the atheists and agnostics. The following fundamental questions will be addressed in detail:

1. Can the theists provide consistent and convincing evidence for the existence of God/gods?
2. What is the Name of the only true God if the universe and life were created by Him only?
3. Is the God in the Hebrew Bible the only true God who created the universe and life?
4. Is Yeshua the true Messiah and the Son of God?
5. Can we construct the world's true chronology without error?
6. Does God direct the history of the whole world?
7. Were all the past numerical prophecies in the Bible fulfilled perfectly?
8. What is the destiny of the world based on the Biblical end-time numerical prophecies and on the true Biblical chronology?

We must begin by addressing the first three questions, since all other questions are related to these three fundamental ones. We can prove that the God of the Hebrew Bible is the true Creator and God of the universe by demonstrating:

1. All the past Biblical numerical prophecies foretold by the true prophets of God were perfectly fulfilled in the time frames specified in the prophecies.
2. The historical events recorded in the Bible are consistent with reliable extra-biblical historical records and astronomical phenomena.
3. The Biblical chronology agrees perfectly with the Chinese chronology, which is constructed here, based on the concurrently recorded historical events and astronomical phenomena.
4. God's perfect number of 7 and its multiples are coded in the orbital motions of the Moon and the Earth. The number 7 has also been coded in the history of the world. The age of the universe in the human view is almost exactly equal to 7^{12} years,

which is constructed from the two perfect numbers of 7 and 12 in the Bible.
5. The God of the Hebrew Bible has directed world history.
6. The science presented in the Bible agrees with the confirmed physical laws.
7. The Word of God does not contradict Itself.

Several Biblical chronologies have been established by some Biblical scholars. However, none of these previous Biblical chronologies is consistent with all the relevant verses in the entire Hebrew Bible nor with the recorded astronomical phenomena and reliable extra-biblical records. In contrast, our current Biblical chronology agrees with all the relevant verses in the complete Hebrew Bible and with the reliable extra-biblical records.

The details of our construction of the Biblical chronology will be presented in Chapter 10. The chronology basically includes the following important events:

1. Adam was created on Nisan 1 (the first day of the first month in the Hebrew calendar) of 3970 BC, which was on April 15 (Friday) in the Julian solar calendar.
2. Noah's flood began on 25 May 2315 BC. Noah and his family left the ark on 3 June 2314 BC, which was one week before Sivan 6 (the 6th day of the third lunar month, the feast day of Pentecost). After Noah's family and all the living creatures had completely left the ark, possibly on the Feast of Pentecost, God established the covenant with Noah and put a rainbow in the sky as a sign of His everlasting covenant with every living creature on the earth.
3. The Israelites were brought out of Egypt on 25 April (Sunday) 1457 BC.
4. Solomon began to build the temple of God on 16 April 977 BC.
5. Solomon dedicated the temple to God on 24 September (Saturday) 969 BC [on Tishri 15 (the 15th day of the 7th month) in the Hebrew calendar].

6. Samaria, the capital of the northern kingdom of Israel, was taken by the Assyrians in the fall of 721 BC.
7. Daniel and his friends were carried to Babylon in the spring of 606 BC (the first exile).
8. Ezekiel, along with about 3,000 priests and prophets, was exiled into Babylon between 29 March and 13 April 598 BC (the second exile). At the same time, the continual daily sacrifices were suspended.
9. Jehoiachin, together with about 10,000 officers, fighting men, and all the craftsmen and artisans, was carried into Babylon on 16 March 597 BC (the third exile).
10. Zedekiah and 831 others were carried into Babylon between July 19 and 27 of 587 BC (the fourth exile), which was near the end of the eighteenth year of Nebuchadnezzar's reign.
11. Solomon's temple was destroyed by the Babylonians on 28 July (Friday) 587 BC, which was on Av 10 (the 10th day of the fifth month in the Hebrew calendar).
12. Yeshua was born on 9 March 5 BC, which was on Nisan 1 (the first day of the first month in the Hebrew calendar).
13. Yeshua was baptized on 24 February 27 AD.
14. John the Baptist proclaimed Yeshua to be the Lamb of God on 5 April 27 AD (Nisan 10).
15. Yeshua was crucified on 5 April (Wednesday) 30 AD and buried just before sunset on April 5. He died at the end of the fourth day, in the fourth year of a sabbatical cycle, and at the end of the fourth millennium from the creation of Adam.
16. Yeshua resurrected just before sunset of 8 April (at the end of Saturday) 30 AD.
17. Yeshua ascended to heaven on 26 May 30 AD, which fell on the Feast of Pentecost.
18. The Church was born on the Feast of Pentecost in 30 AD.
19. The second temple was destroyed on 5 August (Sunday) 70 AD, which was also on Av 10 (the 10th day of the fifth month in the Hebrew calendar).
20. The Dome of the Rock was constructed in the beginning of 69 AH (Islamic calendar), which was after 5 July 688 AD. The

date was most likely on July 12, the 9th day of the 5th month in the Hebrew calendar.
21. The construction of the Dome of the Rock was completed in the end of 72 AH, which was before 24 May 692 AD. The date was most likely on May 8, right after the end of the Islamic Festival of the Sacrifice.
22. Israel's declaration of independence was on 14 May 1948, which was exactly on Sivan 6, on the Feast of Pentecost (if a correct Hebrew lunisolar calendar is used).
23. Israel's war of independence ended on 10 March 1949.

In addition to being consistent with the historical records, our current Biblical chronology reveals the following remarkable features:

1. It shows that many important historical events in the world took place during sabbatical years (see Chapter 14).
2. It shows that Yeshua was crucified and buried at the end of the fourth millennium from the creation of Adam. He was also buried at the end of the fourth day and in the fourth year of a sabbatical cycle.
3. From 1 Nisan 3970 BC to 1 Nisan 3031 (7,000 lunisolar years), there are exactly 2,556,700 days. The average number of days per lunisolar year is neatly expressible in terms of some Biblical numbers: $2{,}556{,}700/7{,}000 = 365.242857 = (7 \times 7 \times 7) + (7+7+7) + 7 \times (1/7 + 1/49 + 1/70)$.
4. Israel's declaration of independence was on the Feast of Pentecost (14 May 1948), which is exactly 274 sabbatical cycles (274×7 years) from the birthday of the Church on the Feast of Pentecost in 30 AD.
5. All of God's covenants including the Noahic covenant, the Mosaic covenant, and the new (Yeshua) covenant were established on the feast days of Pentecost.

Within our current Biblical chronology, all the past numerical prophecies in the Bible (a total of about 20) were fulfilled perfectly within the time frames specified by the prophets of God. The detailed descriptions and interpretations of the numerical prophecies will be given in Part III. Listed below are all the numerical prophecies in the Bible, which we have found:

1. Prophecy of Daniel on seventy weeks (Daniel 9:24-27):

    [24]Seventy weeks are determined for your people and for your holy city, to finish the transgression, to make an end of sins, to make reconciliation for iniquity, to bring in everlasting righteousness, to seal up vision and prophecy, and to anoint the most holy. [25]Know therefore and understand, that from the going forth of the command to restore and build Jerusalem until Messiah the Prince, there shall be seven weeks and sixty-two weeks; the street shall be built again, and the wall, even in troublesome times. [26]And after the sixty-two weeks Messiah shall be cut off, but not to himself; and he shall destroy the city and the sanctuary with the coming prince. The end of it shall be with a flood, and till the end of the war desolations are determined. [27]Then he shall confirm a covenant with many for one week; But in the middle of the week he shall cause sacrifice and offering to cease (fail). And on the wing of abominations shall be one who makes desolate, even until the consummation, which is determined, is poured out on the desolate.

    This prophecy of the 69th week (out of the 70 weeks) was perfectly fulfilled in the baptism and anointing of Yeshua on 24 February 27 AD. The first half of the 70th week was also perfectly fulfilled in Yeshua's earthly ministry from 27 to 30 AD. The last half of the 70th week shall be fulfilled in a future time when Yeshua will come to judge the ungodly and establish the Kingdom of God on earth. The prophetic 70 weeks contain three numerical prophecies, two of them were perfectly fulfilled and one of them will be fulfilled in a future time.

2. Prophecy of Daniel on suspension of 2,300 evening-morning offerings (Daniel 8:13-14):

¹³Then I heard a holy one speaking; and another holy one said to that certain one who was speaking, "How long will the vision be, concerning the daily sacrifices and the transgression of desolation, the giving of both the sanctuary and the host to be trampled underfoot?" ¹⁴And he said to me, "**For two thousand three hundred [2,300] evenings-mornings**; then the sanctuary shall be cleansed."

This prophecy was exactly fulfilled in the events related to the institution of the Festival of Hanukkah by Judas Maccabeus and his brothers in the second century BC. The temple was trampled down on October 29 (Saturday) of 168 BC by the Seleucid king Antiochus IV Epiphanes, and then the continual burnt offerings were taken away. After 1,150 days (2,300 evening or morning burnt offerings were suspended), the temple was cleansed by Judas Maccabeus on 22 December 165 BC. Then the daily burnt offerings were restored. This single numerical prophecy was perfectly fulfilled.

3. The prophetic dream of Nebuchadnezzar on seven times (Daniel 4:10-17):

¹⁰These were the visions of my head while on my bed: I was looking, and behold, a tree in the midst of the earth, and its height was great. ¹¹The tree grew and became strong; Its height reached to the heavens, and it could be seen to the ends of all the earth. ¹²Its leaves were lovely, Its fruit abundant, and in it was food for all. The beasts of the field found shade under it, the birds of

the heavens dwelt in its branches, and all flesh was fed from it. ¹³I saw in the visions of my head while on my bed, and there was a watcher, a holy one, coming down from heaven. ¹⁴He cried aloud and said thus: "Chop down the tree and cut off its branches, strip off its leaves and scatter its fruit. Let the beasts get out from under it, and the birds from its branches. ¹⁵Nevertheless leave the stump and roots in the earth, bound with a band of iron and bronze, in the tender grass of the field. Let it be wet with the dew of heaven, and let him graze with the beasts on the grass of the earth. ¹⁶Let his heart be changed from that of a man, let him be given the heart of a beast, and **let seven times pass over him.** ¹⁷This decision is by the decree of the watchers, and the sentence by the word of the holy ones, in order that the living may know that the Most High rules in the kingdom of men, gives it to whomever He will, and sets over it the lowest of men."

This prophetic dream of Nebuchadnezzar was doubly fulfilled in a short period of 2,520 (7×360) days and in a long period of 2,520 years. The short period was fulfilled in Nebuchadnezzar whose kingship was removed for 2,520 days from 17 March 572 BC. The prophecy was also fulfilled perfectly in the nation of Israel within the long period of 2,520 solar years starting also from 17 March 572 BC. The nation of Israel lost power and sovereignty for exactly 2,520 solar years. The end of the prophetic period was on 10 March 1949 when Israel won the war of independence and established its true sovereignty. This prophetic dream contains two numerical prophecies, which were perfectly fulfilled.

4. Prophecy of Daniel about the period of shattering the holy people's power (Daniel 12:5-7):

⁵Then I, Daniel, looked; and there stood two others, one on this riverbank and the other on that riverbank. ⁶And one said to the man clothed in linen, who was above the waters of the river, "How long shall the fulfillment of these wonders be?" ⁷Then I heard the man clothed in linen, who was above the waters of the river, when he held up his right hand and his left hand to heaven, and swore by Him who lives forever, **that it shall be for a time, times, and half a time; and when he shall have accomplished (ended) shattering the power (strength) of the holy people, all these things shall be finished.**

This prophecy was perfectly fulfilled in the people of Israel. Their power (sovereignty) was completely removed in July 688 AD when the construction of the Dome of the Rock began. The total loss of their sovereignty ended on 14 May 1948 when the nation of Israel was re-established. The day of 14 May 1948 was the feast day of Pentecost and was also in the 1260th year from July 688 AD. This single numerical prophecy was perfectly fulfilled.

5. Prophecy of Daniel on the 1290th day and on the 1335th day (Daniel 12:9-13):

⁹And he said, "Go your way, Daniel, for the words are closed up and sealed till the time of the end. ¹⁰Many shall be purified, made white, and refined, but the wicked shall do wickedly; and none of the wicked shall understand, but the wise shall understand. ¹¹And from the time that the daily sacrifice is taken away and to setting up the abomination of desolation, there shall be days **one thousand two hundred and ninety**

[1,290]. ¹²Blessed is he who waits, and comes to days **one thousand three hundred and thirty-five [1,335]**. ¹³But you, go your way till the end; for you shall rest, and will arise to your inheritance at (toward) the end of the days."

The prophecy on the 1290th day (year) was fulfilled perfectly in the Dome of the Rock, construction of which was finished in May 692 AD. The Dome of the Rock has been sitting on or near the most holy site, the temple site of God. This building should be the abomination of desolation to the God of Israel. The daily sacrifices were taken away in the spring of 598 BC. The 1290th year from the spring of 598 BC fell between the spring of 692 AD to the spring of 693 AD, when the construction of the Dome of the Rock was finished. The prophecy on the 1335th day is yet to be fulfilled. These prophetic words contain two numerical prophecies, one of them was fulfilled perfectly and another will be fulfilled in a future time.

6. Prophecy on the population of Israel at its re-birth (Ezekiel 36:37-38):

³⁷Thus says Yehowah God: "I will also let the house of Israel inquire of Me to do this for them: I will increase their men like a flock. ³⁸**Like a flock offered as holy sacrifices, like the flock at Jerusalem on its feast days, so shall the ruined cities be filled with flocks of men.** Then they shall know that I am Yehowah."

The word of God appears to be qualitative here. In fact, it is a prophecy on the true population of Israel at its re-birth on 14 May 1948. The prophetic population (807,732), which is calculated from verse 38 and the number of flocks on the feast days prescribed in the book of Numbers, matches within 0.21% the published population (806,000) on 15 May 1948 (see http://www.cbs.gov.il/statistical/statistical60_eng.pdf). This single numerical prophecy was perfectly fulfilled.

7. Prophecy of Ezekiel on two destructions of Jerusalem (Ezekiel 4:1-8):

¹You also, son of man, take a clay tablet and lay it before you, and portray on it a city, Jerusalem. ²Lay siege against it, build a siege wall against it, and heap up a mound against it; set camps against it also, and place battering rams against it all around. ³Moreover take for yourself an iron plate, and set it as an iron wall between you and the city. Set your face against it, and it shall be besieged, and you shall lay siege against it. This will be a sign to the house of Israel. ⁴Lie also on your left side, and lay the iniquity of the house of Israel upon it. According to the number of the days that you lie on it, you shall bear their iniquity. ⁵For I have laid on you the years of their iniquity, according to the number of the days, **three hundred and ninety [390] days**; so you shall bear the iniquity of the house of Israel. ⁶And when you have completed them, lie again on your right side; then you shall bear the iniquity of the house of Judah **forty [40] days**. I have laid on you a day for each year. ⁷Therefore you shall set your face toward the siege of Jerusalem; your arm shall be uncovered, and you shall prophesy against it. ⁸And surely I will restrain you so that you cannot turn from one side to another till you have ended the days of your siege.

This prophecy on 390 days was perfectly fulfilled in the destruction of Jerusalem in July 587 BC. Solomon started to build the first temple in the spring of 977 BC, and the temple and Jerusalem were destroyed after

390 years in July 587 BC. Another prophecy on 40 days was fulfilled in the destruction of Jerusalem and the second temple in August 70 AD. Yeshua built the spiritual temple of God (Church) in the spring of 30 AD. The second physical temple and Jerusalem were finally destroyed after 40 years. These prophetic words comprise two numerical prophecies that were fulfilled perfectly.

8. Prophecy of Jeremiah on 17 shekels of silver for a field (Jeremiah 32:6-15):

⁶And Jeremiah said, "The word of Yehowah came to me, saying, ⁷'Behold, Hanamel the son of Shallum your uncle will come to you, saying, 'Buy my field which is in Anathoth, for the right of redemption is yours to buy it.'" ⁸Then Hanamel my uncle's son came to me in the court of the prison according to the word of Yehowah, and said to me, 'Please buy my field that is in Anathoth, which is in the country of Benjamin; for the right of inheritance is yours, and the redemption yours; buy it for yourself.' Then I knew that this was the word of Yehowah. ⁹So I bought the field from Hanamel, the son of my uncle who was in Anathoth, and weighed out to him the money—**seventeen shekels of silver**. ¹⁰And I signed the deed and sealed it, took witnesses, and weighed the money on the scales. ¹¹So I took the purchase deed, both that which was sealed according to the law and custom, and that which was open; ¹²and I gave the purchase deed to Baruch the son of Neriah, son of Mahseiah, in the presence of Hanamel my uncle's son, and in the presence of the witnesses who signed the purchase deed, before all the Jews who sat in the court of the prison. ¹³"Then I charged Baruch before them, saying, ¹⁴"Thus says the Lord of hosts, the God of Israel: "Take these deeds, both this purchase deed which is

sealed and this deed which is open, and put them in an earthen vessel, that they may last many days."¹⁵For thus says the Lord of hosts, the God of Israel: "Houses and fields and vineyards shall be possessed again in this land."

This prophecy of Jeremiah was perfectly fulfilled in the story about the betrayal by Judas, one of Yeshua's twelve disciples. This story was recorded in detail in the Gospel of Matthew. Matthew correctly told us that this prophecy of Jeremiah was fulfilled in the story of Judas (Matthew 27:9). The thirty pieces of silver coins paid to Judas for his betrayal contained exactly seventeen shekels of silver. This single numerical prophecy was perfectly fulfilled.

9. Prophecy of Jeremiah on the 70-year exile to Babylon (Jeremiah 29:10):

¹⁰For thus says Yehowah: "After **seventy [70] years** are completed at Babylon, I will visit you and perform My good word toward you, and cause you to return to this place..."

This prophecy was fulfilled perfectly in the first exile of the Jews in the spring of 606 BC and the first return in the spring of 536 BC. It was also fulfilled perfectly in the last exile of the Jews in July 587 BC and the last return in the fall of 517 BC. This single numerical prophecy was fulfilled exactly.

10. Isaiah's prophecy on the breaking of Ephraim in 65 years (Isaiah 7:3-8):

³Then Yehowah said to Isaiah, "Go out now to meet Ahaz, you and Shear-Jashub your son, at the end of the aqueduct from the upper pool, on the highway to

the Fuller's Field, ⁴and say to him: 'Take heed, and be quiet; do not fear or be fainthearted for these two stubs of smoking firebrands, for the fierce anger of Rezin and Syria, and the son of Remaliah. ⁵Because Syria, Ephraim, and the son of Remaliah have plotted evil against you, saying, ⁶"Let us go up against Judah and trouble it, and let us make a gap in its wall for ourselves, and set a king over them, the son of Tabel"—⁷thus says Yehowah God: "It shall not stand, nor shall it come to pass. ⁸For the head of Syria is Damascus, and the head of Damascus is Rezin. **Sixty-five [65] years Ephraim will be broken, so that it will not be a people."**

The 65-year prophetic period began in the fall of 733 BC when Ahaz started his sole reign. The prophetic period ended in the first year (668 BC) of Asnappar (Ashurbanipal), the last Assyrian king. From 733 BC to 668 BC, there were exactly 65 years. This single numerical prophecy was perfectly fulfilled.

11. Prophecy of Zechariah on the strike of the Jews (Zechariah 13:7-9):

⁷"Awake, O sword, against My shepherd, against the man who is My companion," says Yehowah of hosts. "Strike the shepherd, and the sheep will be scattered; Then I will turn My hand against the little ones. ⁸And it shall come to pass in all the land," says Yehowah, "**That two-thirds in it shall be cut off and die**, but one-third shall be left in it: ⁹I will bring the one-third through the fire, will refine them as silver is refined, and test them as gold is tested. They will call on My name, and I will answer them. I will say, 'This is My people'; and each one will say, 'Yehowah is my God.'"

This prophecy was fulfilled perfectly in the Jews of Europe during the second world war when the Nazis killed about 6 million Jews, two thirds of the Jews living in the whole land of Europe. This single numerical prophecy was perfectly fulfilled.

12. Prophecy of Moses on the ages of the world and the universe (Psalm 90:4):

⁴A thousand years in your sight are like a day that has just gone by, or like a watch in the night.

When Moses said this, he was not speaking figuratively but prophesying the ages of the world and the universe in the modern time using a human clock versus God's clock. The ages of the world and universe in the modern time are about 4 and 14 billion years in terms of the human clock, while their ages are about 6,000 years in terms of God's absolute clock. Moses' prophetic words contain two numerical prophecies, which were perfectly fulfilled (see Chapter 28).

13. Prophecy of Yeshua on his burial and resurrection (Matthew 12:38-40):

³⁸Then some of the scribes and Pharisees answered, saying, "Teacher, we want to see a sign from you." ³⁹But he answered and said to them, "An evil and adulterous generation seeks after a sign, and no sign will be given to it except the sign of the prophet Jonah. ⁴⁰For as Jonah was **three days and three nights** in the belly of the great fish, so will the Son of Man be **three days and three nights** in the heart of the earth."

This single numerical prophecy was fulfilled perfectly in Yeshua according to the Gospels of Matthew and John (see Chapter 31).

14. Prophecy of Yeshua on the destruction of the holy temple (Matthew 24:1-3 and 34):

¹Then Yeshua went out and departed from the temple, and his disciples came up to show him the buildings of the temple. ²And Yeshua said to them, "Do you not see all these things? Assuredly, I say to you, not one stone shall be left here upon another, that shall not be thrown down." ³Now as he sat on the Mount of Olives, the disciples came to him privately, saying, "Tell us, when will these things be [ruined]? And what will be the sign of your coming, and of the end of the age?.... ³⁴Assuredly, I say to you, **this generation will by no means pass away till all these things become [ruined]."**

The average time of one generation in the time of Yeshua was about 42 years according to Matthew's genealogy. The temple was destroyed 40 years after Yeshua made the prophecy. Forty years are indeed less than one generation of his time. This single numerical prophecy was perfectly fulfilled.

15. Yeshua's prophecies on his first century return (Matthew 10:16-23):

¹⁶"Behold, I send you out as sheep in the midst of wolves. Therefore be wise as serpents and harmless as doves. ¹⁷But beware of men, for they will deliver you up to councils and scourge you in their synagogues. ¹⁸You will be brought before governors and kings for my sake, as a testimony to them and to the Gentiles. ¹⁹But when they deliver you up, do not worry about how or what you should speak. For it will be given to you in that hour what you should speak; ²⁰for it is not you who speak, but the Spirit of your Father who speaks in you. ²¹Now

brother will deliver up brother to death, and a father his child; and children will rise up against parents and cause them to be put to death. ²²And you will be hated by all for my name's sake. But he who endures to the end will be saved. ²³When they persecute you in this city, flee to another. **For assuredly, I say to you, you will not have gone through the cities of Israel before the Son of Man comes."**

No Biblical scholar has ever published a correct understanding of this prophecy of Yeshua. The true meaning of the prophecy is that Yeshua would return shortly after he went back to his Father in 30 AD. Appearing as the mighty messenger of God, Yeshua descended to the earth and stayed in the temple of God for about half an hour in the spring of 67 AD. He revealed himself to John the Apostle and asked him to measure the temple of God and prophesied the destruction of Jerusalem exactly after 42 lunar months. This single numerical prophecy was perfectly fulfilled.

This book contains 5 parts, 40 chapters, and 4 appendixes. In Part I, we compare various calendars and show the construction rules of these calendars. After reading this part, readers will become experts in the various calendars. The correct calendars we have used are crucial to the accurate construction of several chronologies. In Appendix D, we list the Hebrew lunisolar calendars for some important years related to the main texts. The Hebrew lunisolar calendar used by modern Israel is based on a computer program, which should be valid within a short period of less than 300 years due to a slight misalignment between the true lunar phases and the solar year. In many of these years, the Israeli calendars are not correct because of their unnecessary and incorrect intercalation of a 13th month. Our Hebrew lunisolar calendars of some important years in Appendix D are based on the exact lunar phases and the calendar rules from the Bible. The calculated Julian solar calendar and the Hebrew lunisolar calendar are superimposed on each other.

Readers could initially skip Part I and come back to it when the calendar's information is needed to understand the latter parts.

In Part II, we will show how to construct the chronology of the Ancient Near East, the chronology of Babylon and Persia, the chronology of ancient China, the Biblical chronology, and the chronology of Judah and Israel's kings, as well as the timelines of Yeshua and Herod. The Biblical chronology is consistent with all reliable extra-biblical records and has uncertainties of less than 6 months. The accurate Biblical chronology is necessary for us to interpret the numerical prophecies correctly. This part may be difficult to understand to those who do not have a strong background in science, history, and the Old-Testament Scriptures. **Readers could initially skip this part and directly jump to Part III.**

In Part III, we will provide detailed descriptions and explanations for the numerical prophecies in the Old-Testament Scriptures. The precise fulfillments of these prophecies suggest that these prophecies must come from the true God who fully orchestrates all the historical events in the exact years specified in the prophecies. No human can predict these events in such a distant future. No pagan god has the power or might to prevent these foretold events from happening in such exact time frames. The prophet Isaiah explained the difference between the true God and false gods in Isaiah 41:21-24:

> "Produce your case," says Yehowah; "bring forth your strong reasons," says the King of Jacob. "Let them bring them forth and show us what shall happen: let them show the former things, what they were, that we may consider them, and know the latter end of them; or declare to us things to come. Show the things that are to come hereafter, that we may know that you are gods: yea, do good, or do evil, that we may be dismayed, and behold it together. Behold, you are of nothing, and your work is nothing: an abomination is he that chooses you."

The true God foretells what will happen in the future and makes it happen exactly according to His words.

In Part IV, we provide clear proof that Yeshua is the true Messiah foretold by the prophets in the Old-Testament Scriptures. We will show that all his own numerical prophecies were fulfilled perfectly and that all of the Old-Testament numerical prophecies about him were fulfilled exactly. In addition to the exact fulfillments of the numerical prophecies, we will also show that some descriptive prophecies about him in the Old-Testament Scriptures were fulfilled.

In Part V, we will present end-time prophecies, which show the destiny of the world and that of mankind. While these prophecies are derived from the Bible, our interpretations may contain personal bias and/or error. Since we show that all the past numerical prophecies were fulfilled perfectly in the times specified in the prophecies, we believe that the end-time numerical prophecies should also be given a measure of earned respect. Uncertainty must be related to our possible misinterpretations of the prophecies.

In order to precisely determine the time and magnitude of solar eclipses, we need to know the delta-T ($\varDelta T$) parameter, which is the arithmetic difference between Terrestrial Dynamical Time and Universal Time. In Appendix A, we present the curve of the delta-T parameter versus year, which is obtained from the known solar and lunar eclipses. In the construction of various chronologies, we used the recorded solar and lunar eclipses, which can be precisely predicted from the Stellarium Program if the reliable delta-T parameters are used. The uncertainties of the predicted eclipse times are less than 2 hours. Because of this accuracy, the constructed chronologies of several regions in the world have small uncertainties.

In Appendix B, we provide experimental evidence for slowing down of the speed of light and the atomic clock. This result is crucial to the understanding of the prophecy of Moses in Chapter 28. If we assume that the speed of light is constant, one infers that the world would be much older than 6,000 years. In contrast, if we use God's absolute clock—in which the speed of light decays—one infers that the world is less than 6,000 years old. Moses' prayer in Psalm 90:4 provides prophetic words about the ages of the world and the universe in the modern time (right before God and His Messiah reign on the earth) in terms of God's absolute clock and the human relative clock.

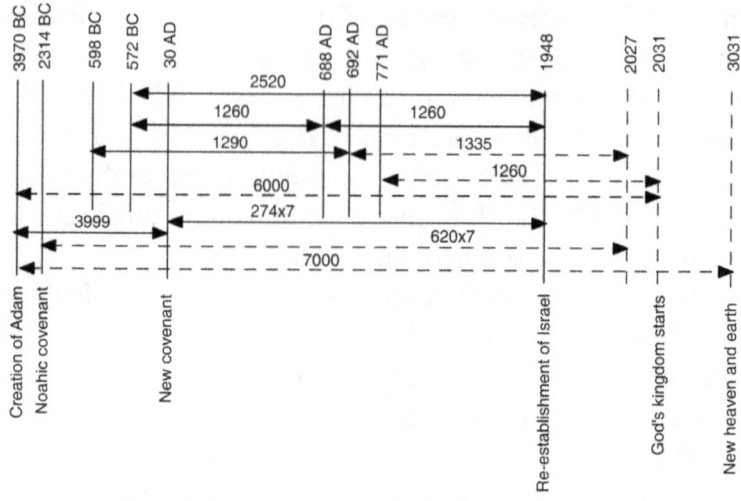

Figure 1: Schematic diagram for the destiny of mankind.

In Appendix C, we modify the standard cosmological model with "cold dark matter" being negative-mass antimatter. The basic assumption of the cosmology model is that the speed of light is constant, which is true if the speed of light is measured by the atomic clock. Our modified model can quantitatively explain all the observed results including: 1) the primordial abundances of ^{7}Li, ^{4}He, ^{3}He, and deuterium, 2) the power spectra of the cosmic microwave background, and 3) the locally measured Hubble constant. The observed quantization of some red shifts is also naturally explained within the model. It is amazing that the age of the universe within our model is almost exactly equal to 7^{12} years.

Unless otherwise specified, the Biblical verses quoted in this book are mostly from New King James Version (NKJV). In the quotations, we have changed "the LORD" back to "Yehowah" according to the original Hebrew Bible and the pronunciation of God's name by the Karaites. We have also changed "Jesus" to "Yeshua" and "Christ" to "Messiah" according to the original Hebrew Gospel of Matthew. An angel of God, who appeared to Joseph in a dream, called our Messiah "Yeshua" while Matthew simply called him "Yeshu," the Galilean pronunciation or a short version of "Yeshua."

In summary, the Biblical chronology and the numerical prophecies in the books of Daniel and Revelation lead to a schematic diagram for the destiny of mankind (Figure 1). The most likely dates of these years are the following: 15 April (1 Nisan) 3970 BC, 10 June (6 Sivan) 2314 BC, 3 April (10 Nisan) 598 BC, 17 March (10 Adar II) 572 BC, 12 July (9 Av) 688 AD, 8 May (16 Iyar) 692 AD, 7 December (25 Kislev) 771 AD, 14 May (6 Sivan) 1948, and 12 May (6 Sivan) 2027, 25 March (1 Nisan) 2031, and 17 March (1 Nisan) 3031. The prophetic periods connected by solid lines were perfectly fulfilled while the prophetic periods marked by dashed lines are to be fulfilled. Readers need to read the entire book with critical thinking in order to make their intellectual judgment on the correctness of the diagram. If readers are convinced of the diagram, they should prepare for the final coming of Yeshua, which are imminent.

PART I
LUNAR AND SOLAR CALENDARS

CHAPTER 1

INTRODUCTION TO LUNAR AND SOLAR CALENDARS

In order to construct the accurate chronologies of several important regions in the world, one must fully understand the calendars used by the Israelites, ancient Babylonians, Persians, and Chinese. In the ancient world, there were essentially three types of calendars: lunar, solar, and lunisolar.

Calendars based solely on the Moon's motion are called lunar calendars. The time it takes the Moon to orbit the Earth is about 29.53 days on average. Therefore, some months in the lunar calendar have 29 days and other months have 30 days. There are twelve lunar months and about 354/355 days in each lunar year. The pure lunar calendar that is based solely on the Moon's motion has been used in the Islamic countries of the Middle East.

Calendars based only on the Sun's motion (relative to the Earth) are called solar calendars. One type of solar calendar was recorded in the book of Enoch and used in the first and second century BC by Essenes, one of the Jewish sects. The normal year in Enoch's solar calendar consists of eight 30-day months and four 31-day months (the third, sixth, ninth, and twelfth month), making a total of 364 days and 52 weeks. Another type of solar calendar called the Julian calendar was proposed by Julius Caesar in 46 BC. The Julian calendar was predominantly used in the Roman world but was gradually replaced by the Gregorian calendar after 1582 AD.

A lunisolar calendar is a calendar whose dates mark both the moon phases and the seasons of the solar year. The normal years in the lunisolar calendar consist of 12 months and each month has 29 or 30 days. Every second or third year is called embolismic year in which a leap month is added to synchronize the lunar year with the solar year. The Hebrew, Chinese, Korean, and Babylonian calendars are all lunisolar. The variations of these lunisolar calendars lie with the differences in the definitions of the first day of a month and the first month of a year, and in the ways of intercalating the leap month. In the Hebrew, Chinese, and Korean calendars, the first day of a month corresponds to a day when the moon is hidden (dark moon). Within this criterion, the full moon mostly falls on the 15th day of a month. Consistently, the recorded lunar eclipses (occurring at the full moon) mostly took place on the 15th day. In contrast, the first day of a month in the Babylonian calendar corresponds to the day when a new crescent is seen in the western sky after sunset. Within this criterion, the full moon mostly falls on the 14th day of a month. That is why the lunar eclipses recorded by the Babylonians occurred mostly on the 14th day.

Remarkably, the Chinese lunisolar calendar (Xia calendar) is quite similar to the Hebrew one. The major difference is that the Chinese New Year starts one month or two months earlier than the Hebrew New Year. According to the instruction of Yehowah, the God of Abraham, Isaac, and Jacob, the first month of a year corresponds to the month in which the Vernal (Spring) Equinox falls. The Chinese Mid-Autumn Festival is celebrated on the 15th day of the 8th month of the lunisolar calendar with a full moon at night. This day mostly corresponds to the 15th day of the 7th month in the Hebrew lunisolar calendar, which is the first day of the Feast of Tabernacles. The original Mid-Autumn Festival was to celebrate the harvest and to give thanks to the heavenly God, which is similar to the Feast of Tabernacles. Later on, this festival developed into moon worship.

We will discuss the Hebrew lunisolar calendar in detail in Chapter 2, the Babylonian lunisolar calendar in Chapter 3, Enoch's solar calendar in Chapter 4, and the Chinese lunisolar calendar in Chapter 5. Understanding these calendars is essential to both the construction of the accurate Biblical chronology and to deciphering the Biblical numerical prophecies. **Readers could initially skip this part (Part I) and directly jump to Part III if they do not have a strong background in science and history.**

CHAPTER 2

THE HEBREW LUNISOLAR CALENDAR

The Hebrew lunisolar calendar has been used by the Israelites since Yehowah brought them out of Egypt. Yehowah commanded the Israelites that the first month of their year start from the month when He brought them out of Egypt (Exodus 12:1-2).

As the Moon goes around the Earth it looks different in the sky. This is because only certain parts of the Moon are reflected. Different lunar calendars in the ancient world use different definitions for the first day of a month. In the Hebrew calendar, the first day corresponds to a day when the Moon is hidden. This criterion is consistent with that for the astronomical new-moon day when the solar eclipse could occur. This is also consistent with the book of Enoch (Enoch 73:6-8):

> And when she receives one-seventh part of the half of her light, her light amounts to one-seventh part and the half thereof. And she sets with the sun, and when the sun rises the moon rises with him and receives the half of one part of light, and in that night in the beginning of her morning [in the commencement of the lunar day] the moon sets with the sun and is **invisible** that night with the fourteen parts and the half of one of them. And she rises on that day with exactly a seventh part, and comes forth and recedes from the rising of the sun, and in her remaining days she becomes bright in the (remaining) thirteen parts.

This criterion also leads to a full moon that most often falls on the 15th day of a month. Within this criterion, a crescent moon can be seen in the morning sky of the last day of a month. This was clearly described in the book of Enoch (Enoch 73:4), "And thus she rises. And her first phase in the east comes forth on the thirtieth morning: and on that day she becomes visible and constitutes for you the first phase of the moon on the thirtieth day together with the sun in the portal where the sun rises."

The Bible encyclopedia *Insight on the Scriptures* (Watchtower Bible and Tract Society of New York, Inc. Brooklyn, NY 1988. Vol. 2, p. 429) also says:

> In postexilic times the *Mishnah* (*Rosh Ha-Shanah* 1:3-2:7) states that the Jewish Sanhedrin met early in the morning on the 30th day of each of seven months in the year to determine the time of the new moon. Watchmen were posted on high vantage points around Jerusalem and carried an immediate report to the Jewish court after sighting the new moon. Upon receiving sufficient testimony, the court announced, "It is consecrated," officially marking the start of a new moon. If cloudy skies or fog caused poor visibility, then the preceding month was declared to have had 30 days, and the new month began on the day following the court assembly. It is also said that further announcement was made by a signal fire lit on the Mount of Olives, which was then repeated on other high points throughout the country. This method was evidently replaced later by the dispatching of messengers to carry the news.

This practice of the Sanhedrin clearly tells us that the lunar month begins on the day after the old crescent before sunrise.

Do the Scriptures reveal anything about the new moon and full moon? Psalm 81:3 (ASV) says: "Blow the trumpet at the new moon, at the full moon, on our feast-day." This verse implies that a full moon falls on the first day of the Feast of Tabernacles, which is the 15th day of the

7th month (Tishri). Similarly, the first day of the Feast of Unleavened Bread falls on the 15th day of the first month (Nisan). According to astronomy, there are about 14 days from the astronomical new moon (dark moon) to the astronomical full moon in the months in proximity to the Equinoxes. This indicates that the full moon is on the 15th day if the dark moon is on the first day of the first or seventh month. Therefore, the Biblical definition of the new moon is identical to the astronomical one. With this definition, a solar eclipse mostly occurs on the first day of a month and a lunar eclipse mostly takes place on the 15th day of a month.

A record of the Christian transition to pagan calendars has been preserved in various sepulchral inscriptions. One of the oldest dated Christian sepulchral inscriptions discovered in Rome referred to dies Veneris (day of Venus). It listed both the Julian and lunisolar dates. The inscription dated 269 AD stated:

> In the consulship of Claudius and Paternus, on the Nones of November, on the day of Venus, and on the 24th day of the lunar month, Leuces placed [this memorial] to her very dear daughter Severa, and to Thy Holy Spirit. She died [at the age] of 55 years, and 11 months [and] 10 days (E. Dichl, *Inscriptiones Latin Christian Veteres*, Vol. 2, p. 193, #3391. See also, J. B. de Rossi, *Inscriptiones Christian Urbis Rome*, Vol. 1, part 1, p. 18, #11).

The "Nones" of November is November 5 which fell on the day of Venus, Friday. This corresponded to the 24th day of the lunar month. On October 13 of 269 AD, an astronomical new moon occurred at 2:06 am in Jerusalem. Within the dark-moon criterion for the Hebrew lunisolar calendar, the day from sunset of October 12 to sunset of October 13 was the first day of Heshvan (the eighth month) and the day from sunset of November 4 to sunset of November 5 was the 24th day of Heshvan, in agreement with the sepulchral inscription. Therefore, this inscription confirms the dark-moon criterion for the first day of the month.

According to *A Dictionary of the Bible* [Volume I (Part I: A - Cyrus) by James Hastings, 2004, page 411], Nisan 1 in 277 AD was on March 22. The astronomical data for the moon-phases show that an astronomical new moon occurred at 0:53 am on March 22 of 277 AD. Within the dark-moon criterion for the Hebrew calendar, the day from sunset of March 21 to sunset of March 22 was Nisan 1, which is in perfect agreement with that recorded in *A Dictionary of the Bible*.

Method of intercalation

A pure lunar year without addition of an intercalary month is about eleven days shorter than the solar year (365.24 days). The pure lunar calendar with 12 lunar months cannot align with the seasons. This is not what God inspires us to follow because Yehowah clearly tells us that there are two seasons each year: summer and winter (Genesis 8:22 and Psalm 74:17). When one side of the Earth has summer, the other has winter and vice versa. There is an imaginary line called the Equator that divides the Earth into the northern and southern hemispheres. When the Sun just crosses the Equator, day and night are of equal length. This is called an Equinox. In the spring, the Equinox (called Vernal Equinox) occurs around March 21 in the current solar calendar. In the fall, the Equinox (called Autumnal Equinox) takes place around September 23.

In order to have two complete seasons each year, the year must align with the Vernal Equinox or the Autumnal Equinox. By intercalating a month every two or three years, one can align the lunar year with the solar year. It was known that every 19-year period, known as the Metonic cycle, the paths of the Sun, Moon, and Earth almost repeat. The Babylonians and Chinese also knew of this cycle. Even with this intercalation and the postponement rules (see below), the mathematically calculated Hebrew lunisolar calendar year is longer by 6 minutes and 40 seconds than the current mean tropical year, so that every 216 years the calculated Hebrew lunisolar calendar will fall a day behind the current mean tropical year. Since the currently used Hebrew calendar is mathematically calculated by matching the correct Hebrew calendar back to as early as the third century AD, they must be out of alignment after so many years have passed from the third century AD.

Therefore, one needs to use the calculated astronomical moon phases to make a correct lunisolar calendar every year. In this way, we have selectively constructed some correct lunisolar calendars from 3971 BC to 3031, which may be used in the main text. These calendars are shown in Appendix D.

One of the most important events for modern Israelites is the rebirth of the nation of Israel on May 14 of 1948. According to the Hebrew calendar used by modern Israelites, this very important day was on Iyar 5 (the fifth day of the second month). But according to our correct Hebrew calendar (see Appendix D), the day was on Sivan 6 (the sixth day of the third month), which was the feast day of Pentecost. Because this event took place exactly in a feast day of Yehowah, it must be orchestrated by the Almighty God.

We know that the first new moon of the year is the month of Nisan. The barley in Israel starts to ripen during this time. The first new moon of the year can occur before or after the Vernal Equinox, but the first day of the Feast of Unleavened Bread, the 15th day of Nisan, cannot precede the Vernal Equinox. **That is, the full moon must be on or after the Vernal Equinox.** Otherwise, we need to add a 13th month (called Adar II) to the prior year.

The rules of postponement

In the current Hebrew calendar, the new moon of the seventh month (Tishri) is calculated based on the so-called "postponement" without fully respecting for the new moon of the first month (Nisan). As Tishri 1 is the only new moon that is assigned as a holy day (Feast of Trumpets), it is most important to determine this new moon. The other holy days must be aligned with it automatically.

The rules of postponement are used to determine which day should be proclaimed as the first day of Tishri. There are generally four postponement rules, two of them being primary while the other two are logical extensions of the first two.

The first rule states that if the calculated new moon of Tishri occurs after noon on a given day, the first day of the month is postponed to the following day. It is unclear whether or not this rule is mandated by the Scriptures.

The other primary rule is that if the calculated new moon of Tishri occurs on Sunday, Wednesday or Friday, the first day of the month is considered to begin on the following day, i.e., Monday, Thursday, or Saturday.

Is there Biblical basis for this? God first gave Moses a detailed list of His Festivals in Leviticus 23:4-44 (also see Table I). The feast days appeared to fall into two categories in terms of the levels of sanctity. There are six of these days in the first category: the first and seventh day of the Feast of Unleavened Bread, the day of Pentecost, the day of Trumpets, the first day of the Feast of Tabernacles and the eighth day. During these six days, **no servile work should be done**. In the second category, the day of Atonement has the same sanctity as the weekly Sabbaths. On these two days, **no work should be done at all**. Clearly these two days are different from the other six days. Furthermore, in describing the Feast of Trumpets, the first day of Tabernacles, and and the eighth day, the Hebrew term "shabbaton," translated "Sabbath," was used. In contrast, for the weekly Sabbaths and the day of Atonement a different descriptive term "shabbat shabbaton" was used, translated as "a Sabbath of rest" (using plural Sabbaths in Greek New-Testament).

Table I: The Annual Festivals of Yehowah God

Festival	Date	Comment
Passover or Preparation day	Before sunset, Nisan 14	Passover lambs are sacrificed.
Feast of Unleavened Bread or Feast of Passover	Nisan 15-21	The feast lasts for 7 days. The first and last days are special sabbaths, that are called by John as "high days." No servile work is permitted.
Pentecost	Sivan 6	A sabbatical day. No servile work is permitted.
Feast of Trumpets	Tishri 1	A sabbatical day. No servile work is permitted.
Day of Atonement	Tishri 10	A sabbatical day. No work whatever is permitted.

Feast of Tabernacles	Tishri 15-21	The feast lasts for 7 days. The first day is the special sabbath. No servile work is permitted.
The eighth day	Tishri 22	A sabbatical day. No servile work is permitted.

Since the weekly Sabbaths and the day of Atonement have a higher level of sanctity, the Levitical priesthood should have implemented the postponement rules. The day of Atonement should not be the preparation day for the weekly Sabbaths (which would occur if the first day of Tishri came on a Wednesday) because no work at all should be done. Similarly, the weekly Sabbaths cannot be the preparation day for the day of Atonement, which would happen if Tishri 1 fell on a Friday or a Sunday. Consequently, Tishri 1 cannot be on Sunday, Wednesday, or Friday.

The first postponement rule may not have to be followed since it was incorporated in the 7th to 8th century AD with no scriptural basis. If we obey the other main rules, Tishri 1 should fall on Monday, Tuesday, Thursday, and Saturday only. Furthermore, the odd-numbered months have 30 days except for the 9th month (Kislev) which could have 29 days; the even-numbered months have 29 days except for the 8th month (Heshvan) which could have 30 days.

In 269 AD, we know that the first day of Heshvan (the 8th month) was on October 13, so Tishri 1 was on Monday, September 13, obeying the second category postponement rules. The astronomical new moon occurred at 16:34 on September 13, which was after noon, but that day was not postponed to the next day. This suggests that the first postponement rule was not obeyed in the third century AD. In 277 AD, Nisan 1 was on March 22 and Tishri 1 was on Saturday, September 15, which is also in agreement with the main postponement rules. The Hebrew lunisolar calendars in Appendix D will follow the second category postponement rules but ignore the first rule.

CHAPTER 3

BABYLONIAN LUNISOLAR CALENDAR

When ancient Israel fell under the dominion of great pagan empires, its calendar was radically changed. In the Hebrew Bible, the months of the year are mostly numbered prior to the exile to Babylon. But after that, Babylonian-like month's names appeared in the books of Zechariah, Esther, Ezra, and Nehemiah. The Babylonian-like months of Nisan, Sivan, Elul, Kislev, Tebet, Shebet, and Adar are used either on their own or along with the numbered months. Nisan was consistently equated with the first month of Exodus (Exodus 12:2) while Nisannu was the first month in the Babylonian calendar.

The Babylonian calendar originated in Babylon (Southern Iraq) in the early second millennium BC and circulated throughout the rest of Mesopotamia in the late second millennium BC. In the first millennium BC, the calendar became the official calendar of the great empires of Assyria, Babylonia, and Persia. After the Jewish Hasmonean state was separated from its Hellenistic Seleucid rulers in the mid-second century BC, the Jews adopted only Babylonian-like month's names but used their own Hebrew lunisolar calendar for the Festivals of God. Since Zechariah, Ezra, and Nehemiah were servants of God, we believe that they also used the Hebrew lunisolar calendar rather than the Babylonian one for the Biblical festivals while under the dominion of the great pagan empires.

The Babylonian calendar was also intercalated every two or three years by the addition of a 13th month (usually by duplicating the 12th month, Addaru, and less frequently by duplicating the sixth month, Ululu). This calendar may be quite similar to the original Hebrew one, but there are significant differences in the intercalation rule and in the definition of the first day of the month.

As mentioned in Chapter 2, the Hebrew calendar is intercalated only in the month of Adar, but not Elul. In the Hebrew calendar, Adar II is intercalated when the full moon after the 12th month falls before the Vernal Equinox. In contrast, the first month of the Babylonian calendar always falls on or after the Vernal Equinox, so only some of the first months in the Babylonian calendar coincide with the first months in the Hebrew calendar.

The first day of a Babylonian month is a day when a new crescent is seen in the western sky after sunset. Within this criterion, the full moon falls mostly on the 14th day of a month. That is why the recorded lunar eclipses by Babylonians mostly took place on the 14th day and the recorded solar eclipses on the last day of a month. The same criterion has been used in the Islamic pure lunar calendar. This definition may be associated with the pagan worship to the moon in the first day of a month when a new crescent is seen in the western sky. In contrast, the God of Israel does not allow His people to worship any visible object, so the first day of a month corresponds to the dark-moon phase, making it impossible for them to worship the visible moon on that day. Therefore, the first day of a Hebrew month is one or two days earlier than that of a Babylonian month.

Table II: The Names of Lunar Months in Different Lunisolar Calendars

	Babylonian	Hebrew	Macedonian (Seleucid)	Macedonian (post-Seleucid)
I	Nisannu	Nisan	Dystros	Xandikos
II	Ajaru	Iyar	Xandikos	Artemisios
III	Simanu	Sivan	Artemisios	Daisios
IV	Duuzu	Tammuz	Daisios	Panemos
V	Abu	Av	Panemos	Loios
VI	Ululu	Elul	Loios	Gorpiaios
VII	Tasritu	Tishri	Gorpiaios	Hyperberetaios
VIII	Arahsamna	Heshvan	Hyperberetaios	Dios
IX	Kislimu	Kislev	Dios	Apellaios
X	Tebetu	Tebet	Apellaios	Audunaios
XI	Sabatu	Shebet	Audunaios	Peritios
XII	Addaru	Adar	Peritios	Dystros

It is worth noting that in the post-Seleucid Macedonian calendar (see Table II), the first month of a year starts from Xandikos, which is equivalent to Nisannu in the Babylonian calendar and to Nisan in the Hebrew calendar. But in the Seleucid Macedonian calendar, the first month of a year starts from Dystros, corresponding to Addaru in the Babylonian calendar and to Adar in the Hebrew calendar. The month Dystros is the month just before the Vernal Equinox. The new-year month in the Seleucid Macedonian calendar is the same as that in the Chinese lunisolar calendar.

CHAPTER 4

ENOCH'S SOLAR CALENDAR

Calendars based on the Sun's motion (relative to the Earth) are called solar calendars. A solar calendar was originally used by Enoch and Noah, and later used in the first and second century BC by the Essenes, one of the Jewish sects. The normal year in Enoch's solar calendar consists of eight 30-day months and four 31-day months (the third, sixth, ninth, and twelfth month), making a total of 364 days and 52 weeks. A new solar year always starts on the Wednesday of the week within which the Vernal Equinox falls. With only 364 days per year, it is clear that the seasons of the calendar would be noticeably off after a few years. To keep the year in phase with the seasons, one needs to find a method to add extra days. In the book of Enoch, there is no explicit suggestion of a rule for adding the days.

Do the Scriptures provide any hint? Matthew recorded in Matthew 18:21-22, "Then Peter came to him and said, 'Lord, how often shall my brother sin against me, and I forgive him? Up to seven times?' Yeshua said to him, 'I do not say to you, up to seven times, but up to seventy times seven.'" Seven appears to be a complete number to Peter, but seventy times seven [490] is the true complete number to Yeshua. Did Yeshua simply speak to his disciples figuratively? No, he may provide a hint about the solar calendar, as demonstrated below.

490 is the least common factor of 7, 49, and 70. The numbers: 7, 49, and 70 often appear in the Hebrew Bible, representing the sabbatical year (the 7th year), jubilee year (the 49th year), and 10 (complete) cycles of the sabbatical year, respectively. In the normal solar year, 52 weeks can be expressed as $(7 \times 7 \times 7) + (7+7+7) = 364$ days. If we simply add one week

in the year number divisible by 7, adding one more week in the year number divisible also by 49 or 70, one can bring the solar calendar into line with the Equinoxes. With this intercalation method, the average number of days per year is equal to 364 + (7/7+7/49+7/70) = 365.242857 within 490 years. The intercalation is complete within one cycle of 490 years. As shown below, the "magic" number 365.242857 for the average number of days per Enoch's solar year is hidden in God's creation.

We will show in Chapters 6 and 10 that the creation year was in 3970 BC and that the average number of days per Hebrew lunisolar year within 7,000 lunisolar years (from Nisan 1 of 3970 BC to Nisan 1 of 3031) is exactly equal to 365.242857 (= 364 + 7/7 + 7/49 + 7/70). We thus see that the mystery of the year length is coded in God's perfect number: 7 and its multiples such as 49 and 70. Because God has 10 commandments, the number 10 is a complete number of God. Another of God's complete numbers is 12, which is related to Israeli 12 tribes, 12 apostles of Yeshua, and 12 months of a year. There are many 12's in chapter 21 of the book of Revelation. It is amazing that the age of the universe in terms of the human clock is exactly equal to 7^{12} years (see Appendix C).

Now let us prove whether our speculation on the intercalation method for Enoch's solar calendar is correct or not. In 3970 BC, the Vernal Equinox fell at 9:17 on April 23 (which is obtained from the Stellarium Program), so the first day of the Enoch solar year was on April 20 (Wednesday). The Julian day number for 20 April 3970 BC is JD 271489 (obtained from the Stellarium Program). After 14 × 490 years = 6,860 years from 3970 BC, it comes to 2891. The first day of the Enoch solar year in 2891 will be on March 21 (Wednesday). The Julian day number for 21 March 2891 is JD 2777055. The total number of days within 6860 Enoch's solar years is 2,777,055 − 271,489 = 2,505,566, so the average number of days per Enoch's solar year within this period is 2,505,566/6,860 = 365.242857. Readers could easily verify the same number of days per Enoch's solar year within any multiple of 490 years from 3970 BC. Thus, we have proved the correct intercalation method, which we have figured out from the hint of Yeshua's words recorded in the Gospel of Matthew.

CHAPTER 5

CHINESE LUNISOLAR CALENDAR

The Chinese calendar (Zhongli 中历) is the traditional calendar that was used in China before the official introduction of the Julian calendar in 1912. The Chinese calendar is also called "peasant calendar" (nongli 农历) or "old calendar" (jiuli 旧历). It is still widely used among the people in mainland China, Hong Kong, Taiwan, and Chinese abroad.

The peasant calendar divides a year into 24 solar terms (ershisi jieqi 二十四节气) whose names indicate agricultural activities. This traditional calendar has been used since the Xia Dynasty and therefore is also called "Xia calendar" (Xiali 夏历). Because the calculation of this calendar is based on the phases of the Moon that has a nature of yin (阴), it is also called "Yin calendar" (Yinli 阴历). The course of the months is related to the new-moon phase. In order to make the calendar align with the seasons, it is necessary to add an intercalary month (runyue 闰月) every two or three years. A year with an intercalary month is called runnian 闰年.

The Chinese calendar is also a lunisolar calendar. At present, a day starts from midnight. But in ancient China, the starting time of a day can be inferred from the historically recorded lunar and solar eclipses. The astronomers in the Shang Dynasty (1781-1116 BC) recorded many lunar and solar eclipses along with the cyclic numbers of days (1 to 60). Interestingly, the cyclic number of days did not change from one sunset to another. This implies that a day should have started at sunset just like in the nation of Israel.

The first month is called zhengyue (正月), but the other months are given regular numbers, like eryue (二月 second month), sanyue (三月

third month), and so on. Each month begins on a new-moon (dark-moon) day. This day is called the first day (chuyi 初一) of the month. There are "long months" (dayue 大月) with lengths of 30 days, and "small months" (xiaoyue 小月) with lengths of 29 days. The beginning of the first month of the traditional peasant calendar is oriented towards the Winter Solstice, the day on which the day is the shortest and the night the longest (December 21 according to the Julian calendar). The New-Year's Day (yuandan 元旦) of the traditional Chinese calendar (Xia calendar) is the day of the second new moon following the Winter Solstice. During the Xia Dynasty (2218-1781 BC) the beginning of the year was on the first day of the first month (zhengyue chuyi 正月初一). During the Shang Dynasty, the first day of the twelfth month of the Xia calendar was the beginning of the year. During the Zhou Dynasty (1116-314 BC), the first day of the eleventh month of the Xia calendar was the beginning of the year. During the Han Dynasty (206 BC-220 AD), the beginning of the year was shifted back to the first day of the first month of the Xia calendar, which has not been changed until today.

Chinese New Year in the Xia calendar shall fall on the new moon that is closest to the solar term li chun (start of spring) that typically falls on February 4. In many normal years, the first month of the Xia calendar corresponds to the 12th month of the Hebrew calendar. The first day of a month and the beginning of a day in ancient China are almost identical to those in ancient and modern Israel.

PART II
WORLD CHRONOLOGY

CHAPTER 6

INTRODUCTION TO THE WORLD CHRONOLOGY

The conventional chronology of ancient Egypt places the beginning of the old kingdom in the 27th century BC. The early period of Egypt started from about 3000 BC. According to the traditional Chinese chronology, the first Chinese emperor, called Yellow Emperor (Huang-Di), began his reign in 2698 BC, which was around the same time as the starting date (about 2686 BC) of the old kingdom of ancient Egypt. The middle chronology of the ancient Near East places the beginning of Mesopotamia's early dynastic period at about 2500 BC. The chronologies of these regions with the oldest civilizations in the world consistently suggest that the earliest human kingdom began from the 27th century BC, which was about 4,700 years ago.

On the other hand, the previous Biblical chronologies established by several Biblical scholars indicate that Adam was created around 4,000 BC, which was about 1,000 years earlier than the early period of Egypt. These Biblical chronologies suggest that the creation of the earth and life should have taken place about 6,000 years ago, which appears to seriously contradict the modern cosmology that points to the earth's age being over 4 billion years. If one only believes in the modern cosmology, one will completely discredit the Biblical chronology and thus the Hebrew Scriptures. If one only believes in the Hebrew Scriptures, one will have to completely disbelieve in the modern cosmology. Is there a possibility that both the modern cosmology and the Hebrew Scriptures are still compatible? Yes, it is possible! We will demonstrate this possibility in Chapter 28.

The previous Biblical chronologies have large uncertainties (at least 300 years) due to their methods of construction as well as variations in the Biblical texts. Our current Biblical chronology, which is based on the Masoretic Text of the Hebrew Bible, has a very small uncertainty (less than 6 months). There are several ways to prove its accuracy. First, we have constructed the Chinese chronology back to 2716 BC with uncertainties of less than 6 months. The accuracy of this chronology is due to the concurrently recorded astronomical phenomena, which can be accurately determined from modern astronomy. It is incredible that the year of Noah's flood (2315 BC), deduced from the Masoretic Text of the Hebrew Bible, is the same as that of China's great flood (2315 BC) recorded in the Bamboo Annals. Moses' historical records, preserved in the Masoretic Text of the Hebrew Bible, accurately trace back to the earliest time (3970 BC) without relying on any astronomical phenomenon. China's history thus proves that the Masoretic Text of the Hebrew Bible is truly inspired by the Almighty God. It is thanks to the Jewish people who have so faithfully preserved the Word of God that we can read and study it today.

Secondly, many important historical events in the world took place in sabbatical years (see Chapter 14). The number "seven" is God's holy number and has been coded in the history of the world. Within our current chronology, Yeshua in the New Testament was crucified in the year (30 AD) that was 3,999 years from the creation of Adam (at the end of the fourth millennium from the creation). He was also buried at the end of the fourth day and in the fourth year of a sabbatical cycle. This cannot be a mere coincidence.

It is convenient to use Julian day (JD) numbers to calculate the number of days for a period. The JD number of 15 April 3970 BC is JD 271485, which is obtained from the Stellarium Program. For the 7,000 lunisolar years from 1 Nisan (15 April) 3970 BC to 1 Nisan 3031 (March 17, JD 2828185), there are 2,556,700 days exactly. The average number of days per year within the 7,000 lunisolar years is: $2,556,700/7,000 = 365.242857 = (7 \times 7 \times 7) + (7+7+7) + 7 \times (1/7+1/49+1/70)$. The average numbers of days per Enoch's solar year is also equal to the "magic" number of $(7 \times 7 \times 7) + (7+7+7) + 7 \times (1/7+1/49+1/70)$, as we discussed in Chapter 4.

In the following chapters, we will show how to construct these chronologies scientifically and logically. If readers want to verify the authenticity of our constructed chronologies and have a strong background in science and history, they may continue to read these chapters carefully. Otherwise, we suggest that they should initially read only the introduction sections of the chapters and skip the sections of "detailed explanations."

CHAPTER 7

THE CHRONOLOGY OF THE ANCIENT NEAR EAST

The chronology of the ancient Near East provides a framework of dates for various events, rulers and dynasties in Mesopotamia. An absolute chronology for the first millennium BC has been well established because it agrees with some recorded astronomical events. Despite over 100 years of scholarly efforts, only a relative chronology has been established for the third and second millennium BC and their absolute chronology has an uncertainty of over 150 years.

A key document to pin down the absolute chronology is the Venus tablet of Ammisaduqa (king of Old Babylon), the preserved record of astronomical observations of Venus during the reign of Ammisaduqa. Since the conjunction of the rise of Venus occurs periodically, the recorded astronomical observations of Venus can provide possible fixed points of reference. Astronomical calculation has been used to fix the first year of the reign of Hammurabi either as 1848 BC, 1792 BC, 1728 BC, or 1696 BC, depending on whether the high (or long), middle, low (or short), or ultra-short chronology is followed. The differences are 56, 64, and 32 years, respectively, which are multiples of 8. This is because Venus goes around the Sun 13.004 times every 8 years.

Here, we have unambiguously established the absolute chronology from the historically recorded rise of Venus, along with other historically recorded solar and lunar eclipses (see Table III). The second column of Table III is the short chronology established previously by others. Currently most historians accept the middle chronology, which parallelly shifts the regnal periods to the earlier times by 64 years compared to the short chronology. The accurate chronology established here is shown in the 4th column of Table III, which is in perfect agreement with all the recorded astronomical phenomena.

Our current chronology shows that the kingdoms in the Ancient Near East appear to have begun from 2266 BC. There were no detailed historical records before 2266 BC, which can be explained by the fact that Noah's flood (2315-2314 BC) should have destroyed everything in this region. Sargon started to reign in 2241 BC, which was 73 years after the flood. If he came to the throne in his 30's, he should have been born about 40 years after the flood. Because Ham should have begotten Cush right after the flood and Cush should have begotten children about 30-40 years from the flood, Nimrod, a grandson of Ham (Genesis 10:6-8), should have been born about 30-40 years after the flood. Comparing the ages and stories of Nimrod and Sargon, we speculate that they might be the same person with different names. Our speculation is consistent with that of Yigal Levin who published his article "NIMROD THE MIGHTY, KING OF KISH, KING OF SUMER AND AKKAD" in 2002 AD (Vetus Testamentum, Vol. 52, Fasc. 3, 2002, pp. 350-366). The current chronology of the Ancient Near East thus provides an independent proof for the accuracy of the Biblical chronology presented in Chapter 10.

The detailed argument and explanation are given below. If readers want to verify the authenticity of our chronology and have a strong background in science and history, they may continue to read this chapter carefully. Otherwise, they could initially skip the "detailed explanations" below.

Table III: The Chronology of the Ancient Near East

(The short chronology in the second column is taken from https://en.wikipedia.org/wiki/Short_chronology)

Ruler	Reign (Short)	Reign (Ultra-short)	Modified reign (Ultra-short)	Regnal length
Lugal-zage-si	2295–2271 BC	2263–2239 BC	2266–2242 BC	24
Sargon	2270–2215 BC	2238–2183 BC	2241–2186 BC	56
Rimush	2214–2206 BC	2182–2174 BC	2185–2177 BC	9
Man-ishtishu	2205–2191 BC	2273–2159 BC	2176–2162 BC	15
Naram-sin	2190–2154 BC	2158–2122 BC	2161–2125 BC	37
Shar-kali-sharri	2153–2129 BC	2121–2097 BC	2124–2100 BC	25
Sarlagab	2129–2126 BC	2097–2094 BC	2100–2097 BC	3
Shulme	2126–2120 BC	2094–2088 BC	2097–2091 BC	6
Elulmesh or Silulumesh	2120–2114 BC	2088–2082 BC	2091–2085 BC	6
Inimabakesh	2114–2109 BC	2082–2077 BC	2085–2080 BC	5
Igeshaush or Igeaus	2109–2103 BC	2077–2071 BC	2080–2074 BC	6
Yarlagab or Yarlaqaba	2103–2088 BC	2071–2056 BC	2074–2059 BC	15
Ibate	2088–2085 BC	2056–2053 BC	2059–2056 BC	3
Yarlangab or Yarla	2085–2082 BC	2053–2050 BC	2056–2053 BC	3
Kurum	2082–2081 BC	2050–2049 BC	2053–2052 BC	1
Apilkin or Habil-kin	2081–2078 BC	2049–2046 BC	2052–2049 BC	3
La-erabum	2078–2076 BC	2046–2044 BC	2049–2047 BC	2
Irarum	2076–2074 BC	2044–2042 BC	2047–2045 BC	2
Ibranum	2074–2073 BC	2042–2041 BC	2045–2044 BC	1
Hablum	2073–2071 BC	2041–2039 BC	2044–2042 BC	2
Puzur-Suen	2071–2064 BC	2039–2032 BC	2042–2035 BC	7
Yarlaganda	2064–2057 BC	2032–2025 BC	2035–2028 BC	7
Si-um or Si-u	2057–2050 BC	2025–2018 BC	2028–2021 BC	7
Tirigan	2050–2050 BC	2018–2018 BC	2021–2021 BC	1
Nammahani	2049–2046 BC	2017–2014 BC	2020–2017 BC	4
Ur-Namma or Ur-Engur	2046–2029 BC	2014–1997 BC	2017–2000 BC	17
Shulgi	**2029–1982 BC**	**1997–1950 BC**	**2000–1953 BC**	**47**
Amar-Suena	1981–1973 BC	1949–1941 BC	1952–1944 BC	9
Shu-Suen	1972–1964 BC	1940–1932 BC	1943–1935 BC	9
Ibbi-Suen	**1963–1940 BC**	**1932–1908 BC**	**1934–1911 BC**	**24**
Emisum	**1940–1912 BC**	**1908–1980 BC**	**1911–1883 BC**	**28**
Samium	**1912–1877 BC**	1880–1845 BC	1883–1848 BC	35

Zabaia	1877–1868 BC	1845–1836 BC	1848–1839 BC	9
Gungunum	1868–1841 BC	1836–1809 BC	1839–1812 BC	27
Abisare	1841–1830 BC	1809–1798 BC	1812–1801 BC	11
Sumuel	1830–1801 BC	1798–1769 BC	1801–1772 BC	29
Nur-Adad	1801–1785 BC	1769–1753 BC	1772–1756 BC	16
Sin-Iddinam	1785–1778 BC	1753–1746 BC	1756–1749 BC	7
Sin-Eribam	1778–1776 BC	1746–1744 BC	1749–1747 BC	2
Sin-Iqisham	1776–1771 BC	1744–1739 BC	1747–1742 BC	5
Silli-Adad	1771–1770 BC	1739–1738 BC	1742–1741 BC	1
Warad-Sin	1770–1758 BC	1738–1726 BC	1741–1729 BC	12
Rim-Sin I	1758–1699 BC	1726–1667 BC	1729–1670 BC	59
Hammurabi of Babylon	1699–1686 BC	1667–1654 BC	1670–1657 BC	13
Samsuiluna of Babylon	1686–1678 BC	1654–1646 BC	1657–1649 BC	8
Rim-Sin II	1678–1674 BC	1646–1642 BC	1649–1645 BC	4
Hammurabi	**1728–1686 BC**	**1696–1654 BC**	**1699–1657 BC**	**42**
Samsu-iluna	1686–1648 BC	1654–1616 BC	1657–1619 BC	38
Abi-eshuh or Abieshu	1648–1620 BC	1616–1588 BC	1619–1591 BC	28
Ammi-ditana	1620–1583 BC	1588–1551 BC	1591–1551 BC	40
Ammisaduqa	**1582–1562 BC**	**1550–1530 BC**	**1550–1530 BC**	**21**
Samsu-Ditana	1562–1531 BC	1530–1499 BC	1530–1493 BC	37
Mursili I	**1556–1526 BC**	**1524–1494 BC**	**1524–1493 BC**	**31**

Detailed explanations

The bold face in Table III highlights the timelines of the kings, which are accurately determined from historically recorded astronomical phenomena including astronomical observations of Venus as well as lunar and solar eclipses.

1. Venus Tablet

The record of astronomical observations of Venus during the reign of Ammisaduqa has been well preserved. The record is difficult to comprehend to those who do not have a strong background in science and history. In the following, we list the detailed record for completeness but only focus on three years (year 1, year 9, and year 17) highlighted by the bold face:

- **Year 1 inferior Venus sets on Shabatu [the 11th month] 15 and after 3 days rises on Shabatu 18;**
- Year 2 superior Venus vanishes East on Arahsamnu 21 and after 1 month 25 days appears West on Tebetu 16;
- Year 3 inferior Venus sets on Ululu 29 and after 16 days rises on Tashritu 15;
- Year 4 superior Venus vanishes East on Dumuzi 3 and after 2 months 6 days appears West on Ululu 9;
- Year 5 inferior Venus sets on Nisan 29 and after 12 days rises on Ayar 11;
- Year 5 superior Venus vanishes East on Kislimu 27 and after 2 months 3 days appears West on Shabatu 30;
- Year 6 inferior Venus sets on Arahsamnu 28 and after 3 days rises on Kislimu 1;
- Year 7 superior Venus vanishes East on Abu 30 and after 2 months appears West on Tashritu 30;
- Year 8 inferior Venus sets on Dumuzi 9 and after 17 days rises on Dumuzi 26;
- Year 8 superior Venus vanishes East on Adar 27 and after 2 months 16 days appears West on Simanu 13;
- **Year 9 inferior Venus sets on Adar [the 12th month] 12 and after 2 days rises on Adar 14;**
- Year 10 superior Venus vanishes East on Arahsamnu 17 and after 1 month 25 days appears West on Tebetu 12;
- Year 11 inferior Venus sets on Ululu 25 and after 16 days rises on II Ululu 11;
- Year 12 superior Venus vanishes East on Ayar 29 and after 2 months 6 days appears West on Abu 5;
- Year 13 inferior Venus sets on Nisan 25 and after 12 days rises on Ayar 7;
- Year 13 superior Venus vanishes East on Tebetu 23 and after 2 months 3 days appears West on Adar 26;
- Year 14 inferior Venus sets on Arahsamnu 24 and after 3 days rises on Arahsamnu 27;
- Year 15 superior Venus vanishes East on Abu 26 and after 2 months appears West on Tashritu 26;

- Year 16 inferior Venus sets on Dumuzi 5 and after 16 days rises on Dumuzi 21;
- Year 16 superior Venus vanishes East on Adar 24 and after 2 months 15 days appears West on Simanu 9;
- **Year 17 inferior Venus sets on Adar [the 12th month] 8 and after 3 days rises on Adar 11;**
- Year 18 superior Venus vanishes East on Arahsamnu 13 and after 1 month 25 days appears West on Tebetu 8;
- Year 19 inferior Venus sets on II Ululu 20 and after 17 days rises on Tashritu 8;
- Year 20 superior Venus vanishes East on Simanu 25 and after 2 months 6 days appears West on Ululu 1;
- Year 21 inferior Venus sets on Nisan 22 and after 11 days rises on Ayar 3;
- Year 21 superior Venus vanishes East on Tebetu 19 and after 2 months 3 days appears West on Adar 22.

If one can explain the observations of Venus in the 1st, 9th and 17th year of Ammisaduqa (see the bolded lines above), one should be able to explain all the other years consistently. These three-year observations of Venus cannot be consistently explained if we use the Babylonian lunisolar calendar established after 700 BC, where the first month always starts on or after the Vernal Equinox. One cannot simultaneously match the records for year 1, year 9, and year 17 if year 0 (the ascension year of king Ammisaduqa), year 8, and year 16 are all regular years with no intercalary month. Only if year 0 is an embolismic year (where an intercalary month is added before year 1 starts) while year 8 and year 16 are regular years, can the records for year 1, year 9, and year 17 agree with the astronomical calculation (see below). It is only possible if the Babylonians in the time of Ammisaduqa used a lunisolar calendar that was similar to the Hebrew lunisolar calendar.

According to the intercalation rule of the Hebrew calendar (see Chapter 2), an intercalary month is added if the time of the full moon after the 12th month falls before the Vernal Equinox. The full moon after the 12th month of 1551 BC was at 23:06 on April 3 of 1550 BC while the Vernal Equinox was at 14:19 on April 4 of 1550 BC. According to the intercalation rule of the Hebrew calendar, a 13th month should have been added for 1551 BC (that is, the year of 1551 BC was an embolismic year). This implies that the year of 1551 BC could have been year 0 of Ammisaduqa. Then the first month of 1550 BC started on April 20 (see Appendix D) when Ammisaduqa should have commenced his first year. In the 18th day of the 11th month of Ammisaduqa's 1st year, which was on 26 February 1549 BC, Venus rose according to the record (year 1), in agreement with the astronomical calculation from the Stellarium Program.

In 1542 BC (8 years after 1550 BC), the Vernal Equinox was at 12:52 on April 4 and the full moon after the 12th month of 1543 BC was at 17:44 on April 5 of 1542 BC. Thus, 1543 BC was a regular year and could have been year 8 of Ammisaduqa. The first month of 1542 BC started in the evening of March 21 (see Appendix D) when Ammisaduqa should have begun his 9th year. In the 14th day of the 12th month of his 9th year, which was on 21 February 1541 BC, Venus rose again according to the record (year 9), which is in perfect agreement with the astronomical calculation from the Stellarium Program (see Figure 2).

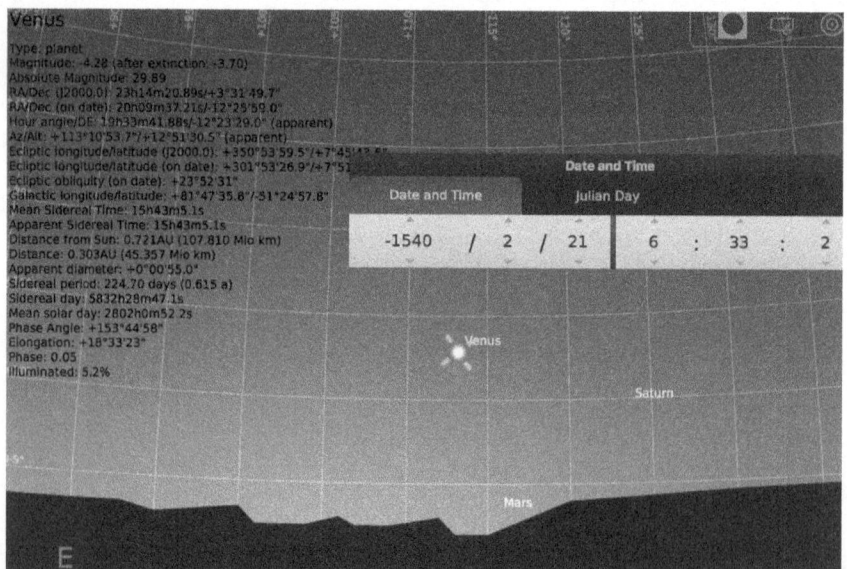

Figure 2: Venus rose on 21 February 1541 BC in Babylon, as predicted from the Stellarium Program.

In 1534 BC (8 years after 1542 BC), the Vernal Equinox was at 5:31 on April 4 and the full moon after the 12th month of 1535 BC was at 12:20 on April 7 of 1534 BC. Therefore 1534 BC was also a regular year and the first month started in the evening of March 23 (see Appendix D) when Ammisaduqa should have started his 17th year. In the 11th day of the 12th month of his 17th year, which was on 22 February 1533 BC, Venus rose again according to the record (year 17), in agreement with the astronomical calculation.

Any backward or forward shift by multiples of 8 years cannot consistently match the recorded Venus rising in year 1, year 9, and year 17 of Ammisaduqa. If the commonly used Babylonian calendar were used to record the Venus rising, no year would have been matched. The recorded astronomical observations of Venus can only be in agreement with the astronomical calculation if the first year of Ammisaduqa was in 1550 BC and the lunisolar calendar used by Ammisaduqa's astronomers was the same as the Hebrew lunisolar calendar first introduced by Moses right after the exodus from Egypt (1457 BC). We thus conclude that the first year of Ammisaduqa must have been in 1550 BC, which confirms the ultra-short chronology listed in Table III.

If the regnal lengths of the kings in the previously established chronology were accurate, the first year of Hammurabi's reign in the ultra-short chronology would be placed in 1696 BC (see the third column of Table III). On the other hand, the recorded lunar eclipse observed in either the 11th or 12th year of Hammurabi (see below) suggests that the first year of Hammurabi should have been between 1697 and 1699 BC. Naturally, this discrepancy can be resolved since the regnal length of Ammi-Ditana was assigned to be 37 years in the previous chronology while his true regnal length was more than 37 years (https://en.wikipedia.org/wiki/Ammi-Ditana). To be consistent with the observed lunar eclipse in the end year of Shulgi (see below), we conclude the first year of Hammurabi to be in 1699 BC, three years earlier than the previously assigned time in the ultra-short chronology.

How would it have been possible for the old Babylonians around 1550 BC to use a lunisolar calendar so like that of the Hebrews? Hammurabi was the sixth king of the First Babylonian Dynasty (https://en.wikipedia.org/wiki/Code_of_Hammurabi). He issued the code of Hammurabi, which he claimed to have received from Shamash, the Babylonian god of justice. The code consisted of 282 laws and was one of the first law codes that emphasized the physical punishment of perpetrators. The code was also one of the earliest examples of "presumption of innocence," where both the accused and accuser had the opportunity to provide evidence.

Scholars have found numerous similarities between the code of Hammurabi and the laws of Moses in the Torah. We do not believe that the Mosaic laws were copied from Hammurabi's code. In all likelihood, both sets of just laws should have been inspired by the same God who is the God of all nations. This same origin explains why the calendar used by the Babylonians during that special period could have been the same as the Hebrew's.

2. Lunar eclipse in the end year of Shulgi

The first lunar eclipse of Ur was described in a tablet (EAE 20). The eclipse was said to take place on the 14th day of the third month, beginning on the first watch in the east, and ending in the west at the beginning of the second watch. The eclipse was thought to mark the end of Shulgi's reign, around 1950 BC, according to the chronology established by the recorded astronomical observations of Venus (see Table III).

The predicted total lunar eclipse on 27 June 1954 BC matches perfectly with the recorded lunar eclipse. The day of 12 June 1954 BC was indeed the 14th day of the third month according to the commonly used Babylonian lunisolar calendar. With a delta-T parameter: $\Delta T = -20 + 31.1 t^2$ (see Appendix A), the predicted eclipse ended at 22:09.

Since sunset was at 18:50 and sunrise was at 4:44 that day, the first watch started at 18:50; the second watch started at 22:08; and the third watch ended at 4:44 (there were three night-watches for the Babylonians and four night-watches for the Hebrews). Therefore, the predicted lunar eclipse ended at 22:09, which was right at the beginning of the second watch, perfectly matching the recorded lunar eclipse.

Since this lunar eclipse marked the end of the reign of Shulgi, the final year of his reign should have been from the spring of 1954 BC to the spring of 1953 BC. Our chronology listed in Table III (the fourth column) fixes the end of Shulgi's reign in the spring of 1953 BC.

3. Lunar eclipse in the end year of Ibbi-Suen

The second lunar eclipse of Ur was described in EAE 21 and 22. It was said that the eclipse took place on the 14th day of the 12th month, beginning in the first watch in the south, and ending in the last watch in the north. The eclipse was thought to mark the end of the reign of Ibbi-Suen and the end of the Ur III Dynasty. The predicted lunar eclipse on 16 March 1912 BC matches the recorded lunar eclipse. The 16th day of March was on the 14th day of the 12th lunar month of 1913 BC.

From the fitted curve of the delta-T parameter (see Appendix A), we find that the delta-T parameter in 1912 BC is given by $\Delta T = -20 + 27.8t^2$. The predicted eclipse has a magnitude of about 1.6, starting at 19:43 and ending at 0:57.

Since sunset was at 17:58 and sunrise was at 6:34 that day, the first watch started from 17:58 and the last watch started at 2:06. The predicted lunar eclipse on 16 March 1912 BC started in the first watch but ended at 0:57, about one hour before the last watch. This small discrepancy between the predicted and observed ending time of the eclipse should be caused by the uncertainty of the delta-T parameter. Indeed, if $\Delta T = -20 + 32t^2$ is used, the predicted eclipse started at 20:35 and ended at 1:51. The ending time of the eclipse was only 15 minutes away from the last watch.

The end of the Dynasty of Ur III was in the spring of 1911 BC, according to the chronology in Table III, which was about one year after this recorded lunar eclipse in the spring of 1912 BC.

4. Lunar eclipse in the 11th or 12th year of Hammurabi

A lunar eclipse was recorded in the 11th or 12th year of Hammurabi (Tablet HC-A 25-115) during the Asqudum eponym. Two total lunar eclipses are predicted to occur on February 18 and August 13 of 1687 BC. If the lunar eclipse was seen on 18 February 1687 BC in his 11th year, then his first year was the year between the spring of 1698 BC and the spring of 1697 BC. If the lunar eclipse was seen on 18 February 1687

BC but in the 12th year of Hammurabi's reign, then his first year was the year between the spring of 1699 BC and the spring of 1698 BC. If the lunar eclipse was seen on 13 August 1687 BC in his 11th year, then his first year was the year between the spring of 1697 BC and the spring of 1696 BC. If the lunar eclipse was seen on 13 August 1687 BC but in his 12th year, then his first year was the year between the spring of 1698 BC and the spring of the 1697 BC. The above logical reasoning leads to a conclusion that the first year of Hammurabi should have been between the spring of 1699 and the spring of 1696 BC. In order to match the lunar eclipse in the last year of Shulgi, the first year of Hammurabi should have been the year between the spring 1699 BC and the spring of 1698 BC. Therefore, the lunar eclipse should have been seen on 18 February 1687 BC and in the 12th year of Hammurabi's reign.

5. Solar and lunar eclipses at the end of the First Babylonian Dynasty

Both solar and lunar eclipses were recorded in EAE 20. The eclipses presaged the end of the First Dynasty of Babylon. The lunar eclipse was seen on the 14th day of the 11th month and started in the last watch in the south. It was partially eclipsed in the west. Two weeks later, the solar eclipse was seen on the 28th day of the 11th month.

There are very few pairs of solar and lunar eclipses in the same month. An additional constraint for the pairs of eclipses is that they both occurred in the 11th month and were two weeks apart. A partial lunar eclipse was predicted to be seen on 5 March 1493 BC and exactly two weeks later, a solar eclipse was predicted to be seen in Babylon on 19 March 1493 BC (see Figure 3). The two dates should have been on the 14th and 28th day of the 11th month of 1494 BC, only if the old Assyrian lunisolar calendar was used to record the eclipses. It is likely that the last king of the First Dynasty of Babylon abandoned the previous Hammurabi's code and reverted to the original Assyrian code (including the use of the old Assyrian calendar), leading to the destruction of his kingdom.

Since there are no other eclipse pairs that could have taken place in the 11th month, the predicted and observed eclipse pairs in the 11th month of 1494 BC completely pin down the time for the end of the

First Dynasty of Babylon. The final year of the First Dynasty of Babylon should have been from the spring of 1494 BC to the spring of 1493 BC. It was destroyed in the early spring of 1493 BC right after the occurrence of the lunar and solar eclipse pairs.

From the fitted curve of the delta-T parameter (see Appendix A), we find that the delta-T parameter in 1493 BC is given by $\Delta T = -20 + 25.95 t^2$. Figure 3 shows the occurrence of the maximum solar eclipse at 12:22 on 19 March 1493 BC. The maximum eclipse factor is 41.3%, which is substantial.

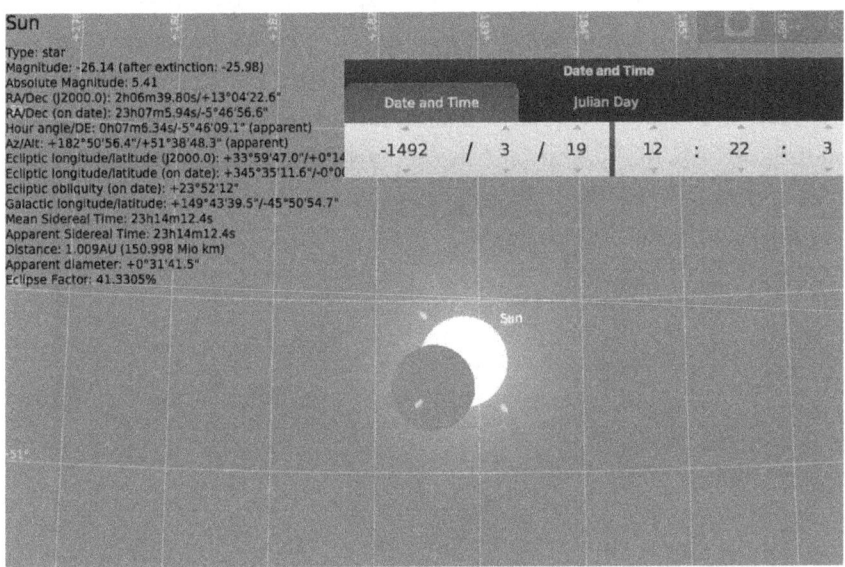

Figure 3: Predicted solar eclipse on 19 March 1493 BC, observed in Babylon.

The predicted lunar eclipse on 5 March 1493 BC has a magnitude of about 1.0. The eclipse started at 2:11 and ended at 6:18 according to the calculation. Since sunset and sunrise on March 5 of 1493 BC were at 17:53 and 6:45, respectively, the third watch should have started at 2:22. Therefore, the starting time (2:11) of the predicted lunar eclipse was very close to the beginning of the last watch, perfectly matching the historical record of the lunar eclipse.

If Babylon fell right after the solar eclipse on 19 March 1493 BC, the last year of Samsu-Ditana was from the spring of 1494 BC to the spring of 1493 BC. Babylon was destroyed in the 12th month of 1494

BC. If this was the case, Samsu-Ditan should have actually reigned for 37 years rather than for 31 years. It is likely that some of the historical records for the latter part of his reign were destroyed after the sacking of Babylon.

According to the short chronology, Mursili I reigned between 1556 and 1526 BC (see the last row of Table III). Within the ultra-short chronology (shifted down by 32 years compared to the short chronology), Mursili I should have reigned between 1524 and 1494 BC instead. It was recorded (see the website: https://en.wikipedia.org/wiki/Mursili_I) that when Mursili I returned to his kingdom after sacking Babylon, he was assassinated in a conspiracy led by his brother-in-law, Hantili I (who took the throne) and Hantili's son-in-law, Zidanta I. This suggests that the city of Babylon should have been destroyed in the last month of 1494 BC if Mursili I reigned until the last month of 1494 BC (the spring of 1493 BC). This is consistent with the conclusion drawn from the recorded eclipse pairs.

CHAPTER 8

CHRONOLOGY OF BABYLON AND PERSIA

Ptolemy's Canon is one of the most important bases for our knowledge of Mesopotamia's ancient chronology. The Canon's increments by whole ancient Egyptian years (365 days per year) have two consequences. The first is that the beginning and ending dates of kings are simplified to the beginning and ending times of ancient Egyptian years, which are off about one day every four years against the Julian calendar. The second is that this list of kings is oversimplified: Kings who reigned for less than one year were not listed. Usually the overlapping year was assigned to the king who died in that year, but not always. The Canon is generally considered by historians to be quite accurate (probably with an error of less than 2 years) but is not the ultimate source for chronology synchronization. Here, we will make a revision on the Canon that only covers the kings from Nabopolassar to Darius III Codomannus, based on the detailed regnal lengths of the kings, which were summarized in *Babylonian Chronology 626 B.C. –A.D.75* by Richard A. Parker and Waldo H. Dubberstein (Wipf and Stock Publishers, 2007).

Table IV: Chronology of Babylon and Persia

	Name (modern)	Regnal length	Dates in our era
1	Nabopolassar	21 years	11/1/626 – 8/15/605
2	Nebuchadnezzar II	43 years	8/16/605 – 10/7/562
3	Amel-Marduk	2 years	10/8/562 – 8/7/560
4	Neriglissar	3 years +8 months	9/1/560 – 4/12/556
5	Labashi-Marduk	1 year + 3 months	4/13/556–7/3/555
6	Nabonidus	17 years	7/4/555 – 10/17/538
7	Darius the Mede (Ugbaru)	13 months	10/18/538– 11/13/537
8	Cyrus the Great	9 years	10/18/538 – 8/9/529
9	Cambyses II	7 years	4/21/529 – 4/7/522
10	Bardiya (Smerdis, Gaumata)	5 months	4/14/522 – 9/9/522
11	Nebuchadnezzar IV	2 months	10/6/522 – 12/7/522
12	Darius I the Great	36 years	2/4/521 – 11/21/485
13	Xerxes I	21 years	11/22/485 – 10/11/464
14	Artaxerxes I Makrocheir	41 years	10/12/464 – 4/9/423
15	Darius II Nothus	20 years	8/12/424 – 10/30/404
16	Artaxerxes II Mnemon	45 years	10/31/404 – 11/24/359
17	Artaxerxes III Ochus	21 years	11/25/359 – 11/15/338
18	Artaxerxes IV Arses	2 years	11/16/338 – 11/44/336
19	Darius III Codomannus	4 years	11/15/336 – 11/13/332

Table IV lists the actual starting and ending dates of the kings. The overlapped time of two adjacent kings was due to coregency. The coregency between Cyrus and his son Cambyses II should have begun from Nisannu 1 of the 9th year of Cyrus, according to a contract tablet which reads: "year 1, ascension year, Cambyses king of Babylon and Lands." [*Krüickmann, Neubabylonische Rechts und Venoaltungstexte* (Leipzig, 1933), No. 92]. Year 1 and the ascension year were the same year only if the king started to reign exactly on the first day of a new year (Nisannu 1). The astronomical clay tablet of BM 33066 records two lunar eclipses in July of 523 BC and in January of 522 BC, which was in the 7th year of Cambyses II. This important astronomical record leads us to set the beginning date of the first year (or ascension year) of Cambyses II to be on Nisannu 1 (April 12) of 528 BC. Since the 9th year of Cyrus was also on Nisannu 1 of 528 BC, the first year of Cyrus must have started on Nisannu 1 of 537 BC, and his ascension date should have been on the third day of the 8th month of 538 BC when he took Babylon. This is one year later than the date generally accepted by historians. The previous Canon contradicts the fact that Cambyses II started to co-reign with his father exactly in the beginning of the new year. The second contradiction is that Labaši-Marduk should have reigned for at least 1 year and 3 months. Any king who reigned for less than one year should not have been in the Uruk King's List. But Labaši-Marduk is in the List and the text of the List contains a lacuna, where one should expect to read a year number for his reign. Therefore, Labaši-Marduk should have reigned for more than one year, in agreement with the modified chronology in Table IV.

The current chronology is also consistent with the third book of Chaldean history by Berosus, as reiterated by Josephus in *Against Apion*, bk. 1, 146-153. The added total regnal length for Neriglissar and Labashi-Marduk was 4 years and 9 months according to Josephus, which was in agreement with the current chronology (see Table IV).

The current chronology is further confirmed by the list of the Kings of Tyre (Table V), which is taken from https://en.wikipedia.org/wiki/King_of_Tyre. The list was constructed from *Against Apion*: bk. 1, 156-158. Josephus stated that Cyrus the Persian took the Babylonian kingdom in **the fourteenth year** of Hiram (*Against Apion*: bk. 1, 159). Since the 14th year of Hiram was between the spring of 538 BC and the spring of 537 BC according to Table V, the third day of the 8th month of 538 BC (when Cyrus took Babylon) was indeed in the 14th year of Hiram. This excellent consistency suggests that our current chronology of Babylon and Persia is more accurate than the generally accepted one.

Table V: Kings of Tyre

King Name	Reign period	Note
Ithobaal III	591-573 BC	Carthage became independent of Tyre in 574 BC
Baal II	573-564 BC	
Yakinbaal	564-564 BC	
Chelbes	564-563 BC	
Abbar	563-562 BC	
Mattan III and Ger Ashthari	562-556 BC	
Baal-Eser III	556-555 BC	
Merbalus	555-551 BC	
Hiram III	551-532 BC	

CHAPTER 9

CHINESE CHRONOLOGY

China is one of the world's most ancient civilizations. China's written history was generally believed to begin from the Shang Dynasty over 3,000 years ago. Ancient historical texts such as the Records of the Grand Historian (about 100 BC) and the Bamboo Annals (the 6th century BC) describe the earlier dynasties (e.g., the Xia Dynasty) before the Shang Dynasty. The Shujing (Shu-king), the Chinese historical classic document, compiled by Confucius (551-479 BC) provides a record of religion, philosophy, customs, and government of the Chinese from the earliest times. The authenticity of these records remains an open question because the earliest recorded historical events had already taken place about 2,000 years before the authors compiled them.

The Chinese chronology after 770 BC (after the Eastern Zhou Dynasty) has been accurately established with no uncertainty. This accuracy is warranted by the fact that the chronology is in perfect agreement with all recorded astronomical data. In contrast, the Chinese chronology prior to 770 BC has not been resolved despite tremendous efforts of Chinese scholars from several different fields since 1996. The Xia-Shang-Zhou Chronology Project (Chinese: 夏商周断代工程, Pinyin: *Xia-Shang-Zhou Duandai Gongcheng*) was a multi-disciplinary project commissioned by the government of China in 1996. The objective of this project was to accurately determine the locations and timelines of the Xia, Shang, and Zhou Dynasties. To achieve better accuracy of the chronology, some 200 experts took part in the project which involved multiple methods such as the radiocarbon dating method, archaeological dating method, historical textual analysis, astronomy, and so on. Preliminary results of the project were released in November of 2000. However, the conclusions have been disputed by many scholars.

The main conclusion of the project is that the first year of King Yi (懿王) of the Western Zhou Dynasty is fixed in 899 BC, which shifts forward the previously assigned year of 935 BC by 36 years. This conclusion is based on an interpretation of a solar eclipse that was seen in the first year of King Yi. This interpretation was published in 1995 by scholars from the Jet Propulsion Laboratory (JPL) and University of California at Los Angeles (UCLA). In this publication, an earlier morning solar eclipse on 21 April 899 BC was attributed to the solar eclipse observed in the first year of King Yi. In the following paragraphs, we will show that because of this incorrect interpretation, the Chinese chronology before the Eastern Zhou Dynasty shifts forward by many years and becomes less accurate than the traditional Chinese chronology established before 1996.

In Table VI below, we have reconstructed the Chinese chronology starting from the first year of Huang-Di (Yellow Emperor) based on all the available astronomical data recorded mostly in the *Bamboo Annals*. The regnal lengths of the kings marked by *"Common Scheme"* in the last column of Table VI are taken from a historical book "中国历史年表, *Timelines of Chinese History*", which was compiled by 柏杨 (Bo Yang), a famous author in Taiwan, China. The book was published in 1977, well before the Xia-Shang-Zhou Chronology Project. The regnal lengths of the kings between Emperor Yao and the Eastern Zhou Dynasty are nearly identical to those listed by James Legge, which were obtained from *Common Scheme*. The regnal lengths marked by *"Bamboo Annals"* are directly taken from the *Bamboo Annals*, where the regnal lengths perfectly match the astronomical data, particularly in the period between Wu-Ding and Di-Xin. The total number of years between Wu-Ding and Di-Xin determined from *Common Scheme* is only one year shorter than that inferred from the *Bamboo Annals*.

Detailed accounts of kings that were recorded in the *Bamboo Annals* are usually reliable. In contrast, short and brief records of kings in the *Bamboo Annals* are not so reliable, possibly because the original detailed records were lost and modified or reconstructed by latter historians. What is amazing is that the astronomical records of some "crucial" kings in the *Bamboo Annals* remain intact, which allow us to precisely determine the beginning and the ending of each kingdom in the early dynasties. In particular, the detailed records of Huang-Di, Yao, Shun, Yu, Zhong-Kang, Gui (Jie), Wu-Ding, Di-Xin, Zhou Cheng-Wang, Zhou You-Wang, and Zhou Ping-Wang can perfectly recover the entire chronology of the Chinese history without noticeable errors due to the concurrently recorded astronomical phenomena. The recorded astronomical phenomena allow us to accurately trace backward the times of the ancient Chinese kings. Below, we will provide some examples to demonstrate how we use the astronomical phenomena to accurately determine the ascension years of Huang-Di, Yao, Shun, Yu, and some other important kings/emperors.

In order to fully understand the section of "detailed explanations" below, one needs to have a strong background in science as well as Chinese history and culture. If readers wish to verify the authenticity of the chronology and are interested in Chinese history and culture, they may continue to read this chapter carefully. Otherwise, they could skip the section of "detailed explanations" below.

The first (ascension) year of Emperor Yao has been verified by 4 independent astronomical phenomena. These astronomical phenomena consistently show that Yao started his reign in the fall of 2376 BC. In Yao's 61st year, which was in 2315 BC, China's "great flood" took place. It is amazing that China's great flood happened in the same year as Noah's flood (see Chapter 10). The accurate timeline of Emperor Yao proves the accuracy of our current Biblical chronology which will be shown in Chapter 10.

Yao's timeline also resolves a 2,000-year controversy as to whether Noah's flood was regional or global. His timeline clearly tells us that God did not destroy all the Chinese people by the flood, and that the Chinese people are not the descendants of Noah. This conclusion is in sharp contrast to a general belief of most Christians: Noah's flood was global and destroyed all humans except for the 8 people in Noah's family. This general belief appears to be supported by the Biblical account of Noah's flood. Nevertheless, with a correct understanding of the Hebrew word "כל kol" (meaning all) in the Hebrew Bible, one can also conclude that Noah's flood should have been regional (for detailed argument of Dr. Michael Heiser for local regional flood from the Biblical text, please see https://drmsh.com/argue-biblical-text-local-regional-flood-instead-global-flood/).

About 2,000 years ago, Flavius Josephus, Jewish priest and historian, agreed with his contemporary historians and wrote: "There is a great mountain in Armenia, over Minyas, called Baris, upon which it is reported that many who fled at the time of the Deluge were saved; and that one who was carried in an ark came on shore upon the top of it; and that the remains of the timber were a great while preserved. This might be the man about whom Moses, the legislator of the Jews, wrote." (*Antiq*. bk. 1, ch.3, sect. 6). The implication of Josephus' writing is that many people apart from Noah's family survived Noah's flood, in agreement with China's historical records.

Since Josephus was a Pharisee and a Jewish priest, he must have understood the Hebrew Scriptures very well. He would not have written the above paragraph concerning the survivors of Noah's flood if his own understanding of the Hebrew Scriptures had convinced him that only Noah's family would have survived from the flood. Therefore, Josephus must have had the same understanding of the Hebrew Scriptures as Dr. Michael Heiser who argued for local regional flood from the Biblical text.

Table VI: Chronology of China

Rulers	Regnal time	Regnal length (year)	Comment
Huang Di 黄帝	2716-2616 BC	100	Huang Di Started to reign in the autumn of 2716 BC; Solar eclipse on 21 September 2666 BC in year 50
Shao Hao 少昊	2616-2533 BC	83	Common Scheme
Xuan Di 玄帝	2533-2455 BC	78	Common Scheme
Di Ku 帝喾	2455-2385 BC	70	Common Scheme
Di Zhi 帝挚	2385-2376 BC	9	Common Scheme
Yao 尧	2376-2276 BC	100	Yao started to reign between 29 August and 17 November 2376 BC. Venus was seen in Yi on 28 August 2334 BC in year 42; solar eclipse on 18 November 2324 BC in year 53; Venus was seen in Yi on 25 June 2306 BC in year 70; five stars (like threaded pearls) were seen on 8 April 2306 BC in year 70.
No king	2276-2271 BC	5	See main text.
Shun 舜	2271-2221 BC	50	Venus was seen in Fang (Scorpius) between 8-19 September 2271 BC right upon his ascension.
Yu 禹	2257-2221 BC	36	Co-reigned with Shun; heavenly word that Shun should resign in favor of Yu in 2257 BC, in the end of year 14.
No king	2221-2218 BC	3	Common Scheme

Yu 禹	2218-2210 BC	8	Bamboo Annals: Yu reigned for 45 years, reigned solely for 8 years.
Qi 啟	2210-2200 BC	10	Common Scheme
Tai Kang 太康	2200-2171 BC	29	Common Scheme
Zhong Kang 仲康	2171-2158 BC	13	Solar eclipse on 22 November 2167 BC in the 9th month of year 5
Xiang 相	2158-2131 BC	27	Common Scheme
Usurpation	2131-2091 BC	40	Common Scheme
Shao Kang 少康	2091-2069 BC	22	Common Scheme
Zhu 杼	2069-2052 BC	17	Common Scheme
Huai 槐	2052-2026 BC	26	Common Scheme
Mang 芒	2026-2008 BC	18	Common Scheme
Xie 泄	2008-1992 BC	16	Common Scheme
Bu Jiang 不降	1992-1933 BC	59	Common Scheme
Jiong 扃	1933-1915 BC	18	Bamboo Annals
Jin 廑	1915-1894 BC	21	Common Scheme
Kong Jia 孔甲	1894-1863 BC	31	Common Scheme
Gao 皋	1863-1852 BC	11	Common Scheme
Fa 發	1852-1833 BC	19	Common Scheme
Gui 癸	1833-1781 BC	52	Solar eclipse on 15 June 1805 BC in year 29

Name	Years	Reign	Notes
Tang 汤	1781-1768 BC	13	Shang Dynasty started.
Tai-Jia 太甲	1768-1735 BC	33	Common Scheme
Wo-Ding 沃丁	1735-1706 BC	29	Common Scheme
Tai-Kang 太康	1706-1681 BC	25	Common Scheme
Xiao-Jia 小甲	1681-1664 BC	17	Common Scheme
Yong-Ji 雍己	1664-1652 BC	12	Common Scheme
Tai-Wu 太戊	1652-1577 BC	75	Common Scheme
Zhong-Ding 仲丁	1577-1564 BC	13	Common Scheme
Wai-Ren 外壬	1564-1549 BC	15	Common Scheme
He-Dan-Jia 河亶甲	1549-1540 BC	9	Common Scheme
Zu-Yi 祖乙	1540-1521 BC	19	Common Scheme
Zu-Xin 祖辛	1521-1505 BC	16	Common Scheme
Wo-Jia 沃甲	1505-1480 BC	25	Common Scheme
Zu-Ding 祖丁	1480-1448 BC	32	Common Scheme
Nan-Geng 南庚	1448-1423 BC	25	Common Scheme
Yang-Jia 阳甲	1423-1416 BC	7	Common Scheme
Pan-Geng 盤庚	1416-1388 BC	28	Common Scheme
Xiao-Xin 小辛	1388-1367 BC	21	Common Scheme
Xiao-Yi 小乙	1367-1339 BC	28	Common Scheme

Name	Reign	Years	Notes
Wu-Ding 武丁	1339-1280 BC	59	Total lunar eclipse on 24 November 1311 BC in the 12th month of year 29
Zu-Geng 祖庚	1280-1269 BC	11	Bamboo Annals
Zu-Jia 祖甲	1269-1236 BC	33	Bamboo Annals
Lin-Xin 廩辛	1236-1232 BC	4	Bamboo Annals
Geng-Ding 庚丁	1232-1224 BC	8	Bamboo Annals
Wu-Yi 武乙	1224-1189 BC	35	Bamboo Annals
Tai-Ding 太丁	1189-1176 BC	13	Zhou Wen-Wang started to reign in 1178 BC in the 12th year of Tai-Ding.
Di-Yi 帝乙	1176-1168 BC	8	Bamboo Annals: Di-Yi died in his 9th year. He should die just after new year and Di-Xin started his first year in the beginning of the 9th year of Di-Yi.
Di-Xin 帝辛	1168-1116 BC	52	Solar eclipse on 10 September 1121 BC in year 48; Solar eclipse on 10 September 1117 BC in year 52; five stars were seen in constellation of Fang on 29 December 1137 BC in year 32. Zhou Wen-Wang died in 1128 BC in the spring of year 41 (total regnal length is 50 years). Di-Xin was executed on 27 January 1116 BC, which was in the second month, in the day of jia-zi (1st day of cycle).
King Wu 武王	1127-1116 BC	11	Wu started to reign in year 42 of Di-Xin.
King Wu 武王	1116-1110 BC	6	Zhou Dynasty started.
King Cheng 成王	1110-1073 BC	37	Solar eclipse on 7 March 1093 BC in the first month of spring of year 18; Common Scheme

King Kang 康王	1073-1047 BC	26	Common Scheme
King Zhao 昭王	1047-996 BC	51	Common Scheme
King Mu 穆王	996-941 BC	55	Common Scheme
King Gong 共王	941-926 BC	15	https://zh.wikipedia.org/wiki/周共王
King Yi 懿王	926-901 BC	25	Solar eclipse on 21 March 926 BC in the first month of year 1; Common Scheme
King Xiao 孝王	901-886 BC	15	Common Scheme
King Yi 夷王	886-878 BC	8	Bamboo Annals
King Li 厉王	878-841 BC	37	Common Scheme
Gong He 共和	841-827 BC	14	Common Scheme
King Xuan 宣王	827-781 BC	46	Common Scheme
King You 幽王	781-770 BC	11	Solar eclipse on 6 September 776 BC, in the day of xin-mao (28th of the cycle) in year 6; Common Scheme
King Ping 平王	770-719 BC	51	Solar eclipse on 22 February 720 BC in the second month of year 51; Common Scheme
King Nan 周赧王	314-256 BC	59	Zhou ended
King Zhao 秦昭王	255-251 BC	4	Qin began to reign in the land of Zhou.
Qin Shi-Huang 秦始皇	220-210 BC	10	Qin United China started.
Han Wang 汉王	206-202 BC	4	Western Han Dynasty started.
Han Gaozu 汉高祖	202-195 BC	7	
Han Ai Di 汉哀帝 (Jianping Era)	6-3 BC		"Comet" seen in the second month of the second year of Jianping (between March 8 and April 7 of 5 BC).

Guangwu Di 光武帝	August 25 AD-March 57 AD	31	Eastern Han Dynasty started.
Three Kingdoms 三国	220-280 AD	60	
Western Jin 西晋	266-316 AD	50	
Eastern Jin 东晋	317-420 AD	103	
Sixteen Kingdoms 十六国	304-439 AD	135	
Northern and Southern Dynasties 南北朝	386-589 AD	203	
Sui dynasty 隋	581-618 AD	37	
Tang dynasty 唐	618-907 AD	289	
Five Dynasties and Ten Kingdoms 五代十国	907-960 AD	53	
Northern Song 北宋	960-1127 AD	167	
Southern Song 南宋	1127-1279 AD	152	
Liao Dynasty 辽	907-1125 AD	218	
Western Liao 西辽	1124-1218 AD	94	
Western Xia 西夏	1038-1227 AD	189	
Jin Dynasty 金	1115-1234 AD	119	
Yuan Dynasty 元	1271-1368 AD	97	
Ming Dynasty 明	1368-1664 AD	276	
Qing Dynasty 清	1636-1912 AD	276	

Republic China 中华民国	1912-1949 AD	37	
People's Republic of China 中华人民共和国	1949 AD-present		

Detailed explanations

In the following, we will demonstrate how we use the recorded astronomical phenomena to accurately determine the ascension years of King Yi, Zhou Cheng-Wang, Huang-Di, Yao, Shun, Yu, Zhong-Kang, and Zhou Wen-Wang. The obtained error-free ascension years of these kings are crucial to our reconstruction of the accurate Chinese chronology.

1. The first year of King Yi

As discussed above, two American scholars from JPL and UCLA published a paper in 1995 to show that the early morning solar eclipse on 21 April 899 BC occurred in the first year of King Yi. Scholars in mainland China simply accepted this conclusion without carefully examining all possible alternatives. This paper was based on the original Chinese text recorded in the *Bamboo Annals*, which reads: "元年丙寅,春正月,王即位,天再旦于郑." The first English translation of this text was given by James Legge: "In his first year, which was *ping-yin* (third day of cycle), when he came to the throne, there were two sunrises in Ching."

There are two problems with the interpretation in the 1995 paper. First, the original Chinese text clearly says that the solar eclipse took place in the first month of spring. The day of 21 April 899 BC could never have been in the first month of spring according to any Chinese lunisolar calendar. Second, if we use an accurate delta-T parameter (see Appendix A), we find that the maximum coverage (90.6%) of the solar eclipse occurred at 5:57, 16 minutes before sunrise at 6:13. There is nothing that could mimic two sunrises.

Since the meaning of "天再旦(Pinyin: *tian zai dan*)" is not unique, the Chinese text could also be translated as: "In his first year, which was *bing-yin* (the third day of a sexagenary cycle), in the first month of spring, when he came to the throne, the sky brightened twice in Zheng."

The basic meaning of "旦" is "sunrise," so "再旦" could mean "one more sunrise." But "旦" could also mean "brighten," so "天再旦" in the Chinese text could also mean that the sky brightens again. Therefore, "天再旦" could simply mimic the phenomenon of a solar eclipse.

A predicted solar eclipse on 21 March 926 BC should have corresponded to the first year of King Yi. The day of 21 March 926 BC was indeed in the last day of the first month of spring according to the Chinese lunisolar calendar (see Chapter 5). Therefore, the first year of King Yi should have been in 926 BC rather than in 899 BC.

2. The 18th year of Zhou Cheng-Wang

Another solar eclipse is predicted to have taken place on 7 March 1093 BC, which matched the recorded solar eclipse in the *Bamboo Annals*: "十八年,春正月,王如洛邑定鼎,凤凰见,遂有事于河。" Our English translation of this text is: "In the 18th year of Zhou Cheng-Wang (King Cheng), in the first month of spring, the king went to Luo (Luo-yang). Phoenixes appeared and sacrifices were offered at the river (Luo River)."

In order to understand why this description refers to a solar eclipse, we need to understand the Chinese culture first. The phoenix is a bird that signifies a union of yin (阴) and yang (阳). The Chinese word 阴 (yin) derives from the word 月(moon) and 阳(yang) from the word 日 (sun). Thus, the meeting of both male and female phoenixes imitates how the Sun and the Moon come together, namely, the course of a solar eclipse. Then, the above text could be re-phrased as: "There was a solar eclipse and sacrifices were offered at the river." Since the people in ancient China considered solar eclipses to be ill omens, they attempted to offer sacrifices to please Heaven. Thus, whenever there is a statement: "Sacrifices were offered," there must have been a solar eclipse. Indeed, we find that the sacrifice events recorded in the *Bamboo Annals* were always associated with the occurrences of solar eclipses.

Remarkably, a solar eclipse is predicted to occur on 7 March 1093 BC. This eclipse should have occurred in the 18th year of King Cheng if the first year of King Yi was in 926 BC (see Table VI). The day of

7 March 1093 BC was on the last day of the first month of spring according to the Chinese lunisolar calendar, which also matches the historical record. Therefore, our consistent interpretations of the two solar eclipses recorded in the Bamboo Annals lead to the only conclusion that the first year of King Yi must have been in 926 BC rather than in 899 BC.

3. The first year of Huang-Di

According to the historical book of Bo Yang, the total number of years between the first year of Huang-Di and the first year of Emperor Yao is 340. It is amazing that the astronomical records in the Bamboo Annals are in perfect agreement with this number.

The Bamboo Annals recorded for Huang-Di: "五十年秋七月庚申，凤鸟至，帝祭于洛水." The English translation reads: "In his (Huang-Di's) 50th year, in the autumn, in the 7th month, on day geng-shen (the 57th day of a sexagenary cycle), phoenixes arrived, and the emperor offered sacrifices at Luo River."

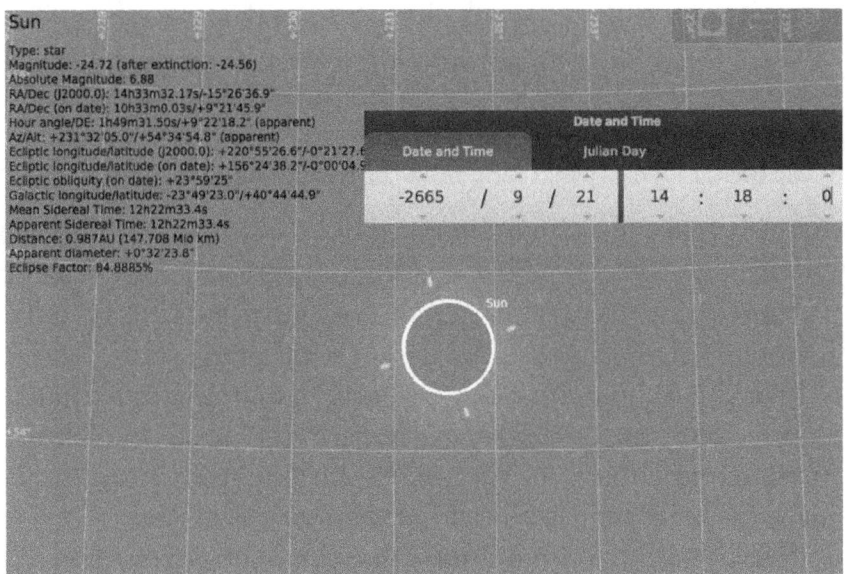

Figure 4: Predicted solar eclipse on 21 September 2666 BC, observed in Xin-Zheng city.

As mentioned above, whenever there is a statement: "Phoenixes arrived (or appeared) and the emperor offered sacrifices…" in the Bamboo Annals, it must refer to a solar eclipse. We searched solar eclipses between 2600-2700 BC using the Stellarium Program and found a solar eclipse in China on 21 September 2666 BC. The day of 21 September 2666 BC was indeed at the end of the 7th month according to the Xia calendar (see below), perfectly matching the record of the Bamboo Annals. If this solar eclipse was indeed the one observed in the 50th year of Huang-Di, the first (ascension) year of his reign should have been after the 8th month of 2716 BC, which corresponded to the 7th month (Tishri) in the Hebrew calendar.

The eclipse was seen in Xin-Zheng city (34°23'40"N 113°44'20"E) on day *gui-wei* (癸未) (the 20th day of a sexagenary cycle) according to the counting method of the Shang Dynasty.

With a delta-T parameter: $\Delta T = -20 + 33.0t^2$, the middle eclipse was at 14:18 with the eclipse factor of 84.89% (see Figure 4).

Since the new moon was at 21:06 on August 22, the first day of the 7th month started from the evening of August 22, and September 21 was in the 30th day of the 7th month. Thus, the month of the solar eclipse exactly matches the historical record. But the day *gui-wei* calculated from the counting method of the Shang Dynasty does not match the recorded one (geng-shen). This is understandable since the chroniclers in the Shang Dynasty may have reset the first day of a sexagenary cycle.

4. The first year of Emperor Yao

If we believe that there were 340 years between the first year of Huang-Di and that of Emperor Yao, Yao should have started his reign in the autumn of 2376 BC. This is confirmed by several independent astronomical phenomena recorded in the Bamboo Annals. For example, the Bamboo Annals recorded: "五十三年，帝祭于洛." The English translation is: "In his (Yao's) 53rd year, the emperor offered sacrifices at Luo River."

Whenever there is a statement: "The emperor offered sacrifices …" in the Bamboo Annals, it must refer to a solar eclipse. This means that there should have been a solar eclipse in his 53rd year (from the autumn of 2324 BC to the autumn of 2323 BC). There was indeed a solar eclipse in China on 18 November 2324 BC, which was observable in Beijing (see Figure 5).

With $\Delta T = -20 + 32.0 t^2$, the middle eclipse occurred at 13:03 with the eclipse factor of 13.6% (see Figure 5).

Since the new moon was at 1:19 on October 20, the first day of the 9th month started from the evening of October 19, and the day of November 18 was in the 30th day of the 9th month. If the observed solar eclipse on 18 November 2324 BC took place in the 53rd year of Yao, he should have started to reign before 18 November 2376 BC.

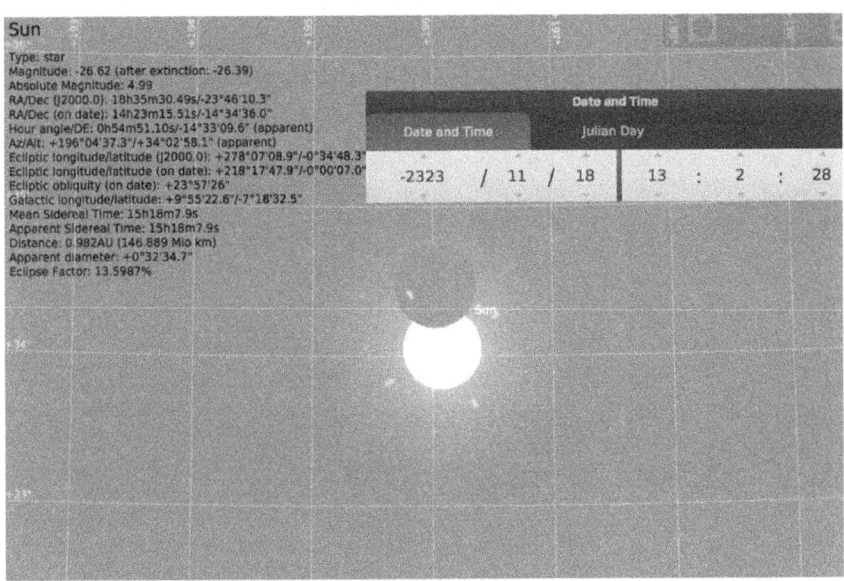

Figure 5: Predicted solar eclipse on 18 November 2324 BC, observed in Beijing, one of the important cities in 冀州 (Ji-Zhou), the territory of Emperor Yao.

There are other astronomical records during the reign of Yao, which can further pin down the starting date of Yao. The Bamboo Annals recorded: "四十二年, 景星见于翼; 帝在位七十年, 景星出翼." Here is the English translation: "In his (Yao's) 42nd year, the brilliant star appeared in constellation Yi; when the emperor came to the throne 70 years, the brilliant star came out of constellation Yi."

"景星" literally means a brilliant star and Venus should be one of the candidates for the brilliant star. The Yi constellation contains Crater and Hydra with Crater being the center of the Yi constellation. The picture in the upper panel of Figure 6 shows that Venus rose from the east in the Yi constellation in the early morning of 18 August 2334 BC. If this happened in the 42nd year of Yao, the first year of Yao was after 18 August 2376 BC, in agreement with the conclusion drawn from the observed solar eclipse in the 53rd year of Yao.

The picture also shows that Venus came out of the Yi constellation in the evening from the west on 25 June 2306 BC (lower panel of Figure 6). If this took place in the 70th year of Yao, the first year of Yao should have been after 25 June 2376 BC.

These combined astronomical records consistently suggest that Yao should have started to reign between August 18 and November 18 of 2376 BC. The number of years that elapsed from the first year of Huang-Di (2716 BC) to the first year of Yao (2376 BC) was precisely 340, which was identical to that determined previously from Common Scheme.

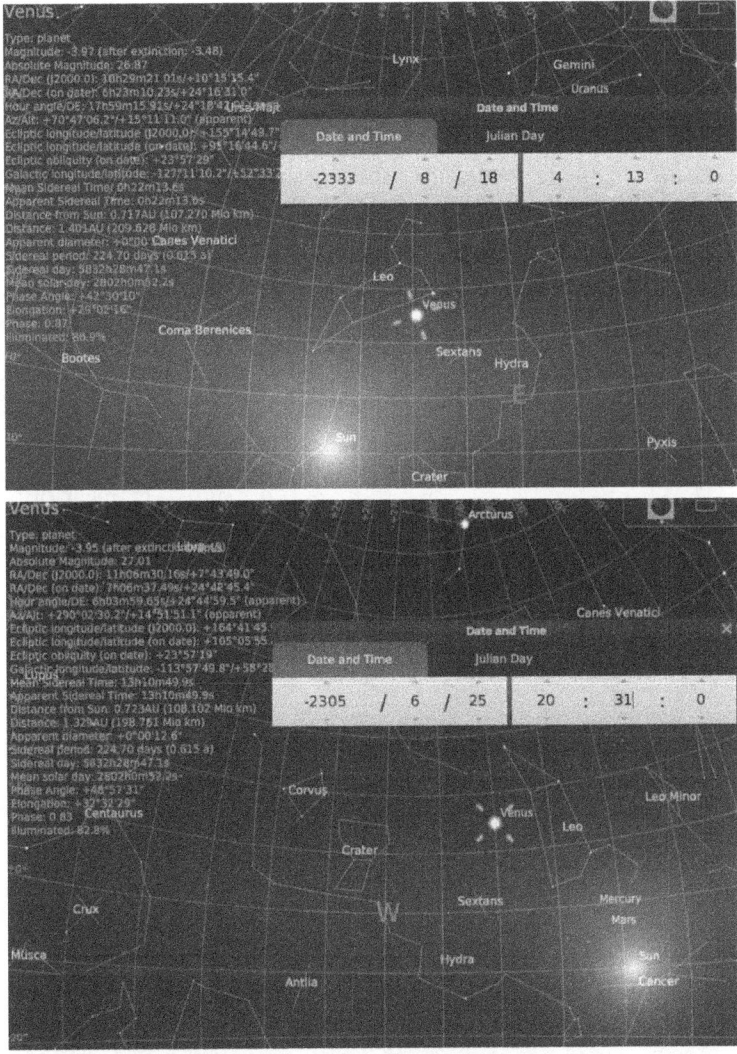

Figure 6: Venus rose in the east in the Yi constellation in the morning of 18 August 2334 BC (upper panel) and Venus came out of the Yi constellation from the west in the evening of 25 June 2306 BC (lower panel).

5. The first year of Emperor Shun

Now we determine the first year of Shun from an astronomical record in his first year. The Bamboo Annals recorded for Shun: "即帝位, 蓂荚生于阶, 凤凰巢于庭, 击石拊石, 以歌《九韶》, 百兽率舞, 景星出于房, 地出乘黄之马." Our English translation reads: "Right upon his (Shun) ascension, the felicitous grew around the stars, the phoenixes nested in the courts. When they beat and tapped the musical stones to perform the *Jiu-Shao* music, all the beasts danced together, the brilliant star came out of the *Fang* constellation, and a Chen-Huang horse came out of the earth."

The picture in Figure 7 shows that Venus came out of *Fang* (*Scorpius*) on 14 September 2271 BC. It was still close to *Fang* until the evening of September 19. This suggests that Shun should have started his reign between 14 and 19 September 2271 BC, which was in the 7th month of 2271 BC.

Since Yao's regnal length was 100 years, there should have been 5 years between the death of Yao and the first year of Shun. The Bamboo Annals recorded: "一百年，帝陟于陶。帝子丹朱避舜于房陵，舜让，不克。朱遂封于房，为虞宾。三年，舜即天子之位." Here is the English translation: "Yao had reigned for 100 years and died. The emperor's son Dan-Zhu kept away from Shun in Fang-ling. Shun tried to yield his throne to Dan-Zhu but was unsuccessful. Dan-Zhu was bestowed as the prince of Fang and was the guest of Yu (Shun). After three years, Shun ascended to the throne of the son of Heaven."

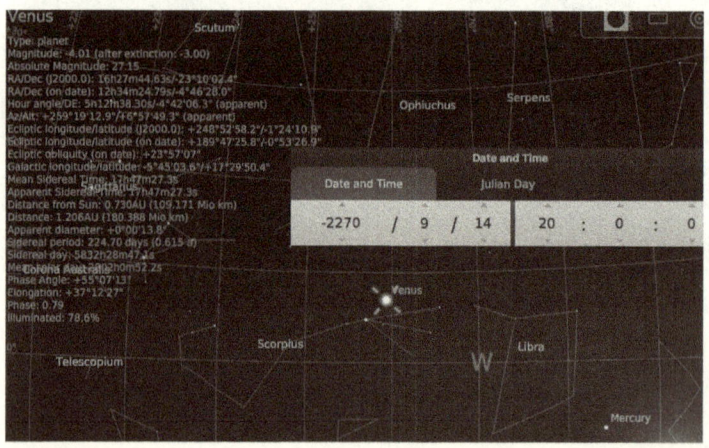

Figure 7: Venus came out of *Fang* (*Scorpius*) on 14 September 2271 BC.

A question arises as to whether "after three years" means three years after Yao's death or three years after Dan-Zhu was bestowed as the prince of Fang. Traditionally, the Chinese historians interpreted "after three years" as "three years after Yao's death." Since there is a gap of about five years between Yao's death and the ascension of Shun according to the astronomical records, "after three years" in the text should mean "three years after Dan-Zhu was bestowed as the prince of Fang." If this is the case, there should have been a gap of two years between Yao's death and the event of Dan-Zhu being bestowed as the prince. Right after Yao's death, Dan-Zhu kept away from Shun possibly because he was afraid of being killed by Shun. But instead, Shun tried to yield his throne to Dan-Zhu although Yao had yielded his throne to Shun in Yao's 73rd year and Shun was the legal successor of the throne. After Shun found that his two-year effort to yield his throne to Dan-Zhu was not successful, he bestowed Dan-Zhu as the prince of Fang. Three years after this, Shun officially ascended to the throne of the son of Heaven when he received a sign from Heaven, that is, the brilliant star came out of the Fang constellation.

6. The first year of Emperor Zhong-Kang

The *Bamboo Annals* recorded: "帝仲康, 元年己丑, 帝即位, 居斟鄩, 五年秋, 九月, 庚戌, 朔, 日有食之, 命胤侯帥師征羲和." Our English translation reads: "In the year of *shi-chou* (the 26th year of a sexagenary cycle), Emperor Zhong-Kang came to the throne and dwelt in Zhenxun. In his 5th year, in the autumn, in the 9th month, on day *geng-shu* (the 47th day of a sexagenary cycle), in the early morning, there was a solar eclipse. Then he ordered the prince of Yin to use military forces to take Xi and He (two drunken astronomers)."

The solar eclipse observed in the fifth year of Emperor Zhong-Kang has been considered to be the first human record of solar eclipses (this information can be found at the website: https://eclipse.gsfc.nasa.gov/SEhistory/SEhistory.html). Since the *Bamboo Annals* recorded two more solar eclipses before this one and the day of the solar eclipse was wrongly assigned (see below), the information in the NASA webpage needs to be updated.

The Chinese word "朔*shuo*" in the above text originally means "new moon" or "dark moon." To be more general, "朔" also means "beginning" and "early morning." Because a solar eclipse always occurs at a new moon, there is no point for the chronicler to say it again. Here, we interpret "朔" as "in the early morning," which describes the time of the solar eclipse.

In ancient China, the day started at sunset just like in the nation of Israel (see Chapter 5). The first day of a month starts in the evening if the conjunction of the Sun and the Moon (dark moon phase) falls before sunrise. On the other hand, the first day of a month starts in the following evening if the conjunction falls after sunrise. Since sunrise occurs at the mid-point of a day, a new month should start from an evening that is the closest to the time of the conjunction. Since a maximally visible solar eclipse is seen in the conjunction after sunrise, a solar eclipse should always occur in the last day of a lunar month. Indeed, only if the solar eclipses happened in the last day of a lunar month, all the solar eclipses recorded in the *Bamboo Annals* can be in perfect agreement with the regnal years of all the kings. Moreover, the *Book of Later Han* recorded every solar eclipse, which always occurred in the last day of a lunar month. This further confirms that the day in ancient China started from sunset.

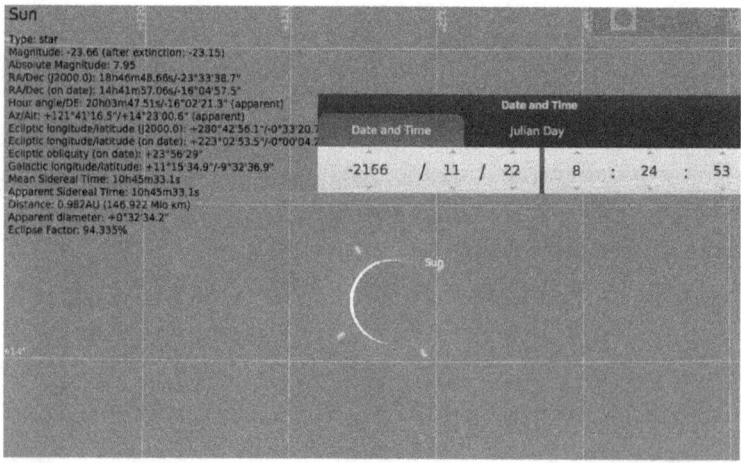

Figure 8: Predicted solar eclipse on 22 November 2167 BC, observed in Zhenxun.

On the other hand, if a day starts from midnight, then morning solar eclipses take place during the first day of a lunar month while afternoon solar eclipses occur during the last day of a lunar month. If a day starts from morning, then solar eclipses always take place in the first day of a month.

The same astronomical phenomenon was also recorded in the Shujing: "乃季秋月朔辰弗集于房." Our English translation is: "In the last month of autumn, in the early morning, the Sun and the Moon did not meet in the lunar mansion of Fang (Scorpio)."

Here, "季秋月" means the last month of autumn, the 9th lunar month. Both records in the *Bamboo Annals* and the Shujing consistently tell us that the solar eclipse occurred in the 9th month, in the early morning, and not in the lunar mansion of Scorpio.

The eclipse was observed in Zhenxun (Gongyi) (34°46'N 112°58'E) on day *yi-yu* 乙酉 (the 22nd day of a sexagenary cycle), according to the counting method of the Shang Dynasty.

With $\Delta T = -20 + 34.52 t^2$, the maximum eclipse was at 8:24 with the eclipse factor of 94.36% (see Figure 8). The eclipse started at 7:20 right after sunrise (at 7:05) and ended at 9:37. The Sun and Moon did not meet in the constellation of Scorpio, but instead about 30 degrees from it. This is consistent with the description that the Sun and the Moon did not meet in the lunar mansion of Scorpio during the solar eclipse.

Since the new moon was at 21:52 on October 23, the first day of the 9th month started from the evening of October 23, and November 22 was in the 30th day of the 9th month, which also matched the historical record. The eclipse was seen between 7:20 and 9:37 in the morning, which was also consistent with the time "朔", "in the early morning." The day calculated from the counting method of the Shang Dynasty does not match the one that was recorded. This is understandable since the chroniclers in the Shang Dynasty may have reset the first day of a sexagenary cycle.

- The number of years between the first year of Shun and the first year of Zhong-Kang also matches the number obtained from Common Scheme. According to the Bamboo Annals, Great Yu started to co-reign with Shun in the 14th year of Shun (from the autumn of 2258 BC to the autumn of 2257 BC). The Bamboo Annals also tells us that Heaven appointed Yu in replacement of Shun in the 14th year of Shun, which should have been around the fall of 2257 BC (near the end of the 14th year of Shun).

7. The first year of Zhou Wen-Wang

Superfluous Book of Zhou (逸周书·小开) recorded: "维三十有五祀，王念曰：" 多口，正月丙子拜望，食无时。汝开后嗣谋，曰：呜呼！于来后之人。余闻在昔曰：明明非常，维德曰为明，食无时，汝日夜何脩非躬？何慎非言？何择非德？" Our English translation reads: "During the sacrifice ceremony in the 35th year of the king (Zhou Wen-Wang), the king said: 'the sacrifice ceremony is holding today in the day of bing-zi (the 13th day of a sexagenary cycle) in the first month because the previous lunar eclipse came untimely (and we missed the sacrifice). To inspire your descendants, you should say, 'Alas, your future generations, I learn that in the past the bright was not always bright except for virtue. Since lunar eclipses could come untimely, why don't you seek virtue by yourself day and night? Why don't you speak your words carefully? Why don't you choose virtue?'"

Several scholars proposed that there was a lunar eclipse on the 13th day of a sexagenary cycle, in the first month, in the 35th year of Zhou Wen-Wang. A lunar eclipse is predicted to occurr on 15 September 1112 BC, which matched the 13th day. But the day of September 15 can never be in the first month. Furthermore, this assignment would lead to the conclusion that the first year of Zhou Wen-Wang would have been in 1146 BC. This is in contradiction with the record of the Bamboo Annals, which shows that the first year of Zhou Wen-Wang was in 1178 BC, in the 12th year of Tai-Ding. He died in the spring of the 41st of Di-Xin according to the Bamboo Annals, which was in 1128 BC. From 1178 BC to 1128 BC, there were 50 years, which was in perfect agreement with the record in the Annals of Zhou: Wen-Wang reigned for 50 years.

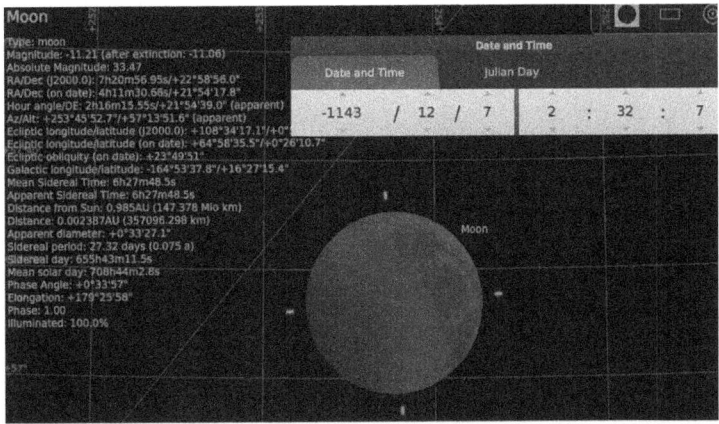

Figure 9: Predicted lunar eclipse on 7 December 1144 BC in Anyang.

If we carefully read the ancient text, we find the subtle meaning of the text. It does not actually say that the king made sacrifices in the first month and in the day of bing-zi because a lunar eclipse happened on that day. It is more logical to say that a lunar eclipse happened in the previous month, but the king missed the sacrificing ceremony because the eclipse took place in a day that was unexpected based on the common knowledge. If this is the correct understanding, there should have been a lunar eclipse in the 12th or 13th month of the previous year of 1144 BC. Indeed, a lunar eclipse was seen in China on 7 December 1144 BC (JD 1303917.27). It was on day xin-hai 辛亥 (the 48th of a sexagenary cycle) rather than on the 13th day (bing-zi).

With $\Delta T = -20 + 28.2t^2$ and the observation point in Anyang (36°6'N114°20'), the maximum eclipse occurred at 2:32 with magnitude of 1.7 (see Figure 9). The new moon was at 17:29 of November 22, so the first day of the month started from the evening of November 22 and the lunar eclipse happened during the night of the 15th day of the month. It is known that a full moon and a lunar eclipse commonly takes place during the night of the 16th day at the end of a year. But this eclipse happened in the 15th day, which was not expected by the king. That is why he wanted to hold a special sacrificial ceremony in the beginning of the year to inspire people to seek virtue because everything, including the previous lunar eclipse, was uncertain except for virtue that is always bright.

We can easily show that the day bing-zi was on 1 January 1143 BC, the 10th day of the first lunar month in the time of Zhou Wen-Wang.

CHAPTER 10

BIBLICAL CHRONOLOGY

We present our Biblical chronology in Table VII, which spans exactly 7,000 years. Adam was created on 1 Nisan (15 April, Friday) 3970 BC and the world will end on 29 Adar 3031. The chronology is purely based on Scriptural passages of the Masoretic Text of the Hebrew Bible and on the proof that Solomon's temple was first destroyed in 587 BC (see Chapter 11). The Biblical verse references and/or comments are provided in the last column of the table. In the second column, we provide years, seasons, and dates.

From the creation of Adam to the birth of Noah, the chronology is straightforward. No detailed explanation is required nor provided. In the following sections, we will provide detailed explanations for certain parts of the chronology that are not so straightforward.

Table VII: Biblical Chronology

Events	Date or season and year	Time elapsed	Verses and/or comments
Creation of Adam	1 Nisan, Friday, 15 April 3970 BC		
Birth of Seth	Spring 3840 BC	130 years	And Adam lived one hundred and thirty years, and begot a son in his own likeness, after his image, and named him Seth. (Genesis 5:3)
Birth of Enosh	Spring 3735 BC	105 years	Seth lived one hundred and five years, and begot Enosh. (Genesis 5:6)
Birth of Cainan	Spring 3645 BC	90 years	Enosh lived ninety years, and begot Cainan. (Genesis 5:9)
Birth of Mahalaleel	Spring 3575 BC	70 years	Cainan lived seventy years, and begot Mahalalel. (Genesis 5:12)
Birth of Jared	Spring 3510 BC	65 years	Mahalalel lived sixty-five years, and begot Jared. (Genesis 5:15)
Birth of Enoch	Spring 3348 BC	162 years	Jared lived one hundred and sixty-two years, and begot Enoch. (Genesis 5:18)
Birth of Mathuselah	Fall 3284 BC	65 years	Enoch lived sixty-five years, and begot Methuselah. (Genesis 5:21)
Birth of Lamech	Spring 3096 BC	187 years	Methuselah lived one hundred and eighty-seven years, and begot Lamech. (Genesis 5:25)
Birth of Noah	Spring 2914 BC	182 years	Lamech lived one hundred and eighty-two years and had a son. (Genesis 5:28)
Beginning of the flood	25 May 2315 BC	599 years	In the six hundredth year of Noah's life, in the second month, the seventeenth day of the month, on that day all the fountains of the great deep were broken up, and the windows of heaven were opened. (Genesis 7:11)

God commanded Noah to leave the ark.	3 June 2314 BC	374 days	And it came to pass in the six hundred and first year, in the first month, the first day of the month, that the waters were dried up from the earth; and Noah removed the covering of the ark and looked, and indeed the surface of the ground was dry. And in the second month, on the twenty-seventh day of the month, the earth was dried. Then God spoke to Noah, saying, "Go out of the ark, you and your wife, and your sons and your sons' wives with you." (Genesis 8:13-15)
Noahic Covenant	10 June 2314 BC	7 days	It may have taken about 7 days to evacuate everything from the ark since it took about 7 days for everything to get into the ark. After everything left the ark, Noah offered burnt offerings to God and God made a Noahic covenant on the day of Pentecost (10 June 2314 BC).
Birth of Arphaxed	Spring 2312 BC	2 years	Shem was one hundred years old, and begot Arphaxad two years after the flood. (Genesis 11:10)
Birth of Salah	Spring 2277 BC	35 years	Arphaxad lived thirty-five years, and begot Salah. (Genesis 11:12)
Birth of Eber	Spring 2247 BC	30 years	Salah lived thirty years, and begot Eber. (Genesis 11:14)
Birth of Peleg	Spring 2213 BC	34 years	Eber lived thirty-four years, and begot Peleg. (Genesis 11:16)
Birth of Reu	Spring 2183 BC	30 years	Peleg lived thirty years, and begot Reu. (Genesis 11:18)
Birth of Serug	Spring 2151 BC	32 years	Reu lived thirty-two years, and begot Serug. (Genesis 11:20)
Birth of Nahor	Spring 2121 BC	30 years	Serug lived thirty years, and begot Nahor. (Genesis 11:22)
Birth of Terah	Spring 2092 BC	29 years	Nahor lived twenty-nine years, and begot Terah. (Genesis 11:24)

Birth of Abraham	Spring 1962 BC	130 years	So the days of Terah were two hundred and five years, and Terah died in Haran. (Genesis 11:32) Now Yehowah had said to Abram: "Get out of your country, from your family and from your father's house, to a land that I will show you. I will make you a great nation; I will bless you and make your name great; and you shall be a blessing. I will bless those who bless you, and I will curse him who curses you; and in you all the families of the earth shall be blessed." So Abram departed as Yehowah had spoken to him, and Lot went with him. And Abram was seventy-five years old when he departed from Haran. (Genesis 12:1-4)
Abraham left Haran and stayed in Canaan.	Spring 1887 BC	75 years	And Abram was seventy-five years old when he departed from Haran. (Genesis 12:4)
Abraham went to Egypt.	Spring 1887 BC	2 months	Now there was a famine in the land, and Abram went down to Egypt to dwell there, for the famine was severe in the land. (Genesis 12:10)
Exodus from Egypt	25 April (15 Nisan) 1457 BC	430 years	Now the sojourn of the children of Israel who lived in Egypt was four hundred and thirty years. And it came to pass at the end of the four hundred and thirty years—on that very same day—it came to pass that all the armies of Yehowah went out from the land of Egypt. (Exodus 12:40-41)
Started to build the temple	16 April 977 BC	480 years	And it came to pass in the four hundred and eightieth year after the children of Israel had come out of the land of Egypt, in the fourth year of Solomon's reign over Israel, in the month of Ziv, which is the second month, that he began to build the house of Yehowah. (1 Kings 6:1) And he began to build on the second day of the second month in the fourth year of his reign. (2 Chronicles 3:2)

Jerusalem fell (the first time).	28 July 587 BC	390.25 years	Lie also on your left side, and lay the iniquity of the house of Israel upon it. According to the number of the days that you lie on it, you shall bear their iniquity. For I have laid on you the years of their iniquity, according to the number of the days, three hundred and ninety days; so you shall bear the iniquity of the house of Israel. (Ezekiel 4:4-5)
Messiah anointed (baptized by John)	24 Feb. 27 AD	611.6 years	Know therefore and understand, that from the going forth of the command (the first lunar month of 457 BC) to restore and build Jerusalem until Messiah the Prince, there shall be seven weeks and sixty-two weeks (483 days); The street shall be built again, and the wall, even in troublesome times. (Daniel 9:25)
Messiah called his disciples.	6 April 27 AD	41 days	John 1:43-51 recorded the event on Nisan 11, when he called his disciples.
Messiah crucifixion	5 April 30 AD	3 years	And after the sixty-two weeks Messiah shall be cut off, but not to himself (actually he was not cut off since he resurrected and ascended to the Father). (Daniel 9:26)
Church started.	26 May 30 AD	50 days	And he shall confirm a covenant with many for one week; But in the middle of the week He shall make sacrifice and offering to be ineffective. (Daniel 9:27). He established his church on the day of Pentecost and replaced sacrifice and offering with baptism. In his first coming, he finished the salvation work for over three years (1143 days) and in his second coming, he will judge the ungodly for less than 4 years (1413 days).

Jerusalem fell (the second time).	4 Sept. 70 AD	40.28 years	...he shall destroy the city and the sanctuary with the coming prince. The end of it shall be with a flood, And till the end of the war desolations are determined. ...And on the wing of abominations shall be one who makes desolate, Even until the consummation, which is determined, Is poured out on the desolate. (Daniel 9:26-27) And when you have completed them, lie again on your right side; then you shall bear the iniquity of the house of Judah forty days. I have laid on you a day for each year. (Ezekiel 4:6)
Messiah will start to reign.	25 March 2031	1961 years	Blessed and holy is he who has part in the first resurrection. Over such the second death has no power, but they shall be priests of God and of Christ and shall reign with Him a thousand years. (Revelation 20:6)
New heaven and new earth (the eternal Kingdom of God will start)	17 March 3031	1000 years	Now I saw a new heaven and a new earth, for the first heaven and the first earth had passed away. Also there was no more sea. (Revelation 21:1)

Creation of Adam

Based on the Scriptural passages of the Masoretic Text of the Hebrew Bible, we deduce that Adam was created in the spring of 3970 BC. But on which day was he created? The Scriptures provide us with insight. First, according to Moses, he must have been created on a Friday, on the sixth day of God's creation week. Second, God told Moses to set up the tabernacle of God on the first day of the first month (Exodus 40:2). Third, God's tabernacle on the earth symbolizes God's dwelling with us (Exodus 25:8, Revelation 21:3). God created man in His image to have dominion over all His creations on the earth (Genesis 1:26) and to have a loving relationship with Him (God dwells with man). When God made Adam and Eve, He stayed in the Garden and lived with them. God dwelled with them in the sixth day. Therefore, Adam should have been created on Nisan 1, during the sixth day of God's creation week.

According to the calculated Hebrew lunisolar calendar, Nisan 1 of 3970 BC should have been on April 14, on Thursday. That is one day off from Friday. This discrepancy can be naturally resolved if we accept the fact that God doubled the length of a day for Joshua, as recorded in the book of Joshua (Joshua 10:12-13). Because the Sun and the Moon appeared to be still and the day length doubled (Joshua 10:13), the Earth's rotation in that day should have been slowed down significantly while the orbital motions of the Sun and the Moon remained intact. After God did this miracle for Joshua, He should have reset the Earth's rotational speed back to the original one.

Because the calculated Hebrew calendar is based on the assumption that there has been no change in the motions of the Moon, the Sun, and the Earth from the creation, the miracle in the time of Joshua should lead to a modification for the calculated Hebrew calendars before the miracle day in 1417 BC, when God doubled its length. The modification causes the first months of all the lunar months in the calculated lunisolar calendars before the miracle day of 1471 BC to be shifted forward by one day to yield the true calendars. In Chapters 7 and 9, we did not make the one-day correction before the miracle day of 1417 BC when we described various astronomical phenomena such as the predicted lunar and solar eclipses. However, the calendars before the miracle day of 1417 BC listed in Appendix D are the true calendars, which have been corrected by the one-day shift. With this correction, Nisan 1 of 3970 BC was on April 15 (Friday) in the true calendar (see Appendix D). This appears to cause a problem: the first day of the 7th month is correspondingly moved to Sunday, which is not allowed according to the rules of "postponement" (see Chapter 2). Since the rules of "postponement" have been designed for observing the Feasts of God, there is no point in respecting these rules before starting the Feasts of God in 969 BC. Therefore, it is permissible for Nisan 1 of 3970 BC to be on April 15 (Friday).

How special is Nisan 1 of 3970 BC? The number of days for the 7,000 lunisolar years from 1 Nisan (April 15) 3970 BC to 1 Nisan (17 March) 3031 can be calculated from the Julian day numbers of these two days. From the Stellarium Program, we find JD 271485 for the day of 15 April 3970 BC and JD 2828185 for the day of 17 March 3031.

Thus, there are 2,828,185 − 271,485 days = 2,556,700 days from Nisan 1 of 3970 BC to Nisan 1 of 3031. The average number of days per year within the 7,000 lunisolar years is 2,556,700/7,000 = 365.242857 = (7×7×7) + (7+7+7) + 7×(1/7+1/49+1/70). It is remarkable that the 365.242857 days for the year length can be perfectly expressed by God's holy number 7 and its multiples. If the first lunisolar year had started from any other year, the average number of days per year within the period of 7000 lunisolar years would not be the "magic" number. If God had not doubled Joshua's day length, neither would one get the "magic" number.

Nisan 1 of 3970 BC should be the beginning of the second year in the lunisolar calendar. The first year was before Nisan 1 of 3970 BC and lasted for only five days in terms of God's absolute clock. The five days may have been very long in terms of the human clock (see Chapter 28).

Noah's flood

Genesis 8:1-5 reads, "Then God remembered Noah, and every living thing, and all the animals that were with him in the ark. And God made a wind to pass over the earth, and the waters subsided. The fountains of the deep and the windows of heaven were also stopped, and the rain from heaven was restrained. And the waters receded continually from the earth. At the end of the hundred and fifty days the waters decreased. And the ark rested in the seventh month, the seventeenth day of the month, on the mountains of Ararat. And the waters decreased continually until the tenth month. In the tenth month, on the first day of the month, the tops of the mountains were seen."

These verses tell us that at the end of 150 days of the flood the waters decreased, and after 150 days from the flood the ark rested on the mountains of Ararat in the 17th day of the 7th month. Verses 3 and 4 talk about two different events which are connected by the Hebrew word "ו" meaning "and." The connection with the word "and" means that the two different events could happen at the same time or sequentially. Since the first event occurred at the end of 150 days after the flood, the second event should have taken place at least 150 days after the flood. We also know that the second event happened in the 17th day of the 7th

month, which was five months after the flood started in the 17th day of the 2nd month (Genesis 7:11). Therefore, the second event took place five months or at least 150 days after the flood. If the author had used a lunisolar calendar to record the flood events, the record would not make any sense because the maximum number of days for 5 lunar months is 148 days, which cannot match the day number of at least 150. Therefore, Moses (in fact Noah himself) must not have used a lunisolar calendar to record the flood.

A solar calendar was described in the book of Enoch (see Chapter 4). Since Enoch was the great grandfather of Noah, it is likely that Noah used Enoch's solar calendar to record the flood events. If this is the case, there should have been 152±1 days from the 17th day of the 2nd month to the 17th day of the 7th month (see the calendar of 2315 BC in Appendix D). The uncertainty of ±1 day is because the exact starting time of the flood and the exact resting time of the ark are unknown. The 152±1 days for the 5 Enoch's months are over 150 days, in perfect agreement with the flood account. Therefore, the ark rested on the mountains of Ararat at least one day after the waters started to decrease at the end of 150 days from the flood.

The first day of the first month in Enoch's solar calendar is always on the Wednesday of the week within which the Vernal Equinox falls. The flood started on the 17th day of the second month, in the six hundredth year of Noah's life (Genesis 7:11). Since the first day of the first month of the coming year was in the six hundred and first year of Noah's life (Genesis 8:13), Noah must have been born on or before the first day of the first solar month.

The flood started on the 17th day of the second month, in the six hundredth year of Noah's life, which was on 25 May 2315 BC (see the calendar of 2315 BC in Appendix D). The rain lasted for 40 days and 40 nights and stopped on 4 July 2315 BC. The 17th day of the 7th solar month in 2315 BC was on October 24 while October 25 was on the feast day of Tabernacles (Tishri 15). Thus, the ark should have rested on the mountains of Ararat right before sunset of October 24 so that Noah's family might have celebrated the Feast of Tabernacles after sunset of October 24.

On the 27th day of the second month of the following year (3 June 2314 BC), in the six hundred and first year of Noah's life, God commanded Noah and his family to leave the ark. Because God commanded them to enter the ark one week before the flood started (Genesis 7:4), one week should have been enough time for them to bring many living creatures into the ark and to place them in prescribed locations. Similarly, it may also have taken one week for them to untie and bring these creatures out of the ark and to clean the waste in the ark. After finishing all the work probably on 10 June 2314 BC, on Sivan 6 (the sixth day of the third lunar month), on the day of Pentecost, Noah built an altar and made burnt offerings to Yehowah. Then Yehowah made a covenant with Noah and set a rainbow in the cloud for the sign of the covenant. This is the everlasting covenant between Yehowah and every living creature: He shall no longer destroy the earth and living things with a flood.

Even after the recent discovery of Noah's ark on Mt. Ararat, Biblical scholars have not been able to provide any convincing explanation as to where the flood fits in history. Our Biblical chronology indicates that Noah's flood began on 25 May 2315 BC and the waters started to decrease after 150 days. It is amazing that Noah's flood took place in the same year as that of China's great flood recorded by both the Bamboo Annals and the Canon of Yao. The Bamboo Annals recorded, "(帝尧)六十一年，命崇伯鲧治河." Our English translation is: "In the 61st year of (Emperor Yao), Yao commanded Chong Bo Gun to control the flood." The *Canon of Yao* also recorded that in his 61st year, Yao appointed Gun to control the flood because the waters of the very destructive flood had embraced the hills and overtopped the great heights, threatening the heavens. China's great flood described in the *Canon of Yao* was similar to Noah's flood (Genesis 7:19), "The waters prevailed exceedingly upon the earth, and all the high hills that under the whole heaven were covered."

According to the Chinese chronology presented in Chapter 9, the first year of Emperor Yao was from the fall of 2376 BC to the fall of 2375 BC. Thus, the 61st year of Yao was from the fall of 2316 BC to the fall of 2315 BC. Noah's flood started on 25 May 2315 BC and the rain was upon the earth 40 days and 40 nights (Genesis 7:12). The period of the flood (from 25 May to 4 July 2315 BC) was indeed in the 61st year of Yao. This proves that the flood recorded by the Chinese was the same as the one recorded in the Hebrew Bible. Since the Chinese chronology is based on concurrently recorded historical events with the astronomical phenomena, it has no uncertainty concerning the time of the flood. Therefore, the Chinese chronology has verified the great accuracy of the Biblical chronology, which is purely based on the Masoretic Text of the Hebrew Bible. This also proves that the Masoretic Text of the Hebrew Bible, which has been so carefully and faithfully preserved by the Jews, is the most accurate Hebrew Bible.

Birth of Abraham

There is some disagreement among Biblical chronologists as to whether Terah was 70 or 130 years old when his son, Abram (later renamed Abraham), was born. The view that Terah was 130 years old at the birth of Abraham is based on the following verses: Acts 7:4, Genesis 11:32, and Genesis 12:4. Acts 7:4 says, "Then he (Abraham) came out of the land of the Chaldeans, and dwelt in Haran, and from there when his father was dead, He (God) moved him into this land in which you now dwell." Now consider also Genesis 11:32, "And the days of Terah were two hundred and five years, and Terah died in Haran," and Genesis 12:4, "... Abram was seventy and five years old when he departed out of Haran." Subtracting 75 from 205 yields 130 for Terah's age at the birth of Abraham.

The view that Terah was 70 years old at the birth of Abraham is based on Genesis 11:26 and Genesis 17:17. Genesis 11:26 says, "And Terah lived 70 years, and begat Abram, Nahor, and Haran." If one assumes that Abram was Terah's firstborn because his name was mentioned first, he would have been born when Terah was 70. However, the first mention of his name does not necessarily mean that Abram was the firstborn.

To prove this point, let's look at the other places in the book of Genesis. Genesis 5:32 states: "And Noah was five hundred years old, and Noah begot Shem, Ham, and Japheth." Like the situation with Terah's begetting of Abraham, Nahor, and Haran, here we read that at the age of 500, Noah begot Shem, Ham, and Japheth. Was Shem the firstborn? Or was Shem mentioned the first because of his significance?

In all likelihood, the evidence indicates that Shem was not the firstborn but was instead born three years after the firstborn.

Genesis 7:6 says, "Noah was six hundred years old when the flood waters were on the earth." Also take account of Genesis 8:13, "And it came to pass in the six hundred and first year, in the first month, the first day of the month, that the waters were dried up from the earth and Noah removed the covering of the ark and looked, and indeed the surface of the ground was dry." Moreover, Genesis 11:10 states, "Shem was one hundred years old, and begot Arphaxad two years after the flood." If Shem was the first-born, he would have been 103 years old at the end of two years after the flood. But Genesis 11:10 reveals that Shem was 100 years old at that time. This proves that Shem was indeed not the first-born but simply mentioned first. In fact, Japheth is older than Shem according to Genesis 10:21, "And children were born also to Shem, the father of all the children of Eber, the brother of Japheth the elder."

Therefore, the firstborn must have been Japheth. Whether or not Shem was older than Ham depends on our understanding of Genesis 9:24, "So Noah awoke from his wine, and knew that his younger son (Ham) had done to him." Here, "younger" translated in NKJV could be also translated into "youngest," as found in other versions of English translation. If "younger" is the only correct translation here, his younger son could refer to the second or the youngest. If the names of Noah's three sons were mentioned according to their importance, Japheth would be mentioned right after Shem, and Ham would be the last because one of his sons Canaan was cursed. In all likelihood, Moses arranged the names from the youngest to the oldest, as in both cases: Noah's begetting of Shem, Ham, and Japheth, and Terah's begetting of Abraham, Nahor, and Haran. Both Shem and Abraham were the youngest.

Genesis 17:17 is another verse that appears to support the view that Terah was 70 years old at the birth of Abraham. In Genesis 17:17, when God told Abraham that he would have a child at the age of one hundred, Abraham fell on his face and laughed, and said in his heart, "Shall a child be born to a man who is one hundred years old? And shall Sarah, who is ninety years old, bear a child?"

Abraham would not have thought that it was strange at all if his own father (Terah) had been 130 years old when he was born. Although this appears to be a reasonable argument, we can discount it by considering the following facts:

1. Abraham didn't seem to have any trouble believing that he could bear a child by Hagar (Sarah's young servant) when he was 86 years old (Genesis 16:16).
2. It would be extremely difficult for Sarah to bear a child at her age. Abraham's own health may have also been deteriorating. This may partially explain his unbelief.
3. Since he had now been living with Hagar for 13 years without bearing additional children, he may have had the idea that he was no longer able to beget.
4. After Sarah had died at the age of 127 (Genesis 23:1-2), Abraham was over 140 years old. He took another wife and had 6 more kids by her (Genesis 25:1-6). This proves that Abraham's age of 99 and Terah's age of 130 had no problem with childbearing.

The above facts show that a man of 100 years old would have still been considered to be able to father children, while a woman of 90 years would be extremely difficult to bear a child. This point is further supported by Genesis 18:11, "Now Abraham and Sarah were old, well advanced in age; and Sarah had passed the age of childbearing." This verse provides a general view of that generation that only Sarah but not Abraham passed the age of childbearing although both were old. Therefore, Abraham's unbelief could be due to the age of his wife Sarah only.

Sojourning of Abraham in Canaan and Egypt for 430 years

When Abraham was 75 years old, he and his family left Haran and went to the land of Canaan (Genesis 12:4-5). He also went down to Egypt and dwelt there when there was a famine in the land (Genesis 12:10). When Abraham left Haran, God blessed him and promised that all the families of the earth shall be blessed in him. From the time when

Abraham settled in Canaan to the time when the children of Israel went out of Egypt, there should have been 430 years. The time interval of 430 years is inferred from Exodus 12:40-41, which says, "Now the sojourning of the children of Israel, who dwelt in Egypt (and Canaan), was four hundred and thirty years. And it came to pass at the end of the four hundred and thirty years, even the selfsame day it came to pass, that all the hosts of Yehowah went out from the land of Egypt." Both Samarian Pentateuch and Greek Septuagint read "who dwelt in Egypt and Canaan."

Abraham is considered to be the father of the nation of Israel. God often refers to Himself as the God of Abraham, Isaac, and Jacob (e.g., Genesis 50:24 and Exodus 3:15). This name of God emphasizes the covenant that God made with Israel. The Israelites have become God's chosen people from the time of Abraham. God repeated the Abrahamic Covenant to three different generations: Abraham, Isaac, and Jacob. All were given the promise of land, many descendants, and blessing. God first called Abram out of Ur of the Chaldees to the land of Canaan, establishing a covenant with him (Genesis 12:1-3). God reaffirmed the same covenant with Abraham's son, Isaac (Genesis 21:12; Genesis 26:3-4), and later with Isaac's son, Jacob (Genesis 28:14–15). God who established and ratified this covenant is rightly called the God of Abraham, Isaac, and Jacob. Therefore, the 430-year period started from the time when Abraham moved to Canaan at his age of 75.

Two thousand years ago, the orthodox Jews understood Exodus 12:40-41 similarly. Josephus stated in *Antiquities of the Jews* (book 13, 61), "Solomon began to build the temple in the fourth year of his reign, on the second month, which the Macedonians call Artemisius, and the Hebrews Jur, five hundred and ninety-two [592] years after the exodus out of Egypt; but one thousand and twenty [1020] years from Abraham's coming out of Mesopotamia into Canaan." This statement implies that there should have been 1020 − 592 years = 428 years from the time when Abraham entered Canaan to the time when the Israelites went out of Egypt. The length of 428 years is close to the length of 430 years stated in Exodus 12:40-41.

Exodus of Egypt to construction of the holy temple (480 years)

Josephus told us that 592 years had elapsed from the exodus from Egypt to the start of the construction of the holy temple. This is inconsistent with 480 years directly quoted from 1 Kings 6:1. Masoretic Text, Targum, and Vulgate all read 480 years except for 440 years in Septuagint. The forty years shorter in Septuagint may be due to mistranslation or a copyist error.

The length of 592 years may be inferred from the Biblical interpretation of the Jews at that time. According to Josephus, the Israelites took 40 years to wander in the wilderness, 30 years to conquer and divide the land, 20 years to be led by Saul (*Antiq.*, bk. 6, 378) after the judge's period, 40 years to be reigned by King David, and 4 years to be reigned by Solomon before he began to build the temple. Adding all the numbers above yields 134 years. The length of the judge's total ruling period is calculated to be 458 years by subtracting 134 years from 592 years. The number of about 460 years could be deduced from the book of Judges on the assumption that the ruling periods of different judges did not overlap. However, this number of 592 years is much different from that of 1 Kings 6:1, suggesting that there were significant ruling overlaps among different judges.

1 Kings 6:1 says, "And it came to pass in the four hundred and eightieth year after the children of Israel were come out of the land of Egypt, in the fourth year of Solomon's reign over Israel, in the month Zif, which is the second month, that he began to build the house of Yehowah." We know that 480 years elapsed between the exodus from Egypt and the time that King Solomon began to build the holy temple, in the fourth year of his reign.

2 Chronicles 3:2 reads: "And he began to build on the second day of the second month in the fourth year of his reign." Solomon started to build the temple in the second day of the second month, in the 4th year of his reign. The date should have been on 16 April 977 BC (also see discussion in Chapter 11).

The lunisolar calendar in 977 BC needs to be carefully constructed according to the intercalation rule: the 13th month is added only if the first full moon after the 12th month falls before the day of the Vernal Equinox.

The first full moon after the 12th month of 978 BC was at 22:15 on March 29 of 977 BC, which was on the Jewish day of March 30. The Vernal Equinox in that year was at 7:35 on March 30, so the full moon fell on the same day as the Vernal Equinox. According to the intercalation rule, the year of 978 BC was a regular year without the 13th month. Therefore, Nisan 1 was on March 16, and the second day of the second month was on April 16 (see the calendar of 977 BC in Appendix D).

The children of Israel came out of the land of Egypt on the 15th day of the first month of 1457 BC (25 April 1457 BC). One can easily show that the time difference of the two events was 480 solar years minus 4 days. This number means that the construction of the holy temple indeed started at the end of the 480th year from the time when the children of Israel were come out of the land of Egypt. This confirms the accuracy of the Biblical statement: "And it came to pass in the four hundred and eightieth year after the children of Israel were come out of the land of Egypt, in the fourth year of Solomon's reign over Israel, in the second day of the second month, that he began to build the house of Yehowah."

From starting to build the temple to the destruction of Jerusalem (390 years)

From the chronology of Judah and Israel's Kings (see Chapter 11), we see that the time interval between the commencement of building Solomon's temple and the destruction of Jerusalem is 390 years. This confirms the prophecy of Ezekiel (Ezekiel 4:4-5), "Lie also on your left side, and lay the iniquity of the house of Israel upon it. According to the number of the days that you lie on it, you shall bear their iniquity. For I have laid on you the years of their iniquity, according to the number of the days, three hundred and ninety days; so you shall bear the iniquity of the house of Israel." Ezekiel's prophecy is about the siege and destruction of Jerusalem as seen from the previous verses (Ezekiel 4:1-3): "You also, son of man, take a clay tablet and lay it before you, and portray on it a city, Jerusalem. Lay siege against it, build a siege wall against it, and heap up a mound against it; set camps against it also, and place battering rams against it all around. Moreover take for yourself an iron plate, and set it as an iron wall between you and the city. Set your face against it, and it shall be besieged, and you shall lay siege against it."

The end-point of the 390-year prophetic period corresponds to the time when Jerusalem was destroyed, but the prophet did not provide any information about the starting point of the prophetic period. Therefore, nobody was able to verify whether this prophecy had been fulfilled. Nevertheless, we can get insight from the following prophecy (Ezekiel 4:6): "And when you have completed them, lie again on your right side; then you shall bear the iniquity of the house of Judah forty days. I have laid on you a day for each year." This second prophecy is about the destruction of Jerusalem for the second time due to the iniquity of the Jews. It is well known that Jerusalem was destroyed in 70 AD, exactly forty years after crucifixion of Yeshua in 30 AD (see the date of Yeshua's crucifixion in Chapter 12). Yeshua referred to his own body as the temple and prophesized that his body would be destroyed and be raised up in three days and three nights. This implies that the resurrected body of Yeshua is the temple of God, which was built after his resurrection, in agreement with Revelation 21:22, "But I saw no temple in it, for Yehowah God Almighty and the Lamb are its temple."

For the second prophecy, the starting point of the 40-year period was the construction of a spiritual temple, which was the resurrected body of Yeshua. By analogy, the starting point of the 390-year prophetic period should have been the starting time of building the physical temple. Indeed, there were 390 years plus about 100 days from the commencement of the construction of Solomon's temple to the destruction of Jerusalem (see Chapter 11).

In Chapter 11, we will show that Jerusalem was destroyed on 28 July (10 Av) 587 BC (the 10th day of the fifth month). This exact time is consistent with the Babylonian chronology (see Chapter 8), which is confirmed by all recorded astronomical phenomena. This fixed point of reference allows us to construct the absolute Biblical chronology very accurately. The accuracy of the chronology can be independently confirmed by the Chinese chronology, which is accurate back to 2716 BC due to the concurrently recorded astronomical phenomena (Chapter 9). The chronology is also in agreement with the chronology of the Ancient Near East (Chapter 7), where the first mighty Mesopotamian king Sargon was actually Nimrod, the Almighty man described in Genesis 10:8-12.

CHAPTER 11

CHRONOLOGY OF JUDAH AND ISRAEL'S KINGS

The Biblical chronology described in Chapter 10 should align perfectly with the chronology of the kings of Israel and Judah if both are accurate. The construction of the latter chronology depends primarily on a series of regnal lengths and cross references within the books of Kings and Chronicles. The ascension of each king is dated in terms of the reign of his contemporary in either the southern kingdom of Judah or the northern kingdom of Israel. The inferred chronology should also align with the chronologies of other ancient civilizations. With this method and some assumptions, Thiele constructed his Biblical chronology, which appears to be accepted by most scholars in this field. Nevertheless, some scholars have maintained that there are weaknesses in his argument such as some unfounded assumptions.

In his desire to resolve the discrepancies between the dates in the books of Kings, Thiele was forced to make some improbable suppositions. Thiele noticed that the cross references given during the long reign of King Asa of Judah had a cumulative error of 1 year for each succeeding reign of the kings of Israel. In order to resolve the discrepancies, he assumed two different methods of reckoning regnal years: the **ascension-year** method in Judah and **non-ascension-year** method in Israel. Under the ascension-year method, if a king died in the middle of a year, the period to the end of that year would be called the "ascension year," and year 1 of the new king's reign would begin at the following new year. Under the non-ascension-year method, the ascension year of a new king would be year 1. He further assumed that the northern kingdom used a spring new year while the southern kingdom used a fall new year.

These assumptions do not have a scriptural basis. If all the Hebrew Scriptures are inspired by God and the true author is God, how is it possible for Him to use different reckoning methods for the two kingdoms? The books of Kings were believed to be written by Jeremiah the prophet of God. How could he be so inconsistent in writing about the two kingdoms? Yehowah appointed Nisan 1 as the beginning of a year for the Israelites after He brought them out of Egypt. There is no place in the Hebrew Scriptures where Yehowah would allow the children of Israel to change the first day of a new year.

Biblical method for reckoning regnal years

If all the Hebrew Scriptures are inspired by God, the chronology derived from the books of Kings and Chronicles should be consistent with any other book in the Hebrew Bible and with other reliable historical and astronomical records outside the Bible. Any unreliable and unproved extra-biblical resources cannot be used to support or discredit the conclusion drawn from Biblical evidence. Here, we will construct the chronology of the kings of Israel and Judah based on all the relevant verses in the Hebrew Bible. It is also in perfect agreement with reliable extra-biblical records and astronomical phenomena.

We will first prove that the authors in the books of Kings, Chronicles, and of Jeremiah used an **anniversary** reckoning method where the regnal years of a king were counted by the anniversaries of his ascension. This method of reckoning regnal years was used in both the northern and southern kingdoms. This anniversary method is inferred from the Scriptures and differs from any method assumed by Thiele. In the cross references, the regnal years of a king are not reckoned from any new year but from the exact ascension date of the referenced king (the anniversary of his ascension). This method does not cause a cumulative error of larger than one year, which allows us to precisely determine the timeline of each king and the total length of each kingdom's lifespan.

How do we know that this is the reckoning method used by the Biblical authors? The reckoning method should not be invented by men, but instead be derived from the Biblical resources. Incredibly, Jeremiah 1 and 52 provide us with this information.

The captivity of Jerusalem took place in the fifth month according to Jeremiah 1:3, "It came also in the days of Jehoiakim the son of Josiah king of Judah, unto the end of the eleventh year of Zedekiah the son of Josiah king of Judah, unto the carrying away of Jerusalem captive in the fifth month." This same event occurred in the eighteenth year of Nebuchadnezzar according to Jeremiah 52:29, "In the eighteenth year of Nebuchadnezzar he carried away captive from Jerusalem eight hundred thirty and two persons." These two verses tell us that Jerusalem's captivity happened in the fifth Hebrew lunar month and in the eighteenth year of Nebuchadnezzar.

Jeremiah also said that Jerusalem and the holy temple were burned down on the 10th day of the fifth Hebrew lunar month in the nineteenth year of Nebuchadnezzar (Jeremiah 52:12). Clearly, there was a day in the fifth month that marked a crossover from the eighteenth to the nineteenth year of Nebuchadnezzar. This crossover day must have been between the first and 10th day of the fifth month and had nothing to do with the Babylonian new-year day. This indicates that Jeremiah used the anniversary method where the regnal years were counted from the anniversary date of Nebuchadnezzar's ascension, which should have been between the first and 10th day of the fifth month.

History indeed tells us that Nebuchadnezzar's father died on the 8th day of the fifth month (August 15) of 605 BC in the Babylonian calendar (ABC 5: Obv. 10), which corresponded to the 10th day of the fifth month in the Hebrew calendar (see the Hebrew calendar of 605 BC in Appendix D). Nebuchadnezzar started his reign just after his father died and the coronation of his kingship was on the first day of the sixth month in the Babylonian calendar (ABC 5: Obv.11). Jeremiah recognized the effective ascension date of Nebuchadnezzar rather than his coronation date.

Having correctly established the reckoning method for regnal years, we can unambiguously prove that the holy temple and Jerusalem were destroyed on the 10th day of the fifth month in the Hebrew calendar and on the anniversary of the nineteenth year of Nebuchadnezzar's reign, which was on 28 July 587 BC (see the Hebrew calendar of 587 BC in

Appendix D). Jerusalem was destroyed in 587 BC rather than 586 BC that most Biblical scholars believe.

The Biblical authors did not always follow a chronological order while writing different stories that were supplementary to each other. They usually wrote the main story sequentially to the end. But when they did add a supplementary material to the main story, the time for the supplementary story was often in the middle of the time interval of the main story. Jeremiah followed this writing style. Verses 52:1-14 present a main story about the siege, captivity, and fall of Jerusalem sequentially and verses 52:15-30 provide a supplementary material about the carrying away of Jerusalem captive. After Jeremiah wrapped the main story with the destruction of the holy temple and Jerusalem (verses 12-14), he then provided more detailed information about the carrying away of Jerusalem captive and the temple's articles. The burning down of Jerusalem must have taken place after the articles of the temple were taken away and the people in Jerusalem left the city. The most likely sequence is this: The articles of the temple and the people of Jerusalem were brought to Nebuchadnezzar at Riblah in the beginning of the fifth month, near the end of the 18th year of Nebuchadnezzar; after the execution of some people at Riblah, the holy temple and Jerusalem were burned down by Nebuzaradan, commander of the imperial guard on the 10th day of the fifth month, on the anniversary of the 19th year of Nebuchadnezzar.

Zedekiah became the king of Judah on Adar 3 of 598 BC and was carried into Babylon around the 10th day of the fifth month of 587 BC. Zedekiah reigned 10 years + 6 months +7 days, which are rounded to 11 years, in agreement with Jeremiah 52:1.

Ezekiel the prophet of God also used the same method to reckon the regnal years of a king, as clearly seen from Ezekiel 24:1, "In the ninth year, in the tenth month on the tenth day, the word of Yehowah came to me: 'Son of man, record this date, this very date, because the king of Babylon has laid siege to Jerusalem this very day.'" Here, the year is counted from the exile day of Jehoiachin, the same day that Zedekiah began to reign. The same event was recorded in Jeremiah 52:4, "So in the ninth year of Zedekiah's reign, on the tenth day of the tenth month, Nebuchadnezzar king of Babylon marched against Jerusalem with his whole army. They encamped outside the city and built siege works all around it." This was also recorded in 2 Kings 25:1. Therefore, in the books of Ezekiel, Kings, and Chronicles, the authors used the same reckoning method as the one used by Jeremiah.

Daniel the prophet of God should have used the same reckoning method as Ezekiel because both grew up in Judah and were carried into Babylon in their youth. Both were the prophets of God and were similar in age. Isaiah the prophet of God recorded the same story about Hezekiah king of Judah as that recorded in the books of Kings and Chronicles. It is only natural that Isaiah should have used the same reckoning method as Jeremiah.

Jewish and Christian tradition identified the author of the books of Chronicles as Ezra. Ezra was also believed to be the author of both Chronicles and Ezra–Nehemiah, but later critical scholars abandoned the books' identification with Ezra and called the anonymous author "the Chronicler." One of the most striking, although inconclusive, features of Chronicles is that its closing sentence is repeated as the opening of Ezra–Nehemiah. If the same author wrote the books of Chronicles, Ezra, and of Nehemiah, we expect that the author should have used the same reckoning method as Jeremiah. This should be the case because the true author of all these Biblical books is God.

Now let us test the above hypothesis. Nehemiah 1:1 and 2:1 show that the month of Kislev (the 9th month) preceded Nisan in the 20th year of Artaxerxes I, and Ezra 7:7-9 shows that Nisan preceded Av (the 5th month) in the 7th year of Artaxerxes I, so that the turning point from one regnal year of Artaxerxes I to another should have occurred between Av and Kislev. If one would use the ascension-year reckoning method, the Persians would have started their new year in the fall, which contradicts the fact that the ancient Persians and Babylonians always started their new year in the spring. Yehowah never allows His servants to write something without respecting facts. In order to be consistent with the anniversary reckoning method used by Jeremiah, Artaxerxes I must have started to reign in the fall. The chronology of Babylonian and Persian kings shown in Chapter 8 indeed shows that Artaxerxes I came to the throne in the 7th month of 464 BC. This further proves that God consistently used the same reckoning method in His inspired books.

Method for reckoning regnal years in Josephus' works

Josephus the Jewish historian of the first century AD appears to have also used the anniversary reckoning method in his account of the Jewish War: "This defeat [of Cestius] happened on the eighth day of the month Dius [Marchesvan/the eighth month] in the twelfth year of the reign of Nero." (*Wars*, bk. 2, ch.19, sect. 9).

It is known that the Roman emperor Claudius was poisoned to death on 13 October 54 AD, which is on the 22nd of Hyperberetaios [Tishri/the seventh month]. If Nero would have come to the throne immediately after the death of Claudius, the defeat of Cestius would not have been in the twelfth year of Nero if counted using the anniversary or non-ascension-year method. The ascension-year method would have been valid in this case but cannot simultaneously explain Josephus' other account: "the second temple was destroyed in Vespasian's second year." (*Wars*, bk. 6, ch. 4, 269). Vespasian was proclaimed emperor by his troops in July of 69 AD and Jerusalem was destroyed on August 5 of 70 AD, which would be in the first year of Vespasian if counted using the ascension-year method.

If we assume that Nero came to the throne after 8 Marchesvan (the 8th month) 54 AD, over 2 weeks after the death of Claudius, we can consistently explain all the accounts of Josephus using the anniversary reckoning method. This assumption may be supported by the historical fact told by Richard Cavendish (*History Today*, Vol. 54, Issue 10, 2004):

> Agrippina apparently delayed announcing the death for a while, to wait for an astrologically favorable moment and until word had been sent to the Praetorian Guard. When the moment came, Nero was escorted to the Praetorian barracks where he was hailed as Imperator. The Senate quickly followed suit and when Nero delivered the expected eulogy of the dead emperor, the senators sniggered. The Senate also decreed the deification of Claudius, which was needed to bolster Nero's position

as "son of the deified." Lucius Annaeus Seneca, who had overseen Nero's education, wrote a mocking account of "The Pumpkinification of the Divine Claudius." It describes the late emperor presenting himself at the gates of Olympus, where the gods contemptuously reject him and pack him off to Hades.

This passage suggests that Nero may have waited over 2 weeks to find an astrologically favorable moment for his ascension. Thus, he may have started his reign after 8 Marchesvan 54 AD.

In summary, all the Biblical writers of the Hebrew Bible and the Jewish historian Josephus have consistently used the anniversary reckoning method to count regnal years of the kings. With the anniversary reckoning method, we are able to construct the chronology of Judah and Israel's kings accurately.

Relative chronology of Judah and Israel's kings

In Table VIII below, we present the relative chronology of Judah and Israel's kings. The chronology is relative to the time when the united kingdom of Israel was divided into the southern kingdom Judah with two tribes (Judah and Benjamin) and the northern kingdom Israel with 10 tribes. We set this time to 0. The letter "F" in the table means "Fall" season (after the Summer Solstice) and the letter "S" means "Spring" season (before the Summer Solstice). The first number inside parenthesis after each king's name marks his regnal length. Half a year or more is rounded to one year and less than half a year is rounded to 0. The second part inside parenthesis is an abbreviated king's name along with an ordinal number "x", meaning that the current king started to reign in the "xth" year of the cross-referenced king. For example, Asa's information (41, Jer20) indicates that King Asa started to reign in the 20th year of Jeroboam, which was abbreviated with "Jer" to save space, and that he reigned for 41 years. "In the 20th year of Jeroboam" means that he had reigned for more than 19 and less than 20 years, depending on whether the time is in the beginning or the end of the year. Some negative numbers are for reference to the reign of a future king. The second parenthesis provides the references for the Biblical verses. In most cases, the uncertainty is less than half a year.

The relative chronology is internally consistent. The rows with **bold face** mean that the king started to reign solely. The regnal length of a king is calculated from the beginning of his reign (or co-reign) to the end when the following king starts to reign solely. With co-regency, the regnal length of each king matches the chronology very well. We describe these co-regency periods in detail as follows: Nadab started to reign at 22S and his reign ended at 24S when Baasha started to reign solely; Baasha started to co-reign with Nadab at 23S and ended his reign at 47S when Elah started to reign solely; Omri started to co-reign with Elah at 47S and ended his reign at 58F when Ahab started to reign solely; Jehoshaphat started to co-reign with Asa and ended his reign at 83S when Jehoram started to reign solely (Jehoram might have co-reigned with Jehoshaphat at 78S for a very short time and been removed by his father); Ahab started to reign at 56S and ended his reign at 77F when Ahaziah started to reign; Jehoahaz started to reign at 120F and ended his reign at 137S when Jehoash started to reign solely; Jehoash started to co-reign with Jehoahaz at 134S and ended his reign at 149F when Jeroboam II started to reign solely; Joash started to reign at 98S and ended his reign at 138S when Amaziah started to reign solely; Amaziah started to co-reign with Joash at 135F and ended his reign at 164F when Azariah started to reign solely; Azariah started to co-reign with Amaziah at 140F and ended his reign when Jotham started to reign at 192F; Jotham started to reign at 192F and ended his reign at 208F when Ahaz started to reign solely; Ahaz started to co-reign with Jotham at 199F and ended his reign at 215S when Hezekiah started to reign solely; Hezekiah started to co-reign with Ahaz at 214F and ended his reign at 244S when Manasseh started to reign.

Table VIII: Relative Chronology of Judah and Israel's Kings

Judah (and Benjamin)	Israel (Ten Northern Tribes)
Rehoboam (17) (1 Kings 14:21) 0F	0F Jeroboam I (22) (1 Kings 14:20)
Abijah (3, Jer18) (1 Kings 15:1) 17F	
Asa (41, Jer20) (1 Kings 15:9) 20F	
	22S Nadab (2, Asa2) (1 Kings 15:25)
	23S Baasha (24, Asa3) (1 Kings 15:33)
	24S Baasha (24, Asa4)
	46S Elah (2, Asa26) (1 Kings 16:8)
	47S Elah (2, Asa27)
	47S Omri (12, Asa27) (1 Kings 16:23)
	47F Omri (12, Asa27)
	56S Ahab (22) (1 Kings 16:29)
Jehoshaphat (25, Asa37) 58S	
	58F Ahab (22, Asa38) (1 Kings 16:29)
Jehoshaphat (25, Ahab4) (1 Kings 22:41-42) 61F	
	77F Ahaziah (2, Jehos17) (1 Kings 22:51)
Jehoram (unknown, Jor-2) (2 Kings 1:17) 78S	
	79S Joram (12, Jehos18) (2 Kings 3:1 & 1:17)
Jehoram (8, Jor5) (2 Kings 8:16) 83S	
Ahaziah (1, Jor12) (2 Kings 9:29 & 8:25) 91S	
Athaliah (6) (2 Kings 9-10; 11:1-4) 92F	92F Jesu (28) (2 Kings 9-10)
Joash (40, Jesu7)(2 Kings 12:1) 98S	
	120F Jehoahaz (17, Joash23) (2 Kings 13:1)
	134S Jehoash (16, Joash37) (2 Kings 13:10)
Amaziah (29, Jehoash2) (2 Kings 14:1-2) 135F	
	137S Jehoash (16, Joash40)
	137F Jeroboam II (41) (2 Kings 15:1)

Amaziah (29, Jehoash2) 138S	
Azariah (52, Zech-38) (2 Kings 15:8) 140F	
	149F Jeroboam II (41, Ama15) (2 Kings 14:23)
Azariah (Jerob27) (2 Kings 15:1) 164F	
	178F Zechariah (0.5, Jerob41) (2 Kings 14:23)
	179S Menahem (10, Aza39) (2 Kings 15:17)
	189F Pehakian (2, Aza50) (2 Kings 15:23)
	191F Pekah (20, Aza52) (2 Kings 15:27)
Jotham (16, Pekah2) (2 Kings 15:32-33) 192F	
Ahaz (16, Hos-12) (2 Kings 17:1) 199F	
Ahaz (16, Pekah17) (2 Kings 16:1) 208F	
	211F Hoshea (9, Joth20) (2 Kings 15:30)
Hezekiah (29, Hos3) (2 Kings 18:1-2) 214F	
Hezekiah (29) (2 Chron. 29:1) 215S	
	220F Samaria fell (Hos9, Hez6) (2 Kings 17:6; 18:10)
Manasseh (55) (2 Kings 21:1) 244S	
Amon (2) (2 Kings 21:19) 299S	
Josial (31) (2 Kings 22:1) 301S	
Jehoiakim (11) (2 Kings 23:36) 332S	
Zedekiah (11) (2 Kings 24:18) 344S	
Jerusalem fell (Neb19) (2 Kings 25:8) 354F	

Absolute chronology of Judah and Israel's kings

In Table IX, we present the absolute chronology by fixing the time of the destruction of Jerusalem to be the fall of 587 BC (which is written as 587F in Table IX to save space). The chronology is consistent with all the Biblical verses without any adjustment. Thiele adjusted his chronology by comparing some extra-biblical events, which have not been proved to be reliable. Here, we only compare it with reliable extra-biblical chronologies. What is so amazing is that they are in perfect agreement with each other.

Since Solomon had reigned for 40 years before Rehoboam started to reign in the fall of 941 BC, he started his reign in the fall of 981 BC. In his 4th year and in the spring of 977 BC, he started to build the holy temple. From the time when Solomon started to build the temple to the time when Jerusalem was destroyed, there were 390 years.

Table IX: Absolute Chronology of Judah and Israel's Kings

Judah (and Benjamin)	Israel (Ten Northern Tribes)
Rehoboam (17) (1 Kings 14:21) 941F	941F Jeroboam I (22)(1 Kings 14:20)
Abijah (3, Jer18) (1 Kings 15:1) 924F	
Asa (41, Jer20) (1 Kings 15:9) 921F	
	919S Nadab (2, Asa2) (1 Kings 15:25)
	918S Baasha (24, Asa3) (1 Kings 15:33)
	917S Baasha (24, Asa4)
	895S Elah (2, Asa26) (1 Kings 16:8)
	894S Elah (2, Asa27)
	894S Omri (12, Asa27) (1 Kings 16:23)
	894F Omri (12, Asa27)
	885S Ahab (22) (1 Kings 16:29)
Jehoshaphat (25, Asa38) 883S	
	883F Ahab (22, Asa38) (1 Kings 16:29)
Jehoshaphat (25, Ahab4) (1 Kings 22:41-42) 880F	
	864F Ahaziah (2, Jehos17) (1 Kings 22:51)

Jehoram (unknown, Jor-2) (2 Kings 1:17) 863S	
	862S Joram (12, Jehos18) (2 Kings 3:1 & 1:17)
Jehoram (8, Jor5) (2 Kings 8:16) 858S	
Ahaziah (1, Jor12) (2 Kings 9:29 & 8:25) 850S	
Athaliah (6) (2 Kings 9-10; 11:1-4) 849F	839F Jesu (28) (2 Kings 9-10)
Joash (40, Jesu7) (2 Kings 12:1) 843S	
	821F Jehoahaz (17, Joash23) (2 Kings 13:1)
	807S Jehoash (16, Joash37) (2 Kings 13:10)
Amaziah (29, Jehoash2) (2 Kings 14:1-2) 806F	
	804S Jehoash (16, Joash37)
	794F Jeroboam II (41) (2 Kings 15:1)
Amaziah (29, Jehoash2) 803S	
Azariah (52, Zech-38) (2 Kings 15:8) 801F	
	792F Jeroboam II (41, Ama15) (2 Kings 14:23)
Azariah (Jerob27) (2 Kings 15:1) 777F	
	763F Zechariah (0.5, Jerob41) (2 Kings 14:23)
	762S Menahem (10, Aza39) (2 Kings 15:17)
	752F Pehakian (2, Aza50) (2 Kings 15:23)
	750F Pekah (20, Aza52) (2 Kings 15:27)
Jotham (16, Pekah2) (2 Kings 15:32-33) 749F	
Ahaz (16, Hos-12) (2 Kings 17:1) 742F	
Ahaz (16, Pekah17) (2 Kings 16:1) 733F	
	730F Hoshea (9, Joth20) (2 Kings 15:30)

Hezekiah (29, Hos3) (2 Kings 18:1-2) 727F	
Hezekiah (29) (2 Chron. 29:1) 726S	
	721F Samaria fell (Hos9, Hez6) (2 Kings 17:6; 18:10)
Manasseh (55) (2 Kings 21:1) 697S	
Amon (2) (2 Kings 21:19) 642S	
Josial (31) (2 Kings 22:1) 640S	
Jehoiakim (11) (2 Kings 23:36) 609S	
Zedekiah (11) (2 Kings 24:18) 597S	
Jerusalem fell (Neb19) (2 Kings 25:8) 587F	

Starting to build Solomon's temple

Solomon began to build the temple in the fourth year of his reign, on the second day of the second month, four hundred and eighty years after the exodus of the Israelites out of Egypt (1 Kings 6:1, 2 Chronicles 3:2). As discussed above, Solomon started to build the temple in the spring of 977 BC (in the second day of the second month), which was on 16 April 977 BC. In the 8th month of his 11th year (970 BC), he finished all the detailed works (1 Kings 6:38). After this, Solomon ministered to make various temple articles. About one year later, he assembled the elders of Israel, heads of the tribes, and the chief fathers of children of Israel, and brought up the ark of the Covenant of Yehowah from the city of David. He dedicated to the temple in the 7th month of 969 BC (1 Kings 6:38, 1 Kings 8:1-2). The dedication of the temple marked the date in which the holy temple was built.

This magnificent event which lasted for three weeks should have been well known to all the neighboring countries. Consequently, the date of the 7th month of 969 BC should have been remembered or recorded by the historians both inside and outside Israel.

Josephus stated: "Let me now pass from these to some Phoenician records concerning our nation and present the evidence drawn from them. Among the Tyrians there are exact public records going back many years, about matters of significance done by them or with each other. It is recorded there that the temple was built by King Solomon in Jerusalem a hundred and forty-three [143] years and eight months before the Tyrians built Karchedon [Carthage]" (*Against Apion*, bk. 1, 106-108). Adding a hundred and forty-three years and eight months to the 7th month of 969 BC yields the 4th month of 825 BC, the date in which the Tyrians built Carthage.

Indeed, the date of the founding of Carthage was 825 BC, which was synchronized (https://en.wikipedia.org/wiki/King_of_Tyre) with an Assyrian record (tribute of Baal-Eser II/Balazeros II to Shalmaneser III in 841 BC) and with the founding of Rome. Pompeius Trogus, a Gallo-Roman historian who lived during the reign of Emperor Augustus, placed the founding of Carthage or Dido's flight from her brother Pygmalion in the seventh year of Pygmalion, and 72 years before the founding of Rome.

At least as early as the first century BC and later, the date most commonly used by Roman writers for the founding of Rome was on 21 April 753 BC. This places the founding of Carthage in 825 (753 + 72) BC. Therefore, our chronology is in perfect agreement with the extra-biblical records.

Sennacherib's attack on Judah

Sennacherib started to attack the fortified cities of Judah in the 14th year of Hezekiah king of Judah (2 Kings 18:13). Hayim Tadmor wrote an article about the last stage of Sargon's military activities in Philistia, which provides an important insight into the beginning year of Sennacherib's attack on the fortified cities of Judah. He wrote in "*Philistia under Assyrian Rule*" [*The Biblical Archaeologist*, Vol. 29, No. 3 (Sept. 1966), pp. 86-102]:

> The year 712 [BC] marked the last stage of Sargon's military activities in Philistia: the war against Ashdod. A year before that, in 713 [BC], Azuri, Ashdod's king, was accused of treachery and deported. His brother Ahimetu was then enthroned in his place (*ARAB II* 30). By the end of 713 [BC] or by the beginning of 712 [BC], 29 anti-Assyrian extremists overthrew Ahimetu and replaced him with a commoner called Yamani. This

usurper, a Philistine, and not the as usually assumed Greek or a Cypriot adventurer, turned out to be an enterprising and ambitious man. According to Sargon's account (*ARAB II* 30; *ANET* 286), he contacted his neighbors — the other Philistine cities as well as Judah, Edom and Moab — in an attempt to stir up a rebellion, and he requested Egypt's aid. Anticipating an Assyrian attack, he fortified Ashdod against siege, building a deep moat and a high wall (*ARAB II* 195; *ANET* p. 287). When news of Ashdod's revolt reached Sargon, he dispatched his army under the leadership of the commander in chief, the turtanu, explicitly referred to in Isaiah 20:1 as the Tartan "who . . . came to Ashdod and fought against it and took it." The campaign is eloquently described in the Annals (*ARAB* 30) and in the "*Display Inscription*" (*ibid.* 62) from *Dur-Sharrukin* (Khorsabad) composed [in] about 707 [BC]. Two wall reliefs, also from *Dur-Sharrukin*, must be related to the same campaign. They show the siege of Amqarruna (= Ekron) and Gabbutunu (= Gibbeton).

Another piece of evidence comes from a small fragment of a tablet recording the Assyrian attack on Azaq (Azekah in Judah). This assault on Azekah (Tell ez-Zakariyeh), if correctly dated to 712 [BC], was undertaken to intimidate Judah into submission and to prevent Hezekiah from aiding Ashdod.

These passages suggest that Azekah was the first city of Judah that the Assyrians attacked in 712 BC, which was in the 14th year of Hezekiah's sole reign according to our chronology above, in agreement with 2 Kings 18:13 and 2 Chronicles 32:1. Since Sargon king of Assyrian was making war against Ashdod in 712 BC, he would not have been able to simultaneously attack Judah to prevent Hezekiah from aiding Ashdod. Therefore, in all likelihood, Sennacherib, the crown prince of Assyria at that time, launched the attack on Azekah and other cities in Judah.

Although Sennacherib was a crown prince at that time, the title of king in the Biblical text could have referred to Sennacherib's future royal title. This can be seen from other Biblical texts concerning Tiglath-Pileser king of Assyria. Before Tiglath-Pileser became king of Assyria, he was a commander and his name was Pul, but the Biblical author called him king of Assyria (2 Kings 15:19,29). There is another example. During the Sennacherib's campaign against Jerusalem, the Scripture says (2 Kings 19:9): "And when he heard concerning Tirhakah king of Ethiopia…" At that time (702 BC), Tirhakah was only a military commander, and he came to the throne over 10 years later (690 BC).

Sennacherib started to attack the fortified cities of Judah in the spring of 712 BC and captured all the fortified cities except for Jerusalem. Hezekiah decided to defend it by counseling with his princes and mighty men to stop the waters from the fountains which were outside the city, by building up the wall that was broken, raising it up to the towers and another wall outside, and repairing Millo in the city of David, and making weapons and shields in abundance (2 Chronicles 32:2-8). It is possible that Sennacherib was unable to take Jerusalem for many years because Hezekiah and the people of Jerusalem repented of the pride of their hearts and Yehowah's protection was still with Jerusalem during the days of Hezekiah (2 Chronicles 32:26).

The pride of Hezekiah's heart was revealed when the ambassadors of the princes of Babylon were sent unto him to inquire of the wonder (Yehowah's miraculous sign and healing) that was done in the land (2 Chronicles 32:31) and Hezekiah showed them all that was in his storehouses—the silver, the gold, the spices and the fine olive oil—his armory and everything found among his treasures. Because Hezekiah did not follow God more closely according to the benefit God did unto him and his heart was lifted up, there was wrath upon him, and upon Judah and Jerusalem (2 Chronicles 32:31). Because of His wrath, God stirred up the heart of Sennacherib to attack the fortified cities of Judah in the spring of 712 BC after the ambassadors of the princes of Babylon visited Hezekiah.

Hezekiah's illness and Yehowah's miraculous healing should have occurred during the end of the 14th year of his sole reign, which was in the spring of 712 BC. This is because his lifespan was extended for 15 years more after the healing (2 Kings 20:6) and his regnal length was 29 years (2 Kings 18:2). Because his heart was proud after Yehowah had done so many favors to him, God was angry with him, leaving and testing him (2 Chronicles 32:31). This raises a high possibility that the initial invasion of Judah by Sennacherib in the spring of 712 BC occurred right after Hezekiah's illness, which also took place in the spring of 712 BC. To humble Hezekiah, Yehowah immediately stirred up the heart of Sennacherib to attack Judah. This is consistent with the pattern of Yehowah's hands, as seen in many other cases (e.g., 2 Chronicles 28:19-20).

As we mentioned before, the Biblical authors often do not follow a chronological time sequence when they write different stories supplementary to each other. Here, we see another example. For the main story of Hezekiah, the Bible starts with 2 Kings 18:1 which says about the first year of Hezekiah's sole reign (from the spring of 726 BC). It continues and finishes the main story until the death of Sennacherib (681 BC). The supplementary story of Hezekiah starts from 2 Kings 20:1, which says "In those days" rather than "Then." The phrase "in those days" means any time during the reign of Hezekiah. Since this supplementary story is very important, it deserves a separate section to describe in length. If this section were to be part of the main story, it would greatly distract the readers. With this writing style, readers might misunderstand the time sequence if they would not meditate on the verses carefully. Yehowah desires His children to read His Word seriously and carefully and to obey His Word with all their hearts.

After 2 Kings 18:13 tells us that Sennacherib began to assault the fortified cities of Judah in the 14th year of Hezekiah (in the spring of 712 BC when Sennacherib was a crown prince), the following verse (2 Kings 18:14) jumps to the story after Sennacherib became king and tried to attack Jerusalem in his third campaign (702 BC). The story appeared to jump so suddenly, but it was quite normal for Biblical writing. Another sudden jump in the story can be found in 2 Kings 19:36-37. Verse 36 tells a story about Sennacherib's withdrawal to Nineveh in 702 BC (the fourth year of his reign) while the following verse says that he was killed by his son in 681 BC, the end year of his reign. With this compact writing style, the author only briefly recorded a few major events regarding the king.

The story described in 2 Kings 18:14-16 must have happened after Hezekiah showed the Babylonians all the treasures in his palace in the spring of 712 BC. Verse 16 tells us that Hezekiah had to strip off the gold with which he had covered the doors and doorposts of the temple of Yehowah, in order to be able to pay the full tribute imposed by Sennacherib. This verse implies that Hezekiah did not have gold in his storehouses, which made it impossible for him to show off his wealth if the Babylonians had visited him after this campaign. This campaign was generally believed to take place in 701 BC, but by carefully comparing the Chronicle on the Reigns from Nabû-Nasir to Šamaš-šuma-ukin (ABC 1), Assysian Eponyn List, the first edition of BM 113203 cylinder, the Sennacherib prism, and the Biblical account, we conclude that this campaign should have occurred in 702 BC. Independent of whether the campaign took place in 701 BC or 702 BC, it definitely happened after Hezekiah's illness, in agreement with the Biblical record.

Battle of Qarqar not related to King Ahab

The inscription on the Shalmaneser III Stela deals with campaigns Shalmaneser made in western Mesopotamia and Syria, fighting extensively with the countries of Bit Adini and Carchemish (https://en.wikipedia.org/wiki/Kurkh_Monoliths). At the end of the Monolith comes the account of the Battle of Qarqar in 853 BC, where an alliance of twelve kings fought against Shalmaneser at the Syrian city of Qarqar. This alliance, comprised of eleven kings, was led by Irhuleni of Hamath, Hadadezer of Damascus, and a large force led by King A-ha-ab-bu of Sir-ila-a-a.

The identification of "A-ha-ab-bu Sir-ila-a-a" with "Ahab of Israel" was first proposed by Julius Oppert in his 1865 *Histoire des Empires de Chaldée et d'Assyrie.*" If this identification were relevant, Ahab would have been still alive in 853 BC and Hadadezer of Damascus would have formed an alliance with Ahab of Israel, although they had been bitterly hostile to each other according to the Biblical record.

According to the Biblical chronology established here based on all the Biblical records, the last year of Ahab was in 863 BC, which was 10 years earlier than the time for the Battle of Qarqar. The Hebrew interlinear words for the name Ahab and for the kingdom of Israel are Achab and Isral, respectively. The Assyrian interlinear words for the king's name and his kingdom described in the inscription on the Shalmaneser III Stela are A-ha-ab-bu and Sir-ila-a-a. If we compare the interlinear words of both languages, they are not a good match. A-ha-ab-bu slightly matches Achab since there is an extra syllable "bu" in A-ha-ab-bu. Isral does not match with Sir-ila-a-a at all. It is to be noted that the name A-ha-ab-bu might be read equally well as Ahappu and be an entirely different name from Ahab, quite probably Hurrian. It is really questionable because nowhere else on Assyrian tablets is Israel given this name. On the monuments Israel was often called mat Humri, the land of Omri. There is no mention of the battle of Qarqar in the Bible.

The Biblical author described in quite detail the battle at Ramoth-gilead together with the preparations for it (1 Kings 22). He later described the attack on Dothan (2 Kings 6:8-23) and the siege of Samaria that followed it. However, he did not say a single word about the battle of Qarqar. Why would this have been the case if Ahab had really been at Qarqar? Now that he gave a vivid account of Ahab's great victory over Ben-hadad (1 Kings 20:1-34) which led even to the capture of the king of Syria himself, it is impossible that the author did not wish to mention a successful expedition of King Ahab. If the battle of Qarqar had been a humiliating defeat for Ahab, we might expect that the Biblical writer would have more willingly recorded it as a divine judgment on the wicked king of Israel, as he recorded the battle at Ramoth-gilead, in which Ahab perished.

Therefore, King Ahab was not in the battle of Qarqar and the date of this battle cannot be used to constrain the chronology of the kings of Judah and Israel.

Samaria taken in the fall of 721 BC

2 Kings 18:9-10 reads: "And it came to pass in the fourth year of King Hezekiah, which was the seventh year of Hoshea son of Elah king of Israel, that Shalmaneser king of Assyria came up against Samaria, and besieged it. And at the end of three years they took it: even in the sixth year of Hezekiah, that is the ninth year of Hoshea king of Israel, Samaria was taken."

These verses tell us that Shalmaneser came up against Samaria in the beginning of the seventh year of Hoshea and in the beginning of the fourth year of King Hezekiah (the fall of 724 BC). After three years, in the end of the 9th year of Hoshea in which was also the end of the 6th year of Hezekiah, Samaria was taken. This took place during the fall of 721 BC, which was about one year later than the date most historians believe.

The date pertaining to the fall of Samaria can be found from extra-biblical records. ABC 1 is one of the historiographical texts about ancient Assyria and Babylonia. In ABC1: Column 1 (https://www.livius.org/cg cm/chronicles/abc1/abc1_col_i.html#column_i), it was recorded: "The fifth year (722/721 BC): Šalmaneser went to his destiny in the month Tebêtu (16 January 721 BC). For five years Šalmaneser ruled Akkad and Assyria. On the twelfth day of the month Tebêtu (16 January 721 BC), Sargon ascended the throne in Assyria."

Moreover, Assyrian cuneiform states that 27,290 captives were taken from Samaria by the hand of Sargon II. Sargon recorded his first campaign on the walls of the royal palace at Dur-Sharrukin (https://en.wikipedia.org/wiki/Assyrian_captivity): "In my first year of reign … the people of Samaria … to the number of 27,290 … I carried away. Fifty chariots for my royal equipment I selected. The city I rebuilt. I made it greater than it was before. People of the lands I had conquered I settled therein. My official (Tartan) I placed over them as governor." (L.ii.4.). Therefore, Samaria should have been taken in the first year of Sargon II, which was from the spring of 721 BC to the spring of 720 BC. The fall of 721 BC was indeed within the first year of Sargon II.

Earthquake and solar eclipse at the end of Jeroboam II

Amos 1:1 says, "The words of Amos, who was among the sheep breeders of Tekoa, which he saw concerning Israel in the days of Uzziah king of Judah, and in the days of Jeroboam the son of Joash, king of Israel, two years before the earthquake." This verse tells us that Amos saw a vision concerning Israel in the days of Uzziah (Azariah) king of Judah, and in the days of Jeroboam II the son of Joash, king of Israel two years before the great earthquake.

We also learned that the earthquake happened in the summertime and caused many to die from Amos 8:1-3, "Thus Yehowah God showed me: Behold, a basket of summer fruit. And He said, 'Amos, what do you see?' So I said, 'A basket of summer fruit.' Then Yehowah said to me: 'The end has come upon My people Israel; I will not pass by them anymore. And the songs of the temple shall be wailing in that day,' Says Yehowah God, 'Many dead bodies everywhere, they shall be thrown out in silence.'"

Amos 8:8 also tells us that the earthquake was very strong, swelling like the River, heaving and subsiding like the River of Egypt. Then the following two verses (Amos 8:9-10) say:

> "And it shall come to pass in that day," says Yehowah God, "**That I will make the sun go down at noon, and I will darken the earth in broad daylight**; I will turn your feasts into mourning, and all your songs into lamentation; I will bring sackcloth on every waist, and baldness on every head; I will make it like mourning for an only son, and its end like a bitter day."

These verses clearly reveal that the solar eclipse would have taken place at noon, which presaged the coming of the great disaster and distress in the summertime (the great earthquake). Jeroboam II king of Israel might have been killed by the great earthquake, as Yehowah said that the end had come upon His people Israel (Amos 8:2). God might have decided to punish the people of Israel and their king through the great earthquake.

There was a solar eclipse on 15 June 763 BC, which was in the summer. From the fitted curve of the delta-T parameter (see Appendix A), we find that the delta-T parameter in 763 BC is given by $\Delta T = -20 + 30.87 t^2$. The predicted solar eclipse started at 8:45 and ended at 11:11. The maximum eclipse occurred at 9:44 (see Figure 10), over five hours after sunrise (4:32), very close to noon.

Since the solar eclipse took place in the summertime and the great disaster (the great earthquake) also happened in the summertime according to Amos 8:1-3, the two events should have occurred one after another. In all likelihood, King Jeroboam II was killed during the earthquake in the summer of 763 BC. Then Zechariah king of Israel should have started his reign in the fall of 763 BC, in perfect agreement with our chronology (Table IX).

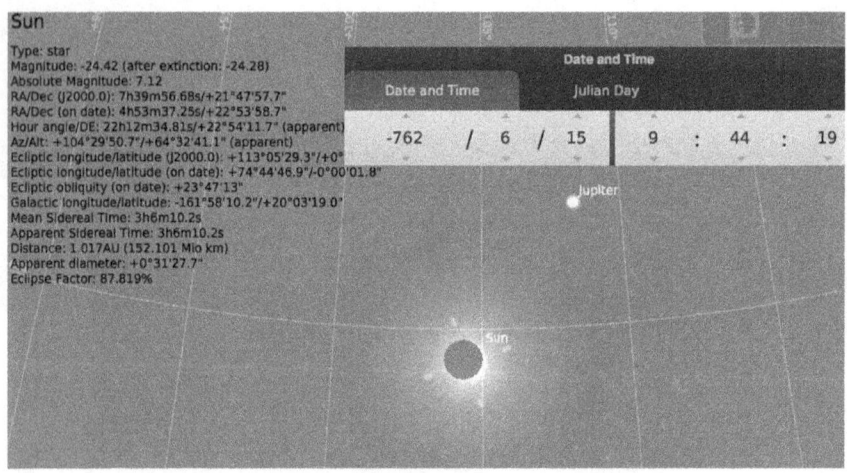

Figure 10: Predicted solar eclipse on 15 June 763 BC, observed in Samaria. Jupiter was visible during the eclipse around noontime.

A major earthquake with a magnitude of about 8.0 occurred in Israel in the eighth century BC. Many scholars have attempted to date the earthquake as accurately as possible [Israel Finkelstein, **Bulletin of American Schools of Oriental Research,** No. 314 (May 1999), pp. 55-70; and references therein]. Yadin in 1975 and Finkelstein in 1999 consistently dated the Hazor's earthquake at 760 BC ± 25 years. Ibrahim and van der Kooij in 1977, 1978, 1991 and Vilders in 1992 dated the earthquake at 770 BC ± 25 years. Dever in 1992 dated

Gezer's earthquake at 760 BC ± 25 years. Ussishkin in 1993 dated Lachish's earthquake at 760 BC ±30 years. A simple average of the 4 data points above yields 762.5 BC ±2.5 years, where ±2.5 years are the standard deviation of the average. The average date of 762.5 BC for the great earthquake is in perfect agreement with the date of the solar eclipse (15 June 763 BC). Similar to the solar eclipse in the spring of 1493 BC, which presaged the end of the First Dynasty of Babylon (Chapter 8), this solar eclipse presaged the end of Jeroboam's reign due to his great sin. This great earthquake should not have occurred naturally but arise from God's divine judgment.

CHAPTER 12

THE LENGTH OF YESHUA'S MINISTRY

In the Biblical chronology constructed in Chapter 10, we have included the timeline of Yeshua. His timeline can be constructed based on the Gospel of Matthew, the Gospel of John, and the book of Revelation. These books are believed to be written by two of Yeshua's twelve disciples. The authenticity of Yeshua's story in these books can be verified by the self-consistency of the timeline and the perfect fulfillment of the numerical prophecies foretold by Yeshua himself and by the prophets of God.

From these reliable Gospels, we can also determine that the length of Yeshua's ministry was about three years. In particular, the Gospel of John explicitly recorded Yeshua's ministry during the first, third, and fourth Passover Festival. Apostle John also recorded a story which took place in a spring between the first and third Passover Festival. Below we will describe them in detail.

First Passover

Yeshua's first Passover (John 2:13) was the one that immediately followed declaration of the Lamb of God by John the Baptist (John 1:29-36) and the first miracle he performed in Cana of Galilee (John 2:1-11). According to the Law (Exodus 12:3), a Passover lamb must be selected on Nisan 10. If Yeshua is the Passover Lamb of God, he must be selected by God on Nisan 10. John the Baptist declared that Yeshua was the Lamb of God when he saw Yeshua coming toward him (John 1:29-34). This declaration should have been made on Nisan 10 in order for Yeshua to be the true Passover Lamb of God. Forty days before John's declaration, Yeshua was baptized (anointed by God Father) and "then was Yeshua led up by the Spirit into the wilderness to be tempted by the devil. And when he had fasted forty days and forty nights, he was afterward hungry." (Matthew 4:1-2). Here, we assume that Yeshua went to John right after he had fasted 40 days and nights.

During Yeshua's first Passover the Jews asked for a sign, and he responded, "'Destroy this temple, and in three days I will raise it up.' The Jews therefore said, 'It took forty-six years to build this temple, and will you raise it up in three days?' But he was speaking of the temple of his body." (John 2:19-21). These passages provide an important clue to establishing the year of Yeshua's first Passover Festival.

What did Yeshua mean by "temple" and how did the Jews interpret his meaning? Yeshua referred to his own body as a temple or shrine as he was standing in the front of the main temple. The Jews thought that he was referring to the physical temple and not to his body. They thought that if Yeshua were to destroy the physical temple, it would not be possible for him to build it again in three days. They responded to Yeshua with the same word "temple," which had taken forty-six years in building. They confronted Yeshua with the impossibility of rebuilding it in three days in contrast to forty-six years in building their physical temple. The Jews knew when the physical temple had begun to be rebuilt but did not understand the spiritual implication of Yeshua's words.

The month and year in which the rebuilding of the temple began can be inferred from the history of Josephus. He wrote: "Now Herod, in the eighteenth year of his reign, and after the acts already mentioned, undertook a very great work, that is, to build of himself the temple of God." (*Antiq.* bk. 15, ch. 11, sect. 1). Herod started his public speech, announcing his intention to rebuild the temple. He promised not to begin the actual rebuilding process until everything was prepared. The preparations would have taken some time, and the actual rebuilding should have begun during Herod's eighteenth year. That is why Josephus emphasized the eighteenth year.

To establish the exact time the temple began to be built during his eighteenth year, it is necessary to backdate from the completion of the Holy of Holies. Josephus wrote, "The temple itself was built by the priests in a year and six months.... They feasted and celebrated this rebuilding of the temple... for at the same time with this celebration for the work about the temple, fell also the day of the king's inauguration." (*Antiq.* bk. 15, ch. 11, sect. 6). The month that fell a year and six months before the anniversary of Herod's inauguration should have been the month of Nisan (the first month) because his inauguration took place in the month of Tishri (the 7th month) of 38 BC, soon after he took Jerusalem in the summertime of 38 BC (see Herod's reign in Chapter 13). Therefore, Herod should have announced his intention to rebuild the temple probably in the beginning of his 18th year (in Tishri of 21 BC) and started to rebuild it in Nisan of 20 BC (in the middle of his 18th year). The construction of the Holy of Holies should have been finished in Tishri of 19 BC and in the 20th anniversary of Herod's inauguration. From the spring of 20 BC to the spring of 27 AD, 46 years had elapsed. This suggests that Yeshua's first Passover was in the spring of 27 AD. From the calendar of 27 AD in Appendix D, we see that Nisan 10 of 27 AD was on 5 April and 40 days before that day was February 24. Yeshua started his earthly ministry in the daytime of Nisan 11 (John 1:35-42), which was on April 6 of 27 AD.

The third Passover

John 6:4-14 records another story in the third Passover:

> Now the Passover, a feast of the Jews, was near. Then Yeshua lifted up his eyes, and seeing a great multitude coming toward him, he said to Philip, "Where shall we buy bread, that these may eat?" But this he said to test him, for he himself knew what he would do. Philip answered Him, "Two hundred denarii worth of bread is not sufficient for them, that every one of them may have a little." One of his disciples, Andrew, Simon Peter's brother, said to him, "There is a lad here who has five barley loaves and two small fish, but what are they among so many?" Then Yeshua said, "Make the people sit down." Now there was much grass in the place. So the men sat down, in number about five thousand. And

Yeshua took the loaves, and when he had given thanks he distributed them to the disciples, and the disciples to those sitting down; and likewise of the fish, as much as they wanted. So when they were filled, he said to his disciples, "Gather up the fragments that remain, so that nothing is lost." Therefore they gathered them up, and filled twelve baskets with the fragments of the five barley loaves which were left over by those who had eaten. Then those men, when they had seen the sign that Yeshua did, said, "This is truly the prophet who is to come into the world."

This story of feeding the five thousand was also recorded in the Gospel of Matthew (Matthew 14:13-21). This story took place after John the Baptist was beheaded by Herod the Tetrarch (Matthew 14:1-12). After this story, both John and Matthew recorded the crucifixion and resurrection of Yeshua during the fourth Passover. Thus, John the Baptist was beheaded about one year before Yeshua's crucifixion.

The fourth and last Passover

The last Passover of Yeshua's ministry is the most documented Passover of all. John 11:55 records, "And the Jews' Passover was near at hand: and many went out of the country up to Jerusalem before the Passover, to purify themselves."

All the Gospels recorded that Yeshua and his disciples had the Passover supper in the beginning of the preparation day (Nisan 14). It seems very difficult to understand why they celebrated the Passover one day earlier than the Pharisees. This mystery can be naturally resolved since Yeshua's disciples were Essenes who followed Enoch's solar calendar. It is remarkable that only in 30 AD did the Essenes' Passover fall one day before the Pharisees' one (see the calendar of 30 AD in Appendix D). In other years around 30 AD, they fell in different weeks. Consequently, 30 AD was the only year in which Yeshua and his disciples could have observed the Essenes' Passover exactly one day before the Pharisees' Passover, and himself be the Passover Lamb of God in the preparation day of the Pharisees' Passover.

From the astronomical data of new moons and full moons, we can unambiguously determine the Hebrew lunisolar calendar (see Appendix D). In the years from 27 to 34 AD, there were two years, 30 and 33 AD, in which Nisan 14 (the preparation day) was on Wednesday. The 15th day of Enoch's first solar month of 30 AD was on Nisan 14 while the 15th day of Enoch's first solar month of 33 AD was on Nisan 21. Only in 30 AD, could Yeshua and his disciples have observed the Essenes' Passover exactly one day before the Pharisees' Passover and then himself be crucified on Wednesday. In Chapter 31, we will prove that Yeshua was crucified on 5 April 30 AD (Wednesday) and resurrected at sunset on 8 April (Saturday). From the day he was declared to be the Lamb of God to the day of his crucifixion, there are exactly three solar years.

After he resurrected in the beginning of Sunday (April 9), he revealed to Marys right after his resurrection (Matthew 28:9; John 20:14-17). He revealed to his disciples in Galilee (Matthew 26:32; Matthew 28:10,16) in the evening of a Sunday (John 20:19). Because it took at least 4 days for Yeshua's disciples to travel from Jerusalem to Galilee on foot, it was impossible for Yeshua to meet his disciples in Galilee on April 9 (right after his resurrection). Therefore, their first meeting must have taken place in the following Sunday evening, which was on April 16 (after sunset of April 15). After he stayed with his disciples for 40 days (Acts 1:3), he then ascended to heaven on 26 May 30 AD (after sunset of May 25), right on the feast day of Pentecost. Before he ascended to heaven, he gave a great commission to his disciples (Matthew 28:19-20): "Go therefore and make disciples of all the nations, baptizing them in the name of the Father and of the Son and of the Holy Spirit, teaching them to observe all things that I have commanded you; and lo, I am with you always, even to the end of the age." Yeshua's disciples would bear witness of him and make disciples of all the nations because they had stayed with him from the beginning (John 15:27). Those who believe in Yeshua through the words of his disciples will be in union with the Father and the Son (John 17:20-21).

The Julian day numbers for 26 May 30 AD and 6 April 27 AD are JD 1732161 and JD 1731015, respectively. From 6 April 27 AD to 26 May 30 AD, there were 1,732,161–1,731,015 = 1,146 days. Since Yeshua spent three days and three nights in the grave, the total length of his ministry on the earth in his first advent was 1,146 − 3 = 1,143 days. The length of his ministry was about three years.

The spring between the first and third Passover

Apostle John clearly recorded Yeshua's ministry in the first, third, and fourth Passover. There appeared to be no direct record of Yeshua's work in the second Passover. Instead, John recorded a story in the spring between the first and third Passover (John 4:31-38):

> ³¹In the meantime his disciples urged him, saying, "Rabbi, eat." ³²But he said to them, "I have food to eat of which you do not know." ³³Therefore the disciples said to one another, "Has anyone brought him anything to eat?" ³⁴Yeshua said to them, "My food is to do the will of Him who sent me, and to finish His work. ³⁵Do you not say, 'There are still four months and then comes the harvest'? Behold, I say to you, lift up your eyes and look at the fields, for they are already white for harvest! ³⁶And he who reaps receives wages, and gathers fruit for eternal life, that both he who sows and he who reaps may rejoice together. ³⁷For in this the saying is true: 'One sows and another reaps.' ³⁸I sent you to reap that for which you have not labored; others have labored, and you have entered into their labors."

Verse 35 implies that the story happened at the time when the fields Yeshua and his disciples passed had already whitened for harvest and there would have been about 4 months until the major harvest. If we know the harvest seasons of Israel, we can pin down the time of the story.

The agricultural year in Israel begins in the fall (after the harvest Festival of Tabernacles) with plowing and sowing. Harvests in Israel begin in the spring in the month of Adar (February/March). The harvest times in the ancient Israel are listed in Table X, which is obtained from the website: http://www.joybysurprise.com/harvest_times_in_israel_.html.

Table X: Harvest Times in Ancient Israel

Months	Weather	Crops & activity
Tishri 7th month(Sep/Oct)	First rains	Plowing begins
Heshvan 8th month(Oct/Nov)		Plowing / grain planting
Kislev 9th month(Nov/Dec)		Grain planting continues
Teveth 10th month(Dec/Jan)	Main rains	
Sebat 11th month (Jan/Feb)		
Adar 12th month (Feb/Mar)	Spring rains	Almond in bloom / flax harvest
Nisan 1st month (Mar/Apr)		Barley harvest begins
2nd month (Apr/May)		Barley harvest completed
3rd month (May/Jun)	Dry season	Wheat harvest begins
4th month (Jun/Jul)		Wheat harvest completed / first figs
Av 5th month (Jul/Aug)	Summer heat	Vintage (grape harvest) begins
Elul 6th month (Aug/Sep)		Date harvest / summer figs

From Table X, one can see that the harvest season in ancient Israel began in Adar (Feb/March) and continued by stages into the fall. The barley harvest begins in the first month Nisan (March-April). The major wheat harvest completes in the 4th month.

Yeshua said that the fields were already white (John 4:35). The color of the barley seeds is white when they are ripe. The color of flax seeds is dark brown or light brown when they are ripe. Therefore, we can conclude that this story should have taken place in the month of Nisan (possibly in the Passover) when the barley harvest began. After about 4 months in the 4th/5th lunar month, the major harvests (wheat and grape harvests) were complete.

CHAPTER 13

HEROD'S REIGN

Herod, also known as Herod the Great, was the Roman client king of Judea which was referred to as the Herodian kingdom. The accurate determination of the Herod's timeline is crucial to the construction of the accurate timeline of Yeshua. The accurate timeline of Yeshua is necessary for us to prove whether Yeshua is the true Messiah.

Details about Herod's life were recorded in The Antiquities of the Jews by Roman-Jewish historian Josephus. Herod also appeared in the Christian Gospel of Matthew as the ruler of Judea who ordered the Massacre of the Innocents at the time of the birth of Yeshua. Moreover, Herod's temple was mentioned in the Gospel of John. Therefore, a reliable determination of his timeline is essential to pinning down the birth date of Yeshua and the starting date of his ministry.

We will use the historical records of Josephus, astronomical information, lunisolar calendar information, and other historical evidence to uniquely determine the date of the first year of Herod's reign. According to Josephus, Herod took Jerusalem in the day of the appointed third month's fasting in the 185th Olympiad (*Antiq.*, bk. 14, ch. 16, sect. 2-4). There is no third month's fasting according to Zechariah 8:19, "Thus says the LORD of hosts; the fast of the fourth month, and the fast of the fifth, and the fast of the seventh, and the fast of the tenth, shall be to the house of Judah joy and gladness, and cheerful feasts; therefore love the truth and peace." Currently, the Jews observe the solemnity of the fast on Tammuz 17/18 (fourth month), Av 9/10 (fifth month), Tishri 3/4 (seventh month), and Tebet 10/11 (tenth month), in agreement with Zechariah 8:19.

Did Josephus make a mistake about the months for fasting appointed by Yehowah God? No, he did not. In fact, his record is correct if we understand that he was using the Babylonian calendar to describe the timeline of the event. In 38 BC the third month in the Babylonian calendar happened to be the fourth month in the Hebrew calendar, while in 37 BC the month's numbers were the same in either calendar (see the calendars of 37 and 38 BC in Appendix D). This fact rules out the possibility that Herod took Jerusalem in the summer of 37 BC since in this year the fasting of the Jews could never have taken place in the third month of the Babylonian calendar. In the summer of 38 BC, which was also in the 185th Olympiad, there was the possibility of a Jewish fasting day in the third month of the Babylonian calendar (and in the fourth month of the Hebrew calendar). If this was the case, the fasting day should have been on Tammuz 17 (June 27) of 38 BC in the Hebrew calendar. Moreover, Jerusalem was besieged during the summertime and in a sabbatical year according to Josephus. Indeed, the year from the spring of 38 BC to the spring of 37 BC is inferred to be a sabbatical year from the confirmed sabbatical year in Chapter 14. Therefore, Herod must have taken Jerusalem in the summer of 38 BC.

Josephus informed us that the war at Actium between Herod and Arabians was at height and the earth was greatly shaken at the beginning of the spring in the seventh year of Herod's reign (*Wars*, bk. 1, ch. 19, sect. 3). Since Herod started to reign in the summer of 38 BC, his seventh year was from the summer of 32 BC to the summer of 31 BC. Therefore, the spring of 31 BC was in the seventh year of Herod's reign.

Josephus also told us that Herod died after a lunar eclipse and before the Passover (*Antiq.*, bk. 17, ch. 6-9). This information allows us to narrow down the year and month Herod died. From 10 BC to 1 AD, there were only two lunar eclipses observable in Jerusalem during the spring season. In 4 BC, a partial lunar eclipse with a magnitude of 1.43 took place on March 13 and the Passover was on April 11. This eclipse is consistent with Josephus' description. In 5 BC, a total lunar eclipse occurred at 20:21 of March 23, one day after the Passover on March 23. This eclipse is inconsistent with Josephus' description. Therefore, Herod must have died between Adar 15 and Nisan 15 of 4 BC.

According to Josephus, Herod had reigned 34 years after he took Jerusalem (*Antiq.*, bk. 17, ch. 8, sect. 1). From June 27 of 38 BC to March 27 of 4 BC, there were 33 years + 9 months, which were rounded to 34 years, in agreement with Josephus' direct statement.

It appears to be generally accepted that the first year of Herod was in 37 BC because the fall of Jerusalem occurred when Marcus Agrippa and Caninius Gallus were consuls of Rome (*Antiq.*, bk. 14, ch. 16, sect. 4), which was in 37 BC according to the accepted chronology for the consuls of Rome. To reconcile with the historical records of Josephus, one must accept that the chronology for Roman consuls may not have been completely accurate: an uncertainty of one year.

In Rome, Herod was unexpectedly appointed king of the Jews by the Roman Senate. Josephus put this in the year of the consulship of Calvinus and Pollio, which would have been 40 BC according to the accepted chronology for the consuls of Rome. This is in contradiction with Josephus' direct statement (*Antiq.*, bk 17, ch. 8, sect. 1): "Herod reigned 37 years [41 to 4 BC] since he was appointed by the Romans." By shifting back by one year in the chronology for the consuls of Rome, we arrive a conclusion that Herod was appointed king of the Jews by the Roman Senate in 41 BC. Therefore, the currently accepted chronology for the consuls of Rome has one year uncertainty in the time of Herod.

CHAPTER 14

SABBATICAL AND JUBILEE YEARS

Unambiguous determination of a sabbatical year can be used to verify the accuracy of the Biblical chronology. An important question arises as to which month a sabbatical year should start. Most modern rabbis believe that a sabbatical year should start from Tishri 1, on the feast day of Trumpets. It is unclear whether this belief has any Biblical basis.

In the books of Moses, the beginning of a year was clearly set on Nisan 1, in the context of a description of the first Passover. "Yehowah said to Moses and Aaron in the land of Egypt: 'This month shall mark for you the beginning of the months; it shall be the first of the months of the year for you.'" (Exodus 12:1-2). This new year celebrated the creation of the Jewish nation through the redemption of the Israelites from Egypt. Nisan, as the first of the months, coincided with the beginning of Jewish national history.

But the Scriptures made no mention of a new year on Tishri 1, which is so central to the Jewish religious experience today. The Scripture's reference to Tishri 1 is a holiday characterized primarily by the blowing of a shofar (trumpet). "In the seventh month, on the first day of the month, you shall observe complete rest, a sacred occasion commemorated with loud blasts. You shall not work at your occupations, and you shall bring an offering by fire to Yehowah." (Leviticus 23:24-25).

According to Josephus (*Antiq.* bk 1, ch. 3, 80-81), Moses appointed Nisan 1 as the beginning of the year after Yehowah brought the Israelites out of Egypt while the new year started on Tishri 1 in Egypt. The statement of Josephus implies that the Israeli new year day of Tishri 1 originates from Egypt.

The Israelites and Egyptians considered the year to begin around the autumn harvest and the beginning of the rainy season, which both signified the start of a new agricultural year. Although the Scriptures never explicitly refer to an autumn new year, the apparent timing of the autumn harvest festivals gives a minor hint of a possible autumn new year. According to Exodus 23:16, the Feast of the Harvest, i.e., the Feast of Tabernacles occurs at "the going out of the year" (b'tzayt ha-shanah), signifying the close of an agricultural year and the beginning of the next agricultural year. The Hebrew word "b'tzayt" used here is the same word used in Exodus 13:8 to refer to the Israelites' going out of Egypt. In other words, the Feast of Tabernacles comes at "the going out" of the agricultural year (that is, just after the end of the old agricultural year). Similarly, in Exodus 34:22, the Feast of the Ingathering, i.e., the Feast of Tabernacles is said to occur at the turn of the year (t'kufat Hashanah).

From the contexts of the Scriptures, one can clearly see that Yehowah appointed Nisan 1 as the beginning of a calendar year for the Israelites and Tishri 1 as the beginning of an agricultural year.

Therefore, the Feast of Tabernacles takes place 14 days after a new agricultural year. Most English Bibles change the literally translated phrase "the going out of the year," "from the end of the year," and "at the turn of the year" into "at the end of the year." The phase "at the end of the year" means the ending part of a year, which is different from the beginning part of a year when the Feast of the Tabernacles celebrates. For Deuteronomy 31:10, the LXX Septuagint English version reads: "And Moses charged them in that day, saying, after seven years, in the time of the year of release, in the Feast of Tabernacles..." In this English translation, the phrase "after seven years" has the same meaning as "from the end of seven years." We believe that the LXX Septuagint English (Greek) version correctly translates this Hebrew verse.

After we have made a clear distinction between the calendar year and the agricultural year, we can discuss whether the sabbatical year should be counted according to the calendar year or the agricultural year. It is claimed that the sabbath year (shmita Hebrew: שמיטה,

literally "release") is the seventh year of the seven-year agricultural cycle mandated by the law for the land of Israel.

Where did Moses tell us that the year of release is counted according to the agricultural cycle? Let's carefully study Deuteronomy 31:10 (LXX): "And Moses charged them in that day, saying, after seven years, in the time of the year of release, in the Feast of Tabernacles …" This verse clearly says that the Feast of Tabernacles occurs after the seventh agricultural year and during the time of the year of release (the sabbatical year). In other words, the sabbatical year continues after the seventh agricultural year ends. **This implies that a sabbatical year is not counted from Tishri 1 but Nisan 1.**

Deuteronomy 31:9-13 also tells us that all the people of Israel should gather for the Feast of Tabernacles during the sabbatical year to read, to hear, to learn, and to observe all the words of the Law of Yehowah. This special holy convocation should take place during the sabbatical year, the Sabbath of Yehowah.

Just as every seventh day is sanctified and set apart as holy, so is every seventh year. The seventh holy day starts from the beginning of a day appointed by God, which is from sunset. The seventh holy year should also start from the beginning of the year appointed by God, which is on Nisan 1. **Therefore, the seventh holy year should be counted from the beginning of the calendar year.**

The above conclusion is also supported by Leviticus 25:20-22 (NIV): "You may ask, 'What will we eat in the seventh year if we do not plant or harvest our crops?' I will send you such a blessing in the sixth year that the land will yield enough for three years. While you plant during the eighth year, you will eat from the old crop and will continue to eat from it until the harvest of the ninth year comes in."

These verses tell us that they would eat the old crop of the sixth year until the harvest of the ninth year comes in. This implies that the crop of the ninth year's harvest must be planted in the eighth year. If the sabbatical year were counted according to the agricultural cycle, the crop planted in the fall of the eighth year would be harvested in the spring and summer of the same eighth year. If the sabbatical year is counted from spring to spring, the crop planted after the fall of the eighth year will be harvested in the spring and summer of the ninth year. Only the latter is consistent with Leviticus 25:20-22.

Although a sabbatical year is not explicitly recorded in the Bible, we can infer it from Chapter 8 of the book of Nehemiah where it records in detail the observation of the Feast of Tabernacles in the 20th year of Artaxerxes I after the wall of Jerusalem was completely repaired (Nehemiah 6:15). According to the chronology of Babylon and Persia in Chapter 8, the 20th year of Artaxerxes I was from the fall of 445 BC to the fall of 444 BC. Nehemiah left Shushan for Jerusalem during the spring of 444 BC, which was on the 20th year of Artaxerxes I (Nehemiah 2:1). The wall of Jerusalem was completely repaired on the twenty-fifth of Elul (Nehemiah 6:15). After that, they celebrated the Feast of Tabernacles in the month of Tishri.

During the Feast, "Day after day, from the first day to the last, Ezra read from the book of the Law of God. They celebrated the Festival for seven days, and on the eighth day, in accordance with the regulation, there was an assembly." (Nehemiah 8:18, NIV). According to Deuteronomy 31:9-13, the people of Israel shall hear the Law of God in the Feast of Tabernacles during the year of release (shmita). Therefore, the year of the wall completion was in a sabbatical year, that is, the sabbatical year was from Nisan 1 of 444 BC to Adar 29 of 443 BC. Once one sabbatical year is determined, we can calculate any other sabbatical year by adding or subtracting multiple 7's.

According to the Biblical chronology in Chapter 10, the first calendar year was from Nisan 1 of 3971 BC to Adar 29 of 3970 BC. The first sabbatical year was then from Nisan 1 of 3965 BC to Adar 29 of 3964 BC. From Nisan 1 of 3965 BC to Nisan 1 of 444 BC, there were 3,521 (503×7) years. Indeed, the Biblical chronology is consistent with the fact that the year starting from Nisan 1 of 444 BC was a sabbatical year.

In Chapter 13, we showed that the summer of 38 BC, when Jerusalem was taken by Herod, was in a sabbatical year. Since the fall of 444 BC was also in a sabbatical year, the sabbatical years of 444 BC and 38 BC must have started in the spring. Otherwise, if a sabbatical year would start from Tishri 1, then Tishri 15 of 444 BC and Tammuz

17 of 38 BC could not have been in sabbatical years simultaneously. Therefore, **a sabbatical year must be counted from Nisan 1.**

Another sabbatical year recorded by Josephus was the year of the siege of Gaza and Tyre. After Alexander took Gaza in September of 332 BC and made haste to go up to Jerusalem, Jaddua the high priest made a request to Alexander that they might enjoy the laws of their forefathers and might pay no tribute on the seventh year. He granted all he requested. After that, the Samaritans also approached to him and petitioned that he would remit the tribute of the seventh year to them, because they did not sow thereon. But he did not grant them that privilege. The story here suggests that the year from the spring of 332 BC to the spring of 331 BC was a sabbatical year. From 444 BC to 332 BC, there were 112 years (7×16 years), which confirms that the year starting from the spring of 332 BC was indeed a sabbatical year.

Simon was killed on January 7 of 135 BC according to 1 Maccabees 16:14: "Now Simon was visiting the cities of the country and attending to their needs, and he went down to Jericho with Mattathias and Judas his sons, in the one hundred and seventy-seventh year, in the eleventh month, which is the month of Shebat." On other hand, Josephus (*Antiq.* bk 13, ch. 7-8) tells us that the year Simon was murdered was a sabbatical year, that is, the year from the spring of 136 BC to the spring of 135 BC was a sabbatical year. From 444 BC to 136 BC, there were 308 years (7×44 years). This confirms that the year starting from the spring of 136 BC was a sabbatical year.

What about a jubilee cycle? Leviticus 25:8-10 gives us a clear instruction, "And you shall number seven sabbaths of years unto you, seven times seven years; and the space of the seven sabbaths of years shall be unto you forty and nine years. And shall you cause the trumpet of the jubilee to sound on the tenth day of the seventh month (Tishri), on the day of Atonement shall you make the trumpet sound throughout all your land. And you shall hallow **the fiftieth year**, and proclaim liberty throughout all the land unto all the inhabitants thereof: it shall be a jubilee unto you; and you shall return every man unto his possession, and you shall return every man unto his family."

These verses tell us that the jubilee starts on the tenth day of the seventh month, on the day of Atonement, which is in the middle of a sabbatical year and just after a 7ᵗʰ agricultural new year. Calendric Signs (4Q319) in the Dead Sea Scrolls also indicate that the jubilee cycle (a period of 49 years) starts and ends in the middle of a sabbatical year. Therefore, a jubilee cycle starts on the day of Atonement in the middle of the first sabbatical year or in the first (or 8th) agricultural year. The fiftieth (agricultural) year is the last year of the jubilee cycle, starting from the day of Atonement in the middle of the 8ᵗʰ sabbatical year and ending on the 9ᵗʰ day of the 7ᵗʰ month of the following year. This fiftieth (agricultural) year shall be hallowed. The new jubilee cycle also starts from the fiftieth (agricultural) year.

Jewish Encyclopedia (http://www.jewishencyclopedia.com/articles/5827-era#anchor2) says: "There is no record in the Bible of the actual beginning of the jubilees nor of their actual ending. **Tradition relates that the fifteenth year after the entering of the Israelites into the land of Canaan was the first year of the first jubilee period.**"

We know that the Israelites entered the land of Canaan in 1417 BC, which was a sabbatical year. The fifteenth agricultural year after the Israelites' entering the land of Canaan was the first year of the first jubilee cycle. Therefore, the first jubilee cycle should have started from the 7ᵗʰ month of 1403 BC (the first agricultural year to the Israelites). The first fiftieth year (the second jubilee cycle started) being hallowed was in 1354 BC. From 1354 BC to 2028, there are 3381 (69×49) years. This implies that the 70ᵗʰ jubilee year to be hallowed should start from the day of Atonement of 2028. From the beginning of the first jubilee in 1403 BC to the day of Atonement in 2028, there are exactly 3430 (70×49) years. According to the Law: A woman who gives birth to a girl shall be deemed to be clean after 80 days. **One expects a very important event may happen in Israel on the day of Atonement of 2028 because that day exactly marks the end of the 70ᵗʰ jubilee circle and exactly 80 years after the nation of Israel was born again.**

In Table XI, we list some important events which occurred in sabbatical years. It is remarkable that the Chinese dynasties always started in sabbatical years before the time of Yeshua Messiah, but after Yeshua's time the pattern changes completely. Among so many dynasties, only the Qin Dynasty appeared to have started in a sabbatical year (1636 AD) if the dynasty started from the reign of the second emperor 皇太极

(*Huang Tai Ji*). However, if the dynasty effectively started from the reign of the first emperor 努尔哈赤 (Nu Er Ha Chi), as should be the case, it began in 1616 AD, which was not in a sabbatical year.

The sudden change of the ruling pattern in China after the time of Yeshua agrees with the statement of Yeshua in John 14:30, "I will no longer talk much with you, for the ruler of this world is coming, and he has nothing in me (no power over me)." Indeed, the Son of God, the seed of the woman, bruised the head of Satan, the serpent of old and the ruler of the world, as prophesized in Genesis 3:15. The Son of God destroyed the works of the devil (sins). The devil has sinned from the beginning while Yeshua and his believers can overcome the sins because the Spirit of God dwells in them. Although the ruler of the world came to the world to bruise the heel of Yeshua, he has no power over Yeshua. After Yeshua went to his Father, the devil has power over the world, but not over the children of God.

China used to be called 神州(the land of God) and the people in the land worshipped the heavenly God. After Yeshua ascended to heaven, the whole world lies under the sway of the wicked one (1 John 5:19). This may explain the sudden change of the ruling pattern in China after the time of Yeshua.

Table XI: Important Events on Sabbatical Years

Events	Date	Starting date of a sabbatical year
Emperor Yao started to reign	Fall 2376 BC	1 Nisan 2376 BC
Emperor Shun started to reign	Fall 2271 BC	1 Nisan 2271 BC
Emperor Yu started to co-reign with Shun (Xia Dynasty started)	Fall 2257 BC	1 Nisan 2257 BC
Shang Dynasty started	Fall 1781 BC	1 Nisan 1781 BC
Zhou Dynasty started	Fall 1116 BC	1 Nisan 1116 BC
Qin Dynasty (United China) started	220 BC	1 Nisan 220 BC
Western Han Dynasty started	206 BC	1 Nisan 206 BC
The end of the First Babylonian Dynasty	March 1493 BC	1 Nisan 1494 BC

The Israelites crossed the Jordan River	10 Nisan 1417 BC	1 Nisan 1417 BC
The first holy temple was built	15 Tishri 969 BC	1 Nisan 969 BC
Jerusalem's wall was repaired	Tishri 444 BC	1 Nisan 444 BC
Yeshua was baptized and anointed	24 February 27 AD	1 Nisan 26 AD
Conquest of Nineveh	August 612 BC	1 Nisan 612 BC
Nebuchadnezzar started to reign	10 Av 605 BC	1 Nisan 605 BC
Alexander the Great started to reign	November 332 BC	1 Nisan 332 BC
The battle of Actium that effectively started the Roman Empire	September 31 BC	1 Nisan 31 BC
America was founded	4 July 1776 AD	1 Nisan 1776 AD

Similarly, Nebuchadnezzar, the most powerful king of the Babylonian kingdom was also raised by God. Nebuchadnezzar's Babylonian kingdom was the first beast in the vision of Daniel. He started to reign in a sabbatical year (605 BC). God also raised Alexander the Great, the king of Greek kingdom (the third beast). Alexander overthrew the city of Tyre and established his kingdom in a sabbatical year. Augustus may have been raised by God as well. He won the important war in the battle of Actium in September 31 BC (in a sabbatical year) to establish the Roman Empire (the fourth beast). The United States of America was established in 1776 AD, which was also in a sabbatical year. This powerful nation should be raised by God to become the closest ally of Israel.

The nation of Israel was effectively established when the Israelites crossed the Jordan River to enter the promised land of God in 1417 BC. The land filled with milk and honey was originally occupied mostly by the Canaanites. But because of their great sins and unrepentance for over 400 years, God decided to destroy them and give the land to His own people, the Israelites. Thus, the nation of Israel was initially established in the spring of 1417 BC, which was in a sabbatical year.

Solomon started to build the temple of God in the spring of 977 BC and dedicated to the temple in the Feast of Tabernacles of 969 BC after he finished its building. The dedication of the temple in Jerusalem was the starting date for the celebration of the Feasts of Yehowah in

Jerusalem, which was the chosen place by God. The dedication also took place in a sabbatical year, marking it as important in the sight of God.

Yeshua was baptized and anointed on 24 February 27 AD. During his baptism, the Father proclaimed him as His beloved Son. This event was prophesized by Daniel about 600 years ago and took place in a sabbatical year.

The great city of Nineveh was conquered in 612 BC, marking the end of the Assyrian Empire. The destruction of Nineveh was prophesized by Nahum and took place in 612 BC, which was also in a sabbatical year. God wanted to destroy it because its people were murderous, and the city was known as the "blood city." God made judgment to the wicked city in a sabbatical year, marking the important divine judgment by God.

PART III
BIBLICAL NUMERICAL PROPHECIES

CHAPTER 15

INTRODUCTION TO BIBLICAL PROPHECIES

Biblical prophecies are the passages in the Holy Bible that reflect the communication between God and His prophets. Prophetic messages widely appear throughout the different books of the Bible. Some of the prophecies are explicitly stated with the definitive numbers of years for their fulfillment. Other prophetic passages are implicitly stated and the interpretations to these prophecies are quite subjective and could vary with the individuals. The prophecies mainly reveal the destinies of various nations surrounding Israel, the nation of Israel itself, the coming of the Messiah and a Messianic Kingdom, and the ultimate destiny of the entirety of mankind.

If Biblical prophecies were all perfectly fulfilled within the time frames specified by God, there is no doubt that the God of the Bible is the only true God who governs every aspect of the universe. Everything must be under His control so that all the prophecies going forth from His mouth must be 100% fulfilled. A proximate or possible fulfillment, or unfulfillment of any prophecy would violate the unique requirement for the prophecy originating from the true God.

According to some Biblical scholars, over 96% of Biblical prophecies have already been fulfilled while the remaining prophecies about the end-times are being or yet to be fulfilled. However, this claim does not appear to be supported by their current interpretations of the prophecies. Here are some examples that clearly discount their claims. The first example is that the Babylonian captivity would have ended when the "70 years" had ended (Jeremiah 29:10). According to the current interpretation, there were only 68 years from the first exile of a small number of hostages including Daniel (Daniel 1:1-4) to the first return of the Israelites (from 605 to 537 BC); only 60 years (from 597 to 537 BC) from the deportation of the 10,000 elites (2 Kings 24:14) including Jehoiachin to the first return; and only 50 years (from 587 to 537 BC) from the destruction of the first temple (2 Kings 25:11) to the first return. This interpretation cannot convince any reasonable person that the numerical prophecy of Jeremiah was perfectly fulfilled.

The second example is Yeshua's prophecy on his resurrection. In Matthew 12:40 Yeshua says: "as Jonas was **three days and three nights** in the whale's belly; so shall the Son of man be **three days and three nights** in the heart of the earth." According to the current interpretation, Yeshua was buried in the evening of a Friday and resurrected before Sunday dawn. How could this interpretation be consistent with the most important Yeshua's prophecy of **three days and three nights**? From Friday night to Sunday morning, there are less than 36 hours, which are only half of the 72 hours (three days and three nights). If this prophecy were not fulfilled, how could Yeshua be the Messiah and the Son of God? Christianity would lose its foundation. How then could someone claim that all the past prophecies in the Bible were perfectly fulfilled?

The current misinterpretations of many Biblical prophecies make us doubt that the God of the Bible is the true God. Furthermore, the currently accepted dates for the Messiah's nativity and crucifixion have pointed in the direction that Yeshua would not be the true Messiah. All the mistakes made by these Biblical scholars and theologians distort the true nature of Christianity so that fewer and fewer intellectuals could become believers.

Here, we will present our correct interpretations of Biblical prophecies based on reliable historical records, astronomical data, and the correct understanding of the Scriptures. Within our interpretations, all the past numerical prophecies in the Bible were perfectly fulfilled in the time frames specified in the prophecies.

There is a basic principle to the interpretations of Biblical prophecies, that is, the day-year principle. A day in prophecy is symbolic of a year of actual time. This principle is based on the following Scriptures: "For forty years—one year for each of the forty days you explored the land—you will suffer for your sins and know what it is like to have me against you." (Numbers 14:34). "Then lie on your left side and put the sin of the people of Israel upon yourself. You are to bear their sin for the number of days you lie on your side. I have assigned you the same number of days as the years of their sin. So for 390 days you will bear the sin of the people of Israel." (Ezekiel 4:5-6).

Here, a year should be a solar year because only the solar year truly represents a year that always has two seasons: summer and winter (Genesis 8:22 and Psalm 74:17). A pure lunar year of 12 months is only 354 or 355 days, which will be off from the seasons if a 13th month is not intercalated every 2 or 3 years. God must know the true length of a year independent of which calendar we use. In both Numbers 14:34 and Ezekiel 4:5-6, what Yehowah really meant for a prophetic day was a solar year with the equal length of summer and winter.

God sees one year as one day, which is also implied in the analogy between the seventh day and the seventh year. The seventh day is the day of God's Sabbath and the seventh year is the year of God's Sabbath. Both the seventh day and the seventh year are sanctified by God and set apart to become the holiest day in a week and the holiest year in a seven-year period respectively.

In God's prophetic language, the phrase "a time" is equal to 360 prophetic days, as inferred from the comparison between Daniel 12:7 and Revelation 12:6. Both verses talk about the same event, which will be discussed in detail below. God never said in the Bible that "a time" is the same as "a year." There are 360 days for "a time," but 365.24 days for "a solar year." Yehowah never confuses His people. He would simply say "a year" if "a time" would be identical to "a year." Daniel did not tell us the exact number of days for "a time" when he wrote the prophecies because God wanted to seal the prophecies until the last days. John the Apostle gave the interpretation for "a time" in Revelation 12, so that Daniel's prophecies could be unlocked after John wrote the book of Revelation. It is interesting that 360 days happen to be very close to a simple average (359.80) of the number of days (365.24) per solar year and that (354.36) per pure lunar year.

In the book of Revelation, John also mentioned a time span of 42 months. Most Biblical scholars believe that 42 months are identical to

1,260 days. John never said that 42 months contain 1,260 days. He was talking about two different events in Revelation 11:2-3. The first event was the trampling of Jerusalem by the Gentiles (in) 42 months while the second event is the prophesying of the two witnesses for 1,260 days. John did not say that the two events would happen simultaneously. John also talked about two events in Revelation 12:14 and Revelation 13:5. He talked about the woman in Revelation 12:14 and about the beast in Revelation 13:5. These are two separate events and John never implied that these two events would take place at the same time.

If a month in the book of Revelation would be a prophetic month, he would have explained it clearly. The book of Revelation is the last book God gave to us. If no other book had specified the meaning of a prophetic month, God would have had John do so in this last book. Such a thing must be very clear to ensure that only one interpretation to His prophecy is correct. If a prophecy has multiple interpretations, it is a vague prophecy and cannot originate from God. Since some of Daniel's prophecies had to be sealed until the last days, God did not allow Daniel to clearly explain the meaning of "a time," so that no one could have understood them in Daniel's time. Even in the first century AD, when John (actually Yeshua) provided the interpretation for "a time" in the book of Revelation, no one could have unlocked Daniel's prophecies in Daniel 12. Only until the rebirth of Israel in 1948 could the true end times be revealed to the wise who might be able to unlock the mysteries according to Daniel 12.

Nowhere does the Bible state that the number of days per a month must be 30. There are 29 or 30 days per month according to the lunar calendar. There are 30 or 31 days per month in Enoch's solar calendar. Why would Yehowah only choose 30 days per month? God never confuses His people. God must follow His own laws prescribed to the world in addition to performing miracles that only He can do. The number of days for 42 months is 1,240.28 according to the lunar calendar and 1,278.37 according to the solar calendar. God only gives us these two calendars and must let us know which calendar He uses to count the month if He has not specified it in His other books.

The idea of a 30-day month is based on the misunderstanding of Genesis 7:11; 8:3-4. Which calendar did Moses use to record the flood event? We have clearly shown that Moses or Noah used Enoch's solar calendar to record the flood (see Chapter 10). We have also shown that Noah's family entered the ark on 25 May 2315 BC (the 17th day of the second Enoch's solar month) and left the ark on 3 June 2314 BC (the 27th day of the second Enoch's solar month). After Noah's family left the ark, God established his covenant with Noah and his descendants and every living creature by setting a rainbow in the clouds. According to His covenant, He will never again destroy humanity and creatures by such a massive flood. This covenant is very likely to have been established on 6 Sivan 2314 BC (10 June 2314 BC), on the feast day of Pentecost, which was one week after they left the ark. This is because on this very day on the Feast of Pentecost, four other important events took place in different years:

1) the old covenant with the Israelites was established on June 14 of 1457 BC
2) Yeshua was conceived by the Holy Spirit on May 23 of 6 BC
3) the Church was born on May 26 of 30 AD
4) Israel was re-born on May 14 of 1948

How amazing and wonderful and precise are God's plans for us? Only the true God can do such wonderful works for us! Hallelujah!

CHAPTER 16

DANIEL'S PROPHECY ON THE 69ᵀᴴ WEEK: MESSIAH ANOINTED

One of the famous numerical prophecies of Daniel is about 70 weeks, which was recorded in Daniel 9:24-25:

> ²⁴**Seventy weeks** are determined for your people and for your holy city, to finish the transgression, to make an end of sins, to make reconciliation for iniquity, to bring in everlasting righteousness, to seal up vision and prophecy, and to anoint the Most Holy. ²⁵"Know therefore and understand, that from the going forth of the command to restore and build Jerusalem until Messiah the Prince, there shall be seven weeks and sixty-two weeks; the street shall be built again, and the wall, even in troublesome times.

These two verses tell us that the length of 70 weeks is determined for the destiny of the holy people (the Israelites), for the holy city (Jerusalem), and for anointing the most holy who is the Messiah and the prince of the nation of Israel. According to the prophecy, the Messiah should have appeared in the 69ᵗʰ week from the time when the command to restore and rebuild Jerusalem was issued. The last day of the 69ᵗʰ prophetic week (one prophetic day is equivalent to one solar year) should correspond to the 483rd year (69×7 = 483) from the time of issuing the command.

In order to check whether this prophecy was fulfilled, we need to know exactly which year the command to restore Jerusalem went forth and which year the Messiah appeared. As we have already shown that Yeshua was claimed by God to be His Son when John the Baptist baptized him on 24 February 27 AD (see Chapter 12). He was declared to be the Lamb of God on Nisan 10 (April 5 of 27 AD) and started his ministry on April 6 of 27 AD, which lasted for 3 years. If Yeshua is indeed the Messiah, the command to restore and rebuild Jerusalem must have been issued in the spring of 457 BC. This is because the 483rd year from the spring of 457 BC is the year from the spring of 26 AD to the spring of 27 AD (please note that 457 BC = −456 because year 0 does not exist). We will show below that the spring of 457 BC was indeed the time when Ezra received a command from King Artaxerxes I in his 7th year of reign. We will also prove that this command has a component of rebuilding the city of Jerusalem, which perfectly matches the prophecy.

Detailed explanations

Two clear commands were described in the book of Ezra. Cyrus king of Persia in the first year of his reign proclaimed the first command (Ezra 1:1-4). Artaxerxes I issued the second command in the seventh year of his reign (Ezra 7:6-26). In the 20th year of Artaxerxes I, the governor Nehemiah asked the king to send him to Jerusalem to repair broken wall (Nehemiah 2:1-6). After the request was granted, Nehemiah asked the king to write two letters (Nehemiah 2:7-8). One letter was addressed to the governors of the region beyond the River so that they permitted Nehemiah to pass through their region. The second letter was given to Asaph the keeper of the king's forest. In this letter, Asaph was asked to provide timber to make beams for the temple gates and the city wall. It is apparent that these two letters were not the commands to restore and rebuild Jerusalem, but only served to help Nehemiah in his work of repairing the city wall. Therefore, only one of the two commands recorded in the book of Ezra was the command to rebuild the city.

Now let us check which command is relevant to the one mentioned by Daniel. In the first year of Cyrus king of Persia, the king issued a decree to rebuild the temple and to allow the exiled Jews to return to Jerusalem. Since Cyrus' decree was only to rebuild the temple but not the city, the returned Jews began to rebuild the temple and lay its foundation (Ezra 3:10-11) while the city remained in ruin (Ezra 4:11-12).

The adversaries of the Jews despised the sanctuary and this holy people who knew God's law. Chapter 4 of the book of Ezra clearly recorded how the adversaries tried to oppose rebuilding the temple and the city with several strategies during a long period from the days of Cyrus to the reign of Artaxerxes I. Some events in this chapter actually happened after the events described in later chapters, which may confuse readers. But if one reads the book carefully, one should be able to understand why the author did not write these events sequentially. It is clear that the author wanted to describe all of the schemes of Israel's adversaries together.

The schemes of the adversaries include the following (Ezra 4) : 1) They gathered to oppose it, 2) they tried to join (infiltrate) so they could manipulate and hinder the process, 3) they wrote an accusation against the Jews to Artaxerxes I, "they are building a rebellious and evil city and will excite sedition," and 4) they asked Artaxerxes I to issue a command to stop rebuilding the city.

Because of the adversaries, the early progress to rebuild the temple in Jerusalem was discontinued until the second year of Darius (Ezra 4:24). In this year, Yehowah spoke to the prophet Haggai concerning the temple. With the encouragement of the prophet, the Jews again started to work by laying the foundation of the temple. The temple was finally finished on the third day of the month of Adar, which was in the sixth year of Darius (Ezra 6:15) and in the spring of 516 BC.

The Jews started to rebuild the city of Jerusalem in the days of Xerxes I (Ezra 4:6) after Darius helped rebuild the temple in 516 BC. However, in the days of both Xerxes I and Artaxerxes I, the adversaries wrote accusations against the Jews who were rebuilding the city (Ezra 4:6-23). During the earlier reign of Artaxerxes I, the adversaries wrote Artaxerxes I in Aramaic script, accusing the Jews of rebuilding a rebellious and evil city. Then Artaxerxes I commanded the Jews to stop rebuilding the city wall. The king also ordered that this city could not resume its reconstruction until he gave a new command (Ezra 4:21).

The king's reply was a great victory for the adversaries who went immediately to the Jews in Jerusalem and compelled them by force to stop their work (Ezra 4:23). Then Yehowah raised up Ezra who was a ready scribe in the Law of Moses. The king granted Ezra **all** his requests because the hand of Yehowah was upon him (Ezra 7:6). Because the king had previously issued the command to temporarily suspend the reconstruction of Jerusalem, it is natural that one of Ezra's requests should have been a reversal of the king's previous cessation command. Apparently, the king granted Ezra all his requests and sent him to investigate Judah and Jerusalem according to the Law of Moses (Ezra 7:14). King Artaxerxes I provided more than enough gold and silver to beautify the temple of God in Jerusalem. The king also said that any silver and gold that was left over may be used for whatever Ezra and his colleagues felt was the will of their God (Ezra 7:18). Since the king had withdrawn his previous cessation decree and issued a new decree to restore Jerusalem, Ezra may have used the rest of the gold and silver to rebuild Jerusalem. This can be seen in the prayer of Ezra in Ezra 9:9. Ezra thanked God for not forsaking them but extending mercy unto them in the sight of the kings of Persia and giving them revival and the wall in Judah and in Jerusalem. Ezra's prayer implies that the Persian king had granted them the permission and provided enough gold and silver to rebuild the house of their God, to repair its ruins, and to rebuild the wall in Judah and in Jerusalem.

In the adversaries' efforts to thwart Jerusalem's reconstruction, they apparently knocked down the rebuilt sections of the wall and burned the gates. This was where Nehemiah came into the picture (Nehemiah 1:3). In the 20th year of Artaxerxes I, Nehemiah heard the sad news that the attempts to rebuild Jerusalem were frustrated again. Nehemiah 1:3 implies that the Jews must have been given permission to rebuild Jerusalem from Artaxerxes I in his decree issued in his 7th year.

Because of the bad news, Nehemiah spoke to Artaxerxes I, who gave him permission to go back and repair the broken wall in Jerusalem (Nehemiah 2), which was rebuilt previously. If Artaxerxes I had not given the Jews the permission to rebuild Jerusalem in his 7th year, there would have been no rebuilt wall in Jerusalem to be knocked down by the adversaries in the 20th year of Artaxerxes I (Nehemiah 1:1-3). If Artaxerxes I had not given the Jews the permission to rebuild Jerusalem in his 7th year, he would not have let Nehemiah go back to repair the broken wall in Jerusalem in his 20th year. Therefore, Artaxerxes's command in his 7th year must have had a component of rebuilding the city of Jerusalem.

With the two letters Nehemiah received from Artaxerxes I in his 20th year, the wall was put up successfully without much trouble (Nehemiah 6:15). Daniel predicted that the street and the wall would be built again in troublesome times after the command to rebuild Jerusalem was issued. Because Nehemiah did not go back to rebuild the street but only to repair the wall, the king's letters in his 20th year could not have included the component of rebuilding the street. Thus, the street must have been rebuilt after Ezra received the command of Artaxerxes I in the spring of his 7th year.

In summary, only the decree of Artaxerxes I to Ezra was the command to restore and rebuild both the temple and Jerusalem while the command of Cyrus was only to allow the Jews to rebuild the temple of God. The street and the wall were rebuilt after Ezra received the command of Artaxerxes I in his 7th year. Then some sections of the wall in Jerusalem were destroyed again by the adversaries in the 20th year of Artaxerxes I. Nehemiah and his colleagues finally finished repairing the wall within 52 days in 25 Elul of 444 BC (Nehemiah 6:15).

Now back to the subject concerning the issuing time for the decree of Artaxerxes I. According to Ezra 7:8, Ezra left Babylon on Nisan 1 and arrived in Jerusalem on the first day of the fifth month in the 7th year of Artaxerxes I. Since Ezra left Babylon on the first day of the month of Nisan, the command must have been issued on or before that day.

Artaxerxes I began to reign on 12 October 464 BC (see Chapter 8). Thus, the 7th year of Artaxerxes I was from 12 October 458 BC to 11 October 457. Since Ezra left Babylon on Nisan 1 and arrived in Jerusalem on the 1st day of the fifth month, in the 7th year of Artaxerxes I, the day that Ezra left for Jerusalem must have been on 1 Nisan of 457 BC (26 March 457 BC).

It is interesting to note that Nisan 1 just coincided with the Vernal Equinox in 457 BC, suggesting that this year is quite special and significant. This day was also the new-year day in both the Hebrew and Babylonian lunisolar calendars. Ezra should have left for Jerusalem immediately after the king issued the command because he prepared his heart to seek the Law of God, to follow it, and to teach it in Israel (Ezra

7:9-10). If he left on the same day, the command should have gone forth on Nisan 1 of 457 BC and on the day of the Vernal Equinox.

Daniel 9:25 is literally translated as, "Know therefore and understand, that from the going forth of the command to restore and build Jerusalem until Messiah the Prince, weeks 7 and weeks 62; the street shall be built again, and the wall, even in troublesome times." Here, the phrases "weeks 7" and "weeks 62" have an unusual word order that may express an idea of counting weeks. If this is the case, the number "7" and "62" in Daniel 9:25 should be understood as ordinal numbers and the Messiah should have been anointed in the 483rd year from the time of issuance of the command to restore and rebuild Jerusalem. The 483rd year from the issuance of the command was the year between the Vernal Equinoxes of 26 AD and 27 AD. Yeshua was baptized by John the Baptist on 24 February 27 AD, which was exactly four weeks before the Vernal Equinox (March 23) of 27 AD. The day when Yeshua was baptized and anointed was indeed in the 483rd year from the time of issuing the command. This cannot be a coincidence. It provides clear evidence that Yeshua is the Messiah anointed by God in the early spring of 27 AD.

CHAPTER 17

DANIEL'S PROPHECY ON THE FIRST HALF OF THE 70TH WEEK

Yeshua was proclaimed to be the Son of God by the heavenly Father during his baptism on 24 February 27 AD, which was towards the end of the 483rd year (the 69th prophetic weeks) from the time (26 March 457 BC) of the issuance of the command to rebuild Jerusalem. This fulfills the prophecy of Daniel 9:25, "Know therefore and understand, that from the going forth of the commandment to restore and rebuild Jerusalem unto the Messiah, the prince, shall be seven weeks, and threescore [60] and two weeks."

In Chapter 16, we provided detailed evidence that this prophecy was fulfilled in Yeshua on the assumption that the 69 weeks from 26 March 457 BC passed without interruption. However, the 69 weeks in Daniel 9:25 had two separated periods: a 7-week period and a 62-week period.

Why did Daniel separate the 69 weeks into two periods? One possible explanation is that there was a gap between the first continuous period of 7 (1×7) weeks and the last continuous period of 63 (9×7) weeks. There should have been no gap from one week to another within the 7-week or within the 63-week period. This gap idea can help unlock the prophecy of the 70th week, which should have also been separated into two periods with a gap according to Daniel 9:27, "Then he shall confirm (strengthen) covenant with many for one week; but in the middle of the week, he shall cause sacrifice and offering to fail (cease). And on the wing of abominations shall be one who makes desolate, even until the consummation, which is determined, is poured out on the desolate."

Daniel 9:27 tells the prophecy of the 70th week during which the Messiah shall strengthen covenant with many but in the middle of the week, he shall cause sacrifice and offering to fail (cease). If this prophecy was fulfilled in Yeshua, the 70th week should have started on 6 April 27 AD when he began his ministry. If this was the case, the 62nd week of the 63-week period should have ended on 6 April 27 AD and the 63rd week of the 63-week period should have started on the same day. Then the beginning time of the 63-week period (434 solar years) was on April 9 of 408 BC. Since the first 7-week period started on 26 March 457 BC, the ending time of this period should have been on 26 March 408 BC. Hence, there was a negligibly small gap of 14 days between 26 March 408 BC and 9 April 408 BC, which justifies the assumption of 69 continuous weeks in the previous chapter.

The second part of verse 27 says that in the middle of the week (the 70th week), he should cause sacrifices and offerings to fail. Here, the Hebrew word "שָׁבַת (shabath)" means "cause to cease" or "cause to fail." In the middle of the 70th week, which was between 30 and 31 AD, the Jews did not cease the sacrifices and offerings after Yeshua was crucified and ascended to heaven in 30 AD. The prophecy would not have been fulfilled in Yeshua if the word "שָׁבַת (shabath)" were translated into "cause to cease." On the other hand, if we translate this word into "cause to fail" or "cause to be ineffective," the prophecy was fulfilled in Yeshua. Indeed, the sacrifices and offerings of the Jews were not accepted by God after 30 AD, as seen from the following statements of the Jews in the Jerusalem or Babylonian Talmud.

In the centuries following the destruction of the temple in Jerusalem (70 AD), the Jewish people began writing two versions of Jewish thought, religious history, and commentary. One was written in Palestine and became known as the Jerusalem Talmud, and the other was written in Babylon and was known as the Babylonian Talmud.

The Jerusalem Talmud reads: "Forty years before the destruction of the temple, the western light went out, the crimson thread remained crimson, and the lot for Yehowah always came up in the left hand. They would close the gates of the temple by night and get up in the morning and find them wide open." (Jacob Neusner, *The Yerushalmi*, p.156-157).

A similar passage in the Babylonian Talmud states: "Our rabbis taught: During the last forty years before the destruction of the temple the lot ['For Yehowah'] did not come up in the right hand; nor did the crimson-colored strap become white; nor did the western most light shine; and the doors of the Hekel [Temple] would open by themselves" (Soncino version, Yoma 39b).

Both passages tell us that God did not accept their sacrifices and offerings between 30 and 70 AD. Before that time, the crimson thread would have been changed into white whenever God had accepted their offerings and forgiven their sins. It was the Messiah who caused their sacrifices and offerings to be ineffective after he ascended to heaven. Solomon in Proverb 15:8 said, "The sacrifice of the wicked is an abomination to Yehowah, but the prayer of the upright is His delight." Because the Jews continued to reject the teachings of the Messiah through his disciples and even persecuted them, their sacrifices and offerings were abominable to Yehowah.

In the Mosaic sacrifice law, sacrifices and offerings can atone the sins unintentionally committed while intentional sins cannot be atoned by the animal sacrifices. Then, how shall the intentional sins be forgiven? In Psalm 40:6-8, David said, "Sacrifice and offering You did not desire; My ears You have opened. Burnt offering and sin offering You did not require. Then I said, 'Behold, I come; In the scroll of the book it is written of me. I delight to do Your will, O my God, and Your law is within my heart.'" Even before the Messiah came, God did not desire and require burnt offering and sin offering. What He really desires is that we delight to do His will, put His law in our heart, and observe it. Sacrifice and offering cannot change our heart.

Yeshua who was the Passover Lamb of God was killed and his blood can redeem our lives (Isaiah 53:4-6,8,10). It is the grace of God! When the Israelites came out of Egypt, all the lives of the Israelites and foreigners (even the Egyptians) could be saved from the wrath of God if the blood of the Passover lamb was on the lintels and the two doorposts of their home. The Passover Lamb of God shed his blood for our sins (Isaiah 53:4-6,8,10) and can redeem us to serve God.

Most Biblical scholars have misunderstood Daniel 9:27. They mistakenly referred to "he" as the antichrist who would confirm the covenant with Israel in the 70th week and break it after three and a half years. According to the Hebrew grammar, "he" must refer to a person previously defined. No antichrist was mentioned in any previous sentence. A Hebrew language expert has clearly proved that "he" in verse 27 refers to the Messiah (see a YouTube video at https://www.youtube.com/watch?v=3EX830ATa2A).

From the context of Daniel 9:24, it is apparent that seventy weeks were decreed for the holy people (the Israelites), for Jerusalem, and for the anointing of the most holy (Messiah) to bring everlasting righteousness. Therefore, the seventy weeks were always related to the Messiah and the destinies of the Israelites and Jerusalem. The 70th week is all about the ministry of the Messiah while at the end of the 69th week, God prepared the way for the Messiah's ministry via the ministry of John the Baptist. John preached the message of repentance in the wilderness of Judea (Matthew 3:1), baptized the Jews who were willing to repent of their sins, anointed Yeshua, and declared him to be the Lamb of God.

Now we discuss the prophecy of Daniel 9:26, "And after the threescore and two [62] weeks shall Messiah be cut off, but not to himself." Here, the 62 weeks refer to the 62 weeks of the second 63-week period. After the 62 weeks (the 69th week), which was in the 70th week, the Messiah shall be cut off. Yeshua was cut off on Nisan 14 of 30 AD, which was in the 70th week. But to him, he was not cut off because he resurrected and would see his seeds and prolong his days (Isaiah 53:10). He was cut off for three days and three nights to bear the iniquities of God's people and justify many (Isaiah 53:11). God shall share a portion with him (Isaiah 53:12) because he was so obedient that he was willing to die for many. Here, it is clear that the prophecy of Daniel 9:26 was also fulfilled in Yeshua.

Daniel 9:26 also tells us that after the Messiah was cut off, the Messiah himself would destroy the holy temple and Jerusalem with a Gentile prince. LXX Septuagint correctly translated the original Hebrew word "עִם" into "with" before the Masoretic Hebrew text was used (while the Masoretic Hebrew word "עַם" with a short line below ע means "people"). Indeed, 40 years after the Messiah was crucified, the Romans destroyed Jerusalem and the temple.

How about the prophecy about the second period of the 70th week? Does the last part of Daniel 9:27 refer to the prophecy on the second period of the 70th week? In Chapter 12, we have shown that the length of Yeshua's ministry in his first advent was 1,143 days. Yeshua shall have to minister for an additional 1,413 days to fulfill the prophecy of the 70th week. Therefore, he should come back to the earth to finish his ministry assigned in the second period of the 70th week, as briefly described in the last part of Daniel 9:27. We will show that Yeshua will come back to pour out his wrath on the ungodly people and to establish the Messianic Kingdom of God on the earth (see Chapter 36).

CHAPTER 18

DANIEL'S PROPHECY ON SUSPENSION OF 2300 EVENING-MORNING BURNT OFFERINGS

In the third year of king Belshazzar's reign, Daniel recorded a prophecy in Daniel 8:13-14:

> Then I heard a holy one speaking; and another holy one said to that certain one which was speaking, "How long shall be the vision concerning the continual burnt offering, and the transgression of desolation, giving both the sanctuary and the host to be trampled underfoot?" And he said to me, "for **two thousand and three hundred [2,300] evenings-mornings**, then shall the sanctuary be cleansed."

This prophecy was fulfilled in the events related to the institution of the Festival of Hanukkah by Judas Maccabeus and his brothers in the second century BC. The temple was trampled down on October 29 (Saturday) of 168 BC by the Seleucid king Antiochus IV Epiphanes, and then the continual burnt offerings were taken away. After 1,150 days (2,300 evening or morning burnt offerings were suspended), the temple was cleansed by Judas Maccabeus on 22 December 165 BC and the daily burnt offerings were restored.

Detailed explanations

From Daniel 8 we understand that the ram represented the kingdom of Persia, and the goat, the kingdom of Greece. In prophecy, beasts often represent kingdoms (Daniel 7:23) and horns represent kings (Revelation 17:12). After Alexander the Great died in 323 BC, the kingdom of Greece was divided into four parts by Alexander's four top generals: Ptolemy, Seleucus, Lycemicus, and Cassander. Ptolemy began a dynasty in Egypt (south) while Seleucus did the same in Syria (north). Lycemicus took over Asia Minor (east) and Cassander took Greece (west).

Now, another character comes to view in the vision of Daniel (Daniel 8:9), "And out of one of them came forth a little horn, which waxed exceeding great, toward the south, and toward the east, and toward the pleasant land." Daniel saw that a little horn would rise from one of the four horns (kings). Then Daniel 8:23 says, "And in the latter time of their kingdoms, when the transgressors are come to the full, a king of fierce countenance, and understanding dark sentences, shall stand up." This verse tells us that this 'horn' would fight against God's people, cause the sacrifices to cease, and make a wreck of the holy place or temple.

Daniel prophesized the vision concerning the daily sacrifices being taken away by the little horn. Daniel 8:26 writes, "And the vision of the evening and the morning which was told is true: therefore shut up the vision; for it shall be many days hence." The evening and the morning in this verse should have referred to the evening and morning offerings because the vision was about the continual burnt offerings (that is, the daily evening and morning offerings), that would have been stopped temporarily many years later. Therefore, Daniel 8:14 foretold that the sanctuary would be cleansed after a total of 2,300 continual evening or morning burning offerings was suspended (or after 1,150 days). The prophecy was made in the third year of king Belshazzar's reign just before Babylon was taken by Cyrus in the eighth month of 538 BC (see Chapter 8).

Has this prophecy been fulfilled? If yes, when was it fulfilled? The story recorded in the first book of Maccabees is consistent with this prophecy. So far, no one seems to have found the exact match of 1,150 days with the story told in 1 Maccabees. The reason for this is that no one has figured out the correct lunisolar calendars for these years. After we have constructed the correct lunisolar calendars for these years based on the astronomical moon-phase data (see Appendix D), we find that the prophecy on the period of 1,150 days was fulfilled.

In the book of Daniel, the little horn clearly refers to the Seleucid kingdom, one of four kingdoms derived from the kingdom of Alexander the Great. The Seleucid king Antiochus IV Epiphanes captured Jerusalem, removed the sacred objects from the temple, and slaughtered many Jews. He imposed a tax and established a fortress in Jerusalem. Antiochus tried to suppress public observance of the Jewish laws to secure control over the Jews. In 168 BC, he desecrated the temple by setting up an "abomination of desolation." He forbade the observance of the Sabbaths and the offering of sacrifices in the holy temple. He also required Jewish leaders to make sacrifices to his idols.

Mattathias called upon the people loyal to the traditions of Israel to oppose the Gentile king, and his three sons (Judas Maccabeus and his brothers) began a military campaign against them (during the Maccabean Revolt). There was a loss of one thousand Jews (men, women, and children) when the Jewish defenders refused to fight on the Sabbaths. In 165 BC the temple was freed and re-consecrated, so that the continual daily sacrifices may begin again. The Festival of Hanukkah was instituted by Judas Maccabeus and his brothers to celebrate this event (1 Maccabees 4:59).

When did the daily sacrifices start to be taken away? The answer can be found in 2 Maccabees 5:23-26 (slightly modified for better reading), "And at Garizim, Andronicus; and besides, Menelaus, who worse than all the rest bare a heavy hand over the citizens, having a malicious mind against his countrymen the Jews. He sent also that detestable ringleader Apollonius with an army of two and twenty thousands, commanding them to slay all those that were in their best age, and to sell the women and the younger sort. He came to Jerusalem pretending peace, till the holy day of the Sabbaths when he commanded his men to arm themselves and to slew all of them that were gone to the celebrating of the Sabbaths. He also searched the city with weapons and slewed great multitudes."

This passage tells us that an army of twenty-two thousand was sent to Jerusalem by Andronicus and Menelaus, and they pretended to be peaceful until the holy Sabbath day. During the Sabbaths, they slewed all the Jews who came to observe the Sabbaths. The evening sacrifice was first taken away on that Sabbaths. Not long after this brutal massacre, they polluted the temple in Jerusalem, called it the temple of Jupiter Olympius, and even erected a desolating sacrilege upon the altar of burnt offerings. This event took place on the fifteenth day of Chislev (Kislev, the 9th lunar month) in the one hundred and forty-fifth year (2 Maccabees 6:1-2; 1 Maccabees 1:54). This day was on 17 November 168 BC according to our lunisolar calendar (see the calendar of 168 BC in Appendix D). Since the brutal massacre and the trample of the temple took place on a Sabbaths (Saturday), not long before erection of a desolating sacrilege on 17 November 168 BC, the Saturday on October 29 of 168 BC, which is 19 days before 17 November 168 BC, may be the starting time of the prophetic period. Any adjacent Saturday around October 29 of 168 BC could also agree with the events recorded in the two books of Maccabees, but we will show that only the day of October 29 of 168 BC can make the prophecy be fulfilled exactly.

When was the sanctuary (temple) cleansed (consecrated)? The first book of Maccabee (1 Maccabees 4:52-53;59) also tells us that in the one hundred and forty-eighth year (165 BC), Judas and his brothers freed the temple. They re-consecrated it and restored daily burnt offerings in the twenty-fifth day of the ninth month (Kislev). According to the lunisolar calendar of 165 BC (see Appendix D), Kislev 25 was on December 22, which was the end time of the prophetic period. From the time that daily sacrifices were taken away on October 29 of 168 BC (JD 1660362) to the time that the sanctuary was cleansed and daily burnt offerings were restored on December 22 of 165 BC (JD 1661512), there were exactly 1,150 days (or exactly 39 lunar months).

Since this prophecy of Daniel was fulfilled in the story recorded in the books of Maccabees, these books should be the inspired Word of God and be included in the Hebrew Bible. Interestingly, Yeshua also celebrated the Festival of Hanukkah in John 10:22-23, "Now it was the Feast of Dedication (Hanukkah) in Jerusalem, and it was winter. And Jesus walked in the temple, in Solomon's porch."

CHAPTER 19

DANIEL'S PROPHECY ON THE 1290TH DAY

Daniel prophesized the time of setting up the abomination of desolation. The detailed prophecy was recorded in Daniel 12:9-11 (JB2000):

> ⁹And he said, Go thy way, Daniel, for these words are closed up and sealed until the time of the fulfillment. ¹⁰Many shall be purified and made white and purged, but the wicked shall get worse; and none of the wicked shall understand, but the wise shall understand. ¹¹And from the time that the daily sacrifice is taken away until the abomination of desolation, there shall be **days a thousand two hundred and ninety [1,290]**.

The prophecy was fulfilled perfectly in the Dome of the Rock, construction of which was finished in May of 692 AD. The Dome of the Rock has been sitting on or near the most holy site, the temple site of God. This building should be an abomination of desolation to the God of Israel. The daily sacrifice was taken away in the spring of 598 BC, as we will show below in detail. The 1290th year from the spring of 598 BC was between the spring of 692 AD to the spring of 693 AD, within which the construction of the Dome of the Rock was finished. This prophecy was fulfilled perfectly.

Detailed explanations

Daily sacrifices (burnt offerings) were suspended several times, as recorded in the Hebrew Bible. The first one was recorded in 2 Chronicles 28:24-25, "Ahaz gathered together the furnishings from the temple of God and cut them in pieces. He shut the doors of Yehowah's temple and set up altars at every street corner in Jerusalem. In every town in Judah he built high places to burn sacrifices to other gods and aroused the anger of Yehowah, the God of his ancestors." The second one was in the time of Ezekiel's exile to Babylon, which was implicitly recorded in 2 Chronicles 36:6-9; Jeremiah 29:1-2; Jeremiah 52:28; and in *Antiq.* bk. 10, ch. 6. From these Biblical verses and Josephus' accounts along with the Jerusalem Chronology, we can figure out the time when the continual daily sacrifice was suspended in the time of Ezekiel.

When was Ezekiel the priest and prophet of God carried into Babylon? Ezekiel 40:1 says: "In the twenty-fifth year of our exile, at the beginning of the year, on the tenth of the month, in the fourteenth year after the fall of the city—on that very day the hand of Yehowah was on me and he took me there."

This verse provides us with a clear hint about when Ezekiel and his companions were exiled to Babylon. We have unambiguously shown that the fall of Jerusalem was in the fifth month of 587 BC (Chapters 10 and 11). This allows us to deduce that the 14th year of the fall of Jerusalem was from the 5th month of 574 BC to the 5th month of 573 BC. Then the very day of Nisan 10 that the hand of Yehowah was upon Ezekiel must have fallen on Nisan 10 of 573 BC. Since Nisan 10 of 573 BC was in the 25th year of Ezekiel's exile, he must have been exiled between Nisan 10 and Av 9 of 598 BC, which is different from the time when Jehoiachin king of Judah was exiled (March 16, 597 BC). This is consistent with the verses (Jeremiah 29:1-2) which imply that the priests and prophets had already been carried into Babylon before Nebuchadnezzar took Jehoiachin, the officers and fighting men, and the craftsmen and artisans—a total of ten thousand (2 Kings 24:14). There were no priests nor prophets in the composition of the ten-thousand captives on March 16 of 597 BC.

Ezekiel gave further hints about his exile in Ezekiel 33:21: "In the twelfth [12th] year of our exile, in the tenth month on the fifth day, a man who had escaped from Jerusalem came to me and said, 'The city has fallen!'" After the fall of Jerusalem in the fifth month of 587 BC, a man escaped from Jerusalem and arrived in Babylon on Tebet 5 of 587 BC. It took about 5 months for the man to run/walk from Jerusalem to Babylon. Since Tebet 5 of 587 BC was in the 12th year of Ezekiel's exile, he must have been exiled after Tebet 5 of 599 BC.

This is consistent with ABC 5 (Jerusalem Chronology) which states: "[Rev.9'] In the sixth year [599/598] in the month of Kislîmu [the 10th month] the king of Akkad mustered his army and marched to the Hatti-land. From the Hatti-land he sent out his companies, [Rev.10'] and scouring the desert they took much plunder from the Arabs, their possessions, animals and gods. In the month of Addaru the king returned to his own land."

This campaign was about one year before the campaign in the spring of 597 BC and should have been related to the siege of Jerusalem when Jehoiakim was king of Judah. The verse in 1 Esdras 1:45 confirms that Nebuchadnezzar took Jehoiachin one year after he took Jehoiakim.

According to Josephus, Jehoiakim submitted to Nebuchadnezzar without resistance immediately after he arrived in Jerusalem (*Antiq.*, bk. 10, ch. 6, 96-97). It is possible that Nebuchadnezzar arrived in Jerusalem in Addaru (the 12th month), and after some days, bound Jehoiakim with bronze shackles and took him to Babylon (2 Chronicles 36:6) in Addaru of 599 BC, corresponding to the Hebrew month of Nisan in 598 BC. Therefore, Ezekiel's exile should have been between 10 and 30 Nisan 598 BC, about one year before Jehoiachin's exile (1 Esdras 1:45).

Josephus said that he also took the principal persons in dignity as captives, 3,000 in number, and led them away to Babylon. Among them was the prophet Ezekiel (*Antiq.*, bk. 10, ch. 6, 98). Nisan 10-30 of 598 BC was also in the 7th year of Nebuchadnezzar according to Jeremiah's anniversary reckoning method but in the 6th year according to the Babylonian non-ascension-year method. Jeremiah also mentioned that in the 7th year of Nebuchadnezzar, 3,023 Jews were carried into exile (Jeremiah 52:28), in agreement with Josephus' account. In the 8th year of Nebuchadnezzar, ten thousand Jews were taken into Babylon along with

Jehoiachin (2 Kings 24:14). Biblical authors in different books talk about two different exiles in different times (separated by about one year).

Ezekiel, Jeremiah, Josephus, and the scribe of the Jerusalem Chronology consistently tell us that about 3,000 principal Jews in dignity were exiled on Nisan 10-30, 598 BC. By besieging Jerusalem, taking away articles in the temple of Yehowah, and carrying away many priests and prophets, Nebuchadnezzar must have trampled down the temple and caused the daily sacrifices to cease in the spring of 598 BC.

There was around a 10-month gap between Jehoiakim's exile and Jehoiachin's reign. A possible explanation is as follows. Nebuchadnezzar took Jehoiakim and his son Jehoiachin together into Babylon, and Jehoiakim died on the way to Babylon. The death of Jehoiakim was recorded in the book of 2 Chronicles 36:6, "Nebuchadnezzar king of Babylon ... bound him in fetters, to carry him to Babylon." Jeremiah prophesied that he died without a proper funeral, describing the people of Judah "shall not lament for him, saying, 'Alas, master!' or 'Alas, his glory!' He shall be buried with the burial of a donkey, dragged and cast out beyond the gates of Jerusalem." (Jeremiah 22:18-19) "and his dead body shall be cast out to the heat of the day and the frost of the night." (Jeremiah 36:30). After Jehoiachin arrived in Babylon, Nebuchadnezzar decided to let Jehoiachin reign in Judah. It could have taken 10 months for the round trip between Jerusalem and Babylon, as inferred from Ezekiel 33:21, which suggests a 5-month distance between Jerusalem and Babylon. Therefore, it is clear that the daily sacrifices were suspended in the spring of 598 BC by Nebuchadnezzar. He might have stopped it again in the spring of 597 BC and again in the summer of 587 BC.

The phrase "abomination of desolation (Hebrew Transliteration: shqutzim mshmm)" is found in three places in the book of Daniel. The first place is in Daniel 9:27, "And he shall confirm the covenant with many for one week: and in the midst of the week he shall cause the sacrifice and the offering to cease (fail), and for the overspreading of abominations he shall make it desolate, even until the consummation, and that determined shall be poured upon the desolate." The second place is in Daniel 11:31, "And forces shall appear on his part, and they shall defile the sanctuary fortress, and shall take away the daily sacrifice, and they shall set up the abomination that makes desolate." The third place is in Daniel 12:11 (YLTV): "and from the time of the turning aside of the perpetual [sacrifice], and to the giving out of the desolating abomination, [are] days a thousand, two hundred, and ninety." In the Gospel of Matthew, the phrase was also used by Yeshua in the Olivet discourse (Matthew 24:15-16): "When you therefore shall see the abomination of desolation, spoken of by Daniel the prophet, stand in the holy place, (whoever reads, let him understand) then let them who are in Judea flee into the mountains."

Daniel and Yeshua used this phrase to speak about an important message concerning the great tribulation in the future or in the end times. The abomination of desolation is a great sign for the coming of the Messiah in the end times, so a correct interpretation to this phrase is crucial to the understanding of the prophecies of Daniel and Yeshua concerning the end times.

The prophecy in Daniel 11:31 was fulfilled in 168 BC when the holy temple was desecrated by the erection of Zeus' statue in its sacred precincts by Antiochus IV Epiphanes. The "abomination of desolation," Yeshua spoke of in Matthew 24:15-16 cannot refer to the one in 168 BC. Although the destruction of Jerusalem in 70 AD could have been a fulfillment of the prophecy foretold by Yeshua, the "abomination of desolation" is a proverbial phrase that could include multiple events and allow for multiple fulfillments.

Now we focus on Daniel 12 where Daniel prophesizes the events related to the end times. If one can identify the "abomination of desolation" in Daniel 12:11, one should be able to figure out the timeline of the end. One of the candidates for the "abomination of desolation" is the Islamic Dome of the Rock, which has been standing on the holiest site of Jerusalem since 692 AD. The building itself is abominable to the Jews because it substitutes the holiest site. To the true Christians, the inscriptions on the wall of the structure are abominable. The inscription given in 692 AD made mosaic declarations: "O you People of the Book, overstep not bounds in your religion, and of Allah speak only the truth. The Messiah, Yeshua, son of Mary, is only an apostle of Allah, and his Word which he conveyed unto Mary, and a Spirit proceeding from him. Believe therefore in God and his apostles, and say not Three. It will be better for you. Allah is only one God. Far be it from His transcendent majesty that he should have a son."

In 1 John 2:22-2, John declares: "Who is a liar but he that denies that Yeshua is the Messiah? He is anti-messiah, that denies the Father and the Son. Whosoever denies the Son, the same has not the Father: [but] he that confesses the Son has the Father also." These inscriptions truly represent the anti-messiah's spirit who denies Yeshua to be the Son of God. The incarnation of the anti-messiah's spirit will in the last day open his mouth in blasphemy against God, His name, His tabernacle, and those who dwell in heaven (Revelation 13:6).

When did the construction of the Dome of the Rock begin? Historians such as Sibt Ibn al-Jawzi (1256 AD) say that the construction of the Dome of the Rock began in 69 AH (after the Hijra) and finished in 72 AH. The inscriptions were placed on the walls of the Dome of the Rock in 72 AH. Creswell thinks that placing the inscriptions marks completion of the Dome of the Rock. His thought is consistent with the passage, "The work of construction began in 688 AD and the building work lasted four years, from 688 AD to 692 AD." (*A History of Palestine*, 634-1099 by Moshe Gil, 1997, Cambridge University Press. ISBN 9780521599849, page 92). In order to match a total of four years for completion, the construction should have started from the beginning of 69 AH and completed at the end of 72 AH.

Therefore, the construction of the Dome of the Rock should have started from the first month of 69 AH (5 July-3 August 688 AD) and ended in the 12th Islamic month (Dhu al-Hijjah) of 72 AH during which Muslim pilgrims should have congregated. The Hajj is performed on the eighth, the ninth, and the tenth of this month. The day of Arafah takes place on the ninth of the month. Eid al-Adha, the "Festival of the Sacrifice," begins on the tenth day and lasts for 4 days (please see https://en.wikipedia.org/wiki/Eid_al-Adha). In all likelihood, the Islamic inscriptions may have been displayed on the 14th day of Dhu al-Hijjah right after the end of "Festival of the Sacrifice" on the 13th day of the month.

The first day of an Islamic lunar month is a day when a new crescent is seen in the western sky after sunset (see https://en.wikipedia.org/wiki/Islamic_calendar). The Stellarium Program shows that a new crescent could barely be seen in the western sky in the evening of April 23 of 692 AD (the visibility was only 1.8%). If this crescent was actually observed, the first day of Dhu al-Hijjah of 72 AH was on April 24 of 692 AD and the 14th day on May 7. If this crescent was too dim to be observed, the first day should have been on April 25 and the 14th day on May 8 (JD 1973938). From May 8 of 692 AD to May 12 of 2027 (JD 2461537), there are 487,599 days = 1,335×365.2427 days, which are exactly equal to 1,335 solar years.

We believe that Daniel 12:11 has been mistranslated in most English-translated versions of the Bible. By comparing with the interlinear Hebrew-English version, we find that Young's literal translation and the Jubilee Bible 2000 are the correct translations. Young's literal translation of Daniel 12:11 reads, "and from the time of the turning aside of the perpetual [sacrifice], and to the giving out of the desolating abomination, [are] days a thousand, two hundred, and ninety." The phrase "from A" is in parallel to the phrase "to B" and they should always be used together when one talks about a time interval from "time A" to "time B." In most English translated versions of the Bible, the sentence does not have "to time B" for a time interval of 1290 days, which is incorrect structurally. In Daniel 12:11, the literally translated phrase "and to B" is awkward in English but natural in Hebrew. Another example can be found in Jeremiah 12:12 (ASV): "Destroyers are come upon all the bare heights in the wilderness; for the sword of Jehovah devours **from** the one end of the land **and to** the other end of the land: no flesh has peace." Here, the Hebrew word "and" is translated into "even" in some English translations. In most English translations, the Hebrew word "and" is simply omitted.

Therefore, Daniel 12:11 should be better translated as, "The setup of the desolating abomination shall be in the 1290th day from the time of the turning aside of the perpetual sacrifice." The Hebrew phrase "days 1290" should be understood as the 1290th day, similar to the case for the phrase "weeks 69" (see discussion in Chapter 16). The phrase "days 1335" in Daniel 12:12 should also be understood as the 1335th day. A similar phrase can be found in Jeremiah 52:29 (literally): "In year(s) 18 of Nebuchadnezzar, he carried away captive from Jerusalem 832." Here, the Hebrew word "שָׁנָה" has been translated into "year" for 318 times and into "years" for 451 times by NASB translation. The phrase "year(s) 18" has been translated as the 18th year.

The prophecy in Daniel 12:11 thus means that the time period from the turning aside of the perpetual sacrifice to setting up the "desolation of abomination" should have been between 1,289 and 1,290 years.

We have shown above that the time that the perpetual sacrifice was turned aside was in the spring of 598 BC. From the time when the perpetual sacrifice was turned aside in the spring of 598 BC to the time when the construction of the Dome of the Rock was finished in May of 692 AD, there was about 1,289.2 years (between 1,289 and 1,290 years). Therefore, the prophecy on the 1290th day in Daniel 12:11 was fulfilled perfectly in the completion of the Dome of the Rock. The prophecy on the 1335th day has not been yet fulfilled. We will discuss it in Chapter 37.

CHAPTER 20

PROPHETIC DREAM OF NEBUCHADNEZZAR ON SEVEN TIMES

Daniel recorded a prophetic dream of Nebuchadnezzar in Daniel 4:10-17:

¹⁰"These were the visions of my head while on my bed: I was looking, and behold, a tree in the midst of the earth, and its height was great. ¹¹The tree grew and became strong; Its height reached to the heavens, and it could be seen to the ends of all the earth. ¹²Its leaves were lovely, Its fruit abundant, and in it was food for all. The beasts of the field found shade under it, the birds of the heavens dwelt in its branches, and all flesh was fed from it. ¹³I saw in the visions of my head while on my bed, and there was a watcher, a holy one, coming down from heaven. ¹⁴He cried aloud and said thus: 'Chop down the tree and cut off its branches, strip off its leaves and scatter its fruit. Let the beasts get out from under it, and the birds from its branches. ¹⁵Nevertheless leave the stump and roots in the earth, bound with a band of iron and bronze, in the tender grass of the field. Let it be wet with the dew of heaven, and let him graze with the beasts on the grass of the earth. ¹⁶Let his heart be changed from that of a man, let him be given the heart of a beast, and **let seven times pass over him.** ¹⁷This decision is by the decree of the watchers, and the sentence by the word of the holy ones, in order that

the living may know that the Most High rules in the kingdom of men, gives it to whomever He will, and sets over it the lowest of men.'...."

This prophetic dream of Nebuchadnezzar was doubly fulfilled in a short period of 2,520 (7×360) days and in a long period of 2,520 years. The short period was fulfilled in Nebuchadnezzar whose kingship was removed for 2,520 days from 17 March 572 BC. The prophecy was also fulfilled perfectly in the nation of Israel within the long period of 2,520 solar years starting also from 17 March 572 BC. The nation of Israel lost their power and sovereignty for exactly 2,520 years. The end of the prophetic period was on 10 March 1949 when Israel won the war of independence and established its true sovereignty.

Detailed explanations

Nebuchadnezzar dreamed that a great and strong tree was chopped down and its stump would regrow after a period of "seven times." Daniel interpreted that the great tree was the king himself and he would lose his kingdom for a period of "seven times" after which his kingdom would be restored. This prophecy was initially fulfilled in Nebuchadnezzar himself 12 months after his prophetic dream (Daniel 4:28-36). Here, the phrase "seven times" means $7 \times 360 = 2,520$ prophetic days or years. The prophecy was initially fulfilled in a short period according to the prophetic days (2,520 days), which was about 7 years.

It is possible that the prophecy would be fulfilled in a long period according to the prophetic years, corresponding to 2,520 years from the time when Nebuchadnezzar temporarily lost his sanity and kingship. In the short period, the great tree referred to Nebuchadnezzar, the great Gentile king. In the long period, the great tree may refer to the holy nation of Israel established by God Himself.

In many parts of Scriptures, Israel was referred to as a tree planted by God. Psalm 44:1-3 says, "We have heard with our ears, O God, our fathers have told us, The deeds You did in their days, In days of old: You drove out the nations with Your hand, But them You planted; You afflicted the peoples, and cast them out. For they did not gain possession of the land by their own sword, nor did their own arm save them; But it was Your right hand, Your arm, and the light of Your countenance, because You favored them."

The verses in Psalm 80:8-11 also tell us, "You have brought a vine out of Egypt; You have cast out the nations, and planted it. You prepared room for it, and caused it to take deep root, and it filled the land. The hills were covered with its shadow, and the mighty cedars with its boughs. She sent out her boughs to the Sea, and her branches to the River."

Jeremiah prophesized God's judgment against Israel in Jeremiah 11:16-17, "Yehowah called your name, Green Olive Tree, lovely and of good fruit. With the noise of a great tumult He has kindled fire on it, and its branches are broken. For Yehowah of hosts, who planted you, has pronounced doom against you for the evil of the house of Israel and of the house of Judah, which they have done against themselves to provoke Me to anger in offering incense to Baal."

Israel was the Green Olive Tree, lovely and of good fruit, planted by God Himself, but the great sins committed by the children of Israel provoked the anger of God and He would cut off its branches and left only the stump. This prophecy was in parallel with the prophetic dream of Nebuchadnezzar in Daniel 4:12-13, "Its leaves were lovely, its fruit abundant, …, and there was a watcher, a holy one, coming down from heaven. He cried aloud and said thus: 'Chop down the tree and cut off its branches, strip off its leaves and scatter its fruit….'"

The tree in the Nebuchadnezzar's dream not only represented his own kingdom but also the kingdom of Israel. The prophetic dream implies that the punishment for the sins of Nebuchadnezzar would last for 2,520 days while the punishment for the sins of the children of Israel would be for 2,520 years.

God had set up a kingdom (the nation of Israel) to represent his rulership on the earth. God allowed that kingdom to become "a ruin" because its rulers had become unfaithful, but He foretold that He would give kingship to "the one who has the legal right." (Ezekiel 21:25-27). The Bible identifies Son of Man as the one who was legally authorized to receive this everlasting kingdom (Daniel 7:13-14).

What does the tree being chopped down mean? Just as the chopping down of the tree represented the complete removal of Nebuchadnezzar's kingship and power, it also represented complete removal of the power of the nation of Israel. The house of Israel was destroyed by the Assyrians in the fall of 721 BC. Nebuchadnezzar destroyed Jerusalem and the house of Judah in July of 587 BC. Earlier in 572 BC, he also destroyed the Jewish remnant who did not obey God's will to stay in Jerusalem but rather escaped to Egypt for protection (see discussion below). This fulfilled the prophecy of Jeremiah against the remnant of Judah who set their faces to go into the land of Egypt to dwell there (Jeremiah 44:11-12). After these Jews were consumed by sword and famine, the power of the Israelites was mostly removed, just as the great tree was chopped down; its branches were cut off, and its leaves were stripped off. Only the stump and the roots were left on the tree, bounded with a band of iron and bronze, wet with the dew of heaven.

Interestingly, the band of bronze and iron links the tree prophecy to the great-image prophecy of Daniel in Chapter 2. Bronze and iron are the last two metals of the great image, indicating that the children of Israel will be given to the hands of bronze and iron kingdoms. The bronze kingdom represents the Greek kingdom, and the iron kingdom refers to the Roman kingdom. History tells us that the children of Israel were persecuted by both Greek and Roman kingdoms. In contrast, the Persian kingdom (represented by silver metal) did not persecute the children of Israel but rather helped them.

When did Nebuchadnezzar temporarily lose his sanity and kingship? We can obtain an insight from Daniel 4:29-31, "At the end of the twelve months he was walking about the royal palace of Babylon. The king spoke, saying, 'Is not this great Babylon, that I have built for a royal dwelling by my mighty power and for the honor of my majesty?' While the word was still in the king's mouth, a voice fell from heaven: 'King Nebuchadnezzar, to you it is spoken: the kingdom has departed from you!'"

At the end of the twelve months from the time of his prophetic dream, Nebuchadnezzar boasted about his own achievement, glory, and honor when he was walking about the royal palace of Babylon. Right after he boasted, he lost his sanity and was driven out of his palace for about seven years.

His insanity must have happened in a consecutive period of seven years, where no royal chronicle of him was recorded. The Jerusalem Chronicle recorded Nebuchadnezzar's activities and campaigns consecutively down to the 11th year (the 9th month of 594 BC) of his reign. The books of Jeremiah and 2 Kings record his siege of Jerusalem in the 9th month of the 9th year of Zedekiah, which was in 589 BC. The Bible also tells us that Nebuchadnezzar destroyed Jerusalem in the 5th month of 587 BC, which was in his 19th regnal year. Right after his destruction of Jerusalem, he started to besiege Tyre in the spring of 586 BC and ended the siege in the spring of 573 BC. His army labored strenuously against Tyre, every head was made bald, and every shoulder rubbed raw, yet neither he nor his army received wages from Tyre (Ezekiel 29:18). The 13-year siege of Tyre should have frustrated and disappointed him, so he would not have been boastful when he returned from the siege of Tyre in the spring of 573 BC. In contrast, his heart could possibly have become very proud after he plundered Egypt with great success: taking away her (Egyptian) wealth, carrying off her spoil, and removing her pillage (Ezekiel 29:19-20).

A Babylonian campaign against Egypt took place in the spring of 567 BC, as recorded in the cuneiform tablet fragment (BM 33041) and the Elephantine stela. Although no detail was given for the campaign, it ended with the Babylonians being defeated by the Egyptians. Naturally, this defeated campaign against Egypt cannot be the successful one Ezekiel talked about in Ezekiel 29:19-20. From the spring of 567 BC to his death in October 562 BC, there were less than 6 years, so his insanity could not have started after 567 BC.

In the first day of the first month (Nisan 1) in the 27th year after captivity of Jehoiachin (Ezekiel 29:17), God said to Ezekiel (Ezekiel 29:21), "In that day I will cause the horn of the house of Israel to spring forth,..." These verses imply that the horn or the power of the house of Israel had been removed before Nisan 1 of that year (the 27th year after captivity of Jehoiachin), and that God would cause the horn or the power of Israel to spring forth again in a future time. Because the captivity of Jehoiachin happened on March 16 of 597 BC, March 27 (Nisan 1) of 571 BC was in the 27th year after captivity of Jehoiachin.

Therefore, Nebuchadnezzar's insanity and Israeli loss of power should have taken place before 1 Nisan 571 BC.

Ezekiel 29:19-20 has been mistranslated by all the English Bibles except for the Yang Literal Transition Bible. The correct translation should be as follows:

> [19]Therefore thus said Yehowah God: "Behold, I was giving the land of Egypt unto Nebuchadnezzar king of Babylon; and he took her multitude, and took her wealth, and took her plunder; and it was the wages for his army. [20]I gave him the land of Egypt for his labor for which he served against it, because they wrought for me, affirmation of Yehowah God."

In verse 20, God had already given Nebuchadnezzar the land of Egypt at the time when He spoke to Ezekiel on Nisan 1 of 571 BC. The tense of "give" here is Qal-Perfect, meaning that the action has been completed. To be consistent with verse 20, the participle "giving" in verse 19 should be the continuous action starting from the past. Since the tenses of the following verbs in verse 19 are of Conjunction Perfect, their tenses should be consistent with that of the participle "giving," which is the Past Continuous Tense. Therefore, in verses 19-20, God spoke of the things that had happened before Nisan 1 of 571 BC, just as He spoke about the siege of Tyre in verse 18, which had happened.

Our correct understanding of these verses leads us to conclude that Nebuchadnezzar's campaign against Egypt to completely remove the power of the escaped men of Judah should have taken place before 1 Nisan 571 BC. From the Jerusalem Chronicle, we see that Nebuchadnezzar often made campaigns in the 9th or 10th month and returned to Babylon in the 12th month, and that he conducted campaigns year by year without cease. If this was the case, the earliest date for the campaign against Egypt should have been in the 9th or 10th month of 573 BC (since the siege of Tyre ended in the spring of 573 BC). He then returned to Babylon in the 12th month of 573 BC (in the spring of 572 BC) after he defeated the Egyptians and consumed all the men of Judah in the land of Egypt. Because of the great victory in the land of Egypt, he boasted and then immediately lost his kingship (Daniel 4:28-33). Then the clock of the two prophetic periods: 2,520 days for Nebuchadnezzar and 2,520 years for the nation of Israel, started to tick in the spring of 572 BC. If this was the case, Nebuchadnezzar must have had the prophetic dream in the spring of 573 BC right after he ended his siege of Tyre.

If Nebuchadnezzar became insane in the spring of 572 BC, then the Babylonian campaign against Egypt in the spring of 567 BC could not have been led by Nebuchadnezzar himself because this was within the period of his insanity (from the spring of 572 BC to the spring of 565 BC). This could naturally explain why the Babylonian army was defeated in 567 BC; it was because the army was not led by Nebuchadnezzar.

Jeremiah prophesized about the destiny of the Egyptian king Apries (Hophra) in Jeremiah 44:30, "Thus says Yehowah; Behold, I will give Pharaoh-hophra king of Egypt into the hand of his enemies, and into the hand of them that seek his life; as I gave Zedekiah king of Judah into the hand of Nebuchadnezzar king of Babylon, his enemy, and that sought his life."

This prophecy suggests that Apries should have been carried into Babylon after he was defeated in Nebuchadnezzar's campaign against Egypt, just as Zedekiah king of Judah was taken into Babylon. Nebuchadnezzar did not kill Apries but imprisoned him in Babylon just as he did to Zedekiah. Nebuchadnezzar became proud and God punished him for his sin right after he plundered Egypt, having accomplished the mission of God, as prophesized by Jeremiah (Jeremiah 44:27), "Behold, I will watch over them for harm, and not for good: and all the men of Judah that are in the land of Egypt shall be consumed by the sword and by the famine, until there is an end of them."

After Nebuchadnezzar was driven out of the palace due to his insanity, he had no control of his kingdom and his usurpers took power and administered the royal affairs. The usurpers may have released Apries and let him go back to Egypt to take his kingdom back from Amasis (the previous general of Apries). This would have led to a civil war between Amasis and Apries in Egypt that lasted for approximately two years (from 572 BC to 570 BC). After Apries was defeated by Amasis in October of 570 BC, he went back to Babylon and turned himself up in the royal court of Babylon. He then persuaded Nebuchadnezzar's usurper to conduct a campaign against Amasis in March of 567 BC. During the campaign, Amasis defeated the Babylonian army and captured Apries. Amasis allowed Apries to live for a short time, but because many Egyptians complained about keeping their enemy alive, he delivered Apries to the people, and they strangled him.

Which day did Nebuchadnezzar lose his kingship after he completely consumed all the men of Judah in the land of Egypt in the spring of 572 BC? After the author of the book kept asking God for a hint about the exact day, he realized that the prophetic dream of Nebuchadnezzar should have happened in a special day since it was guided by God. Suddenly, Ezekiel 40:1 came to his mind. The Hebrew Nisan 10 in this verse may have been the day of Nebuchadnezzar's prophetic dream since Ezekiel received on this same day a vision about the construction of the temple of God in the far future. God first mentioned the day of Nisan 10 in Exodus 12:3, "Speak to all the congregation of Israel, saying: 'On the tenth day of this month every man shall take for himself a lamb, according to the house of his father, a lamb for a household.'" On this day, the Passover lamb was selected and kept until the 14th day of the month for sacrifice. On this special day, our Savior, Yeshua, was declared to be the Lamb of God (John 1:35-36), and after three years he rode on a colt into Jerusalem on the same day (John 12:12-15).

We have proved that the day in Ezekiel 40:1 was on 10 Nisan 573 BC (or 9 Addaru 574 BC in the Babylonian calendar). This should have been the day that Nebuchadnezzar had his prophetic dream after the 13-year siege of Tyre. After 12 lunar months, it came to 10 Adar II 573 BC (the intercalated month), corresponding to 9 Addaru 573 BC in the Babylonian calendar and 17 March 572 BC in the Julian calendar. On this special day, the clock for both prophetic periods started to tick.

Nebuchadnezzar's prophetic dream was initially fulfilled upon himself within a short period of time according to the prophetic days. 2520 days elapsed from 17 March 572 BC to 9 February 565 BC. Nebuchadnezzar's kingship should have been restored on 9 February 565 BC. The long-term portion of this prophecy was fulfilled upon the nation of Israel. From 17 March 572 BC (JD 1512575) to 10 March 1949 (JD 2432985), there were 920,410 days = 2,520×365.24206 days

= 2,520 solar years. This means that the true sovereignty (power) of the nation of Israel should have been restored on 10 March 1949.

One might notice that the Jewish state was re-established on 14 May 1948, which was about 10 months before 10 March 1949. However, the sovereignty of the nation of Israel had not yet been completely established on that day. When the re-creation of the Jewish state was declared, only a provisional government was put in place. The following day, the armies of four Arab countries Egypt, Syria, Transjordan, and Iraq, launched the 1948 Arab–Israel War (or the Israeli War of Independence). The contingents from Yemen, Morocco, Saudi Arabia, and Sudan joined the war. The apparent purpose of the war was to abolish the Jewish state at inception.

After about 8 months of fighting, a ceasefire was declared, and temporary borders were established. Jordan annexed what became known as the West Bank, including East Jerusalem, and Egypt took control of the Gaza Strip. The elections for the Constituent Assembly were held on 25 January 1949. On 16 February 1949, the first Knesset elected Chaim Weizmann as the first President of Israel. The first government was formed on 8 March 1949 with David Ben-Gurion as Prime Minister. On 10 March 1949, the forces of Israel secured southern Negev, reaching the southern tip of Palestine, and taking it without a battle. Israel's soldiers raised a hand-made Israeli flag ("The Ink Flag") at 16:00 on 10 March 1949. The raising of the Ink Flag was the end of the war, marking the beginning of Israeli true sovereignty. Israel was admitted as a member of the United Nations by majority vote on 11 May 1949.

Therefore, the sovereignty (independence) of the nation of Israel was truly re-established on 10 March 1949 when the Israel's War of Independence ended. It is so amazing that exactly 2,520 solar years elapsed from 17 March 572 BC to 10 March 1949. This precisely fulfills the prophecy of "seven times" or 2,520 years appointed by God for the nation of Israel.

CHAPTER 21

DANIEL'S PROPHECY ON THE PERIOD OF SHATTERING THE HOLY PEOPLE'S POWER

Daniel prophesized a period within which the power of the holy people would be completely removed. The detailed prophecy was stated in Daniel 12:5-7:

> ⁵Then I, Daniel, looked; and there stood two others, one on this riverbank and the other on that riverbank. ⁶And one said to the man clothed in linen, who was above the waters of the river, "How long shall the fulfillment of these wonders be?" ⁷Then I heard the man clothed in linen, who was above the waters of the river, when he held up his right hand and his left hand to heaven, and swore by Him who lives forever, that it shall be **for a time, times, and half a time**; and when he shall have accomplished (ended) shattering the power (strength) of the holy people, all these things shall be finished.

This prophecy was perfectly fulfilled in the Jews. Their power (sovereignty) was completely removed in July of 688 AD when the construction of Dome of the Rock began. The total loss of their sovereignty ended on 14 May 1948 when the nation of Israel was re-established. The day of 14 May 1948 was the feast day of Pentecost and was also in the 1260th year from July of 688 AD. The prophecy was fulfilled perfectly.

Detailed explanation

After the second temple in Jerusalem was destroyed in 70 AD, worship overseen by the high priests in Jerusalem ceased. The site was covered in rubble, and a pagan temple dedicated to Jupiter was set up on the Temple Mount when Hadrian became Caesar (117-138 AD). Hadrian installed on the mount two statues: one of Jupiter and the other of himself. Hadrian not only set up a center of worship to Jupiter, but also expelled the Jews from Jerusalem, only allowing them to come into the city on the fast day of Tisha B'av, the ninth day of the fifth lunar month Av. This appears to have caused a second (115-117 AD) and third (132-136 AD) Jewish revolt with the intent of recapturing Jerusalem and reconstructing the holy temple. However, the Romans managed to crush each of these revolts.

History shows that about 1200 years of Islamization had caused Jerusalem to be more desolate physically and/or spiritually prior to 1948. During this period, most of the Jews were forced to leave the Palestinian region and be scattered around the world. By the early 1800's there were only 550 Jews in this region.

Jerusalem was temporarily desolated in 70 AD, again in 135 AD, and conquered again in 639 AD when Khalifah Omar marched into Jerusalem during the Islamic First Jihad. Nevertheless, before the construction of the Islamic Dome of the Rock began in 688 AD, the Jews still had a little power and were able to access Jerusalem and its temple site. In the earlier Umayyad Caliphate period, Muawiyah the first Caliph of the Umayyad Caliphate (661-680 AD) treated Jews, Samaritans, and Manichaeans well and allowed everyone in his regions to live as they wanted (see https://military.wikia.org/wiki/Muawiyah_I).

In July of 688 AD when the construction of the Dome of the Rock began, the Muslims might have used military forces to drive all the Jews out of Jerusalem. The Jews were thus scattered around the world and very few survived in the Palestinian region. They had become powerless and could no longer have accessed Jerusalem and the temple site. They appeared to be completely forsaken by God. Even in the places they were scattered into, they were persecuted and killed by the ungodly and even by many Protestants and Roman Catholics. In the second world war, Nazis killed two thirds of the Jews in Europe (about 6 million) under the name of God. During the period between 688 AD and 1948, the Jews completely lost their power. Therefore, the month of July of 688 AD marks the beginning of shattering the power of the holy people.

On 14 May 1948, the Jews were finally brought back to their homeland and the State of Israel was re-established, marking the end of shattering their power. Indeed, the day of 14 May 1948 was in the 1260th year from July of 688 AD (in the first month of 69 AH). This is the perfect fulfillment of Daniel's prophecy in Daniel 12:7. Here, the phrase "a time, times, and a half" means 1260 prophetic days/years according to Revelation 12:6.

The same prophecy was recorded in Revelation 12:6, "Then the woman fled into the wilderness, where she has a place prepared by God, that they should feed her there one thousand two hundred and sixty days." Here, the woman refers to the nation (children) of Israel. Many years after Yeshua ascended to heaven, the holy people were completely removed from the city of Jerusalem. They fled into the wilderness and were not allowed to approach Jerusalem for 1,260 years.

The starting date for the construction of the Dome of the Rock may be very special to the Jews because it marked total deprivation of their right to access the holiest site (the greatest calamity to the Jews). Because the holy temple was destroyed twice on the 9th/10th day of the fifth Hebrew month and because the first Islamic month of 69 AH happened to be in the fifth month of the Hebrew calendar (see the calendar of 688 AD in Appendix D), it is likely that the construction of the Dome of the Rock might have started on the 9th day of the fifth month of 688 AD, which was on July 12.

The Israelites started to lose their rulership as early as in the spring of 572 BC. The total length of their loss of sovereignty was prophesied to be seven times (2,520 years), as explained in Chapter 20. The half of the seven times in Daniel 12:7 was the last half period of the seven times, during which the Jews completely lost their power and sovereignty. When the shattering of the holy people's power ended on 14 May 1948, God restored their rulership. The true sovereignty (independence) of the nation of Israel was finally re-established on 10 March 1949 when the Israel War of Independence ended.

The numerical prophecies in the book of Daniel can be summarized in Figure 11. The most likely dates of these years are the following: 3 April (10 Nisan) 598 BC, 17 March (10 Adar II) 572 BC, 12 July (9 Av) 688 AD, 8 May (16 Iyar) 692 AD, 14 May (6 Sivan) 1948 AD, and 12 May (6 Sivan) 2027 AD. All the numbers: 1260, 1290, 1335, and 2520 are ordinal. The prophecy on the number 1335 (dashed line in Figure 11) is yet to be fulfilled while the prophecies on all the other numbers were perfectly fulfilled.

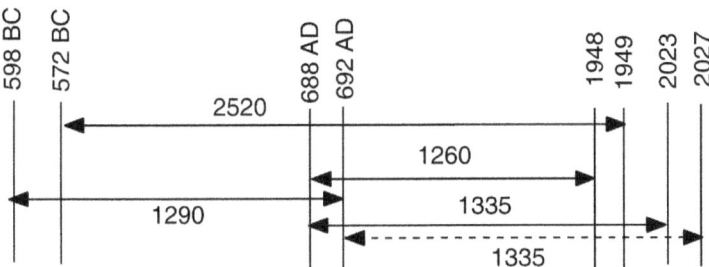

Figure 11: Schematic diagram of Daniel's numerical prophecies.

CHAPTER 22

EZEKIEL'S PROPHECY ON THE POPULATION OF ISRAEL AT ITS RE-BIRTH

In Ezekiel 36:37-38, Ezekiel prophesized the population of the nation of Israel in the latter time when Jerusalem was re-populated:

> ³⁷Thus says Yehowah God: "I will also let the house of Israel inquire of Me to do this for them: I will increase their men like a flock. ³⁸Like a flock offered as holy sacrifices, like the flock at Jerusalem on its feast days, so shall the ruined cities be filled with flocks of men. Then they shall know that I am Yehowah."

Here, the English word "flock" is translated from the original Hebrew word צאן (tson), which means "small cattle," "sheep and goats," and "flock." The English word "cattle" means "cows," "oxen," "bulls," "stock," and "livestock." What Ezekiel prophesized was that the total number of the sacrificed animals in the appointed Feasts of God at Jerusalem is equal to the total number of the Israelites when Yehowah brought them back to the holy land.

The number of the holy sacrifices in the appointed Feasts of God in Jerusalem is clearly prescribed in Numbers 28:16-31 and 29:1-40. There are three appointed Feasts in Jerusalem: Feast of Unleavened Bread, Feast of Weeks, and Feast of Tabernacles. Deuteronomy 16:16 says: "Three times a year all your males shall appear before Yehowah your God in the place which He chooses: at the Feast of Unleavened Bread, at the Feast of Weeks, and at the Feast of Tabernacles; and they shall not appear before Yehowah empty-handed." This verse tells us that the men of the Israelites shall go to Jerusalem during the three appointed holy Feasts and make animal sacrifices to Yehowah in the holy temple.

During the Feast of Unleavened Bread, 14 young bulls, 7 rams, 49 lambs, and 7 goats were to be offered. The total number of animals sacrificed is 77. During the Feast of Weeks, 2 young bulls, 1 ram, 7 lambs, and 1 goat were to be offered. The total number of animals sacrificed is 11. During the Feast of Tabernacles, 70 young bulls, 14 rams, 98 lambs, and 7 goats were to be offered. The total number of the animals sacrificed is 189. The total number of the animal sacrifices each year for the three Feasts is equal to 77+11+189 = 277.

According to the Biblical chronology in Chapter 10, Solomon began to build the holy temple on the second day of the second month of 977 BC. The temple's work was finished in 969 BC and Solomon dedicated the temple in the 7th month of 969 BC. The first Feast of Tabernacles took place in the 7th month of 969 BC. From the 7th month of 969 BC to the 14th day of the 7th month of 1947, there were 2,915 years. The total number of flocks that were supposed to be offered is 2,915×277 = 807,455. The declaration of the re-establishment of the nation of Israel took place at the end of 14 May 1948, which was exactly on the Feast of Weeks according to the correct Hebrew lunisolar calendar. From the 15th day of the 7th month of 1947 to the end of 14 May 1948, there were three complete Feasts, and an additional 277 sacrifices were supposed to be offered. Hence the total number of the sacrifices, which were supposed to be offered at the temple of Jerusalem just before the re-birth of the nation of Israel is 807,455 + 277 = 807,732.

It is remarkable that the number prophesized by Ezekiel exactly matches the population of the nation of Israel on 15 May 1948, which was 806,000 according to the statistics published in http://www.cbs.gov.il/statistical/statistical60_eng.pdf. Israeli population estimated from the statistics is only 0.21% lower than that prophesized by Ezekiel about 2,500 years ago. This consistency proves that Ezekiel is a true prophet of God. We should thus believe his prophecies about the war near the time of the Messianic Kingdom (Ezekiel 38-39) and about the rebuilding of the third temple during the Messianic Kingdom (Ezekiel 40-48).

CHAPTER 23

EZEKIEL'S PROPHECY ON TWO DESTRUCTIONS OF JERUSALEM

Ezekiel prophesized about two destructions of the city of Jerusalem. The detailed prophecy was recorded in Ezekiel 4:1-6:

> ¹You also, son of man, take a clay tablet and lay it before you, and portray on it a city, Jerusalem. ²Lay siege against it, build a siege wall against it, and heap up a mound against it ; set camps against it also, and place battering rams against it all around. ³Moreover take for yourself an iron plate, and set it as an iron wall between you and the city. Set your face against it, and it shall be besieged, and you shall lay siege against it. ⁴Lie also on your left side, and lay the iniquity of the house of Israel upon it. According to the number of the days that you lie on it, you shall bear their iniquity. ⁵For I have laid on you the years of their iniquity, according to the number of the days, **three hundred and ninety [390] days**; so you shall bear the iniquity of the house of Israel. ⁶And when you have completed them, lie again on your right side; then you shall bear the iniquity of the house of Judah **forty [40] days**. I have laid on you a day for each year.

Ezekiel's prophecy is about the siege and destruction of Jerusalem as seen from Ezekiel 4:1-3. The verses in Ezekiel 4:4-5 tell us that the prophet must lie on his left side for 390 days to bear the iniquity of the house of Israel for 390 years (one day for one year). Similarly, the prophet had to lie on his right side for 40 days to bear the iniquity of the house of Judah for 40 years.

A possible interpretation of this prophecy is that 390 and 40 years refer to two independent periods and that at the end of each period, Jerusalem would be besieged and destroyed. Jerusalem would be destroyed twice due to the iniquity of the house of Israel and the iniquity of the house of Judah.

Ezekiel did not provide any information about the starting point of the 390-year period. No one would be able to figure out what event should be related to the starting point of the 390-year prophetic period before finding out the starting point for the second 40-year prophetic period. It is well known that Jerusalem was destroyed in the 9th day of the fifth lunar month of 70 AD, forty years after the crucifixion of Yeshua in 30 AD (see the proof of the date of Yeshua's crucifixion in Chapter 31). Yeshua referred to his own body as the temple and prophesized that his body would be destroyed and raised up in three days. This implies that the resurrected body of Yeshua is the temple of God, which was built after his resurrection, in agreement with Revelation 21:22, "But I saw no temple in it, for Yehowah God Almighty and the Lamb are its temple."

For the 40-year prophetic period, the starting point was from the building of a spiritual temple, which was the resurrected body of Messiah Yeshua. By analogy, the starting point of the 390-year prophetic period should have been the time when the physical temple began to be built. Indeed, we have proved in Chapter 11 that there were 390 years plus about 100 days from the beginning of the construction of Solomon's temple to the first destruction of Jerusalem in the 10th day of the fifth lunar month of 587 BC.

Yeshua also prophesized the destruction of Jerusalem in Matthew 23:37-39; 24:1-2. Yeshua's prophecy about his own crucifixion and resurrection was recorded in Matthew 12:38-41:

^{38}Then some of the scribes and Pharisees answered, saying, "Teacher, we want to see a sign from You." ^{39}But he answered and said to them, "An evil and adulterous generation seeks after a sign, and no sign will be given to it except the sign of the prophet Jonah. ^{40}For as Jonah was three days and three nights in the belly of the great fish, so will the Son of Man be three days and three nights in the heart of the earth. ^{41}The men of Nineveh will rise up in the judgment with this generation and condemn it, because they repented at the preaching of Jonah; and indeed a greater than Jonah is here.

Yeshua foretold that he would resurrect after being buried three days and three nights just as the prophet Jonah was in the belly of the great fish for three days and there nights. He also told the scribes and Pharisees that he is greater than Jonah. Jonah prophesized that Nineveh would be destroyed within 40 days. The people of Nineveh believed Jonah's warning and turned away from their evil ways, so God relented from the disaster that He would have brought upon the city. Yeshua foretold that the men of Nineveh would rise up to judge this generation and condemn it because they repented at the preaching of Jonah while this generation did not repent in the 40-year grace period at the preaching of Yeshua who is even greater than Jonah. From this, Yeshua knew that God would not spare the holy city because of the evils that the leaders of His people committed. God gave Nineveh the grace period of only 40 days, but to His own people, He granted a grace-period of 40 years in hopes of their repentance.

CHAPTER 24

JEREMIAH'S PROPHECY ON 17 SHEKELS OF SILVER

Matthew 27:9-10 concludes the final story of Judas Iscariot with a quotation from the Hebrew Scripture showing how the events around his final days were predicted. In the New King James Version of the Bible, it is translated as:

> ⁹Then was fulfilled what was spoken by Jeremiah the prophet, saying, "And they took the thirty pieces of silver, the value of Him who was priced, whom they of the children of Israel priced, ¹⁰and gave them for the potter's field, as Yehowah directed me."

These verses can be more literally translated as:

> ⁹This fulfilled what was spoken by Jeremiah the prophet, saying, "And they took the thirty silver coins, the price of the (one) had been set, which had been set by the children of Israel, ¹⁰and used them to buy the potter's field, as Yehowah directed me."

What Matthew means in these two verses is that the chief priests took the thirty silver coins to buy the potter's field, whose price had been set by the children of Israel in the time of Jeremiah the prophet.

In the book of Jeremiah, Jeremiah received the word from God about 17 shekels of silver, which was recorded in Jeremiah 32:6-15,

⁶And Jeremiah said, "The word of Yehowah came to me, saying, ⁷'Behold, Hanamel the son of Shallum your uncle will come to you, saying, "Buy my field which is in Anathoth, for the right of redemption is yours to buy it."' ⁸Then Hanamel my uncle's son came to me in the court of the prison according to the word of Yehowah, and said to me, 'Please buy my field that is in Anathoth, which is in the country of Benjamin; for the right of inheritance is yours, and the redemption yours; buy it for yourself.' Then I knew that this was the word of Yehowah. ⁹So I bought the field from Hanamel, the son of my uncle who was in Anathoth, and weighed out to him the money—**seventeen shekels of silver**. ¹⁰And I signed the deed and sealed it, took witnesses, and weighed the money on the scales. ¹¹So I took the purchase deed, both that which was sealed according to the law and custom, and that which was open; ¹²and I gave the purchase deed to Baruch the son of Neriah, son of Mahseiah, in the presence of Hanamel my uncle's son, and in the presence of the witnesses who signed the purchase deed, before all the Jews who sat in the court of the prison. ¹³Then I charged Baruch before them, saying, ¹⁴"Thus says the Lord of hosts, the God of Israel: "Take these deeds, both this purchase deed which is sealed and this deed which is open, and put them in an earthen vessel, that they may last many days."¹⁵For thus says the Lord of hosts, the God of Israel: "Houses and fields and vineyards shall be possessed again in this land."

In this passage, the prophet tells us that he purchased a field in Anathoth from Hanamel, his uncle's son, with a price of **17 shekels of silver**. The deed was sealed and kept in an earthen vessel that may have lasted for many days (verse 14). The houses, fields, and vineyards would be possessed again in this land by purchasing them according to the price of **17 shekels of silver** sealed in the original purchase deed.

Why did God instruct Jeremiah to keep the purchase deed for many days? This was because God had the foreknowledge that the chief priests would purchase the potter's field with the price according to the original purchase deed. Since Anathoth is located about 3 miles north of Jerusalem, it is likely that the field Jeremiah purchased should have been the potter's field Matthew referred to.

What silver coins did the chief priests pay Judas Iscariot for his betrayal? According to the information in https://en.wikipedia.org/wiki/Shekel, it was customary among the Jews to annually offer a half-shekel coin to the temple treasury, for the upkeep and maintenance of the temple precincts and on the purchase of public animal-offerings during the second temple period. This practice did not only apply to the Jews living in the land of Israel, but also to the Jews living outside the land of Israel. This information leads us to believe that the chief priests paid Judas half-shekel coins, which were offered by the Jews.

In 2008, a Judaea half-shekel coin was discovered in Horvat Ethry. The coin was minted in 67/68 AD and weighed 6.69 grams. It has "Half Shekel" imprinted in Hebrew, chalice with beaded rim, date above/"Jerusalem is holy" in Hebrew, sprig of three pomegranates (see the website: https://en.wikipedia.org/wiki/File:JUDAEA_Half_Sheke.jpg).

Since an ancient shekel in the time of Jeremiah was equal to 11 grams, one 6.69-gram Judaean half-shekel coin in the time of Messiah should have weighed 6.69 grams/(11 grams/ancient shekel) = 0.6082 ancient shekels. Then 30 Judaean half-shekel coins should have weighed 30×0.6082 ancient shekels = 18.245 ancient shekels.

If Matthew is right, the 30 Judaean half-shekel coins with the weight of 18.245 ancient shekels must contain exactly 17 shekels of silver. If we know the purity of the silver coins, we can calculate their silver content. It was known that the Tyrian shekel coins were issued by the Tyrians between 126 BC and 56 AD. After the Roman Empire closed down the mint in Tyre, the Roman authorities allowed the Jewish Rabbani to continue minting Tyrian shekels in Palestine, but with the requirement that the coins should continue to bear the same image and text to avoid objections that the Jews were given autonomy. They were replaced by the First Jewish Revolt coinage in 66 AD. This information leads us to believe that the Judaea half-shekel coin should have the same purity as the Tyrian shekel coin, which contained about 94% of silver.

With 94% of silver in the coins, the 30 Judaean half-shekel coins should have contained 17.15 ancient shekels of silver, very close to 17 ancient shekels priced for the field in the time of Jeremiah. According to the information in https://en.wikipedia.org/wiki/Denarius, the Denarius coin between 64 and 68 AD actually contains 93.5% silver. Using this more accurate number for the purity, we find that the 30 Judaean half-shekel coins contain 17.06 ancient shekels of silver, in excellent agreement with the prophecy of Jeremiah.

Matthew was right about the perfect fulfillment of the prophecy of Jeremiah. However, Biblical scholars claim that the purchase of the potter's field was the fulfilment of a prophecy of Zechariah in Zechariah 11:12-13:

> [12]Then I said to them, "If it is agreeable to you, give me my wages; and if not, refrain." So they weighed out for my wages thirty pieces of silver. [13]And Yehowah said to me, "Throw it to the potter"—that princely price they set on me. So I took the thirty pieces of silver and threw them into the house of Yehowah for the potter.

Matthew usually quoted the Hebrew Bible liberally from the source materials. But the verses in Matthew 27:9-10 do not exactly match any Hebrew Bible text. The closest Hebrew Bible text is Zechariah 11:13. One immediate complication with this verse is that if it quotes Zechariah, why does the author attribute it to Jeremiah? This misattribution has been noted since the earliest days of Christianity, and a number of explanations have been given. Many scholars have accepted that this was simply a mistake on the part of the writer. Other arguments to preserve Biblical inerrancy are that Jeremiah was a shorthand to refer to any of the prophets. All these arguments are handwave and have no foundation.

Now we have proved that Matthew did not make a mistake in quoting the prophecy of Jeremiah. The correctness of Matthew concerning the prophecy of Jeremiah further demonstrates that the author of the Gospel of Matthew was a true disciple of Yeshua, who was the true witness of Yeshua's ministry and recorded the words of Yeshua exactly. We will also show that several other numerical prophecies of Yeshua recorded in the Gospel of Matthew were perfectly fulfilled in the events recorded in the Gospel of John and the book of Revelation. All these facts prove that the Gospel of Matthew, the Gospel of John, and the book of Revelation are the inspired Word of God.

The Gospel of Matthew is the earliest Gospel written by Matthew, one of the twelve disciples of Yeshua, as demonstrated in the Acts of Barnabas. The book of the Acts of Barnabas tells us that Mark and Barnabas used the Gospel of Matthew to preach after they departed from Paul. If the book of the Acts of Barnabas truly recorded the story of Barnabas, we may conclude that the Gospel of Mark was not the earliest Gospel but a short and modified version of the Gospel of Matthew.

CHAPTER 25

JEREMIAH'S PROPHECY ON 70 YEARS

In the first year of Nebuchadnezzar, the prophet Jeremiah foretold that the nation of Judah would fall to Nebuchadnezzar king of Babylon. He predicted that the city of Jerusalem and its temple would be destroyed, and that the Jews would be carried into Babylon. He also prophesized that the nation of Judah (as well as other nations) would serve the king of Babylon for 70 years (Jeremiah 25:11); after 70 years were completed at Babylon, God would bring the Jewish captives back to Jerusalem (Jeremiah 29:10).

This prophecy of the 70 years was fulfilled perfectly in the first exile of the Jews to Babylon in the spring of 606 BC and in the last exile in July of 587 BC. The first group of the Jews went back to Jerusalem in the spring of 536 BC in the first year of Cyrus. The last group went back to Jerusalem in the fall of 517 BC in the sixth year of Darius.

Detailed explanations

In the book of Ezra, we were told that the 70 years ended in the first year of Cyrus king of Persia (Ezra 1:1) and that the Jews arrived in Judah before the 7th month (Ezra 3:1). Since it took at least 4 months to travel from Babylon to Jerusalem by foot (Ezra 7:9), they should have left Babylon in the spring.

What does the first year of Cyrus mean? This cannot be the first year of Cyrus' reign over Persia because he was the Persian king long before he took Babylon in October of 538 BC (see Chapter 8). Therefore, the first year of Cyrus should refer to his sole reign over Babylon.

Darius the Mede is mentioned in the book of Daniel as the king of Babylon between Belshazzar and Cyrus the Great, but he is not known in history. Because of this, most scholars view Darius the Mede as literary fiction and even regard the book of Daniel as an apocalypse rather than a book of prophecy. They even speculate that Daniel the prophet of God never existed. They claim that the contents of the book form a cryptic allusion to the persecution of the Jews by the Syrian king Antiochus IV Epiphanes, and that the stories in chapters 1-6 are legendary in character, and that the visions of chapters 7-12 were added during the persecution of Antiochus. They even claimed that the book itself was completed after 164 BC. These absurd claims are completely disproved by the perfect fulfillments of all the past numerical prophecies recorded in the book (see our previous chapters).

In Daniel 6, there are two main historical figures, Darius the Mede, who was made king of Babylon, and Daniel who was appointed by Darius as the principal governor there. The problem is the name Darius because no ruler of Babylon was known by this name prior to the time of Darius I of Persia. It is stated in Daniel 5:31 that he was about 62 years old when he received the kingdom, and the kingdom which he received is identified as that of the Chaldeans (Daniel 9:1). The first year of his reign is written twice in verses 9:1 and 11:1, but no later regnal years are mentioned in any part of the book. He was apparently succeeded by Cyrus according to verse 11:1 since in the third year of Cyrus Daniel looked back to the first year of Darius. He was the son of Ahasuerus and the "seed of the Medes" (verse 9:1). Daniel 9:1 also tells us that he "was made" king over this realm, which clearly implies that a more powerful person appointed him to govern the kingdom of Babylon. According to ABC 7 (Nabonidus Chronicle), Ugbaru, the governor of Gutium (an area closely associated with Media in Babylonian sources), the commander of Mede-Persian troops that conquered Babylon, was appointed by Cyrus after Babylon was taken. He reigned in Babylon from October 18, 538 BC to November 13, 537 BC (see Chapter 8). He only reigned for 13 lunar months + 8 days. After Ugbaru died, Cambyses son of Cyrus did not become king of Babylon but was still the crown prince after Nisan 4 of 537 BC, as inferred from line iii. 24-27 of ABC 7. This historical record clearly indicates that Ugbaru the Mede was made king of Babylon by Cyrus. After Ugbaru died 13 months later, Cyrus became the king of Babylon and of Persia.

The above scenario was further supported by the titularies used in the datelines of economic documents written in Babylonia during that period. In these documents, the titles of kings went through three stages of development: 1) for Neo-Babylonian kings, "king of Babylon," 2) for early Persian kings, "king of Babylon, king of Lands," and 3) for later Persian kings, "king of Lands."

But there is one significant exception to this pattern, and that is the title used for Cyrus during his ascension year and first year. The titularies of tablets tell us that Cyrus only took the title "king of Lands" during his ascension year and for most of his first year of reign. Only in the later part of his first year was "king of Babylon" added to "king of Lands" in titularies of tablets dated to Cyrus. During the four months of his ascension year and the first ten months of his first year, Cyrus carried only the title "king of Lands" and did not carry the additional title "king of Babylon" in these written economic documents. This fact suggests that Cyrus was not the official king of Babylon during the first fourteen months after he took Babylon, but Ugbaru the Mede was the sole king of Babylon during this period. It is remarkable that the regnal length of 14 months derived from the written economic documents was very close to that of 13.2 months inferred from Nabonidus Chronicle. This consistency proves the true nature of history during that period.

Does Ugbaru the Mede match with Darius the Mede in the book of Daniel? Both are the seeds of Medes; both reigned in Babylon for about 14 months; both were made kings; and both were succeeded by Cyrus. The difference in their names should be understandable if Darius was his Persian throne name. Since he was originally a Median and eventually became a Persian king, it is likely that he changed his original Median name to a new Persian name. This is a common practice for many immigrants. The Bible also gives several examples of this practice. For example, the Assyrian king Tiglath-Pileser III was known by his throne name, but his original name was Pulu before he came to the throne (1 Chronicles 5:26, 2 Kings 15:19,29). The Assyrian king Shalmaneser V changed his original name of Ululayu to the Akkadian name Shalmaneser. He continued to use Ululayu for his throne name as king of Babylon, but this has not been found in any authentic official source. Since the throne name Darius was only used for about one year, the official document Nabonidus Chronicle only recorded his original name Ugbaru, which had been used for many years and was well known by the scribes. This naturally explains why historians do not know the throne name of Darius. Because Daniel was appointed to be the principal governor by this king and closely interacted with him, it is natural that Daniel recorded his lesser-known throne name.

Daniel tells us that Darius was the son of Ahasuerus (Daniel 9:1). The name of Ugbaru's father was not recorded in history, so we cannot prove or disprove whether Ugbaru was the son of Ahasuerus. It is known that Ahasuerus is a very popular Persian name. The ancient Zend writings say that in ancient times the Medes, Persians, and Bactrians were the same, having one common language, the Zend, and one religion. It is quite natural that Ugbaru's father has such a common name.

Furthermore, all the prophecies of Daniel have been fulfilled or are yet to be fulfilled, as we show in several separate chapters. The exact fulfillment of each prophecy is an acid test for any prophetic book. Only prophecies revealed by the Almighty God can be fulfilled exactly.

Above arguments lead us to conclude that Cyrus started to reign over Babylon from 13 November 537 BC. Since we know that some Jews started to leave from Babylon in the spring and in the first year of Cyrus, this event must have happened in the spring of 536 BC. In order for the Jews to complete their service to Babylonians for 70 years, they must have been carried into Babylon before the spring of 606 BC.

According to Daniel 1:1-4, Nebuchadnezzar besieged Jerusalem, took some of the articles of the house of God, and carried some young Jewish men into Babylon to serve him in the third year of Jehoiakim. Thus, the first group of the Jews were exiled to Babylon in the third year of Jehoiakim.

When was in the third year of Jehoiakim? The starting date of Jehoiakim's reign can be determined from the Battle of Megiddo (609 BC) recorded in 2 Kings 23:29 and 2 Chronicles 35:20-24 [see https://en.wikipedia.org/wiki/Battle_of_Megiddo_(609_BC)]. In the spring of 609 BC, the Egyptian Necho II personally led a sizable force to help the Assyrians. At the head of a large army, consisting mainly of his mercenaries, Necho II took the coastal route Via Maris into Syria and proceeded through the low tracts of Philistia and Sharon. He prepared to cross the ridge of hills but found that his way was blocked by the Judean army. Josiah king of Judah aligned with the Babylonians to block Necho's advance at Megiddo. There was a fierce battle during which Josiah was killed. Leaving a significant force behind, Necho II returned to Egypt. On his way back to Egypt, he found that Jehoahaz had been selected to succeed his father Josiah. Necho II deposed Jehoahaz and replaced with Jehoiakim and brought him back to Egypt as his prisoner (2 Kings 23:31; 2 Chronicles 36:1-4).

These passages clearly tell us that Jehoiakim started to reign before Necho II marched back to Egypt and after the end of the Battle of Megiddo (the battle started in June or July of 609 BC). The time when the Egyptian army returned to Egypt can be inferred from ABC 3 (Fall of Nineveh Chronicle) which states: "The seventeenth year [of Nabopolassar, 609 BC], in the month Du'ûzu [the fourth month], Aššur-uballit, king of Assyria, with a large army from Egypt crossed the river Euphrates and marched against Harran to conquer it. They captured [lacuna]. They defeated the garrison which the king of Akkad had stationed inside. When they had defeated it they encamped against Harran. Until the month Ulûlu [the 6th month] they did battle against the city but achieved nothing. The king of Akkad went to help his army but did not join battle. He went up to Izalla and the numerous cities in the mountains [lacuna] he set fire to their [lacuna]."

The above description suggests that the Battle of Megiddo should have ended before the 6th month and that Necho II appointed Jehoiakim as king of Judah in the beginning of the 6th month of 609 BC when he marched back to Egypt.

The fourth year of Jehoiakim was from Elul (the 6th month) of 606 BC to Elul of 605 BC when Nebuchadnezzar started to reign (Jeremiah 25:1). It is known that Nebuchadnezzar started his reign on Av 9 of 605 BC, which was between Elul of 606 BC and Elul of 605 BC, the fourth year of Jehoiakim. Thus, the third year of Jehoiakim was from Elul of 607 BC to Elul of 606 BC when Daniel and his friends were taken to Babylon (Daniel 1:1,3,6). In the second year of Nebuchadnezzar (between Av 9 of 604 BC and Av 8 of 603 BC), he had dreams (Daniel 2:1) and Daniel was called to interpret the dreams (Daniel 2:24-45) after he had stayed in Babylon for three years (Daniel 1:5,18). The passages in Daniel 1 and 2 imply that Daniel and his friends were carried into Babylon after Elul of 607 BC and before Av 8 of 606 BC. It most likely happened in Elul of 607 BC because Nebuchadnezzar made his first campaign in 607 BC and conquered all the mountains as far as the district of Urartu and returned to Babylon in the month of Elul (ABC 4: 5-12). Although Nebuchadnezzar was a crown prince at that time, the title of king in the Biblical text could refer to Nebuchadnezzar's future royal title.

Nebuchadnezzar returned to Babylon in the month of Elul and would have arrived in Babylon over the course of about 10 days on horseback. In contrast, the Jewish captives would go to Babylon on foot. It would have taken at least 4 months for them to arrive in Babylon (Ezra 7:9). It is likely that they arrived in Babylon to serve the Babylonians in the 11th/12th month of 607 BC, which was in the spring of 606 BC. From the spring of 606 BC to the spring of 536 BC, 70 years elapsed. Jeremiah's prophecy on the 70 years was perfectly fulfilled on the first group of the Jews who were carried into Babylon.

Jeremiah's prophecy on 70 years was also fulfilled upon the last group of the Jews being carried into Babylon. This group of the Jews were taken to Babylon when Jerusalem and the holy temple were destroyed in July of 587 BC. In the book of Ezra, we are told that the holy temple was finally rebuilt after Darius king of Persia issued a decree to allow the Jews to rebuild the temple. "Now the temple was finished on the third day of the month of Adar, which was in the 6th year of the reign of King Darius." (Ezra 6:15). We know that Darius started to reign on 4 February 521 BC (see Chapter 8). The sixth year of Darius was from the 11th lunar month of 517 BC to the 11th lunar month of 516 BC. Therefore, the temple was rebuilt on Adar 3 of 517 BC, which was in the spring of 516 BC. It is likely that Darius issued the decree around the fall of 517 BC and some of the Jews went back to Jerusalem to help rebuild the temple. From July of 587 BC to the fall of 517 BC, there were 70 years.

CHAPTER 26

ISAIAH'S PROPHECY ON THE BREAKING OF EPHRAIM IN 65 YEARS

During the days of Ahaz's sole reign, Rezin king of Syria and Pekah king of Israel went up to Jerusalem to make war but could not prevail against it. But the hearts of the people in Jerusalem were moved like the trees, moving with the wind. Then Yehowah God asked Isaiah to speak to Ahaz (Isaiah 7:4-8):

> [4] "Take heed, and be quiet; do not fear or be fainthearted for these two stubs of smoking firebrands, for the fierce anger of Rezin and Syria, and the son of Remaliah. [5] Because Syria, Ephraim, and the son of Remaliah have plotted evil against you, saying, [6] 'Let us go up against Judah and trouble it, and let us make a gap in its wall for ourselves, and set a king over them, the son of Tabel'— [7] thus says Yehowah God: "It shall not stand, nor shall it come to pass. [8] For the head of Syria is Damascus, and the head of Damascus is Rezin. **Sixty-five years Ephraim will be broken,** so that it will not be a people."

Isaiah's prophecy of sixty-five years for the breaking of Ephraim is the only numerical prophecy in the book of Isaiah. If this numerical prophecy were not fulfilled, many of his other descriptive prophecies would not be trustable.

When were the remnants of Israel (Ephraim) completely removed from the land of Israel? We are looking for a date when Ephraim, the northern tribe of Israel, was completely broken so that they were no longer a people (nation). If we can pin down the time of the complete removal, we can prove or disprove the only numerical prophecy of Isaiah.

The beginning time of the 65-year prophetic period should have been after Ahaz started his sole reign in the 17th year of Pekah king of Israel (2 Kings 16:1). According to the chronology of Judah and Israel's kings we have constructed above (see Chapter 11), Ahaz started his sole reign in the fall of 733 BC. Ahaz walked in the way of the kings of Israel, even making his son pass through the fire (2 Kings 16:3). Then Rezin king of Syria and Pekah king of Israel went up to Jerusalem to make war against Judah. Therefore, the beginning time of the 65-year prophetic period should have been in the fall of 733 BC.

Most Biblical scholars believe that the breaking of Ephraim coincided with the fall of the city of Samaria in the fall of 721 BC. If this were true, the prophetic period would be only 12 years and this numerical prophecy would not have been fulfilled. Then Isaiah would not be the true prophet of God.

If we carefully check the Hebrew Scriptures, we find that after the fall of Samaria, Ephraim was not completely broken yet. At the end of the 9th year of Hoshea, the king of Assyria took Samaria, and carried the children of Israel away to Assyria, and placed them in Halah, by the Habor, the River of Gozan, and in the cities of the Medes (2 Kings 17:6). Then the king of Assyria brought people from Babylon, Cuthan, Ava, Hamath, and from Sepharvaim, and placed them in the cities of Samaria (2 Kings 17:24). In the beginning of their dwelling in Samaria, they did not fear Yehowah. Therefore Yehowah sent lions among them, killing some of them (2 Kings 17:25`). After this, these foreigners were afraid of the God of Israel and spoke to the Assyrian king about the lions and the reason why this terror happened (2 Kings 17:25-26). Then the king commanded one of the Israel's priests to go back to Samaria and dwell there to teach the foreigners the rituals of the God of Israel (2 Kings 17:27). So one of Israeli priests came back to Samaria, dwelt in Bethel, and taught these foreigners how they should have feared the God of Israel (2 Kings 17:28).

Because this Israeli priest, along with his family and his companions, still dwelt in Samaria to teach the foreigners the rituals of the God of Israel, Ephraim was not completely broken after the fall of Samaria. These foreigners feared the God of Israel but served their own gods according to their own rituals (2 Kings 17:33,41). In contrast, the remnants of Israel did not fear the God of Israel although they were just brought back to teach the foreigners how to fear Him (2 Kings 17:34). They continued to practice their former rituals and did not follow the statutes, ordinances, laws, and commandments of God (2 Kings 17:34).

These passages consistently tell us that Ephraim was not completely broken after the king of Assyria took Samaria in the fall of 721 BC. This is because God brought back some Israelites to Samaria to teach the foreigners how to fear Him.

When were all the Israelites removed from Samaria? We can get an important clue from the book of Ezra (Ezra 4:1-2,10). When some of the Judean captives returned to Jerusalem from Babylon to rebuild the temple of God, their attempts were immediately frustrated by some Samarians (Ezra 4:1). These foreign immigrants were placed in Samaria by the two Assyrian kings, Esarhaddon (Ezra 4:2) and Asnappar (Ezra 4:10), many years after Samaria was taken by the Assyrians. This immigration process started from the fall of Samaria (721 BC) and continued until the later reign of Esarhaddon (681-669 BC) and the earlier reign of Asnappar (669-631 BC). Presumably, the foreign immigrants continued to move to Samaria until all the Israelites were completely removed from the city. Thus, the implication of Ezra 4:2,10 may be that some of the Israelites should have continued to live in Samaria till the earlier year or most likely the first year of Asnappar (Ashurbanipal), which was around 668 BC. From 733 BC to 668 BC, there were 65 years.

The exact year of the complete removal of the Israelites from the land of Israel may be hinted by the significance of the number 13 in prophecy. According to a book by Bullinger, the number 13 has a connection with "rebellion, apostasy, defection, corruption, disintegration." Both Ezekiel's 390 years and Isaiah's 65 years support his view. The 390 years (30×13) are for the iniquity and rebellion of Israel.

Isaiah's 65 year (5 × 13 years) prophetic period began in the fall of 733 BC when Israel-Ephraim attacked Judah. As discussed above, the period most likely ended in the fall of 668 BC, which was in the first year of Ashurbanipal, the last king of Assyria. Isaiah also prophesied that Ephraim would be completely broken by a king of Assyria counted from the day that Ephraim departed from Judah (Isaiah 7:17). This prophecy of Isaiah implies that there may be an amazing connection among the three dates of Ephraim's breaking, Ephraim's attacking Judah, and Ephraim's departure from Judah. From the chronology of Judah and Israel's kings (Chapter 11) we know that Ephraim departed from Judah in the fall of 941 BC. From the fall of 941 BC to the fall of 668 BC, there were 273 years = 21 × 13 years. From the fall of 941 BC to the fall of 733 BC, there were 208 years = 16 × 13 years. The three numbers of 273, 208, and 65 are the multiples of 13, suggesting that these events were related to the iniquity and rebellion of Ephraim-Israel.

CHAPTER 27

ZECHARIAH'S PROPHECY ON STRIKING DOWN THE LITTLE SHEEP

Zechariah prophesized about striking down the little sheep. The detailed prophecy was recorded in Zechariah 13:7-9:

> ⁷"Awake, sword, against my shepherd, against the man who is close to me!" declares Yehowah Almighty. "Strike the shepherd, and the sheep will be scattered, ⁸and I will turn my hand against the little ones. In all the land (the whole land)," declares Yehowah, "**two-thirds will be struck down and perish**; yet one-third will be left in it. This third I will put into the fire; ⁹I will refine them like silver and test them like gold. They will call on my name and I will answer them; I will say, 'They are my people,' and they will say, 'Yehowah is our God.'"

The declaration of the Almighty God: "Strike the shepherd, and the sheep will be scattered" was cited by Yeshua in Matthew 26:31 to confirm that this prophecy was fulfilled in himself and his disciples. Here, "the shepherd" refers to Yeshua himself and "the sheep" to his disciples. The original Hebrew phrase "all the earth" in verse 8 was translated into "all the land." "All the earth" does not necessarily mean the whole world. It could refer to a single piece of land.

Verse 8 prophesized about the little sheep after the prior prophecy (verse 7) was fulfilled. So the prophetic event in verse 8 must have taken place after 30 AD when Yeshua was crucified. Verse 8 says that two-thirds of the little sheep in the whole land will be killed, and one-third will be put into the fire for refinement. Verse 9 says that they will call on the name of Yehowah and Yehowah will answer them and call them His people. Therefore, the prophetic event in verse 8 shall take place right before God answers their prayers and calls them His people.

Ezekiel prophesized that the long desolated holy land would be re-populated by God's people who would be brought back from the sword (that is, from a war) and from the Gentile nations (Ezekiel 38:8). This prophecy of Ezekiel was precisely fulfilled in the re-establishment of the State of Israel on 14 May 1948. During World War II, about 6 million Jews in Europe were killed by German Nazis and some survivors of the holocaust were brought back to the holy land after the war.

Zechariah's prophecy also implies that the little sheep shall be struck down and perish by the sword during a war. The war Zechariah referred to cannot be the Jewish war that took place before the Jewish nation was destroyed by the Romans in 70 AD. During and after the Jewish war, God did not answer the prayers of the Jews, but instead destroyed the holy temple and Jerusalem and drove them into many nations. God did all these and hid His face from them because of their iniquity, transgressions, uncleanness, and unfaithfulness (Ezekiel 39:23-24). Ezekiel also prophesized that God hid His face from His people until they were brought back to the holy land (Ezekiel 39:28-29). As we have discussed in Chapter 17, God started to hide His face from the Jews in 30 AD after Yeshua was crucified. God restored His relationship with His people in 1948 when He brought them back to the holy land (Ezekiel 39:28-29). The total number of the years during which God hid His face from the Jews is $1,948 - 30 = 1,918 = 7 \times 274$.

The war Zechariah talked about must have been the second world war because after this war, God brought the children of Israel back to the long-desolated land and started to call them His people (Ezekiel 39:28-29). Furthermore, the population of the holy land on 15 May 1948 was exactly equal to the number prophesized by Ezekiel (see Chapter 22). It was the Almighty God who brought His people back to the holy land from the sword (Ezekiel 38:8). Therefore, the prophecy of Zechariah on the little sheep must have been fulfilled in the second world war.

In World War II, the German Nazis tried to destroy all the Jews in the world. This brutal holocaust appears to be the work of Satan who always wants to eliminate the Jews. Nevertheless, God did not completely stop Satan's evil plot and allowed him to kill two-thirds of the little sheep. God protected the remaining one third from being killed but refined them through the great suffering. After the refinement, God brought some survivors of the holocaust into the holy land and started to hear the prayers of His people. God has helped them win 6 major wars in the Middle East since He brought them back to the holy land in 1948. With the protection of God, they have dwelled there safely (Ezekiel 39:26).

How about the killed two thirds of the little sheep? God must have His own plan. Otherwise, He would not have let so many little sheep be killed by the evil Nazis. The slain little sheep should be among the "dry bones" described in Ezekiel 37. They appeared to be cut off like the shepherd Yeshua. Just as God raised Yeshua from his grave, He shall also bring the killed little sheep out of their graves and put His spirit into them (Ezekiel 37:12-14). They will be raised up and become an exceedingly great army (Ezekiel 37:10). The resurrected little sheep will live in the holy land after God shall destroy all the ungodly. Then God and his Messiah will reign over them in the holy land for evermore (Ezekiel 37:25-27).

Table XII: Annihilation of the Jewish Population of Europe in Pre-War Countries, Compiled by Lucy S. Dewildowicz

(*A Holocaust Reader*, Lucy S. Dewildowicz, page 381)

Country	Pre-war Jewish population	Estimated killed	Percent killed
Poland	3,300,000	3,000,000	90%
Baltic states	253,000	228,000	90%
Germany and Austria	240,000	210,000	90%
Bohemia and Moravia	90,000	80,000	89%
Slovakia	90,000	75,000	83%
Greece	70,000	54,000	77%
Netherlands	140,000	105,000	75%
Hungary	650,000	450,000	70%
Byelorussian SSR	375,000	245,000	65%
Ukrainian SSR	1,500,000	900,000	60%
Belgium	65,000	40,000	60%
Yugoslavia	43,000	26,000	60%
Romania	600,000	300,000	50%
Norway	1,800	900	50%
France	350,000	90,000	26%
Bulgaria	64,000	14,000	22%
Italy	40,000	8,000	20%
Luxembourg	5,000	1,000	20%
Russian SFSR	975,000	107,000	11%
Finland	2,000	?	?
Denmark	8,000	?	?
Total	8,861,800	5,933,900	67%

The land Zechariah talked about should have been the whole land of Europe where the holocaust took place. Only in this land were the Jews killed or put into the fire for the refinement through the great suffering and distress. The Jews outside this land were not considered in the prophecy because they were not killed nor put into the fire.

Indeed, the figures from Lucy Devidowicz (see Table XII) show that in the land of Europe, the German Nazis killed 67% of the Jews, which was indeed two-thirds of the Jews in the land of Europe at that time. Right after this holocaust, some remnants of the Jews were brought back to their own land and the nation of Israel was re-established on 14 May 1948. It is amazing that the nation of Israel can be resurrected after so many years (about 1,900 years) from its destruction. God is faithful and never breaks His words.

Table XIII: Annihilation of the Jewish Population of Europe in Pre-War Countries, Compiled by the Federal Agency for Civic Education of Germany (29 April 2018)

Country	Pre-war Jewish population	Estimated killed	Percent killed
Albania	200	100	50%
Austria	206,000	65,000	31.50%
Belgium	90,000	25,000	27.80%
Bulgaria	48,400	142	0.30%
Czechoslovakia	357,000	260,000	73%
Denmark	7,800	116	1.49%
Estonia	4,300	1,000	23%
Finland	2200	7	0.32%
France	300,000	76,000	25.33%
Germany	500,000	165,000	33%
Greece	70,000	58,800	84%
Hungary	445,000	270,000	60.70%
Italy	46,000	7,500	16.30%
Latvia	93,500	70,000	74.90%
Lithuania	150,000	145,000	96.70%
Luxembourg	3,600	1,200	33.30%
Netherlands	140,000	102,000	72.90%
Norway	1,800	758	42.10%
Poland	3,400,000	3,000,000	88.25%
Romania	757,000	287,000	38%
Russian SFSR	3,000,000	1,000,000	33.30%
Yugoslavia	68,500	60,000	87.60%
Total	9,689,500	5,594,623	57.74%

We also show the figures from the Federal Agency for Civic Education of Germany, which was published on 29 April 2018 (see Table XIII). The percentage of the killed Jews is 57.74%, significantly lower than 67% obtained earlier by Lucy Devidowicz. This discrepancy is due to the fact that the figures for Russian SFSR and Germany are not reliable in Table XIII. Since the Jewish population in Russian SFSR was over 30% of the total in Table XIII, any uncertainty of this figure can greatly change the average death percentage.

One important difference between the two tables is that Table XIII does not list Byelorussian SSR and Ukrainian SSR. Presumably, the figures of Russian SFSR in Table XIII should include the figures of Byelorussian SSR and Ukrainian SSR because they both were the parts of the former Soviet Union. If we add the Jewish populations of Byelorussian SSR, Ukrainian SSR, and Russian SFSR in Table XII, we find that the total Jewish population of these three regions is 2,850,000, which is 5.3% lower than the population of 3,000,000 for Russian SFSR in Table XIII. Therefore, it is very likely that the figures for Russian SFSR in Table XIII should be the figures summed over the three regions in Table XII.

The total number of the Jews killed in the three regions in Table XII is 1,252,000, which is 25% higher than 1,000,000 in Table XIII. Therefore, Table XIII's percentage (33.3%) of the killed Jews in these regions is 10.6% lower than Table XII's percentage (43.9%). From the website: https://en.wikipedia.org/wiki/The_Holocaust, we find that the number of the Jews killed in the former Soviet Union is about 1,300,000 and that the Jewish population in this region is 3,020,000. The percentage of the Jews killed in this region is calculated to be 43.0%, which is very close to Table XII's percentage (43.9%). We thus conclude that the death percentage in Table XIII is unreliable and must be corrected.

It is unclear whether the Federal Agency for Civic Education of Germany tried to mislead the world by significantly underestimating the death percentage of the German Jews or made an honest mistake. The Jewish population in Germany in 1933 was 523,000-525,000. But by the end of 1938, approximately half the German Jewish population had left Germany. So, the total Jewish population in Germany was about

250,000 at the end of 1938. Between November 1933 and December 1939, about 53,000 German Jews immigrated to Palestine. So by 1941 when the holocaust started, the Jewish population in Germany should have been about 200,000. Since the number of killed Jews in Germany was 165,000, the death percentage is calculated to be about 82.5%, which is close to 87.5% for both Germany and Austria listed in Table XII. Because the death percentage for the German Jews in Table XIII is calculated from the German Jewish population in 1933 (rather than in 1941), the number (33%) is misleading. The same mistake was made for the Austrian Jews.

CHAPTER 28

PROPHECY OF MOSES ON THE AGES OF THE WORLD AND THE UNIVERSE

In Psalm 90:4, Moses prays: "A thousand years in your sight are like a day that has just gone by, or like a watch in the night." This verse appears to be a figurative speech concerning the time in God's sight. This seems to indicate that God exists from eternity to eternity and is thus timeless. But when the author of this book mediated on this verse, he had a feeling that it might be related to the ages of the world and the universe, which Moses learned from God. In a poetic form, "day" in the first half of this verse should refer to the daytime to form a contrast to "night" in the last half. The Hebrew word "day" originally means the daytime. In John 11:9-10, Yeshua answered, "Are there not twelve hours in the day? If anyone walks in the day, he does not stumble, because he sees the light of this world. But if one walks in the night, he stumbles, because the light is not in him." In verse 9, Yeshua confirms that there are twelve hours in a day. Here, the word "day" must mean the daytime because he talked about the night in verse 10 to form a contrast to the "day" in verse 9.

How many years should have passed from the creation of the world to the coming of the Messianic Kingdom. According to the Biblical chronology, there are 6,000 solar years (Chapter 10). The world was created by God in the spring of 3970 BC. 6,000 solar years shall have passed from the creation of the world to the beginning of the Messianic Kingdom according to God's clock. On the other hand, when we use the human clock (e.g., an atomic clock) to measure the same period, it would be much longer if the tick rate of the atomic clock were to slow down over time. Indeed, we have experimentally demonstrated that the tick rate of the atomic clock, which is intrinsically proportional to the speed of light, slows down over time (see Appendix B).

If the speed of light was extremely large before the fourth day of the creation week in Genesis, the atomic clock should have ticked extremely quickly. On and after the fourth day, God should have slowed down both the speed of light and atomic clocks so that humans should have seen the world similarly to what we see today.

Before we provide our interpretation to the prophetic words of Psalm 90:4, let's review the creation week of God, which is recorded in Genesis 1:1-39:

> [1]In the beginning God created the heavens and the earth. [2]The earth was without form, and void; and darkness was on the face of the deep. And the Spirit of God was hovering over the face of the waters. [3]Then God said, "Let there be light"; and there was light. [4]And God saw the light, that it was good; and God divided the light from the darkness. [5]God called the light Day, and the darkness He called Night. So the evening and the morning were the first day. [6]Then God said, "Let there be a firmament in the midst of the waters, and let it divide the waters from the waters." [7]Thus God made the firmament, and divided the waters which were under the firmament from the waters which were above the firmament; and it was so. [8]And God called the firmament Heaven. So the evening and the morning were the second day. [9]Then God said, "Let the waters under the heavens be gathered together into one place, and let the dry land appear"; and it was so. [10]And God called the dry land Earth, and the gathering together of the waters He called Seas. And God saw that it was good. [11]Then God said, "Let the earth bring forth grass, the herb that yields seed, and the fruit tree that yields fruit according to its kind, whose seed is in itself, on the earth"; and it was so. [12]And the earth brought forth

grass, the herb that yields seed according to its kind, and the tree that yields fruit, whose seed is in itself according to its kind. And God saw that it was good. [13]So the evening and the morning were the third day. [14]Then God said, "Let there be lights in the firmament of the heavens to divide the day from the night; and let them be for signs and seasons, and for days and years; [15]and let them be for lights in the firmament of the heavens to give light on the earth"; and it was so. [16]Then God made two great lights: the greater light to rule the day, and the lesser light to rule the night. He made the stars also. [17]God set them in the firmament of the heavens to give light on the earth, [18]and to rule over the day and over the night, and to divide the light from the darkness. And God saw that it was good. [19]So the evening and the morning were the fourth day. [20]Then God said, "Let the waters abound with an abundance of living creatures, and let birds fly above the earth across the face of the firmament of the heavens." [21]So God created great sea creatures and every living thing that moves, with which the waters abounded, according to their kind, and every winged bird according to its kind. And God saw that it was good. [22]And God blessed them, saying, "Be fruitful and multiply, and fill the waters in the seas, and let birds multiply on the earth." [23]So the evening and the morning were the fifth day. [24]Then God said, "Let the earth bring forth the living creature according to its kind: cattle and creeping thing and beast of the earth, each according to its kind"; and it was so. [25]And God made the beast of the earth according to its kind, cattle according to its kind, and everything that creeps on the earth according to its kind. And God saw that it was good. [26]Then God said, "Let Us make man in Our image, according to Our likeness; let them have dominion over the fish of the sea, over the birds of the air, and over the cattle, over all the earth and over every creeping thing that creeps on the earth." ²⁷So God created man in His own image; in the image of God He created him; male and female He created them. ²⁸Then God blessed them, and God said to them, "Be fruitful and multiply; fill the earth and subdue it; have dominion over the fish of the sea, over the birds of the air, and over every living thing that moves on the earth." ²⁹And God said, "See, I have given you every herb that yields seed which is on the face of all the earth, and every tree whose fruit yields seed; to you it shall be for food. ³⁰Also, to every beast of the earth, to every bird of the air, and to everything that creeps on the earth, in which there is life, I have given every green herb for food"; and it was so. ³¹Then God saw everything that He had made, and indeed it was very good. So the evening and the morning were the sixth day.

In the second chapter of the book of Genesis, the first three verses are also related to the creation week (Genesis 2: 1-3):

¹Thus the heavens and the earth, and all the host of them, were finished. ²And on the seventh day God ended His work which He had done, and He rested on the seventh day from all His work which He had done. ³Then God blessed the seventh day and sanctified it, because in it He rested from all His work which God had created and made.

Genesis 1:1 clearly says that in the very beginning God created the heavens and the earth. The word "create" means "bring something into existence." God brought the heavens and the earth into existence in the beginning of the universe. In the second verse, it was stated that the earth was without form and it was void and had no light. Before the first day, the earth was covered by waters and there was no dry land.

The Spirit of God was hovering over the face of the waters on the first day of His creation week. In verse 3, God said, "let there be light" and there was light. It is likely that God might have initiated nuclear fusion in some stars like the Sun and some planets. These bright stars and/or planets were able to luminate the earth to separate day from night. On the second day, God made the firmament (atmosphere), seas, lands, and mountains on the earth. The word "make" means "do something for," which is different from the word "create." It is possible that God initiated tectonic movement processes to form the dry lands, mountains, and seas on the earth. On the third day, God brought forth grass, herbs that yield seeds, and fruit trees that yield fruits. On the fourth day, God made the Sun, the Moon, and the other stars. Just like the Earth, these heavenly bodies had already existed before the first day of the creation week. On the fourth day, God may have perfected them and placed them at optimal positions so that the conditions on the earth should have been perfect for every living creature on the earth. Having made the Sun and the Moon perfect in the fourth day, God created the living creatures in the sky and seas on the fifth day. On the sixth day God created the living creatures on the earth and created man in His own image. On the seventh day, God ended His creation work and rested. God blessed the seventh day and sanctified it.

From the creation sequence, we can see that the solar system had already existed before the first day of the creation week. The other eight planets revolving around the Sun had already existed but did not emit light. The waters had already existed before the Spirit of God was hovering above the surface of the waters on the first day. The radiometric dating of the meteorites from the solar system consistently indicate that the ages of the meteorites are 4.566 billion years [J. Baker et al., Nature **436**, 1127 (2005)]. The first day of the creation week should have been less than 4.566 billion years ago.

One of the oldest detrital zircons from Jack Hills of Western Australia was radiometrically dated as 4.404 billion years ago [S. A. Wilde et al., Nature **409**, 175 (2001)]. This suggests the existence of the continental crust of the earth about 4.404 billion years ago. The oxygen isotope ratios found in the oldest detrital zircon also imply the existence of the continental oceans (waters) about 4.404 billion years ago. Since the waters had already existed before the first day of the creation week and the oceans were made on the third day, the age of the world may be about 4.400 billion years.

According to Moses, 1,000 years in God's sight are like a daytime that has just gone by. A daytime is equal to half a day when the day and night have the same length at the Vernal and Autumnal Equinoxes. If Moses referred to the daytime at the Equinoxes, then 1/2 day (12 hours) in God's clock is equivalent to 1,000 years in the human clock, or a whole day (24 hours) in God's clock is equivalent to 2,000 years in the human clock. Since the world was created about 6,000 years ago according to the Biblical chronology (in God's clock), this first equivalence principle of Moses implies that the age of the world should be about 6,000 × 365.24 × 2,000 years = 4.383 billion years according to the human clock, which is in excellent agreement with the radiometrically dated age of the earth.

Moses also said that 1,000 years in God's sight are also like a night watch. This second equivalence principle of Moses implies that a night watch in God's clock is equivalent to 1,000 years in the human clock. We know that a whole day is equal to 8 night-watches at the Equinoxes. But at the Winter Solstice, the night is longest, and one night-watch in Israel is equal to 3.496 hours at present and 4.0 hours at the beginning of the world (Enoch 72:26). If the night length decreases linearly with time, one night-watch in Israel is calculated to be 3.79 hours in the time of Moses (around 1457 BC). Then, the whole day (24 hours) is equal to 6.33 night-watches at the Winter Solstice in the time of Moses. If Moses referred to the longest night-watch in his time, the second equivalence principle of Moses suggests that a whole day in God's clock should be equal to 6,330 years in the human clock. Since God created the heavens and the earth (the universe) about 6,000 years ago in terms of His clock, this second equivalence principle of Moses implies that the age of the universe should be about 6,000 × 365.24 × 6,330 years = 13.87 billion years in terms of the human clock. It is remarkable that the age of the universe inferred from our modified cosmological model is very close to 7^{12} years = 13.84 billion years (see Appendix C). Within the standard Lambda-CDM concordance model, the age of the universe was calculated to be 13.799±0.021 billion years in 2015 (see https://en.wikipedia.org/wiki/Age_of_the_universe). In both models, the age of the universe is close to 13.8 billion years, in excellent agreement with 13.87 billion years inferred from Psalm 90:4.

Moses' two equivalence principles about the relativity of time in Psalm 90:4 are thus the prophetic words about the ages of both the world and the universe in terms of the human clock. According to our Biblical chronology (see Chapter 10) or in God's absolute clock, the ages of both the world and the universe are about 6,000 years, but in the human clock, they are about 4.4 and 14 billion years, respectively.

The radiometrically dated age is proportional to the lifetimes of the radioactive elements, which should be inversely proportional to the speed of light. When the speed of light should have approached infinity before the fourth day, the lifetimes of the radioactive elements should have been very short. If this is the case, the very long time of the world before the fourth day, which is measured by various radioactive elements with the present lifetimes, should have been just a few days in terms of God's absolute clock.

We have shown that both the speed of light and the atomic clock are slowing down with time (see Appendix B). About twenty years ago, some cosmologists proposed a theory of varying speed of light [J. Magueiyo, Rep. Prog. Phys. **66**, 2025 (2003)]. In order to resolve the horizon problem usually tackled by inflation, they assumed that the speed of light should have approached infinity at the very beginning of the universe. In a similar manner, we propose that the speed of light should have approached infinity prior to the fourth day in which God placed the Sun, the Moon, and other planets around the earth at the optimal positions to mark the seasons, days, and years. God may have very quickly slowed down the speed of light and the atomic clock before that day. The slow-down rate should have become negligibly small on and after the fourth day.

PART IV
PROOF FOR YESHUA BEING THE MESSIAH

CHAPTER 29

INTRODUCTION TO THE TRUE MESSIAH

Yeshua himself claimed to be the Son of God, the Son of Man, and the Messiah according to the Gospel of Matthew. The Gospel of John and the book of Revelation tell us that Yeshua is the incarnation of the Word of God who was with God in the beginning even before the creation of the world. To prove Yeshua to be the Messiah, the Gospels and some writings of his disciples must be in perfect agreement with the Scriptures in the Hebrew Bible, which we have proved to be the true Word of God by demonstrating the perfect fulfillments of all the numerical prophecies (see Part III).

We will not discuss any other New Testament writing that is not directly from his disciples for the following reasons. First, these writings do not directly record the words and acts of Yeshua. Second, we cannot unambiguously prove the identities of the authors who wrote the New Testament epistles.

For the above reasons, we only focus on the Gospel of Matthew, the Gospel of John, and the book of Revelation, which are generally believed to be written by the disciples of Yeshua. If these three books are in perfect agreement with the Scriptures in the Hebrew Bible and all the prophecies of Yeshua recorded in these books are fulfilled exactly, then these books must be truthful and inspired by God just as the Hebrew Bible. After this conclusion is well established, then any other writing that is not consistent with the teachings in these three books must be treated with caution.

The Messiah must be the Son of Man according to Daniel's vision (Daniel 7:13-14), "I was watching in the night visions, and behold, one like the Son of Man, coming with the clouds of heaven! He came to the Ancient of Days, and they brought him near before Him. Then to him was given dominion and glory and a kingdom, that all peoples, nations, and languages should serve him. His dominion is an everlasting dominion, which shall not pass away, and his kingdom the one which shall not be destroyed."

The Son of Man came to the Ancient of Days (God the Father) and was given dominion and glory and a kingdom, which is everlasting. All peoples, nations, and languages should serve him. These verses tell us that the Son of Man is the Messiah, who is the king of kings and the lord of the lords on the earth.

The Messiah must be the Son of God according to Psalm 2:

> [1]Why do the nations rage, and the people plot a vain thing? [2]The kings of the earth set themselves, and the rulers take counsel together, against Yehowah and against His Messiah, saying, [3]"Let us break their bonds in pieces and cast away their cords from us." [4]He who sits in the heavens shall laugh; Yehowah shall hold them in derision. [5]Then He shall speak to them in His wrath, and distress them in His deep displeasure: [6]"Yet I have set My King On My holy hill of Zion." [7]"I will declare the decree: Yehowah has said to me, '**you are My Son, today I have begotten you.** [8]Ask of me, and I will give you the nations for your inheritance, and the ends of the earth for your possession. [9]You shall break them with a rod of iron; You shall dash them to pieces like a potter's vessel.'" [10]Now therefore, be wise, O kings; Be instructed, you judges of the earth. [11]Serve Yehowah with fear, and rejoice with trembling. [12]**Kiss the Son**, lest he be angry, and you perish in the way, when his wrath is kindled but a little. **Blessed are all those who put their trust in him.**

Psalm 2:7 clearly tells us the Messiah is the Son of God. The Son of God will rule the nations with a rod of iron and shall dash the rulers on the earth to pieces like potter's vessel. All the kings and judges of the earth must be wise, be instructed, serve Yehowah with fear, rejoice with trembling, and kiss the Son. If they do not respect the Son and if his wrath is kindled only a little, they will thus perish. Blessed are all those who put their trust in the Son.

Therefore, the Hebrew Bible teaches us that the titles: the Son of Man, the Son of God, and the Messiah are given to the same being. If Yeshua is the Messiah, he is also the Son of Man and the Son of God. The Gospels of Matthew and John agree with the teachings of the Hebrew Bible. Matthew recorded Yeshua's statement that there is only one teacher the Messiah (Matthew 23:8). John also stated (John 1:17): "For the law was given through Moses, but grace and truth came through Yeshua Messiah." Therefore, only the Messiah is the true teacher and only his interpretation of the Hebrew Bible is truthful.

In order to unambiguously prove that Yeshua is the true Messiah, all the numerical prophecies about the Messiah in the Hebrew Bible must be perfectly fulfilled in Yeshua and all the numerical prophecies foretold by Yeshua himself must also be fulfilled exactly. If Yeshua were a false messiah, none of his prophecies would be fulfilled.

We have shown that the 70-week prophecies in Daniel 9:26-27 were perfectly fulfilled in Yeshua (Chapters 16 and 17). We have further shown that Ezekiel's 40-day prophecy on the destruction of Jerusalem was also fulfilled perfectly in Yeshua (Chapter 23). These are the numerical prophecies. No one would be able to fabricate stories about Yeshua to perfectly match these numerical prophecies. This is because the writers in the time of the Messiah (2,000 years ago) could not have figured out the exact starting times of the prophecies if they had not been inspired by God. In the following chapters, we will show that all the numerical prophecies foretold by Yeshua himself were fulfilled perfectly. The perfect fulfillments of Yeshua's own prophecies prove that he is the true Messiah.

In addition to the perfect fulfillments of these numerical prophecies, there are other descriptive prophecies in the Hebrew Bible (e.g., the books of Isaiah and Zechariah). Many rabbis in modern Israel still do not believe these clear descriptive prophecies on the Messiah. They attempt to provide alternative interpretations to the prophecies, which appear reasonable but are not correct and self-consistent. In the following chapters, we will also present some descriptive prophecies on the Messiah in the Hebrew Bible to see if Yeshua is the true Messiah foretold by these prophets of God.

CHAPTER 30

YESHUA MESSIAH FROM SOME DESCRIPTIVE PROPHECIES

All Christians believe that the prophecy on the sin-bearing servant in Isaiah 53 was fulfilled in Yeshua about 2,000 years ago. This prophecy has been used to prove that Yeshua is the true Messiah. However, many of the modern Jewish rabbis interpret the sin-bearing servant in Isaiah 53 as the nation of Israel. They believe that Yeshua is not the sin-bearing servant and cannot be their Messiah.

Sin-bearing servant in Isaiah 53

It is impossible that the sin-bearing servant in Isaiah 53 is the nation of Israel. If the sin-bearing servant in Isaiah 53 were the nation of Israel, how is it possible that the nation of Israel would be buried with the wicked and with the rich (Isaiah 53:9)? It is obvious that this sin-bearing servant is a single person and does not represent the nation of Israel. In the previous chapters of the book of Isaiah, God calls Israel his servant and witnesses (Isaiah 43:10). Here, the word "servant" has singular form but represents the people of Israel (plural meaning) because the parallel word "witnesses" has plural form. In Isaiah 53, the sin-bearing servant has singular form and singular meaning. Similarly, the Hebrew word "seed" has singular form in Genesis 13:16 but plural meaning: descendants. But in Genesis 3:15, the word "seed" has singular form and singular meaning because the singular pronouns "he" and "his" are used together.

In Isaiah 49:3, a servant whose name is called Israel is declared. It is this verse that causes the modern Jewish rabbis to misattribute the sin-bearing servant in Isaiah 53 to the nation of Israel or Jacob. This servant Israel cannot refer to Jacob because God had hidden this servant (Isaiah 49:2) until the time of Isaiah while Jacob had been known a long time before Isaiah. At the time of the prophecy, God made this hidden servant known. This servant will bring Jacob back to Yehowah God (Isaiah 49:5), raise up the tribes of Jacob, and restore the preserved ones of Israel (Isaiah 49:6). If this servant were Jacob, how would verses 5 and 6 make sense? This servant will also be the light of the Gentiles and bring the salvation of God to the ends of the earth (Isaiah 49:6).

This servant is called Israel by God just as many Jews in modern Israel are called "Israel." The same name for multiple persons is very common in many cultures. There are many Joshua's and Peter's in the United States.

Why does God also call this servant Israel? The name of an Israelite has a special meaning. For example, Moses called Hosea, the son of Nun, Yehoshua. Hosea means salvation and Yehoshua (Joshua) means "Yehowah is salvation." Yehoshua became a regent of Yehowah on the earth, who led the Israelites and brought them into the promised land of God.

Jacob was called "Israel" after he wrestled with the angel of God. For a meaning of the name Israel, NOBSE Study Bible Name List and BDB Theological Dictionary unanimously go with the verb "שרה" of which the meaning is unsure. NOBSE reads God Strives, and BDB proposes El Persists or El Perseveres. Israel is a compound name of El Sarah, which means "he will rule as God." Alfred Jones thinks that the mysterious verb "שרה" might very well mean "to be princely," and assumes that the name Israel consists of a future form of this verb, which hence would mean to become princely. So, Jones interprets the name Israel as "he will be prince with God."

If Israel could mean "he will rule as God" or "he will be prince with God," Israel could be a name of the Messiah who will co-reign with God in the Kingdom of God on the earth. The Messiah is the prince of God and will co-reign with God forever. Therefore, the Son of Man, the Son of God, the Messiah, Yeshua, Israel, the Lamb of God, and the Word of God should all refer to the same being who is the only begotten Son of God.

The angel (messenger) of God who bears the Name of Yehowah in the books of Moses and the mighty angel (messenger) of God in the book of Revelation are also the only begotten Son of God. The Son who bears the Name of his Father is the special messenger of God in both "Old" and "New" Testaments. He is the regent of God and speaks and acts on behalf of God the Father. Yeshua said (John 1:18): "No one has seen God at any time. The only begotten Son, who is in the bosom of the Father, has declared Him." Yeshua's teaching is consistent with the books of Moses. According to both Moses and Yeshua, Abraham, Isaac, Jacob, and Moses did not actually see God the Father, but the Messenger (the Son) of God.

The sin-bearing servant is the prince of [new] Israel, who will bear the sins of the tribes of [old] Israel and restore the preserved ones of [old] Israel. Hosea the prophet rebuked the great sins of [old] Israel and prophesized in Hosea 10:15 and 11:1, "Thus, it shall be done to you, O Bethel, because of your great wickedness. At dawn the king of [old] Israel shall be cut off utterly. For a child Israel, I shall love him, and out of Egypt I shall call my son." These two verses should not be placed in different chapters because they belong to a complete prophecy of God. The verbs "be done," "be cut," and "call" in these two verses are all in perfect tense while the verb "love" is in consecutive imperfect tense. The tense in the NKJV of Hosea 10:15 is correct because the perfect tense in Hebrew language can be used as future tense to express assurance about the action being expressed by the verb. Thus, its use is to emphasize assurance about whatever is being expressed in the sense that the "completeness" of that event is an assured conviction and truth. This is especially true when a prophet of God spoke prophecy, which must be fulfilled in a future date. That is why the verbs in Isaiah 9:6 are in perfect tense in Hebrew, but they are changed to future tense in NKJV. In Hosea 11:1, the verb "love" is in consecutive imperfect tense, which directly points to the future tense. Then the other verbs in perfect tense are consistently attributed to future tense because they are consecutive to the verb "love," which is in future tense. The same grammar structure is also found in Isaiah 9:6 where Isaiah prophesied the birth of a child in a future time. In this verse, two verbs are in consecutive imperfect tense and all the others are in perfect tense, meaning that all the actions must be taken in a future time.

With the correct tense of Hosea 11:1, we can understand that God will love the new child whose name is also called Israel, and He will also call him out of Egypt. In the time of Hosea, the prophet knew that [old] Israel had been already inflicted by the Egyptians for about 400 years and God had brought them out of Egypt. If the new child Israel in Hosea 11:1 were Jacob, it is meaningless to prophesize something that had already happened. In both verses, Hosea simply prophesized that the king of [old] Israel shall be cut off completely because of the great wickedness while the everlasting prince whose name is also called Israel shall be called out of Egypt. This prophecy was fulfilled in Yeshua, the prince of [new] Israel (Matthew 2:15). The prince of [new] Israel will restore the preserved remnants of [old] Israel and bring God's salvation to the ends of the earth (Isaiah 49:6). God has also made his mouth like a sharp sword (Isaiah 49:2) and he will strike the nations with the sharp sword out of his mouth (Revelation 19:15). He will rule the nations with a rod of iron (Revelation 19:15; Psalm 2:9). Therefore, Hosea and Isaiah both prophesized that the servant of God, whose name is called Israel, would be called out of Egypt, bear the sin of the people of God, become the light of the Gentiles, and bring God's salvation to all the nations. Matthew correctly understood the prophecy and attributed this sin-bearing servant to Yeshua Messiah (Matthew 2:15). The angel of God who spoke to John called himself fellow servant of God (Revelation 22:9). We will show in Chapter 33 that the angel of God is actually Yeshua Messiah who serves God to execute His Word faithfully. He called his disciples as his brethren even after he resurrected (Matthew 28:10) and received all the authority in heaven and on earth (Matthew 28:18). He is the humble servant of God, and we shall all follow him.

Misinterpretation of Isaiah 9:6

God's only begotten Son, who exercises God's power on behalf of his Father, who is the counselor of God Almighty the Everlasting Father (Isaiah 9:6), who is the prince of peace (Isaiah 9:6).

Isaiah 9:6 has been mistranslated into every language. Here we provide the verse from a Hebrew Interlinear Bible (Scripture 4 All):

> That boy he-is-born to us son he-is-given to us and she-shall-become the chieftainship on shoulder-blade-of him and he-shall-call name-of him one-marvelous one-counseling El masterful Father-of-future chief-of well-being.

When we add punctuation, the verse reads:

> That boy he-is-born to us, son he-is-given to us, and she-shall-become the chieftainship on shoulder-blade-of him, and he-shall-call name-of him one-marvelous, one-counseling El masterful Father-of-future, chief-of well-being.

If we accept this interlinear translation, we can re-phrase this verse as:

> A boy is born unto us, a son is given unto us, and the government shall be upon his shoulder. And his name shall be called the wonderful, the counselor of God Almighty the Everlasting Father, and the prince of peace.

The phrase "one-counseling El masterful Father-of-future" should mean "the one who will counsel El masterful Father-of-future," that is, the counselor of God Almighty the Everlasting Father.

Another Hebrew Interlinear Bible for Isaiah 9:6 reads:

> For a child is born unto us a son is given unto us and will be the government upon his shoulder and will be called his name wonderful counselor God Almighty Everlasting Father prince of peace.

Here, "counselor" should be "counseling" because this verb is in the participle form. By adding punctuation and changing "counselor" to "counseling," we finally rephrase this verse as:

> A child is born unto us, a son is given unto us, and the government shall be upon his shoulder. And his name shall be called **the wonderful** counseling God Almighty the Everlasting Father, and **the prince of peace**.

Both interlinear versions tell us that the Son is called **the wonderful who counsels God the Father, and the prince of peace**. The Son is **the counselor** of God Almighty the Everlasting Father and **the prince of peace**. The Son will co-reign with his Father in the everlasting Kingdom of God. The Son is not the same as the God Almighty Yehowah. The Son is the Messenger of God, who bears the Name of Yehowah. The God Almighty, the Ancient of Days, or Yehowah God is **unbegotten** (Revelation 1:4,8) while the Son is **begotten**. The Father and the Son are not equal, as Daniel clearly told us in Daniel 7:13-14.

Some rabbis in modern Israel interpret the child in Isaiah 9:6 as referring to Hezekiah king of Judah. No human has been called "God Almighty Everlasting Father." If the Messiah who is the king of kings and the lord of lords on the earth cannot be called "God Almighty Everlasting Father," how could an earthly king have more privilege than the everlasting prince of God (the Messiah)? The title "God" (meaning the god) is reserved for the heavenly Father only. Because Christians called their Messiah "God Almighty Everlasting Father" due to mistranslation (misinterpretation) of Isaiah 9:6, the rabbis were angry and mocked them as being ignorant. Yet in a similar manner, the rabbis blaspheme God when they refer to Hezekiah king of Judah as "God Almighty Everlasting Father." Yeshua declared (Matthew 23:9): "Do not call anyone on the earth your father; for One is your Father, He who is in heaven." Only the Father in heaven is called Everlasting Father. Yeshua also declared that my Father is greater than I (John 14:28). Yeshua's teaching is perfectly truthful.

Isaiah's prophecy on the time of a virgin birth

During the days of Ahaz's sole reign in the fall of 733 BC (see Chapter 11), Rezin king of Syria and Pekah king of Israel, went up to Jerusalem to make war against Judah, but could not prevail against it. But the hearts of the people in Jerusalem were moved like the trees moving with the wind. Then Yehowah God asked Isaiah to speak to Ahaz (Isaiah 7:4-8), "Take heed, and be quiet; do not fear or be fainthearted for these two stubs of smoking firebrands, for the fierce anger of Rezin and Syria, and the son of Remaliah. Because Syria, Ephraim, and the son of Remaliah have plotted evil against you, saying, 'Let us go up against Judah and trouble it, and let us make a gap in its wall for ourselves, and set a king over them, the son of Tabel'— thus says Yehowah God: 'It shall not stand, nor shall it come to pass. For the head of Syria is Damascus, and the head of Damascus is Rezin. Sixty-five years Ephraim will be broken, so that it will not be a people…'"

Pekah king of Israel wanted to take over Judah to reign over the whole land of Israel. Yehowah God does not allow this to happen because He has His own plan. His plan is that the Messiah He has chosen will reign the whole nation of Israel, and that both the northern and southern kingdoms of Israel will be broken. The northern kingdom Ephraim will be broken in 65 years and the southern kingdom Judah will be broken a little later.

When Ahaz refused to ask Yehowah God for a sign, He gave Ahaz a sign (Isaiah 7:14-16):

> Behold, the virgin shall conceive and bear a son, and shall call his name Immanuel. Curds and honey he shall eat, that he may know to refuse the evil and choose the good. **For before the child shall know to refuse the evil and choose the good, the land that you dread will be forsaken from the faces of two of her kings.**

The prophecy on the virgin birth was interpreted by Matthew to be the birth of Yeshua. If this interpretation were incorrect, the foundation of Yeshua's faith would be completely collapsed. Most modern Jewish rabbis strongly criticize this interpretation because they believe that this child is not the Messiah and the Hebrew word "עַלְמָה (almah)" should not be translated into "virgin."

The Hebrew word "עַלְמָה" means "a young woman" or "virgin." God wanted to give a sign to Ahaz when He foretold a child's birth. If a young woman gives birth of a male child, it is not a sign at all. Any normal young woman can give birth to a male child. From the context, the best meaning of the word "עַלְמָה" is "virgin."

A crucial question arises as to when the child shall be born. The child cannot be the newborn son of Isaiah because his son's name was called "Maher-Shalal-Hash-Baz." (Isaiah 8:3) rather than "Immanuel." Isaiah prophesized that before the child (the son of Isaiah) would have knowledge to cry his father and mother, the riches of Damascus and the possessions of Samaria would be taken away to the face of the king of Assyria (Isaiah 8:4).

Before Ahaz died in the fall of 727 BC, the king of Assyria went up against Damascus and took it, carried its people to Kir, and killed Rezin (2 Kings 16:9). In 730 BC, Hoshea became king of Israel and did evil in the sight of God (2 Kings 17:1-2). Shalmaneser king of Assyria came up against him and Hoshea became his vassal and paid him tribute money (2 Kings 17:3). The prophecy of Isaiah about his own son was fulfilled in these events that happened in 730 BC when his son was about two years old.

When should the virgin have given her birth? The child conceived by the virgin must have been born after the land that Ahaz dreaded had been forsaken from the faces of two of her kings (Isaiah 7:16). What is the land that Ahaz dreaded? The land could not have been a city because the land had kings. The land could not have been the land of the northern Israel because it was disowned once from the face of one king (Hoshea) in 721 BC. Therefore, this prophecy of Isaiah means that the child would be born after Syria had been disowned twice from the faces of her two separated kings.

The land of Syria was first taken by the Assyrians from the face of Rezin king of Syria in 730 BC. This was the first time that the land was disowned from the face of one of her kings. The land was then governed by kings of Assyria until 605 BC. It fell into the hands of Pharaoh Necho II after 605 BC. In 572 BC, the land of Syria was conquered by Neo-Babylonians. In the 4th century BC, the land was taken by Alexander the Great and eventually fell into the hands of the Seleucid Empire. Then Itureans rose their power in the declining period of the Seleucid Empire in the second century BC. They dominated vast stretches of Syrian territory and even penetrated the northern parts of Israel as far as the Galilee.

The exact origin of the Itureans is under debate. Some scholars identify them as Arabs while the others as Aramaean people. If the Itureans were Aramaean people, the land of Syria should have been owned again by the original Aramaean people in the second century BC. In the first century BC the Iturean kingdom had its center in the kingdom of Ptolemy. Ptolemy reigned between 85 and 40 BC and was succeeded by his son Lysanias. About 23 BC, Iturea and the adjacent provinces fell into the hands of Zenodorus, the son of Lysanias. During his reign, the Roman emperor Augustus gave the Iturean kingdom to Herod the Great despite Zenodorus' resistance. Thus, the land of Syria was again disowned from the face of her king (Zenodorus) between 23 and 20 BC.

If the Itureans were Aramaean people, the prophecy of Isaiah was fulfilled in the birth of Yeshua in 5 BC (see Chapter 34). Yeshua was indeed born after the land of Syria was disowned for the second time around 20 BC. After Isaiah prophesized this in the fall of 733 BC (see Chapter 27), the land of Syria was disowned for the first time around 730 BC when the son of Isaiah was about two years old and had knowledge to cry his father and mother.

CHAPTER 31

YESHUA'S PROPHECY ON HIS BURIAL AND RESURRECTION

When was Yeshua crucified, buried, and resurrected? This question has not been answered since the beginning of Christianity. Almost all Christians have just followed the Roman Catholic Good Friday-Easter Sunday tradition, accepting that Yeshua was crucified on a Friday afternoon, buried just before sunset of that Friday, and resurrected on the following Sunday morning. This timeframe includes Friday night, the daylight portion of Saturday, and Saturday night. The time interval is clearly two nights and one day—**not three days and three nights**, as Yeshua promised as his only sign: "Then some of the scribes and Pharisees answered, saying, 'Teacher, we want to see a sign from you.' But he answered and said to them, 'An evil and adulterous generation seeks after a sign, and no sign will be given to it except the sign of the prophet Jonah. For as Jonah was **three days and three nights** in the belly of the great fish, so will the Son of Man be **three days and three nights** in the heart of the earth.'" (Matthew 12:38-40).

Yeshua's own words clearly suggest that he would be **three days and three nights** in the grave just as Jonah was **three days and three nights** in the whale's belly. How long did Jonah stay inside the whale's belly? The Scripture says: "Now Yehowah had prepared a great fish to swallow up Jonah. And Jonah was in the belly of the fish **three days and three nights**" (Jonah 1:17). The Scripture continues to say: "Then Jonah prayed unto Yehowah his God out of the fish's belly, ... And Yehowah spoke unto the fish, and it vomited out Jonah upon the dry land." (Jonah 2:1-10).

Yeshua himself also said, "Behold, we are going up to Jerusalem, and the Son of Man will be betrayed to the chief priests and to the scribes; and they will condemn him to death and deliver him to the Gentiles to mock and to scourge and to crucify. And **the third day** he will rise again." (Matthew 20:18-19). Here, Matthew tells us that Yeshua would rise again **the third day** by directly quoting Yeshua's own words.

According to our current understanding of the language, "**three days and three nights**" and "**the third day**" are not the same. How could the same author write the same thing using apparently contradictory wordings? Did Matthew or Yeshua say something contradictory to each other? If this would be the case, how would this Gospel be inspired by the Almighty God and how would Yeshua be the Son of God and the Messiah?

Understanding of "the third day"

Did the Gospel's writer make such an obvious mistake? Absolutely not! It is important to note that like the Romans, the Jews counted day and year exclusively, following Babylon's way during the second temple period. For the Jews, a day starts and ends from one sunset to next. For example, if today is Wednesday, "In the first day" means the day between today's sunset and sunset of Thursday, and "in the third day" means the day between sunset of Friday and sunset of Saturday. "The third day" without the preposition "in" means the end of the third day (see below). Therefore, if Yeshua was buried on sunset of Wednesday and rose just at sunset of Saturday, it is correct to say that he resurrected the third day. If Yeshua was buried at sunset of Wednesday and resurrected at sunset of Saturday, he had stayed in the grave for three days and three nights, just as what Yeshua said in Matthew 12:38-40. According to Matthew's account, Yeshua was indeed buried at sunset of his crucifixion day (Matthew 27:57). The fact that Yeshua was crucified during the daytime of that Wednesday and rose on sunset of that Saturday is indeed consistent with Matthew 27:63, "Sir, we remember while he was still alive, how that deceiver said, '**After three days** I will rise.'"

Yeshua's own words confirm that the Jews at his time followed the Babylonian counting of hour, day or year. Yeshua taught us how to count the hour in Matthew 20:1-16:

> [1]"For the kingdom of heaven is like a landowner who went out early in the morning to hire laborers for his vineyard. [2]Now when he had agreed with the laborers for a denarius a day, he sent them into his vineyard. [3]And he went out **about the third hour** and saw others standing idle in the marketplace, [4]and said to them, 'You also go into the vineyard, and whatever is right I will give you.' So they went. [5]Again he went out about the sixth and the ninth hour, and did likewise. [6]And **about the eleventh hour** he went out and found others standing idle, and said to them, 'Why have you been standing here idle all day?' [7]They said to him, 'Because no one hired us.' He said to them, 'You also go into the vineyard, and whatever is right you will receive.' [8]So **when evening had come**, the owner of the vineyard said to his steward, 'Call the laborers and give them their wages, beginning with the last to the first.' [9]And when those came who were hired **about the eleventh hour**, they each received a denarius. [10]But when the first came, they supposed that they would receive more; and they likewise received each a denarius. [11]And when they had received it, they complained against the landowner, [12]saying, '**These last men have worked only one hour**, and you made them equal to us who have borne the burden and the heat of the day.' [13]But he answered one of them and said, 'Friend, I am doing you no wrong. Did you not agree with me for a denarius? [14]Take what is yours and go your way. I wish to give to this last man the same as to you. [15]Is it not lawful for me to do what I wish with my own things? Or is your eye evil because I am good?' [16]So the last will be first, and the first last. **For many are called, but few chosen.**"

This passage tells us that a daytime is divided into twelve hours. The passage also implies that if the Sun rises at 6:00 am and sets at 6:00 pm, then "the first hour" of the day is at 7:00 am, "the third hour" at 9:00 am, "the ninth hour" at 3:00 pm, "the eleventh hour" at 5:00 pm, and "the twelfth hour" at 6:00 pm. Those who came at the eleventh hour worked only one hour toward the end of the day at the twelfth hour (verses 9 and 12).

Therefore, the Scriptures clearly teach us that "the third hour" means the time at which exactly three hours have passed from the beginning of a day. "The third hour" without the preposition "in" means the end of the third hour. By analogy, "the third day" means the day exactly three days after a new day starts, that is, at the end of the third day.

The Gospel of John recorded the detailed events day by day in John 1:28-51 and John 2:1-2. From these events, we can clearly see the meaning of "the third day." John 1:28 tells us that the testimonies of John the Baptist took place in the Jordan river. After this verse, John 1:29 recorded: "**The next day** John saw Yeshua coming toward him, and said, 'Behold! The Lamb of God who takes away the sin of the world!'" John testified that Yeshua was the Lamb of God **the next day**, which was in the first day, relative to the day recorded in John 1:28. Then verses 35 and 36 say: "**Again, the next day**, John stood with two of his disciples. And looking at Yeshua as he walked, he said, 'Behold the Lamb of God!'" John introduced Yeshua the Lamb of God to two of his disciples in the second day. In the third day, Yeshua found Philip in Galilee, as recorded in John 1:43, "**The following day** Yeshua wanted to go to Galilee, and he found Philip and said to him, 'Follow Me.'" In the same day, Yeshua also found Nathanael (see verses 45-51). Then John 2:1 says, "**The third day** there was a wedding in Cana of Galilee, and the mother of Yeshua was there." The wedding in Cana of Galilee should have taken place in the evening of the same day when Yeshua met Philip and Nathanael in Galilee. In the evening (at sunset) of the wedding ceremony, the third day was approaching the end, so John used "the third day" to tell us that the wedding started exactly at sunset of that day. From the day when John the Baptist made the testimonies in the Jordan river to the evening of the wedding ceremony, three days and three nights had passed.

During the first Passover right after Yeshua performed the first miracle (changing water to wine) at Cana, he said to the Jews, "Destroy this temple, and in three days I will raise it up." (John 2:19). Here, Yeshua spoke of the temple of his body, which will be raised up in three days (three days later) after it is destroyed.

Therefore, all these verses in the Gospels of Matthew and John consistently suggest that Yeshua resurrected exactly three days and three nights after his burial. In contrast, most Biblical scholars believe and teach a false idea that Yeshua was only buried for half that time. Even Clarke's Commentary, in explaining Matthew 12:40, follows this false tradition, established as early as the mid-second century AD. Despite many attempts of scholars and theologians to "prove" one day and two nights **cannot** mean three days and three nights.

Yeshua's crucifixion and burial

Yeshua's crucifixion took place on the 14th day of Nisan, the first month of a year assigned by God, which is the preparation day of the Passover (John 19:14). Yeshua was nailed on the cross around the sixth hour (John 19:14), in agreement with Matthew 27:45, "Now from the sixth hour there was darkness over all the land unto the ninth hour." The darkness should have started right after Yeshua was nailed on the cross.

Yeshua died around 3:00 pm (the ninth hour) (Matthew 27:45-50). With Governor Pilate's permission, Joseph of Arimathaea procured the body, wrapped it in linen (John 19:40), and placed it in the sepulcher. By evening (just before or at sunset) of that day, the burial was complete (Matthew 27:57). The burial took place on **the preparation day** of the Passover, shortly before or at sunset. The **preparation day** preceded the Feast of Unleavened Bread, which was also called the Feast of Passover. The first day of the Feast was called a high Sabbath or "high day" (John 19:31), which is held annually to memorialize the day in which the almighty God brought the Israelites out of Egypt. The midnight of Nisan 15 is the Passover of Yehowah. John 19:31 especially emphasizes that the next day after Yeshua's crucifixion was a special Sabbath that is different from the weekly Sabbaths (in plural form). It was on this special Sabbath that the high priest and the Pharisees came to

Pilate to ensure that Yeshua's tomb was securely guarded and sealed (Matthew 27:62-66).

John 19:31 also tells us that Yeshua cannot be crucified on a Friday. If his crucifixion were on a Friday, the next day would be the weekly Sabbaths rather than a high Sabbath. Below we will prove that Yeshua resurrected at the very beginning of the first day (Sunday), which was right after the end of the weekly Sabbaths. We have proved that the only year of Yeshua's crucifixion, which was consistent with the Gospels of Matthew and John, was 30 AD (see Chapter 12). According to the Hebrew lunisolar calendar of 30 AD (see Appendix D), the preparation day of the Feast of the Passover in 30 AD is indeed on Wednesday. From sunset of Wednesday to sunset of Saturday, there are exactly three days and three nights, in agreement with Yeshua's own prophecy about his resurrection.

Some Biblical scholars and theologians argued that the darkness from the sixth hour to the ninth hour during Yeshua's crucifixion, as recorded in Matthew 27:45, was related to a solar eclipse. This argument does not have any scientific foundation. First, solar eclipses only take place in either the first or the last day of a lunar month while Yeshua's crucifixion occurred in the middle of the lunar month Nisan. Second, solar eclipses last for less than 6 minutes, much shorter than 3 hours. Therefore, the darkness cannot be caused by a natural solar eclipse.

Another possibility is that God might have miraculously darkened the sky by darkening the sun or by heavy clouds. Yeshua prophesized that the sun would be darkened, and the moon would not give its light immediately after the end-time tribulation (Matthew 24:29). This type of darkness should not happen in a dark-moon phase when a solar eclipse can take place. This is because at this moment the moon does not give its light even if the sun is not darkened. This miraculous darkness prophesized by Yeshua shall happen in a day when both the sun and the moon are supposed to be seen by the people in different parts of the world. If the sun had been miraculously darkened from 12:00 to 3:00 pm during Yeshua's crucifixion, the full moon in China would not have given its light from 6:00 to 9:00 pm and Chinese chroniclers would have recorded such an unusual phenomenon in the sky. However, they recorded all the natural eclipses around the year of Yeshua's crucifixion (during the reign of Emperor Guang-Wu in the Later Han Dynasty) but nothing else. This fact suggests that such a phenomenon should never have taken place during Yeshua's crucifixion. Alternatively, the darkness recorded by Matthew should have been caused by heavy clouds.

The Book of Later Han recorded two solar eclipses in the 30th day of the 9th month in the 6th year of Emperor Guang-Wu (30 AD) and in the 30th day of the 3rd month in Guang-Wu's 7th year (31 AD). These two solar eclipses are predicted to have taken place in China around 7:00 am on November 14 of 30 AD and around 9:00 am on May 10 of 31 AD, respectively. The dates of the predicted solar eclipses perfectly match the ones recorded in the Book of Later Han (Volume 1b). Thus, the Chinese chroniclers accurately recorded these natural astronomical phenomena but no miraculous phenomenon in the sky around the year of Yeshua's crucifixion.

The time of Yeshua's resurrection

Most Christians believe that Yeshua resurrected in the early morning of Sunday. Most English translated Bibles explicitly say that the women (several Mary's) went to the tomb of Yeshua in the early morning shortly after he was resurrected.

If the Gospels of Matthew and John are all inspired by God, they must be consistent with each other. John 20:1 (NKJV) says: "Now on the first day of the week Mary Magdalene went to the tomb early, while it was still dark, and saw that the stone had been taken away from the tomb."

The Greek word "prior" in John 20:1 was translated into "early," which means the early part of the first day of the week. Since a day starts from sunset to the Jews, the early part of the first day of the week could have corresponded to the time just after sunset of Saturday.

If the Greek word "prior" is translated into "early," then John 20:1 can be translated as: "Now at the early time of the first day of the week, Mary Magdalene went to the tomb, while it was yet (already) dark, and saw that the stone had been taken away from the tomb." The Greek word "ετι" in John 20:1 should best match the English word "yet" rather than "still." The adverb "yet" has the meanings of "now," "right now," "at this time," and "already."

The Gospel of Matthew even provides a precise time of Yeshua's resurrection. Matthew 28:1 has also been mistranslated. The original Greek text reads: "Ὀψὲ δὲ σαββάτων, τῇ ἐπιφωσκούσῃ εἰς μίαν σαββάτων (after then, the Sabbaths it being dawn towards the first day of the week)." Here, Saturday is written in the plural (sabbaton), while Sunday is written as eis mian sabbaton. These two phrases have exactly the same meaning and specify the hour that falls on the Saturday evening when the Sunday is about to begin. The first word of the phrase, opse (ὀψὲ), when it is used with a day of the week, means: "at dusk," "at nightfall," or "at evening." The word "opse" can also mean "at the end" of an event.

Now, let's take a look at the second phrase of the Ancient Greek text of Matthew "epiphoskouse eis mian sabbaton (ἐπιφωσκούσῃ εἰς μίαν σαββάτων)," which is usually translated as "it began to dawn toward the first day of the week." This is where the serious misunderstanding occurs. This particular translation leads to an entirely incorrect understanding, since the modern reader thinks that it is referring to dawn (early morning). This is not the case. When the Jews used the expression "the break/light of a new day," they did not mean at daylight in the morning, but "the night of the new day has come to light." Consequently, for the Jews, the "daybreak" of the new day corresponds to the evening time. In the Gospel of Luke, Luke specifies the time of Yeshua's burial with the phrase: καὶ ἡμέρα ἦν παρασκευῆς, καὶ σάββατον ἐπέφωσκεν, i.e., "it was the day of Preparation, and Sabbath was about to begin (literally, it began to dawn toward Sabbath)" (Luke 23:54). This phrase in Luke "it began to dawn toward Sabbath" and the phrase in Matthew "it began to dawn toward the first day of the week" use the same verb "epiphosko" and specify the same time, right at sunset (at daybreak). This means that the women departed to see the tomb just at sunset of Saturday right after the weekly Sabbaths. Before they arrived at the tomb, an angel of Yehowah descended from heaven, rolled back the stone from the door, and sat on it right after sunset (Matthew 28:2). After the women arrived in the tomb at the beginning of Sunday and entered the tomb, the angel clothed with a long white robe talked to them that Yeshua had risen (Matthew 28:5-6).

Mary Magdalene saw the empty tomb at the beginning of that Saturday night when there was already darkness, but she did not see the risen Yeshua—unlike the Virgin Mary, who saw him and touched him. Mary Magdalene returned to the tomb later that night, along with Peter and another disciple whom Yeshua loved (John 20:1-2), and when she remained alone after the two disciples had left, she then saw the risen Yeshua.

It is interesting that our correct translation of these verses is backed up by all the ancient translations of the New Testament, such as the Latin translation by St Jerome (Vulgata), the Syriac Peshitta, the Ethiopian, the Arabic, the Armenian translation of the fifth century, etc. They attest that Yeshua resurrected just at sunset of Saturday and Mary Magdalene and the other Mary's visited the tomb afterward.

In *"The Report of Pilate the Procurator Concerning Our Lord Yeshua Christ"*, sent to the August Cæsar in Rome, Pilate stated:

> And the fear of the earthquake remained from the sixth hour of the preparation until the ninth hour. And on the evening of the first day of the week there was a sound out of the heaven, so that the heaven became enlightened sevenfold more than all the days. And at the third hour of the night also the sun was seen brighter than it had ever shone before, lighting up all the heaven. And as lightnings come suddenly in winter, so majestic men appeared in glorious robes, an innumerable multitude, whose voice was heard as that of a very great thunder, crying out: "Yeshua that was crucified is risen: come up out of Hades, ye that have been enslaved in the underground regions of Hades." And the chasm of the earth was as if it had no bottom; but it was as if the very foundations of the earth appeared along with those that cried out in the heavens and walked about in the body in the midst of the dead that had risen. And he that raised up all the dead, and bound Hades, said: "Say to my disciples, 'He goes before you into Galilee; there shall you see him.'"

Pilate's letter to August Cæsar tells us that on the evening of the first day of the week there was a sound out of the heaven and that the heaven became enlightened sevenfold more than all the days. His statement is consistent with Matthew 28:2-3: "And behold, there was a great earthquake; for an angel of Yehowah descended from heaven, and came and rolled back the stone from the door, and sat on it. His countenance was like lightning, and his clothing as white as snow." Pilate's report, if reliable, confirms that Yeshua had already resurrected in the evening of the first day of the week.

CHAPTER 32

YESHUA'S PROPHECY ON THE DESTRUCTION OF THE HOLY TEMPLE

Yeshua prophesized about the destruction of the temple of God within about 40 years in Matthew 24:1-3 and 34:

> ¹Then Yeshua went out and departed from the temple, and his disciples came up to show him the buildings of the temple. ²And Yeshua said to them, "Do you not see all these things? Assuredly, I say to you, not one stone shall be left here upon another, that shall not be thrown down." ³Now as he sat on the Mount of Olives, the disciples came to him privately, saying, "Tell us, when will these things be [ruined]? And what will be the sign of your coming, and of the end of the age?…" ³⁴Assuredly, I say to you, **this generation will by no means pass away till all these things become [ruined]**.

In verse 2, **all these things** Yeshua refers to are the buildings of the temple, which shall be thrown down (ruined) completely. In verse 3, his disciples asked him three independent questions: (1) When will [all] these things be [ruined]? This question is related to the buildings of the temple, which Yeshua prophesized to be ruined completely; (2) what will be the sign of Yeshua's return; and (3) what will be the sign of the end of the age?

Yeshua did not answer these three questions sequentially. He answered and said to them: "Take heed that no one deceives you. For many will come in my name, saying, 'I am the Messiah,' and will deceive many." (Matthew 24:4-5).

In these verses, Yeshua told his disciples that before all these things (the buildings of the temple) were ruined, many false messiahs would come in his name and deceive many. Yeshua warned his disciples not to be deceived by the false messiahs. Here he answered the first question of his disciples.

In verses 6-14, Yeshua said:

> "And you will hear of wars and rumors of wars. See that you are not troubled; for it is necessary for them to take place, but the end is not yet. For nation will rise against nation, and kingdom against kingdom. And there will be famines, pestilences, and earthquakes in various places. All these are the beginning of sorrows. And they will deliver you up to tribulation and kill you, and you will be hated by all nations for my name's sake. And many will be offended, will betray one another, and will hate one another. And many false prophets will rise up and deceive many. And because lawlessness will abound, the love of many will grow cold. But he who endures to the end shall be saved. And this gospel of the kingdom will be preached in all the world as a witness to all the nations, and then the end will come."

In these verses, Yeshua answered the third question of his disciples: What will be the signs before the end of the age?

In verses 15-20, Yeshua said:

> "Therefore when you see the 'abomination of desolation,' spoken of by Daniel the prophet, standing in the holy place (whoever reads, let him understand), then let those who are in Judea flee to the mountains. Let him who is on the housetop not go down to take anything out of his house. And let him who is in the field not go back to get his clothes. But woe to those who are pregnant and

to those who are nursing babies in those days! And pray that your flight may not be in winter or on the Sabbath."

In these verses, Yeshua answered the first question of his disciples again. Yeshua prophesized the destruction of Jerusalem and the temple of God. The event of the Romans (the Gentiles) standing in the holy place was an abomination to God because no foreigner who is uncircumcised in flesh and heart is allowed to enter the holy temple of God (Ezekiel 44:6-9). Yeshua foretold that the Jews could escape from the tribulation by fleeing to the mountains when they saw the Romans stand in the holy place.

In verses 21-22, Yeshua stated:

"There will indeed then be great tribulation (literally translated), such as has not been since the beginning of the world until this time, no, nor ever shall be. And unless those days were shortened, no flesh would be saved; but for the elect's sake those days will be shortened."

In these verses, Yeshua answered the third question of his disciples: What will be the signs before the end of the age?

In verses 23-28, Yeshua told his disciples:

"And if anyone says to you, 'Look, here is the Messiah!' or 'There!' do not believe it. For false messiahs and false prophets will rise and show great signs and wonders to deceive, if possible, even the elect. See, I have told you beforehand. Therefore if they say to you, 'Look, he is in the desert!' do not go out; or 'Look, he is in the inner rooms!' do not believe it. For as the lightning comes from the east and flashes to the west, so also will the coming of the Son of Man be. For wherever the carcass is, there the eagles will be gathered together."

Here, Yeshua provided a general guidance to identify false messiahs and false prophets in any time. Since false messiahs and false prophets had appeared before the temple was destroyed (Matthew 24:4-5) and continued to appear till the end times, this general guidance is necessary for his true believers not to be deceived. The general guidance is that Yeshua will come down from heaven as the lightning coming from the east and flashing to the west. The resurrected Yeshua should never appear in the desert nor in the inner rooms (secret chambers). If anyone tells you that he has seen the resurrected Yeshua in the desert or in the inner rooms, what he has seen is not Yeshua but a false messiah. Even if the false messiah and his prophets could perform great signs and wonders, do not believe them because they do these to deceive you, even the elect.

In verses 29-31, Yeshua said:

> "Immediately after the tribulation of those days the sun will be darkened, and the moon will not give its light; the stars will fall from heaven, and the powers of the heavens will be shaken. And the sign of the Son of Man will appear in heaven, and all the tribes of the earth will mourn, and they will see the Son of Man coming on the clouds of heaven with power and great glory. And he will send his angels with a great sound of a trumpet, and they will gather together his elect from the four winds, from one end of heaven to the other."

In these verses, Yeshua answered the third question of his disciples: What will the signs of his coming in the end times be? He also foretold his disciples that he would return with power and great glory and would first gather his true believers before he would pour out the wrath of God upon the ungodly.

In verses 32-34, Yeshua said:

> "Now learn this parable from the fig tree: When its branch has already become tender and puts forth leaves, you know that summer is near. So you also, when you see all these, know that it is near, at the doors! Assuredly, I

say to you, **this generation will by no means pass away** till all these things become (ruined)."

In these verses, Yeshua answered the first question of his disciples again: When will all these things become (ruined)?

The Greek word "Γίνομαι" (transliteration: ginomai) in verse 34 has the following meanings: come into being; come to pass; happen; **become** (signifying a change of condition, state or place). In most English translations, "ginomai" is translated as "happen" or "take place." Then verse 34 reads: "Assuredly, I say to you, this generation will by no means pass away till all these things take place." If all these things would refer to the end-time events, this prophecy of Yeshua would not be fulfilled because the end did not come one generation after his prophecy. If "ginomai" is translated as "become," verse 34 reads: "Assuredly, I say to you, this generation will by no means pass away till all these things **become** [ruined]." This verse naturally answered the first question of his disciples: When will [all] these things be [ruined]?

In these verses, Yeshua actually prophesized the time for destruction of the temple of God. He foretold that the temple would be destroyed in the summertime (verse 32) and within a generation (verse 34) from his prophecy. In Chapter 1 of the Gospel of Matthew, the author counted 14 generations from captivity of Jeconiah (Jehoiachin) into Babylon to the birth of Yeshua. It is known that Jehoiachin was taken into Babylon in the spring of 597 BC (see Chapter 11). In Chapter 34, we will prove that Yeshua was born in the spring of 5 BC. Therefore, the average number of years per generation is calculated to be (597-5)/14 = 42.3. Yeshua prophesized this in the spring of 30 AD and the temple was destroyed in the summer of 70 AD. Therefore, the temple of God was destroyed about 40.5 years (slightly less than a generation) after the time of his prophecy. This prophecy of Yeshua was fulfilled perfectly.

A similar prophecy on the destruction of Jerusalem can be found in Matthew 12:41: "The men of Nineveh will rise up in the judgment with this generation and condemn it, because they repented at the preaching of Jonah; and indeed [one] greater than Jonah is here."

There is an implied prophecy in his statement. Before this statement, Yeshua prophesized that he would resurrect after he would be buried for 3 days and 3 nights just as happened to Jonah. In Matthew 12:41, Yeshua foretold God's judgment and condemnation on this generation because they did not repent at the warning of Yeshua. Jonah the prophet prophesized the destruction of Nineveh within 40 days. The men of Nineveh repented at the warning of Jonah. Yeshua who is greater than Jonah prophesized the destruction of Jerusalem within one generation. God gave a 40-day warning to the men of Nineveh through His prophet Jonah. In contrast, God gave a 40-year warning to the men of Jerusalem through His only begotten Son. Unfortunately, the Jews did not repent, and God's wrath poured out on His people, as also prophesized by Daniel (Daniel 9:26-27). The Romans destroyed Jerusalem ruthlessly in 70 AD and killed over 1 million Jews, 40 years after Yeshua's warning.

CHAPTER 33

YESHUA'S PROPHECIES ON HIS FIRST CENTURY RETURN

Matthew 10: 16-23 recorded the prophecy of Yeshua on the time of his return:

> [16]"Behold, I send you out as sheep in the midst of wolves. Therefore be wise as serpents and harmless as doves. [17]But beware of men, for they will deliver you up to councils and scourge you in their synagogues. [18]You will be brought before governors and kings for my sake, as a testimony to them and to the Gentiles. [19]But when they deliver you up, do not worry about how or what you should speak. For it will be given to you in that hour what you should speak; [20]for it is not you who speak, but the Spirit of your Father who speaks in you. [21]Now brother will deliver up brother to death, and a father his child; and children will rise up against parents and cause them to be put to death. [22]And you will be hated by all for my name's sake. But he who endures to the end will be saved. [23]**When they persecute you in this city, flee to another. For assuredly, I say to you, you will not have gone through the cities of Israel before the Son of Man comes.**"

This prophecy of Yeshua suggests that his return should have taken place before his disciples had gone through all the cities of Israel. Yeshua also prophesied that his disciples would be persecuted and flee from one city to another. Before they went through all the cities of Israel or before the persecution was over, Yeshua should have returned. This is his first return he foretold his disciples. He also foretold his final return in Matthew 24:26-31.

If the prophecy of his first return would not have been fulfilled, Yeshua would not be the true Messiah and Savior. We will show that this prophecy was fulfilled in the spring of 67 AD when he returned to instruct John to measure the temple of God and to prophesy the destruction of Jerusalem in 42 months.

Just as the Spirit of God took Ezekiel from Babylon to Jerusalem (Ezekiel 8:3), the angel of God may have taken John from Patmos Island to the temple of God in Jerusalem. After John was given a reed-like measuring rod, the mighty angel stood and said to John, "Rise and measure the temple of God, the altar, and those who worship there. But leave out the court, which is outside the temple, and do not measure it, for it has been given to the Gentiles. And they will trample down the holy city, forty-two [42] months." (Revelation 11:1-2).

In most English translations, the preposition "for" has been added before 42 months. When "for" is added, the prophecy would read: "And they (the Gentiles) will trample down the holy city for 42 months." Since the holy city Jerusalem has never been trampled down continuously for 42 months, most Biblical scholars believe that this prophetic event shall take place in the end times after the third temple of God is rebuilt.

Since there is no "for" in the original text of Revelation 11:2 and the verb is in the future indicative active mode [describing a future action (snapshot) at a particular time], we can interpret this verse alternatively. If we add "in" before 42 months, the prophecy will read: "And they (the Gentiles) will trample down (destroy ruthlessly) the holy city in 42 months." This interpretation can be justified by analogy with John 2:20. The interlinear English translation of this verse is:

> The Jews therefore said: "46 years [ago] this temple was erected [and is still under construction] and you will raise it up in three days?"

Here, the verb "**οἰκοδομέω** (oikodomeó)" means "erect a building" and "build a house." The verb "**οἰκοδομήθη**" in the above sentence is in the aorist indicative passive form. The Greek aorist tense in the indicative mood simply describes a past action (snapshot at a particular time). Therefore, the erection of the temple (the commencement of the temple's construction) is a past action relative to the time when the Jews spoke to Yeshua.

We have shown that the temple was erected (started to be built) in the spring of 20 BC, which was 46 years before the Jews spoke to Yeshua (see Chapter 12). Since these Jews knew that the construction of the temple started 46 years ago [and was still under way], their statement can be rephrased as: "The temple has been under construction for 46 years and you will raise it up in three days?"

In the Greek text of John 2:20, there is no preposition before 46 years nor adverb after 46 years. Adding the adverb "ago" after 46 years correctly conveys the meaning of this verse: The temple was erected 46 years before the Jews spoke to Yeshua. By analogy, adding the proposition "in" before 42 months in Revelation 11:2 conveys the idea that Jerusalem will be destroyed ruthlessly 42 months after this prophecy of the mighty angel. If this interpretation is correct, the book of Revelation was written 42 months before Jerusalem was destroyed.

Who is the mighty angel of God described in Revelation 10:1-3? The face of the mighty angel was like sun and his feet like pillars of fire (10:1), and a rainbow was on his head. He had a little book open in his hand and cried out with a loud voice like roaring of a lion (Revelation 10:3). In Matthew 17:2, we see that when Yeshua was transfigured into his glorious body, his face did shine as the sun. In Revelation 5:5, the slain Lamb was declared to be the lion of the tribe of Judah. From these descriptions, the mighty angel is likely to be Yeshua himself.

How is it possible that Yeshua is the angel of God? Yehowah God told Moses (NKJV with no modification): "Behold, I send an Angel before you to keep you in the way and to bring you into the place which I have prepared. Beware of Him and obey His voice; do not provoke Him, for He will not pardon your transgressions; for My name is in Him. For My Angel will go before you and bring you in to the Amorites and the Hittites and the Perizzites and the Canaanites and the Hivites and the

Jebusites; and I will cut them off. ..." (Exodus 23:20-23). These verses tell us that because the Angel bears the name of Yehowah God, He is the regent of God, who acts and speaks on behalf of Yehowah God Himself. That is why the Angel of Yehowah and Yehowah Himself are inter-exchangeable in the five books of Moses. For example, "And the Angel of God, who went before the camp of Israel, moved and went behind them; and the pillar of cloud went from before them and stood behind them. So it came between the camp of the Egyptians and the camp of Israel. Thus it was a cloud and darkness to the one, and it gave light by night to the other, so that the one did not come near the other all that night." (Exodus 14:19-20). These verses tell us that the Angel of God went before the Israelites by day in a pillar of cloud to lead the way, and by night in a pillar of fire to give them light. This contrasts with Exodus 13:21 where Moses tells us that Yehowah Himself did the same things for the Israelites.

Who does bear the name of Yehowah? Moses called Hoshea (meaning salvation), the son of Nun, Yehoshua (Numbers 13:16). The name of Yehoshua is the compound name of Yehowah and Hoshea, which means "Yehowah is salvation." Yehoshua the son of Nun was a man and a leader of the Israelites. Yehoshua cannot be the Angel of God because he did not go before the Israelites by day in a pillar of cloud to lead the way, and by night in a pillar of fire to give them light. The name of Yeshua is the same as Yehoshua. Yeshua the son of Jozadak (Ezra 3:2) should not have been the Angel of God. The name of the Messiah is called Yeshua because he will save his people from their sins (Matthew 1:21). Since the name of the Messiah bears the name of Yehowah, he should be the Angel of God mentioned in the books of Moses. If this is true, no one in the Hebrew Bible (Tanakh) directly saw Yehowah God Himself, but His Angel who bears His Name. That is why Yeshua said, "No one has seen God at any time. The only begotten Son, who is in the bosom of the Father, he has declared Him." (John 1:18). Yeshua also said, "All the things have been delivered to me by my Father, and no one knows the Son except the Father, nor does anyone know the Father except the Son, and the one to whom the Son wills to reveal Him." (Matthew 11:27). Therefore, Yeshua's own words confirm that the Angel of God in the Old Testament is actually the Son of God who bears the Name (Yehowah) of his Father. The Son of God speaks and acts in the Name of his Father.

Because the messenger of God fully represents God, he speaks and acts with the same authority as God. In ancient China, the messenger of an emperor also speaks and acts with the same authority as the emperor. Whoever knows the identity of the messenger, he/she must bow down to him because he is like the emperor.

The capitalization of the words such as "Angel", "He", "His", and "Him" in these verses implies that the NKJV translators have referred to the Angel (Messenger) of God as the Son of God. Therefore, the author of the present book is not the only one who identifies the Angel of God in the Hebrew Bible as the only begotten Son of God.

One can clearly identify the Angel of God as Yeshua Messiah from Revelation 22:6-7. In Revelation 22:6-7, the angel said to John: "These words are faithful and true. And the Lord God of the holy prophets sent the angel of Him to show His servants the things which must shortly take place. Behold, I am coming quickly! Blessed is he who keeps the words of the prophecy of this book." From verse 22:6, we see that God sent the angel of Him to show His servants—things which must shortly take place. The angel also said to John (verse 22:7), "Behold, I am coming quickly..." In this verse, "I" must refer to the angel who talked to John and was one of the seven angels who had the seven bowls (Revelation 21:9). Who is coming quickly? It is the angel of God who is coming quickly. It is Yeshua Messiah who is coming quickly. In fact, the words recorded in Revelation 22: 9-16 are all from the angel of God. From the contents of these words, it is apparent that the angel must be Yeshua Messiah.

Therefore, the mighty angel in the book of Revelation is Yeshua himself. This conclusion is further supported by the verse: "And I will give power to my two witnesses, and they will prophesy one thousand two hundred and sixty days, clothed in sackcloth." (Revelation 11:3). Since the mighty angel gives power to his two witnesses who are the two olive trees and the two lampstands before the God of the earth, he must have great power and authority. No other angel in the Hebrew Bible has authority and power comparable to the Angel of Yehowah who bears His Name and executes all authority of Him. Yeshua the Son of

God was given all authority in heaven and earth after he resurrected (Matthew 28:18) and was restored to his original glory before the world was created (John 17:5). Yeshua also declared that all the things the Father has are his (John 16:15). The Son of God has authority to send the Holy Spirit (the Spirit of the Truth) from the Father to his disciples to testify of him (John 15:26) and to guide his disciples into all truth (John 16:13). Therefore, only the Son of God has such a great authority to give power to his two witnesses.

Who are the two witnesses of the mighty angel? When Yeshua was transfigured into his glorious body, Moses and Elijah also appeared to three disciples of Yeshua (Matthew 17:3). This implies that Moses and Elijah are the two witnesses of Yeshua. The two witnesses in the book of Revelation should also be Moses and Elijah because they will perform miracles (Revelation 11:5-6) similar to those performed by Moses and Elijah in the past and because Yeshua stated that Elijah would come in a future time (Matthew 11:14). The future time for Elijah to come should be right before the great day of Yehowah in the end times, which was prophesized in Malachi 4:5, "Behold, I will send you Elijah the prophet before the coming of the great and dreadful day of Yehowah." The great and dreadful day of Yehowah (probably the third woe) will take place after the 7th trumpet and the second woe (see Chapter 40). The two witnesses sent by the mighty angel of God will prophesize 1260 days before the 7th trumpet sounds (Revelation 11). One of the witnesses, Elijah, will be sent by Yehowah Himself according to Malachi 4:5. The apparent contradiction between Malachi and Revelation can be naturally resolved if the mighty angel of God is Yeshua himself who received all the power and glory from his Father after his resurrection. Yeshua has the authority to send the Spirit of Truth from his Father to his disciples after he sat on the right-hand side of his Father. Therefore, the mighty angel of God must be Yeshua himself in order for Moses and Elijah to be his witnesses.

When was John on Patmos Island? The time must have been in the period when the disciples of Yeshua were persecuted (Revelation 1:9). We know that Nero severely persecuted the Christians and the Jews between 64 and 68 AD. But most Biblical scholars believe that John was on Patmos Island around 90 AD when Domitian was the Roman emperor (81-96 AD). There is no historical record of severe persecution of Christians during the reign of Domitian.

We will use the historical records of Josephus about the Jewish war to determine the time of John's writing of the book of Revelation. Josephus told us (*Wars*, bk. 6, ch. 5, sect. 3):

> Thus were the miserable people persuaded by these deceivers, and such as belied God himself; while they did not attend nor give credit to the signs that were so evident, and did so plainly foretell their future desolation, but, like men infatuated, without either eyes to see or minds to consider, did not regard the denunciations that God made to them. Thus there was a star resembling a sword, which stood over the city, and a comet, that continued a whole year. Thus also before the Jews' rebellion, and before those commotions which preceded the war, when the people were come in great crowds to the feast of unleavened bread, **on the eighth day of the month Xanthicus [the first month], and at the ninth hour of the night [about 3 am], so great a light shone round the altar and the holy house, that it appeared to be bright day time; which lasted for half an hour. This light seemed to be a good sign to the unskillful, but was so interpreted by the sacred scribes, as to portend those events that followed immediately upon it.** At the same festival also, a heifer, as she was led by the high priest to be sacrificed, brought forth a lamb in the midst of the temple. Moreover, the eastern gate of the inner [court of the] temple, which was of brass, and vastly heavy, and had been with difficulty shut by twenty men, and rested upon a basis armed with iron, and had bolts fastened very deep into the firm floor, which was there made of one entire stone, was seen to be opened of its own accord about the sixth hour of the night. Now those that kept watch in the temple came hereupon running to the captain of the temple, and told

him of it; who then came up thither, and not without great difficulty was able to shut the gate again. This also appeared to the vulgar to be a very happy prodigy, as if God did thereby open them the gate of happiness. But the men of learning understood it, **that the security of their holy house was dissolved of its own accord, and that the gate was opened for the advantage of their enemies. So these publicly declared that the signal foreshowed the desolation that was coming upon them.** Besides these, a few days after that feast, on the one and twentieth day of the month Artemisius [the second month], a certain prodigious and incredible phenomenon appeared: I suppose the account of it would seem to be a fable, were it not related by those that saw it, and were not the events that followed it of so considerable a nature as to deserve such signals; for, before sun-setting, chariots and troops of soldiers in their armor were seen running about among the clouds, and surrounding of cities. Moreover, **at that feast which we call Pentecost**, as the priests were going by night into the inner [court of the temple,] as their custom was, to perform their sacred ministrations, they said that, in the first place, **they felt a quaking, and heard a great noise, and after that they heard a sound as of a great multitude, saying, "Let us remove hence."**

This passage tells us that before the Jewish war started (in April of 67 AD), there were two astronomical phenomena: A star resembling a sword stood over the city and a comet appeared. The Chinese astronomers also recorded these two astronomical phenomena separated by about 7 months. The separation between the revolt of the Jews (in the fall of 66 AD) and the starting of the Jewish war (in April of 67 AD) was also about 7 months. So, what Josephus tells us is that the two astronomical phenomena took place about one year before the revolt of the Jews and before the starting of the Jewish war, respectively. Since the original Greek text does not have punctuation, the English translation may read as: "Thus there were a star resembling a sword (which stood over the city) and a comet, which were a whole year before the Jews' revolt and before those commotions (which preceded the war), respectively."

The Chinese recorded a comet-like star on 29 July 65 AD: "孝明永平八年六月壬午，长星出柳张，三十七度，犯轩辕，刺天船，陵太微，气至上阶，凡见五十六日去." Our English translation reads:

> On the day of *ren-wu* (the 19th day of a sexagenary cycle) in the sixth month, in the eighth year of the Yong-Ping reign-period of King Xiao-Ming (29 July 65 AD), a long star (extending 37 degrees) was seen. The head of the star was within Hydra. It falls into Leo Major, stabs towards Perseus, and crosses over the supreme-palace enclosure. Its halo tail reaches the upper steps of Ursa Major. The star disappeared after 56 days.

Figure 12 simulates the above description of the long star. The Chinese word "刺" (which means "stab") suggests that the long star was like a sword. The "sword" stabs towards Perseus.

Since the revolt of the Jews took place in the fall of 66 AD and the long star was seen in August and September of 65 AD, the separation of the two events was indeed about one year, in agreement with the account of Josephus.

The Chinese astronomer also recorded a comet on 20 February 66 AD: "On the day of wu-shen (the 45th day of a sexagenary cycle) in the first month, in the ninth year of the Yong-Ping reign-period of King Xiao-Ming, a "guest star" (comet) appeared in α-Altair (ninth lunar mansion) with a length of 8 feet. It went out of sight after appearing for 50 days."

This comet appeared in February, March, and in early April of 66 AD, which was also about one year before the commotions which preceded the Jewish war (in April of 67 AD).

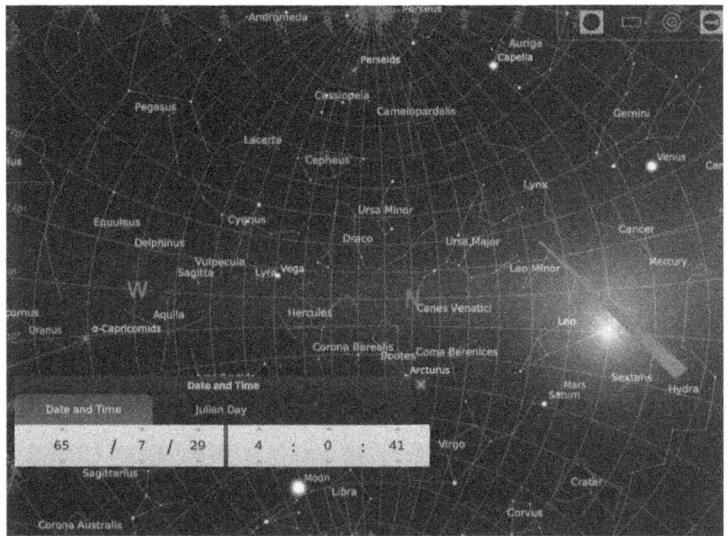

Figure 12: A comet-like long-star was like a sword (indicted by an arrow), which appeared on 29 July 65 AD and was recorded by the Chinese astronomer. The "sword" stabs (points) towards Perseus.

Josephus tells us that on the eighth day of the month Xanthicus [the first Macedonian month] of 67 AD, the Jews came in great crowds for the feast of unleavened bread. At the ninth hour of the night (about 3:00 am) in the 9th day, a great light shone around the altar and the temple for half an hour, and it appeared like the daytime due to the great light.

This miraculous event recorded by Josephus may be related to the event described in Revelation 11:2. This verse tells us that the mighty angel and John were inside the holy temple of God and the angel instructed John to measure the temple of God, the altar, and those who worshipped there. Since the face of the angel was like the sun, the altar and the holy temple must have been brightened like the daytime at his presence. Those who worshipped there must have seen the great light. Josephus should have eye witnessed it or obtained the information from those who worshipped there. The mighty angel must have chosen this particular time to let his people witness the miraculous event as a warning sign.

The 9th day of the month Xanthicus of 67 AD happened to be the 9th day of the month Nisan in the Hebrew calendar (see Appendix D), which was on April 12 and on Sunday. Yeshua also revealed to John on Sunday according to Revelation 1:10-11 (Hebraic-Roots Version):

> [10]And I was in the spirit on the first [day] of the week. And I heard from behind me, a great voice as a shofar, [11]That said, those [things] that you see, write in a book and send to the seven assemblies: to Ephesus, and to Smyrna, and to Pergamos, and to Thyatira, and to Sardis, and to Philadelphia, and to Laodicea.

It is interesting to note that the Hebrew version of Revelation does not identify the first day of the week as the Lord's Day. In the Greek version, the first day of the week was changed into the Lord's Day. Since the original book of Revelation was written in Hebrew (see the proof in the beginning part of The Hebraic-Roots Version Scripture), the change of the Lord's Day to the first day of the week did not originate from God.

If Yeshua prophesied the destruction of Jerusalem in the holy temple on 12 April 67 AD (the 9th day of the month Xanthicus or Nisan), exactly 42 lunar months after the prophecy should have been on **the 8th day of the month Gorpeius [the sixth month] (September 3) of 70 AD** or on the 9th day of the month Elul in the Hebrew calendar (the Macedonian calendar in 70 AD was one day later than the Hebrew calendar). This date can be easily figured out considering the fact that there was one embolismic year from 67 to 70 AD. From 12 April 67 AD to 3 September 70 AD, there were 1240 days = 42×29.524 days = 42 lunar months

According to the prophecy of the mighty angel, Jerusalem should have been destroyed by the Gentles 42 months from the time of his prophecy. If this prophecy was fulfilled perfectly, Jerusalem should have been destroyed on **the eighth day of the month Gorpeius of 70 AD**. This is indeed the case. According to Josephus (*Wars*, bk. 6, ch. 10, sect. 1), "And thus was Jerusalem taken, in the second year of the reign of Vespasian [70 AD], **on the eighth day of the month Gorpeius**. It had been taken five times before though this was the second time of its desolation."

The perfect fulfillment of this prophecy also pins down the exact time of John's writing of the revelation of Yeshua and the exact time of Yeshua's first return. Therefore, we are certain that on 12 April 67 AD (Sunday) John wrote the book of Revelation, and Yeshua (the mighty angel) returned to the earth, revealing himself only to John. Yeshua's first return on 12 April 67 AD perfectly fulfills the prophecy of Yeshua in Matthew 10:23: His return should have taken place before his disciples went through all the cities of Israel and before the end of the severe persecution of his disciples in 68 AD. Yeshua's first return on Nisan 9 of 67 AD was to prophesize and to warn the pending judgment of God on His people. It is the Messiah who destroyed Jerusalem and the temple with the Gentile's prince, as prophesized in Daniel 9:26-27 (see Chapter 17).

His return in 67 AD also fulfilled a puzzling prophecy of Yeshua, which was recorded in the Gospel of John (John 21:21-23): "Peter, seeing him, said to Yeshua, 'But Lord, what about this man?' Yeshua said to him, 'If I will that he remains till I come, what is that to you? You follow me.' Then this saying went out among the brethren that this disciple would not die. Yet Yeshua did not say to him that he would not die, but, 'If I will that he remains till I come, what is that to you?'" Indeed, John was still alive in 67 AD at Yeshua's first return but Peter had died before 67 AD.

His return in 67 AD fulfilled one more puzzling prophecy of Yeshua, which was recorded in Matthew 16:28, "Assuredly, I say to you, there are some standing here who shall not taste death till they see the Son of Man coming in his kingdom (royal power)." Here, Greek word "βασιλεία" means "kingdom," "sovereignty," and "royal power." The best English translation of "βασιλεία" in this verse should be "royal power," because this verse is in parallel with Matthew 16:27, "For the Son of Man will come in the glory of his Father with his angels, and then he will reward each according to his works." Verse 27 talks about his final return in the glory of his Father to judge the whole world while verse 28 refers to his return in 67 AD in his royal power. In 67 AD, John, Jude, and Simon were still alive while all the other disciples of Yeshua were martyred (please see the martyrdom of the 12 disciples of Yeshua at http://www.about-jesus.org/martyrs.htm). This fact clearly confirms Yeshua's prophecy that he would come in royal power at the time when some of his disciples were still alive.

The perfect fulfillment of this numerical prophecy proves that the Gospels of Matthew and John and the book of Revelation are the inspired Word of God. This also provides clear evidence for Yeshua being the true prophet of God, as foretold by Moses in Deuteronomy 18:17-22.

CHAPTER 34

BIRTHDAY OF YESHUA MESSIAH

On December 25, Christians around the world gather to celebrate Yeshua's birthday. Was Yeshua Messiah really born on December 25? If not, when was the exact date of his birth? Although the Scriptures do not directly tell us the exact birthday of Yeshua, can we identify it? Great efforts have been made to obtain the exact birthday of Yeshua for about 2,000 years, no consensus has been reached so far. Here, we attempt to determine the true birthday (9 March 5 BC) of Yeshua from Biblical, astronomical, and historical records.

Yeshua's birth on Nisan 1

In order to identify the true birthday of Yeshua, we need to find hints from the Scriptures. In the previous chapters, we have proved that Yeshua is the Messiah, the Son of God, the Son of Man, the Word of God, the Passover Lamb of God, the Messenger of Yehowah God who bears the Name of Yehowah. He is the regent of Yehowah God, speaking and acting on behalf of Yehowah.

Matthew cited the Hebrew Bible, saying, "Behold, a virgin (young woman) shall be with child, and shall bring forth a son, and they shall call his name Emmanuel, which being interpreted is, God with us." (Matthew 1:23). Matthew tells us that the birth of Yeshua signifies "God is with us" or "God dwells among us."

Apostle John stated (John 1:14): "And the Word became flesh and dwelt among us, and we beheld his glory, the glory as of the only begotten of the Father, full of grace and truth." John also declared that the Word was with God from the beginning (John 1:1). He speaks and acts exactly according to what his Father tells him. "No one has seen God at any time. Only the begotten Son, who is in the bosom of the Father, has declared Him." (John 1:18). The Son of God appeared to Moses as the Messenger of God, who bears the Name of Yehowah (Exodus 23:20-23). The Messenger of God is the same as the Word of God because he speaks the Word of God on God's behalf and with the same authority of God. The Son of God became flesh and directly appeared to the Israelites on behalf of his Father. This is the most direct signature of "God's dwelling among us."

Moses also told us that the tabernacle (the simple tent-sanctuary) was the portable earthly meeting place of God with the children of Israel from the time of the exodus of Egypt. The tabernacle is the symbol of "God dwelling among us" in the time of Moses (Exodus 25:8) and in the eternal Kingdom of God (Revelation 21:3).

Since both the tabernacle and the incarnated Son of God (the Messiah) symbolize the dwelling of God among us, setting up God's tabernacle in the time of Moses should have been a foreshadow of the Messiah's birth. God instructed Moses, "On the first day of the first month (Nisan 1) shall you set up the tabernacle of the tent of the congregation. And you shall put in it the ark of the testimony, and cover the ark with the veil." (Exodus 40: 2-3). "And it came to pass in the first month in the second year, on the first day of the month, that the tabernacle was raised up." (Exodus 40:17). Moses indeed set up the tabernacle on Nisan 1. This provides a strong hint that Yeshua should have been born on Nisan 1 if he is the true Messiah and his name is called Emmanuel.

When should Yeshua have been conceived if he was born on Nisan 1? We can find a hint from the starting time of building the tabernacle. In the third month—according to Jewish sage, the first day of that month (Exodus 19:1, NIV) marks the time more explicitly, that is, 45 days after the exodus from Egypt on the first Passover (Nisan 15). Moses spent one day on the mountain (Exodus 19:3), one day returning the people's answer (Exodus 19:7-8), three days of preparation, making the whole time 50 days from the first Passover to the promulgation of the Law (Ten Commandments) and the establishment of God's covenant with the Israelites. Hence on the Feast of Pentecost, that is, in the sixth day of the third Hebrew lunar month (Sivan 6), the covenant of God with the Israelites was established. After God made the covenant, He called Moses out of the midst of a cloud and Moses went up into the mountain in the seventh day of the third lunar month (Exodus 24:16-18). It was on the 7th day of the third month, Moses went up into the mountain and was instructed by God to build the tabernacle.

From the promulgation of the Law on the day of Pentecost (14 June 1457 BC) to setting up the tabernacle on the next Nisan 1 (31 March 1456 BC), there were 290 days, which is close to the duration of a woman's pregnancy in the ancient time (in ancient China, the normal pregnancy lasted about 10 lunar months from the time of conception, that is, about 295 days). Since the power of the Spirit of God made Virgin Mary conceive Yeshua, the conception should have also taken place on Pentecost, the very day the almighty God selected for the promulgation of His law.

Yeshua is not only the Messiah but also the Passover Lamb of God. According to the Hebrew Bible, the Passover lamb must be one year old, implying that the Passover lamb must be born in the month of Nisan. Therefore, Yeshua must have been born on Nisan 1 in order for him to be both the Messiah and the Passover Lamb of God.

Messiah's birth on Nisan 1 (March 9) of 5 BC

Matthew's account of Yeshua's nativity gives us a hint that he must have been born before Herod died, "Now when Yeshua was born in Bethlehem of Judea in the days of Herod the king, behold, there came wise men from the east to Jerusalem." (Matthew 2:1). It has been generally accepted that Herod died in the spring of 4 BC. In Chapter 13, we have unambiguously proved that Herod indeed died near the end of March of 4 BC.

According to the Law, a prophet must be at least 30 years old. Ezekiel was called to be the prophet of God in the 30th year of his life (Ezekiel 1:1). Since Yeshua was also the prophet Moses foretold (Deuteronomy 18:18), he must have been at least 30 years old when he began to minister and speak the words of God. In Chapter 12, we have shown that Yeshua was declared to be the Lamb of God by John the Baptist on Nisan 10 of 27 AD and called his disciples on Nisan 11 of 27 AD (April 6). If he was born on 1 Nisan 5 BC, he was 31 years old when he started to minister on Nisan 11 of 27 AD.

Nisan 1 of 5 BC was on March 9 according to the astronomical new moon data and the rules for the Hebrew lunisolar calendar (see Appendix D). If Yeshua was indeed born on 9 March 5 BC, his birthday should be consistent with the star of Bethlehem recorded by Matthew (2:1-12). If Yeshua was born on 9 March 5 BC, Yeshua should have been conceived on the Feast of Pentecost of 6 BC, which was on May 24. From 24 May 6 BC to 9 March 5 BC, there were 290 days.

The star of Bethlehem

The star of Bethlehem was recorded in Matthew 2:1-12:

> [1]Now after Yeshua was born in Bethlehem of Judea in the days of Herod the king, behold, wise men from the East came to Jerusalem, [2]saying, "Where is He who has been born King of the Jews? For we have seen his star in the East and have come to worship Him." [3]When Herod the king heard this, he was troubled, and all Jerusalem with him. [4]And when he had gathered all the chief priests and scribes of the people together, he inquired of them where the Messiah was to be born. [5]So they said to him, "In Bethlehem of Judea, for thus it is written by the prophet: [6]'But you, Bethlehem, in the land of Judah, are not the least among the rulers of Judah; For out of you shall come a ruler who will shepherd My people Israel.'" [7]Then Herod, when he had secretly called the wise men, determined from them what time the star appeared. [8]And he sent them to Bethlehem and said, "Go and search carefully for the young child, and when you have found him, bring back word to me, that I may come and worship him also." [9]When they heard the king, they departed; and behold, the star which they had seen in the East went before them, till it came and stood over

where the young child was. ¹⁰When they saw the star, they rejoiced with exceedingly great joy. ¹¹And when they had come into the house, they saw the young child with Mary His mother, and fell down and worshiped him. And when they had opened their treasures, they presented gifts to him: gold, frankincense, and myrrh. ¹²Then, being divinely warned in a dream that they should not return to Herod, they departed for their own country another way.

The account in the Gospel of Matthew describes how the Magi saw a star which they believed to herald the birth of the Messiah-King of Jews and how they followed the star to find the child and presented their gifts to him.

The star of Bethlehem has been considered to be mythical and unrelated to a real astronomical phenomenon. Here, we show that the star of Bethlehem was a new sword-like star near α-Altair, which was observed by the Chinese astronomers in the second Chinese lunar month of 5 BC, which was between March 9 and April 7.

There are several characteristics of the star of Bethlehem recorded in Matthew's Gospel. The characteristics are as follows:

1. It should be a star which had newly appeared. The best candidate should be a bright nova or supernova.
2. The star was seen in the east by the Magi in the time of the Messiah's birth (Matthew 2:2). When they came to Jerusalem and were sent to Bethlehem by Herod, the star in the east went ahead of them during their journey to Bethlehem, which is due south of Jerusalem. This implies that the star slowly moved through the sky from the east to the south during traveling of the Magi from their country to Jerusalem.
3. The star "stood over" Bethlehem. Matthew 2:9 records that the star "went ahead of them and "stood over" the place where the child was." According to Matthew, the star, as viewed from Jerusalem, "stood over" Bethlehem.

4. The Magi should have arrived in Bethlehem after Mary the mother of Yeshua was ceremonially clean. This should have been at least 40 days after she gave birth to the male child (Yeshua) according to Leviticus 12:1-4: "If a woman has conceived, and borne a male child: then she shall be unclean seven days; as in the days of her customary impurity shall she be unclean. And in the eighth day the flesh of his foreskin shall be circumcised. And she shall then continue in the blood of her purification three and thirty days; she shall touch no hallowed thing, nor come into the sanctuary, until the days of her purification be fulfilled."

A "comet"-like star observed by the Chinese astronomers meets the above characteristics. It was newly formed and "stood over" in the sky. The phrase "stood over" or "hung over" was uniquely applied to describe a comet in ancient literature. For example, Josephus stated: "a star, resembling a sword, stood over the city" (*Wars*, bk. 6, ch. 5, sect. 3). We have shown that he refers to a long star (extending 37 degrees) observed also by the Chinese astronomers on 29 July 65 AD. This star appeared for 56 days according to the Chinese record. Unlike a Halley comet that travels in the sky about 2-5 degrees per day, the long star does not change its position in the sky. Although the ancient Chinese astronomers did not clearly distinguish between a long star (possibly bright nova or supernova) and a comet, the detailed descriptions of their sky behaviors (e.g., position and brightness) were different. Josephus also made the distinction between a sword-like star and a comet, both of which were observed before the Jewish war that started in April of 67 AD (*Wars*, bk. 6, ch. 5, sect. 3).

A sword-like star for the Messiah appears to be foretold in the Hebrew Bible in Numbers 24:15-19 (Balaam fourth Oracle): "And he took up his oracle, and said, Balaam the son of Beor has said, and the man whose eyes are open has said: He has said, who heard the words of God, and knew the knowledge of the Most High, who saw the vision of the Almighty, falling into a trance, but having his eyes open: I shall see him, but not now: I shall behold him, **but not near: there shall come a star out of Jacob, and a scepter shall rise out of Israel**, and shall crush the forehead of Moab, and destroy all the children of Sheth. And Edom shall be a possession, Seir also shall be a possession for his enemies; and Israel shall do valiantly. Out of Jacob shall come he that shall have dominion, and shall destroy him that remains of the city."

The Oracle foretold that a star would come out of Jacob and a scepter would rise out of Israel in far future to have dominion over the nations. Here, the second sentence essentially repeats the first sentence to imply that a new star resembling a scepter will come out of Israel. The new star resembling a scepter (sword) is the star of the Messiah who will rule the nations with a rod of iron and with a sharp sword in his mouth. Therefore, a long star resembling a sword should be the best candidate for the star of Bethlehem.

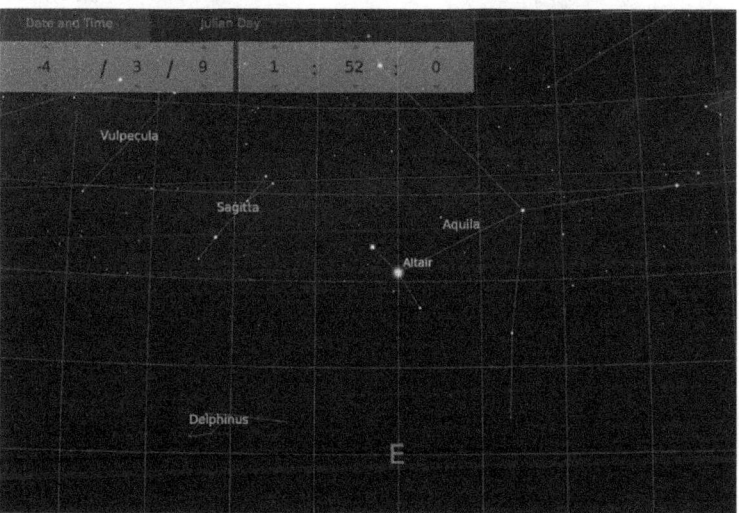

Figure 13: Sky view from Baghdad on 9 March 5 BC, as predicted from the Stellarium Program. The position of α-*Altair* at 1:52 was at 90 degrees, due east of Baghdad.

The Chinese chronicle (in *Qian Han Shu*) recorded: "In the second year of the reign period of Jian-Ping, second month, a *hui-xing* (comet) appeared in *qian-niu* for more than 70 days."

This record tells us that during the interval between March 9 and April 7 of 5 BC (the second Chinese month), a comet was visible for more than 70 days near α-*Altair*. Although *hui-xing* refers to a comet, it could also refer to a bright nova. For example, both the Chinese and

European astronomers used the word "comet" to describe the supernova of 1572 AD. Since the "comet" did not move in the sky, it must be a long star resembling a sword.

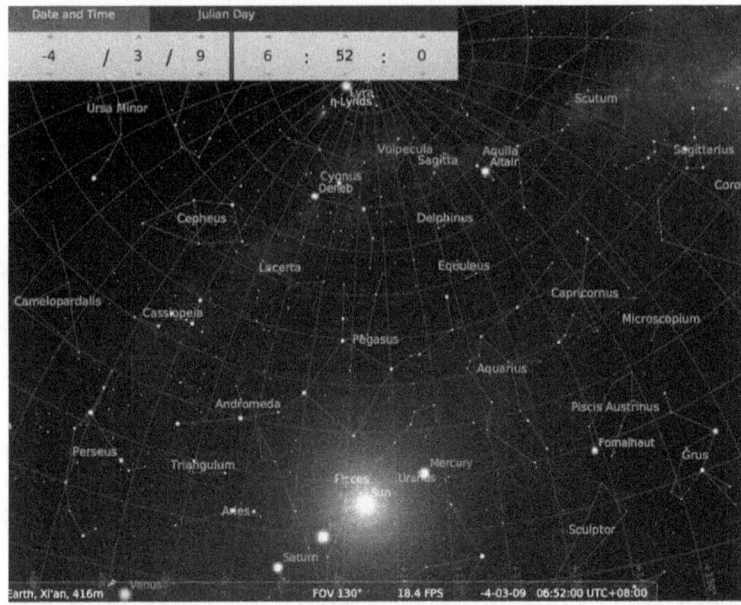

Figure 14: Predicted sky view from Xi-An, China on 9 March 5 BC. The position of α-*Altair* at 6:52 was about 150 degrees, south-east of Xi-An.

In Figures 13 and 14, we show the predicted sky views on 9 March 5 BC, which were observed from Baghdad (close to Babylon) of Iraq and from Xi-An (the capital city of Eastern Han Dynasty) of China, respectively. The sky views are predicted from the Stellarium Program. The position of α-*Altair* at 1:52 on March 9 of 5 BC was due east of Babylon (see Figure 13). If the comet-like star appeared near α-*Altair* at 1:52 Babylon time, it was seen in the direction of due east (the cardinal compass point is at 90 degrees), in agreement with Matthew 2:2. The Jerusalem time was at 0:52 on 9 March 5 BC, which was on Nisan 1. The Xi-An time was at 6:52 on 9 March 5 BC, which was the first day of the second Chinese month. The position of α-*Altair* seen from Xi-An was at about 150 degrees, south-east of Xi-An (see Figure 14). The comet-like star near α-*Altair* should have been visible in China at this time because it was about 20 minutes before sunrise. The comet-like star could have been seen in China on any clear day of the second

Chinese month if the new star appeared for 70 days and was first seen at 0:52 Jerusalem time on 9 March 5 BC, the time when Yeshua was born.

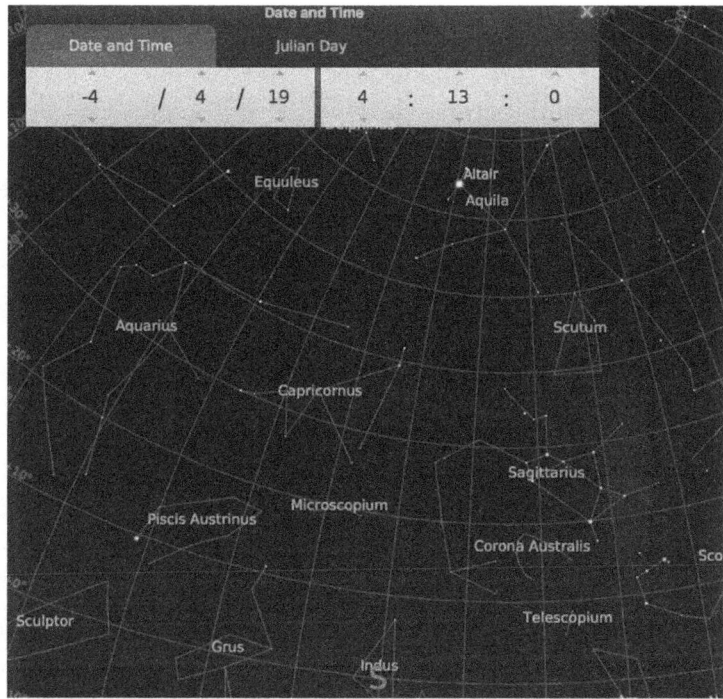

Figure 15: Predicted sky view from Jerusalem on April 19 of 5 BC. The position of α-*Altair* at 4:13 was at 180 degrees, due south of Jerusalem.

After the Magi saw the star in the east on March 9, they may have immediately left Babylon for Jerusalem. How long did they take to travel from Babylon to Jerusalem? The distance is about 900 miles if they traveled through the Fertile Crescent. If they rode on their donkeys, they should have been able to travel 25 miles per day comfortably. So it is reasonable that the Magi took about 6 weeks from first sighting the star until their arrival in Jerusalem.

On 19 April of 5 BC, six weeks after Yeshua was born, the position of α-*Altair* at 4:13 was at 180 degrees, due south of Jerusalem (see Figure 15). This is consistent with Matthew's account (Matthew 2:9). The six weeks were still well within the period (10 weeks) of visibility of the Chinese comet-like star. The Magi should have been able to see the star in the early morning when the sky was clear. If they rode on their donkeys and traveled to the west, they should not have been able to see the star even if the sky was clear in the morning. If the Magi arrived in Jerusalem on 18 April 5 BC and the sky was not clear, they could not have seen the comet-like star when they left Jerusalem for Bethlehem in the early morning of April 19. Due to a possible divine interference, the sky may have suddenly become clear around 4:00 am to allow the Magi to see the star in the due south of Jerusalem. Since both Bethlehem and the star were due south of Jerusalem, the comet-like star appeared to "hang over" Bethlehem to the eyes of the Magi.

This new comet-like star is indeed the best candidate for the star of Bethlehem described in the Gospel of Matthew. Is it significant that the star was born near α-*Altair*. We know that α-*Altair* is the brightest star in the constellation of *Aquila* and the 12th brightest star in the night sky. The ancient Babylonians called α-*Altair* the eagle star. The ancient Chinese called it *Niu Lang Xing* (the oxherd star). In the vision of Ezekiel, he saw the appearance of the glory of Yehowah God. Within it there came the likeness of four living creatures (Ezekiel 1:5) and each one had four faces, one like the face of a man, one like the face of a lion, one like the face of an ox, and one like the face of an eagle (Ezekiel 1:10). His vision tells us that eagle is one of the four perspectives of the likeness of the glory of Yehowah God. This is also consistent with Exodus 19:4, "You have seen what I did unto the Egyptians, and how I bore you on eagles' wings, and brought you unto myself." Since there were four eagle faces in the vision of Ezekiel, Yehowah God carried the Israelites on the wings of eagles (plural form) and brought them into Himself. Therefore, we may assign α-*Altair* into the Star of the Father and the new sword-like star into the star of the Messiah.

PART V
END-TIME PROPHECIES: WORLD DESTINY

CHAPTER 35

INTRODUCTION TO THE END-TIME PROPHECIES

For years people have proclaimed and set dates for the time of the end, yet none of these proclamations has been actualized. Approximately 2,000 years ago, Yeshua's disciples came to him with similar questions. "Now as he sat on the Mount of Olives, the disciples came to him privately, saying, 'Tell us, when will these things be [ruined]? And what will be the sign of your coming, and of the end of the age?'" (Matthew 24:3).

Yeshua then explained what would happen during the end times preceding his final return, "But about that day or hour no one knows, not even the angels in heaven, nor the Son, but only the Father." (Matthew 24:36).

The verb "know" in the English translation of Matthew 24:36 is in the present tense, meaning that only the Father knows the day or hour while all the others (including Yeshua) will never know them. On the other hand, Yeshua said: "Remember therefore how you have received and heard; hold fast and repent. Therefore if you will not watch, I will come upon you like a thief, and you will not know what hour I will come upon you." (Revelation 3:3). This verse implies that if we remain vigilant, we might be able to know the hour so that his coming might not be like a thief. This appears to contradict his own words in Matthew 24:36. By carefully examining the original Greek texts, one can readily discover that the tenses of the verbs are present perfect. Therefore, the correct English translation of Matthew 24:36 should be: "But about that day and hour no one has known, not even the angels in heaven, nor the Son, but only the Father." This means that before Yeshua was crucified, no one, including himself, had known the day and hour except for the Father.

Yeshua's statement at that time agrees with what Daniel stated in Daniel 12:9-10: "He replied, 'Go your way, Daniel, because the words are rolled up and sealed until the time of the end. Many will be purified, made spotless and refined, but the wicked will continue to be wicked. None of the wicked will understand, but those who are wise will understand.'" Daniel's prophecies about the end times were sealed by God at the time they were written. The end-time prophecies were sealed until the time of the end during which the wise will understand the prophecies and keep themselves pure and spotless. Yeshua in Revelation 3:3 warns his saints to be alert before his coming in the last days.

Yeshua also said that his coming would be like the days of Noah. God told Noah that the flood would come in seven days. Noah knew the day and hour, but no other man knew about the flood until it came and swept them all away. To the wicked, the calamities will come like the coming of a thief. But God may reveal the time to the wise by unlocking the sealed prophecies, as written in Daniel 12:9-10.

Only in the last days shall our knowledge increase rapidly (Daniel 12:4) to unveil the sealed end-time prophecies if we study the Scriptures diligently. Thus, unlocking the end-time prophecies right before the coming of the Messiah is not heretical. In contrast, it is perfectly aligned with the teachings of Yeshua Messiah and the prophets in the Hebrew Bible.

CHAPTER 36

DANIEL'S PROPHECY ON THE LAST HALF OF THE 70TH WEEK

In Chapters 16 and 17, we have unlocked the major part of Daniel's prophecy on the 70 weeks in Daniel 9:24-27. Here, we discuss the prophecy on the last half of the 70th week. Before we do this, we repeat the verses of Daniel 9:26-27 below:

> ^{26}And after the sixty-two weeks messiah shall be cut off, but not to himself; And he shall destroy the city and the sanctuary with the coming prince. The end of it shall be with a flood, and till the end of the war desolations are determined. ^{27}And he shall confirm a covenant with many for one week; but in the middle of the week he shall cause sacrifice and offering to fail. And on the wing of abominations shall be one who makes desolate, even until the consummation, which is determined, is poured out on the desolate.

In Chapter 17, we proved that the 70th week started on 11 Nisan 27 AD. The Messiah was crucified on 14 Nisan 30 AD, which was in the middle of the 70th week. Thus, the crucifixion of Yeshua in 30 AD confirmed the prophecy in the first part of Daniel 9:26. The second part of verse 26 means that to the Messiah himself, he was not actually cut off. He was not cut off because he resurrected 3 days and 3 nights after his crucifixion. The resurrected Messiah went back to heaven and sat on the right-hand side of his Father on the Feast of Pentecost of 30 AD. The third part of verse 26 tells us that the Messiah would destroy the city and the sanctuary with the coming prince. Yeshua himself also prophesied the destruction of the temple and the city when he was with his disciples. God gave the Jews a grace period of 40 years hoping for their repentance at the preaching of His only begotten Son. Since they did not repent, God poured out His wrath to His people and destroyed the temple and city in 70 AD. We also know that Yeshua received all authority from his Father after his resurrection (Matthew 28:18). Therefore, it was the Messiah and God who destroyed the temple and the city because of their unrepented sins and evil works. Josephus also said that it was the divine wrath of God that led to the destruction of Jerusalem and the holy temple.

In the first half of the 70th week, Yeshua confirmed the covenant with many and caused sacrifices and offerings to fail (cease) in the middle of the week. He finished God's work of salvation within about three years. He then ascended to heaven and the clock of the 70th week was paused. The total length of his ministry in his first advent was 1143 days (see Chapter 12). In his final advent, the clock of the 70th week may be re-initiated on 6 Sivan 2027, on the feast day of Pentecost. From 6 Sivan (12 May) 2027 to 1 Nisan (25 March) 2031 (when the Kingdom of God starts), 1413 days will elapse. The 1413 days can be calculated from the Julian day number JD 2461537 for 12 May 2027 and JD 2462950 for 25 March 2031. We will see below that the 1413 days are hidden in the events recorded in the book of Revelation. This should be the second half of the 70th week during which the Messiah will finish God's work of judgment and ultimate salvation. Since 1143 days +1413 days = 2556 days = 7×365.143 days, the time for the entirety of the 70th week is indeed very close to 7 solar years (2556.7 days). A difference of less than one day could be due to the fact that we do not know exactly the starting and ending hours of the two periods and that we do not consider the very short time of his work in 67 AD (see Chapter 33). A schematic diagram in Figure 16 summarizes Daniel's 70 weeks (490 years). The two dashed lines in the Figure indicate two gap-periods: two weeks and 1997 years.

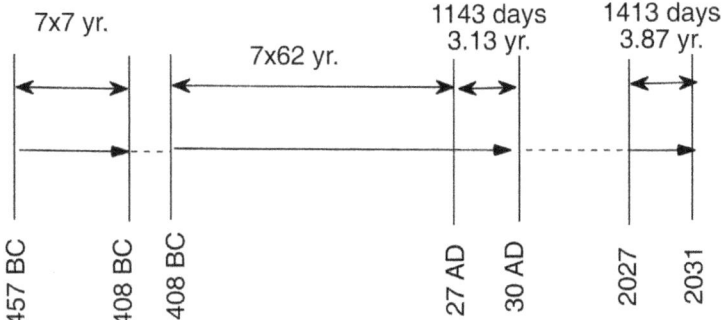
Figure 16: Schematic diagram of Daniel's 70 weeks.

CHAPTER 37

DANIEL'S PROPHECY ON THE 1335TH DAY

Daniel prophesized about the 1335th day that are connected to the end times. The detailed prophecy was recorded in Daniel 12:11-13,

> [11]And from the time that the daily sacrifice is taken away and to setting up the abomination of desolation, there shall be days one thousand two hundred and ninety. [12]Blessed is he who waits, and comes to **days one thousand three hundred and thirty-five [1335]**. [13]But you, go your way till the end; for you shall rest, and will are to your inheritance at the end of the days.

The two prophetic numbers: 1290 and 1335 in Daniel 12:11-13 may be seamessly connected together. In Chapter 19, we unlocked the first number: 1290. The end point of the 1290-year period was fulfilled perfectly in the second lunar month of 692 AD when the construction of the Dome of the Rock was complete. The Dome of the Rock sitting on the holy site of God is **the abomination of desolation** to God. From this moment, the Gentiles completely took over the holy site and God's holy people were completely dispersed from the holy city to become powerless. Right after the first prophecy on "days 1290," the second prophecy on "days 1335" should have followed immediately. This may imply that the starting time of the second prophetic period (1335) should have been the ending time of the first prophetic period (1290).

As we have seen from other prophecies, there is a possibility of double fulfillments of these numbers. In the first fulfillment of a prophecy, in a long period, one day is equivalent to one year, so "days 1290" were fulfilled according to "years 1290." The end point of the "years 1290" prophetic period was in May of 692 AD (possibly on May 8), which was the starting point of the subsequent "years 1335" prophetic period. Adding 1,335 years to the month of May 692 AD, we arrive in May 2027.

In the second fulfillment of a prophecy, in a short period, one prophetic day is literally one day, so "days 1335" should also be fulfilled according to "days 1335." By checking the Hebrew lunisolar calendar, we find that Sivan 6 of 2027 is in the 1335th day of Tishri 1 (September 16) of 2023 (the Feast of Trumpets). It is amazing that the day of 6 Sivan 2027 simultaneously matches both end points of the long "years 1335" period (starting from 692 AD) and the short "days 1335" period (starting from 1 Tishri 2023). Moreover, there are also exactly 1,413 days from 6 Sivan 2027 to 1 Nisan 2031, and the 1,413 days simultaneously match the last half of the 70th week (Chapter 36) and the events mentioned in the book of Revelation (see below). The connections of these prophetic numbers are shown schematically in Figure 17.

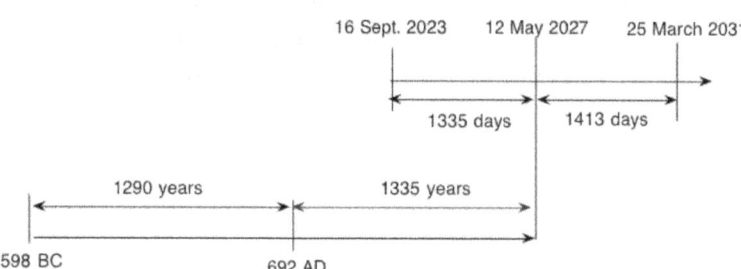

Figure 17: The prophetic periods from the books of Revelation and Daniel.

On the day of 1 Nisan 2031, Yeshua shall start to co-reign with his Father. Daniel prophesied for the 70th week (the last week of the 70 weeks) to be for the Messiah's work on the earth before his reign. In his first advent, he spent 1,143 days on the earth in doing God's work of salvation (from 6 April 27 AD to 26 May 30 AD and excluding 3 days and 3 nights in the grave). In his final advent, he will spend 1,413 days on the earth doing God's work of judgment before he starts to reign. The combined number of days for the first and final advents of Yeshua is 2,556, which is very close to 7 solar years (2,556.7 days).

What is amazing is that the 1,413 days of the last part of the 70th week are also hidden in the book of Revelation. Between the first and seventh trumpet, John mentioned three time periods: five months, 1,260 days, and 3.5 days. Five lunar months = 147.5 days, so 147.5 days +1,260 days +3.5 days = 1,411 days, which are two days less than 1,413 days. The extra 2 days should be for all other events, as we will describe in Chapter 40.

How important is the Feast of Pentecost? From Chapter 15, we know that both the Noahic Covenant and the Mosaic Covenant were established on the feast days of Pentecost. If we use a correct Hebrew calendar for 1948 (see Appendix D), we find that the declaration of re-establishment of the nation of Israel was also on the Feast of Pentecost. We also know that Yeshua ascended to heaven on the Feast of Pentecost in 30 AD. In a like manner, we expect that he may also come down with glory on the Feast of Pentecost to harvest the first fruits before he pours out his wrath to judge the whole world. When the Lamb of God stands on Mount Zion, he will bring 144,000 saints who are the first fruits of God (Revelation 14:1-4). The first fruits must be harvested on the Feast of Pentecost. Therefore, these saints should be raptured on the Feast of Pentecost before the Lamb pours out his wrath.

CHAPTER 38

DANIEL'S PROPHECY ON THE FOURTH BEAST

Daniel prophesized about the fourth beast that would be destroyed in the end times. The detailed prophecy was written in Daniel 7:23-28:

²³Thus he said: "The fourth beast shall be a fourth kingdom on earth, which shall be different from all other kingdoms, and shall devour the whole earth, trample it and break it in pieces. ²⁴The ten horns are ten kings who shall arise from this kingdom. And another shall rise after them; he shall be different from the first ones, and shall subdue three kings. ²⁵He shall speak pompous words against the Most High, shall persecute the saints of the Most High, and shall intend to change times and law. **Then the saints shall be given into his hand for a time and times and half a time.** ²⁶But the court shall be seated, and they shall take away his dominion, to consume and destroy it forever. ²⁷Then the kingdom and dominion, and the greatness of the kingdoms under the whole heaven, shall be given to the people, the saints of the Most High. His kingdom is an everlasting kingdom, and all dominions shall serve and obey him." ²⁸This is the end of the account. As for me, Daniel, my thoughts greatly troubled me, and my countenance changed; but I kept the matter in my heart.

Daniel 7:1-14 records Daniel's vision of four beasts that represent the four kingdoms on the earth before Messiah's everlasting Kingdom (Daniel 7:1-14). The first refers to the kingdom of Babylon, the second to the kingdom of Persia and Media, the third to the kingdom of Greece, and the fourth to the kingdom of Rome. The fourth kingdom would be different from all the previous ones, and would devour the whole earth, tread it down, and break it into pieces. Out of this kingdom would arise ten kings.

When the eleventh king arose, three of the previous kings would have fallen. After this king secured the power, he would speak great words against the Most High and persecute the saints of the Most High until **a time and times and half a time**. Since the phrase "**a time and times and half a time**" means 1,260 prophetic days/years, we conclude that the power of the eleventh king would be removed in the 1260th year from its establishment.

Who is the eleventh king and when did he secure the power and become more powerful than the other 7 kings? History tells us that after the western Roman Empire, ten kingdoms arose:

Ostrogothic Kingdom (493-553 AD)
Visigothic Kingdom (418-720 AD)
Kingdom of Lombard (468-774 AD)
Mauri Kingdom (533-698 AD)
Sub-Roman British Kingdom (410-597 AD)
Kingdom of Burgundy (411 to 534 AD)
Frankish Kingdom (481-843 AD)
Vandal Kingdom (435 AD-534 AD)
Alamanni Tribal Kingdom (3rd century-911 AD)
Kingdom of the Suebi (409-585 AD)

The main religion of the Ostrogothic, the Visigothic, and the Vandal Kingdoms was Arianism, which was a heretical Christian faith according to Catholicism. Because of conflict in religion, these three kingdoms were destroyed by the Eastern Roman Empire and were never reestablished. The other seven kingdoms mostly fell before 774 AD but revived later on. For example, most territories of the Alamanni Kingdom were within the territory of modern Germany; the territories of the kingdom of Burgundy are within modern Switzerland and Austria; the Mauri Kingdom has become the modern state of Mauritania. These 10 kingdoms after the Western Roman Empire appear to fit well the ten kings (horns) in the vision of Daniel.

There was an important historical event that took place in 756 AD. The Frankish king Pepin the Short conferred upon Pope Stephen II the territories belonging to Ravenna, which extended the temporal rule of the Popes beyond the duchy of Rome. This donation provided a legal basis for the establishment of the Papal States. The seeds of the Papal States as a sovereign political entity were planted in the 6th century AD during the period of the Eastern Roman Empire under Emperor Justinian I. But the sovereignty of the Papal States had not come until Charlemagne became the sole king of the Frankish Kingdom in December 771 AD. He continued his father's policy towards the papacy and became its protector to guarantee the sovereignty of the Papal States.

Before 771 AD, the sovereignty of the Papal States was still challenged by the very existence of the Kingdom of Lombard. After 771 AD, Charlemagne protected the Papal States and guaranteed its sovereignty. For example, the territory ruled by the papacy was invaded by Desiderius on 1 February 772 AD. Pope Adrian I then sought the assistance of Charlemagne. Charlemagne entered Italy with a large army and besieged Desiderius in his capital of Pavia in 773 AD. He banished Desiderius to the Abbey of Corbie in France in 774 AD, and adopted the title "King of the Lombard" himself. Charlemagne reached the height of his power in 800 AD and was crowned as Emperor of the Romans by Pope Leo III on Christmas Day at Rome's Old St. Peter's Basilica.

Since all Holy Roman emperors considered their kingdoms to be the descendants of Charlemagne's Empire, the effective date of the Holy Roman Empire's establishment should have been in December 771 AD when Charlemagne became the sole king of the Frankish Kingdom. Only after this date was the sovereignty of the Papal States guaranteed by the Roman emperors. Most historians believe that the Papal States was terminated on 20 September 1870 AD. In fact, this was the fourth disestablishment, but it still, in fact, exists at present.

The Holy Roman Empire is the small horn of the fourth beast. Because this small horn spoke pompous words against the Most-High, persecuted His saints, and intended to change times and law, he will be destroyed forever after the saints are given into his hand for a time and times and half time (Daniel 7:25). This prophecy means that in the 1260th year from the starting of the small horn, he and the fourth beast will be destroyed forever (Daniel 7:11).

Since the first emperor Charlemagne was crowned by Pope Leo III on 25 December 800 AD, historians set the year of 800 AD as the commencement of the Holy Roman Empire. In fact, he became the sole ruler of the Frankish Kingdom and the protector of the Papal States in December of 771 AD when his brother died suddenly and unexpectedly. The sudden and unexplained death of Charlemagne's brother in December 771 AD made him the sole ruler of his kingdom. This should have been a divine interference of God. Therefore, the Holy Roman Empire should have begun in December 771 AD.

This point is further supported by analogy to the coronation date of Nebuchadnezzar. The Jerusalem Chronicles indicate that Nebuchadnezzar was crowned as the king of Babylon on the first day of the sixth Babylonian month of 605 BC. However, God counted his reign to start on the day when his father died: the 8th day of the fifth month of 605 BC. In the same day of 587 BC (the 8th day of 5th month in the Babylonia calendar is the 10th day of the fifth month in the Hebrew calendar), Jerusalem and the holy temple were burned down. God counted this day to be the first day of the 19th year of Nebuchadnezzar's reign. Moreover, the 9th or 10th day of the fifth month in the Hebrew calendar is the fast day of the Israelites, as commanded by God. Therefore, the death of Nebuchadnezzar's father on this special day should have also been a divine interference of God.

If the Holy Roman Empire began in December 771 AD, the 1260th year from this date should be the year between December 2030 and December 2031 (see Figure 1 in Introduction). The destruction of Babylon the Great, the city of Rome—marking the end of the fourth beast—should occur shortly after 25 March 2031 (see Chapter 40).

CHAPTER 39

POSSIBLE INTERPRETATION OF CHAPTERS 12-13 OF REVELATION

Revelation 12:1 says: "Now a great sign appeared in heaven: a woman clothed with the sun, with the moon under her feet, and on her head a garland of twelve stars." The woman in this verse should be identified as the nation of Israel. The woman was clothed with the sun, crowned with twelve stars, and with the moon under her feet. These symbols are similar to the ones described in Genesis 37:6-9:

> So he said to them, "Please hear this dream which I have dreamed: There we were, binding sheaves in the field. Then behold, my sheaf arose and also stood upright; and indeed your sheaves stood all around and bowed down to my sheaf." And his brothers said to him, "Shall you indeed reign over us? Or shall you indeed have dominion over us?" So they hated him even more for his dreams and for his words. Then he dreamed still another dream and told it to his brothers, and said, "Look, I have dreamed another dream. And this time, the sun, the moon, and the eleven stars bowed down to me."

It is clear that in Joseph's dream, the sun and moon symbolized his father Israel and his mother Rachael while the stars represented his eleven brothers and himself. This dream was fulfilled when Joseph became the second most powerful man in Egypt.

The components of the sun, moon, and twelve stars represent the nation of Israel, the people of Israel, or the chosen people of God. Several prophets of God also referred to Israel as a "woman" (Isaiah 54:5-6; Jeremiah 4:31; Micah 4:9-10).

Revelation 12:5 says, "She bore a male child who was to rule all nations with a rod of iron. And her child was caught up to God and His throne." The male child in this verse is Yeshua Messiah since he is to rule all the nations with "a rod of iron." (Revelation 12:5). The dragon in Revelation tried to devour the child at the moment of his birth (Revelation 12:4), which may refer to Herod's attempt to kill the infant Yeshua (Matthew 2:16). He was snatched up to the right-hand side of his Father's throne after he was crucified and resurrected. After Yeshua ascended to heaven, a church in Jerusalem, mainly comprised of his disciples and the Jews, was established. The Gospel was preached over the cities of Israel and even to the Gentiles. But most Jews did not believe in the Gospel and persecuted Yeshua's believers. Forty years after Yeshua's crucifixion, God's wrath poured out on the unrepented Jews and God destroyed the holy temple and the holy city, as prophesized by Yeshua, Daniel, and Ezekiel.

Although Jerusalem was destroyed and almost desolated, the Jews could still approach the city and the temple site. Even in the bad years, they were allowed to pray on the fast day of the 9th or 10th day of the fifth month Av. However, by 688 AD when the construction of the Dome of the Rock began, the Jews were completely expelled from the city and scattered into many other countries. This may be consistent with Revelation 12:6, which says: "Then the woman fled into the wilderness, where she has a place prepared by God, that they should feed her there one thousand two hundred and sixty days."

Since the woman fled into the wildness after Yeshua ascended to heaven, this cannot refer to Mary's flight to Egypt after her birth to Yeshua (Matthew 2:13-14). Furthermore, "the wilderness" refers to any place outside the city of Jerusalem. Revelation 12:6 thus prophesized that the woman representing the people of Israel were exiled from Jerusalem and fled into many other places (the wilderness) for 1260 years. The beginning time of the 1260-year period should have been July 688 AD when the Dome of the Rock began to be built. In the 1260th

year of their exile out of Jerusalem in 688 AD, they were brought back to Jerusalem in 1948. This prophecy was indeed fulfilled exactly (see Chapter 21).

This prophecy in Revelation 12:6 is similar to Daniel 12:5-7 where Daniel prophesized that the power of the holy people would be completely shattered for 1260 years. When the Jews were forced to leave the holy land in 688 AD, they became powerless, being persecuted and killed by the ungodly and evil rulers of the countries they were scattered into. During this period God hid His face from His people because of their iniquity, transgressions, uncleanness, and unfaithfulness (Ezekiel 39:23-24).

Daniel further prophesized that after the exiled holy people were brought back to the holy land, the clock of the end times started to tick. This is consistent with Revelation 12:7-9:

> And war broke out in heaven: Michael and his angels fought with the dragon; and the dragon and his angels fought, but they did not prevail, nor was a place found for them in heaven any longer. So the great dragon was cast out, that serpent of old, called the Devil and Satan, who deceives the whole world; he was cast to the earth, and his angels were cast out with him.

War will break out in heaven and the dragon and his angels will be cast down to the earth. What is the timeline for this event? According to the books of Daniel and Revelation, this should happen after 1948. Revelation 12:13-16 says:

> Now when the dragon saw that he had been cast to the earth, he persecuted the woman who gave birth to the male child. But the woman was given two wings of a great eagle, that she might fly into the wilderness to her place, where she is nourished for a time and times and half a time, from the presence of the serpent. So the serpent spewed water out of his mouth like a flood after the woman, that he might cause her to be carried

away by the flood. But the earth helped the woman, and the earth opened its mouth and swallowed up the flood which the dragon had spewed out of his mouth.

The dragon (the devil) will persecute the woman (the nation of Israel) after he is cast down to the earth. The nation of Israel will be carried into the wildness again and be nourished for 1260 days. The 1260 days here should be literally 1260 days during the end times. It is important to note that the 1260 days in verse 14 are different from the ones in verse 6. In verse 6, the woman herself will flee into the wilderness while in verse 14 she will fly into the wilderness with two eagle wings provided by God. In verse 6, the event occurred after Yeshua was caught up into God and his throne and before Satan and his angels are cast down to the earth, while the event in verse 14 should take place after they are cast down from heaven.

These events described in Revelation 12:7-16 have not happened yet up to now in 2020. After the dragon is cast down to the earth, he will try to destroy the nation of Israel again. He will attempt to destroy them by war, but they will flee into the wilderness with God's help. When shall they flee to the wilderness. Yeshua said: "When you see the 'abomination of desolation' spoken by Daniel the prophet, standing in the holy place, then let those in Judea flee to the mountains." (Matthew 24:15-16). This prophecy should have multiple fulfillments. The first fulfillment should have been in 70 AD when the Romans stood in the holy temple. Since the Romans, the Gentles are not allowed to enter the holy temple, the event of the Romans standing in the holy temple was the "abomination of desolation" to the God of Israel. History tells us that only those Jews who fled to the mountains were not killed by the Romans. The second fulfillment should have been in 692 AD when the Dome of the Rock had been built on the site of the holy temple. The Dome of the Rock is the "abomination of desolation" to the God of Israel and the time (692 AD) of its completion should correspond to the starting time of the long 1335-day prophetic period (see Chapter 37). The third fulfillment shall be in the end-time when the "abomination of desolation" should stand again in the holy place or an event of the "abomination of desolation" should happen in the holy place. Since the starting time of the short 1335-day prophetic period should be on 1 Tishri 2023 (see Chapter 37), it is likely that on or after 1 Tishri 2023, the "abomination of desolation" should stand in the holy place or an event of the "abomination of desolation" should happen in the holy place. According to Yeshua's suggestion, the people of modern Israel should flee into the wilderness on or after 1 Tishri 2023. The wilderness could be the earthly nations such as the United States. The earthly nations who are the friends of Israel will defend Israel and defeat the nations that are called by Satan to attack Israel. In verse 15 "flood" may symbolize "war" and in verse 16 "the earth" may refer to the earthly nations.

After Satan finds that he cannot destroy the nation of Israel, he will be very angry and make war with the other offspring of the woman, who keep the commandments of God and have the testimony of Yeshua. These are the true Gentile believers of Yeshua who have been called into the Kingdom of God through the blood of Yeshua. The Gentile believers in Yeshua are also called the people of Israel, the chosen people of God, and thus belong to the offspring of the woman.

In Revelation 13:1, the beast from the sea should have been the Roman Empire, the fourth beast seen by Daniel. One of its heads (kingdoms) was mortally wounded but will be healed after the dragon gives his power to him. The beast will have authority and make war for 42 months (Revelation 13:5). In Revelation 13:11, the second beast from the earth may be the Roman Catholic Church who looks like a lamb and speaks like a dragon. The leader of the church, the false prophet, will perform great signs to deceive those on the earth (Revelation 13:13-14). He will deceive people on the earth to make an image of the first beast. He will also have the power to give breath to the image of the first beast so that it can speak and cause many who do not worship the image to be killed (verse 15). He will cause all, both small and great, rich and poor, free and slave, to receive a mark on their right hands or on their foreheads (verse 16). The mark is the name of the first beast or the number of the name of the beast. The number of the name of a man who should be the leader of the beast kingdom is 666 (verse 18). If any one does not receive the mark, he may not buy and sell (verse 17).

When will the dragon be cast down to the earth to persecute the woman? We speculate that it should occur around the Feast of Trumpets (Tishri 1) of 2023. A great war against the nation of Israel will also take place after 16 September 2023. Satan will deceive many nations to make a war against the nation of Israel. The United States of America and its allies will side with Israel to help them fly into the wilderness where they will be nourished for 1260 days.

When Satan gives power to the two beasts to make war with Gentile's Yeshua believers for 42 months, many true believers will be killed because of their refusal to worship the image of the first beast and to receive the mark of the beast.

Most Biblical scholars misinterpret Daniel 9:27 (see Chapter 17). They think that the anti-messiah will make a peace covenant with Israel for three and a half years. Then he will break the covenant and bring great tribulation to Yeshua's believers and the Israelites for next three and a half years.

The seven heads on the first beast represent the seven kingdoms in the history of the Roman Empire (the fourth beast in Daniel vision). The seven kingdoms should be:

1) The United Roman Empire
2) The Western Roman Empire
3) The Eastern Roman Empire
4) The Holy Roman Empire
5) The Ottoman Empire
6) Divided Europe
7) The European Union

The deadly wounded head is the Holy Roman Empire and will be healed after Satan is cast down to the earth and gives power to the deadly wounded head.

The Roman Empire in the whole period was the fourth beast in Daniel's vision. John also calls each of the seven kingdoms within the fourth beast a beast. The Holy Roman Empire is one of the seven beasts that was gravely wounded. It will be called the eighth beast after it ascends out of the bottomless pit and is healed by the power of

Satan. It will re-appear for a short time and then go to perdition. This interpretation is consistent with Revelation 17:8-11.

The ten horns on the beast are the ten kings of the healed Holy Roman Empire (the eighth beast). They will receive authority for one hour as kings with the beast. They will make war with the Lamb, and the Lamb will overcome them (Revelation 17:12-14).

The harlot (the woman) who sits on the beast is the Roman Catholic Church who reigns over the kings of the earth (Revelation 17:18). The headquarter of the Roman Catholic Church sits in the great city Rome that has seven hills. Mecca and New York both have seven hills, but they could not be the city Revelation refers to because no blood of holy apostles and prophets of God was found in these two cities (Revelation 18:20). The holy apostle Peter was crucified in Rome rather than in Mecca or New York. The city of Rome, Babylon the Great, will be totally burned by the 10 horns (Revelation 17:16).

CHAPTER 40

POSSIBLE SEQUENCE OF THE WORLD EVENTS IN NEAR FUTURE

Three numbers (1290, 1335, and 1260) in the prophecies of Daniel and three numbers (5 months, 1260 days, and 3.5 days) in the book of Revelation allow us to consistently figure out a possible sequence of the end-time events (see Table XIV below). It is important to note that this chapter contains conjecture.

On 16 September 2023 (after sunset of September 15, Jerusalem time), which is on the Feast of Trumpets, an event of the "abomination of desolation" should take place in the holy place or the "abomination of desolation" should stand in the holy place. The Feast of Pentecost on 12 May 2027 is on the 1335th day from the Feast of Trumpets in 2023. On that special day, the true believers of Yeshua may be raptured, and 144,000 Israelites shall be sealed and protected by God. These things shall happen in the 6th seal, as described in Revelation 6:12-17, 7:1-17. The 6th-seal events are like those described in Matthew 24:29-31,40-41.

Immediately after the rapture, the first, second, third, and fourth trumpet will sound and there will be struck of vegetation, of the seas, of the waters, and of the heavens. All these events shall take a short time (about two days). When the fifth trumpet sounds, the locusts from the bottomless pit will start to strike men without the seal of God for 5 lunar months (147.5 days). At the end of the 5 months, the first woe will end (Revelation 9:12). After the sixth trumpet sounds on 9 October 2027 (the 8th day of the 8th month), two prophets will prophesy for 1260 days and be killed on 22 March 2031 (possibly just after sunset of 21 March). After 3.5 days, they will resurrect and ascend into heaven on 25 March 2031 (maybe in the morning). The second woe will end at this moment. Right after this, the 7th trumpet will sound, and the mystery of God will be completed. The Almighty God and the Messiah will start to reign on 25 March 2031, which is on the first day of Nisan (the first month). After this, the nations will be angry and God's full wrath will be poured out, then the rewards will be given to His prophets and saints (after resurrection of the dead), and finally all God's enemies will be destroyed (Revelation 11:17-18).

The third woe immediately following the second woe should be God's wrath of the 7th bowl because the wrath of the 6th bowl is poured out before Revelation 16:15 (Hebraic-Roots Version), "Behold, He comes as a thief, blessed is he who watches and keeps his garments, lest he walk naked and they see his shame." The HRV text makes more sense than the Greek text, "Behold, I am coming as a thief, blessed is he who watches and keeps his garments, lest he walk naked and they see his shame." In the HRV text, "He" refers to the Almighty God Yehowah while "I" in the Greek text refers to Messiah Yeshua who revealed the end-time prophecy to John. The Messiah shall come down from heaven in the sixth seal and Yehowah God shall come after Elijah the prophet (Malachi 4:5). Yehowah God and His Messiah will start to reign right after the 7th trumpet sounds. Therefore, the wrath of the 6th bowl should be placed before the 7th trumpet.

One of the two witnesses should be Elijah the prophet since he has the power to shut heaven and prevent rainfall in the days of his prophecy (Revelation 11:6) as he did in the ancient times. Another witness should be Moses since he has the power to turn water into blood (Revelation 11:6), as he did in the land of Egypt. In the first coming of the Messiah, John the Baptist came before the Messiah. John prepared the way for the ministry of the Messiah in his first advent. In his final advent, the Messiah will first come down from heaven to prepare the way for his Father's coming. The Messiah will finish God's work of salvation and judgment in the second part of the 70th week in Daniel's prophecy. Yeshua will also send his two witnesses to prophesize 1260 days before Yehowah descends from heaven.

The wrath of the 7th bowl will begin after God and His Messiah start to reign over the nations on the earth. In the wrath of the 7th bowl, there will be great hail and a mighty earthquake that causes many cities to fall. The great Babylon will be judged and destroyed. This should be before the marriage of the Lamb. The great Babylon is an integrated kingdom of the Roman Catholic Church and the Western Roman Empire. This church cannot be invited to the supper of the marriage of the Lamb. Only the true disciples of the Messiah who have performed righteous acts will be invited. On 14 Nisan 30 AD before his crucifixion, Yeshua Messiah told his disciples (Matthew 26:29), "But I say to you, I will not drink of this fruit of the vine from now on until that day when I drink it new with you in my Father's Kingdom."

The final war in the great day of God Almighty should be after the destruction of the great Babylon. This war should be the one described in Ezekiel 38-39, in Zechariah 14, and in Revelation 19:11-21. The three spirits of demons will gather the armies of the nations in Armageddon at the end of the sixth bowl and fight against Jerusalem after the 7th trumpet. Zechariah 14 tells us that Jerusalem will be taken initially and afterward Yehowah God will fight for Jerusalem and strike all the people who fight against Jerusalem. The verses in Revelation 19:11-21 reveal that the Messiah, who is the king of the kings and the lord of the lords, will lead the heavenly armies to fight against the armies of the beast and defeat them. Similar to the description in Ezekiel 39:17-20, all the birds that fly in the midst of heaven will eat the flesh of all the beast armies. In the war, the beast and the false prophet (the second beast) will be cast into the lake of fire and Satan will be cast into the Abyss and shut there for one thousand years.

After one thousand years, Satan will be released to deceive the nations and to gather around Jerusalem to encircle it before 17 March 3031 (Nisan 1). Fire will come down from heaven and devour them, and Satan will be cast into the lake of fire. That will be the final judgment of God and all the dead will be resurrected and judged by God. Those whose names are not written in the book of life will be thrown into the lake of fire. Then there will be a new heaven and a new earth, and the new Jerusalem will come down from heaven on 17 March 3031. From Nisan 1 of 3031, God and His Messiah will reign in the eternal Kingdom of God forever.

Blessed are those who follow His commandments, that they may have the right to access the tree of life, and to enter through the gates of the holy city of new Jerusalem (Revelation 22:14). Outside (the city), are dogs, sorcerers, the sexually immoral, murderers, idolaters, and whoever loves and practices a lie (Revelation 22:15). If the above translation of Revelation 22:15 were correct, who are the people outside the city? Will these ungodly people have a right to live outside the city in the eternal Kingdom of God? If yes, this idea is in contradiction with Revelation 21:8, which tells us that those who commit the similar sins shall be cast into the lake of fire and destroyed (burned up).

In order to resolve the above contradiction, we may check the Interlinear Greek-English Bible to see if there is an alternative translation. The Greek word "exo" means "outside" and "without." Revelation 21:7 talks about the blessing of the people who have overcome while Revelation 21:8 talks about the curse of the people who commit these great sins. In a similar manner, Revelation 22:14 talks about the blessing while Revelation 22:15 addresses the curse. If "exo" means "without," Revelation 22:15 could be translated as: "Without [blessing] are dogs, sorcerers, the sexually immoral, murderers, idolaters, and whoever loves and practices a lie." This translation makes more sense. Only those who have kept the commandments of God are blessed and may have a right to access the tree of life and to enter the city (Revelation 22:14). In contrast, those who have committed the great sins are cursed and shall be cast into the lake of fire after the final judgment (Revelation 21:8).

Table XIV: Possible Sequence of the World Events in Near Future

Date	Event marks	Event description
15 September 2023 (after sunset, Jerusalem time)		On or after the Feast of Trumpets, an event of the "abomination of desolation" should take place in the holy place or the "abomination of desolation" should stand in the holy place.
11 May 2027 (after sunset)	6th seal	On the Feast of Pentecost, the true believers will be raptured; 144,000 Israelites will be sealed and protected by God.
11 May 2027 (after sunset)	7th seal, 1st trumpet, 2nd trumpet, 3rd trumpet, 4th trumpet	Struck of vegetation, of the seas, of the waters, and of the heavens.
13 May 2027 (after sunset)	5th trumpet	The locusts from the bottomless pit will start to strike men without seal of God for 5 lunar months.
8 Oct. 2027 (after sunset)	6th trumpet, 1st woe ends	Two prophets will start to prophesy for 1260 days.
A short time before 21 March 2031	6th bowl	Euphrates River will be dried; Three spirits of demons will gather the kings of the earth for the battle of the Great day of God Almighty.
21 March 2031 (after sunset)		The two witnesses of Yeshua will be killed.
25 March 2031 (after sunrise)	7th trumpet, 2nd woe ends	The two witnesses will rise from death; God and Messiah will start to reign on 1 Nisan.
After 25 March 2031 and before 7 April 2031	7th bowl, 3rd woe	God's full wrath will be poured out; Babylon will be judged.
On 7 April (14 Nisan) 2031		The marriage supper of the Lamb

Right after 7 April 2031		God and His Messiah will defeat the beast and its armies (Ezekiel's war or Armageddon war); Satan will be chained for 1000 years; Some saints will rise and reign with God for 1000 years.
Right before 17 March 3031		War of Gog and Magog
On 17 March 3031		Eternal Kingdom of God will start (new earth, new heaven, and new Jerusalem).

APPENDIXES

APPENDIX A

THE DELTA-T PARAMETER FOR ECLIPSES

The orbital positions of the Sun and Moon required by eclipse predictions, are calculated using Terrestrial Dynamical Time (TD) because it is a uniform time scale. However, world time zones and daily life are based on Universal Time (UT). In order to convert eclipse predictions from TD to UT, the difference between these two timescales must be known. The parameter delta-T (ΔT) is the arithmetic difference between the two as ΔT = TD − UT. Before 500 BC, the value of ΔT can be extrapolated from measured values using the long-term mean parabolic trend: $\Delta T = -20 + bt^2$ seconds, where t = (year−1820)/100 and b = 32.

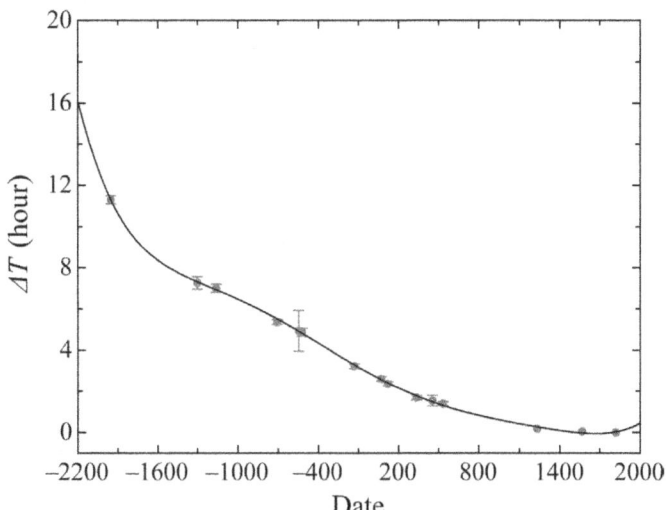

Figure A1: The ΔT parameter as a function of the Julian year

The ΔT parameters can be reliably obtained from the recorded total solar eclipses and from the recorded lunar eclipses with detailed beginning and ending times. The observed locations (coordinates) must also be given. The uncertainties of the ΔT parameters for total solar eclipses can be reliably determined. For lunar eclipses, the uncertainties of the ΔT parameters depend on how accurately the ancient astronomers recorded the beginning and ending times of the eclipses. Figure A1 shows the ΔT parameter as a function of the Julian year. The parameters are obtained from the total solar eclipses mostly observed in China and some in the Near East. The data are fitted with a sixth-order polynomial function (see the solid line in Figure A1):

$$\Delta T = 2.8124 - 0.0035158 j + 1.0979 \times 10^{-6} j^2 + 6.827 \times 10^{-10} j^3 - 5.1087 \times 10^{-13} j^4 - 1.3103 \times 10^{-16} j^5 + 1.1221 \times 10^{-19} j^6$$

In the above equation, j is a Julian year. Positive j refers to a year after Messiah (AD) and negative j to a year before Messiah (BC). For example, $j = 30$ for 30 AD and $j = -130$ for 131 BC.

For any year before 2200 BC, we will use this fitted curve to calculate ΔT in hours. After we calculate ΔT value, we obtain b value by solving equation: $\Delta T = -20 + bt^2$, here $t = (j-1820)/100$ and ΔT is in seconds.

APPENDIX B
PAPER ON THE NONCONSTANCY OF THE SPEED OF LIGHT

Are atomic clocks and the speed of light slowing down?
Peter Zhao

Taizhou Research Institute, Zhejiang University, China

Abstract

We report our time-keeping results for four extremely precise quartz watches of different ages against the world atomic clock that keeps the Coordinated Universal Time. Compared with the quartz clocks, the atomic clock has been slowing down with a rate of 84.3±2.5 ppb per year for the last 40 years. Because quantum theory predicts that the frequency or the tick rate of the atomic clock is linearly proportional to the speed of light in vacuum and because the frequency of the quartz vibration should not increase with time, our data suggest that both the atomic clock and the speed of light should slow down over time. The present result agrees with other independent experiments on as-maintained electrical units in the 1960's and with the theoretical prediction of both the general theory of relativity and Maxwell's equations.

Introduction

When the cesium-based atomic clock was used to measure the time or frequency f, the speed of light in vacuum c was found to be time-independent between 1972 and 1983 (variation is less than 0.4 ppb per year). The c value was determined according to the formula: $c = \lambda f$, where

λ is the wavelength of the emitted light of an atom. Because the Rydberg constant R_∞ is found to be time-independent within the experimental uncertainties of less than 1 ppb per year [1-4] and because $1/\lambda \propto R_\infty$ (see the Bohr model of hydrogen spectra for example), λ is also expected to be time independent. Since the tick rate of a cesium-based atomic clock is linearly proportional to c (see our theoretical proof below), the c value "measured" from such emissive experiments will always be a constant independent of whether c is intrinsically time-dependent or not. Therefore, the constancy of the speed of light cannot be tested by cesium atomic clocks.

The general theory of relativity appears to predict that the vacuum permittivity ϵ_0 should be time-dependent [5-7]. In generalizing Maxwell's equations to the coordinates of general relativity, Møller [5] showed that ϵ_0 is a function of the Friedmann radius $a(t)$, which is time dependent. The same conclusion was also reached by Landau and Lifshitz [6]. In the 1990's, Sumner re-considered the equations of Einstein and Maxwell together [7] and also showed that the energy of the electrical field is proportional to $1/a(t)$ and $\epsilon_0 \propto a(t)$. As seen below, the vacuum permeability μ_0 should be a true constant, the relationship $c = 1/\sqrt{\epsilon_0 \mu_0}$ leads to $c \propto 1/\sqrt{\epsilon_0}$, which is time dependent.

The fine-structure constant α and the Rydberg constant R_∞ are time-independent within the experimental uncertainties of less than 1 ppb per year [1-4]. According to the general theory of relativity and the Maxwell's equations, the mass and charge of a point particle also remain constant as spacetime geometry changes [7]. The simple relationship [8]: $m_e = \frac{2R_\infty h}{c\alpha^2}$ and time independency of the electron mass m_e lead to the time-dependent Planck "constant" $h \propto c$ while the relationship [8]: $\alpha = \frac{e^2 c \mu_0}{2h}$ and time independency of the electron charge e imply that μ_0 is a true constant independent of whether c changes over time or not.

Here, we report our time-keeping results for four extremely precise quartz watches of different ages against the world atomic clock that is used to keep the Coordinated Universal Time (UTC). These watches were made in 1980, 1991, 2007, and 2013, and have accuracies rated as ±5, ±10, ±10, and ±5 seconds per year, respectively. By carefully comparing the tick rate of the world atomic clock with those of the quartz watches, we find that the world atomic clock is slowing down by

2.66±0.08 seconds every year or by 84.3±2.5 ppb every year. Because the frequency of the atomic clock is linearly proportional to the light speed c, our data suggest that both the atomic clock and the speed of light slow down over time.

Theory

In atomic physics, hyperfine structure in an atom arises from interaction between the nucleus and outer electrons. This interaction leads to small shifts or splits in the energy levels. For a nuclear magnetic dipole moment placed in the magnetic field of an electron cloud, the relevant term in the Hamiltonian is given by [9]:

$$\hat{H}_D = 2g_I \mu_B \mu_N \frac{\mu_0}{4\pi} \frac{\mathbf{I} \cdot \mathbf{N}}{r^3},$$

where g_I is the nuclear g-factor, μ_N is the nuclear magneton, $\mathbf{I}$ is the nuclear spin, μ_B is Bohr magneton, and

$$\mathbf{N} = \mathbf{I} - \left(\frac{g_s}{2}\right)[\mathbf{s} - 3(\mathbf{s} \cdot \hat{\mathbf{r}})\hat{\mathbf{r}}],$$

where g_s is the free electron g-factor and $\mathbf{s}$ is the spin of an electron. Using the relationship [8]:

$$\mu_N = \mu_B \frac{A_r(e)}{A_r(p)},$$

where $A_r(e)$ and $A_r(p)$ are the masses of one mole of electrons and protons, respectively, and [8]

$$\mu_B = \sqrt{\frac{c\alpha^5 h}{32\pi^2 \mu_0 R_\infty^2}},$$

We obtain

$$\hat{H}_D = \frac{g_I c\alpha^5 h}{64\pi^3 R_\infty^2} \frac{A_r(e)}{A_r(p)} \frac{\mathbf{I} \cdot \mathbf{N}}{r^3}.$$

The frequency f of the electromagnetic radiation used for the Cs atomic clock is given by

$$f = \frac{E}{h} \propto \frac{g_I c\alpha^5}{64\pi^3 R_\infty^2} \frac{A_r(e)}{A_r(p)} \qquad (1)$$

Because the values of $A_r(e)/A_r(p)$, a, and R_∞ are found to be time-independent [1-4], Eq. 1 confirms that the frequency or the tick rate of the cesium-based atomic clock is linearly proportional to the speed of light c. In fact, because the wavelength of the emitted light of any atom is a constant (independent of time) due to the constancy of R_∞, this linear c dependence of the frequency is valid for any atomic clock.

In using atomic clocks to measure c, workers simply count a fixed number of ticks within a prescribed time. But since the tick rate itself is proportional to the thing being measured (i.e., c), this is not a proper method for measuring c.

On the other hand, the quartz clock is based on the vibrational frequency of the quartz crystal, which is proportional to $\sqrt{E_Y/\rho_m}$, where ρ_m is the mass density of the crystal and E_Y is the Young's modulus. Furthermore, $E_Y/\rho_m = E_Y a^3/M$, where a is the lattice constant and M is the total mass of the atoms within a unit cell. There is no reason why $E_Y a^3$ and thus the frequency of the quartz vibration should increase with time. If the frequency of the quartz vibration would keep increasing with time, then phonon energies in a crystal, which are proportional to the vibration frequencies, would keep increasing with time. This violates the law of energy conservation. Due to aging, the frequency of the quartz vibration follows a logarithmic function and decreases with time after a short time [10]. Furthermore, since radiations like X-ray always reduce the frequency of quartz vibration [11], the tick rate of a quartz clock should always decrease over time due to the presence of cosmic rays.

The quartz crystal resonator or oscillator in quartz clocks is in the shape of a small tuning fork, precisely cut to vibrate at 32768 Hz, corresponding to 2^{15} cycles per second. A quartz cantilever with a length of 3 mm and a thickness of 0.3 mm has a fundamental frequency of about 33 kHz. The crystal should be tuned to exactly 32768 Hz, which is hard to achieve. Alternatively, the crystal is made to oscillate at a slightly higher frequency, but then modified with inhibition compensation. After manufacturing, each module is calibrated against a precision clock (which is the world atomic clock at the time of its manufacture) to keep accurate time by programming the digital logic to skip a small number of crystal cycles at regular intervals. Therefore, through calibration with the world atomic clock in their manufacture dates, the quartz watches with different ages simply "memorize" the tick rates of the world atomic clock in the different manufacture dates of the watches.

If the tick rates of both atomic and quartz clocks would be time independent, the quartz watches with different manufacture dates would run with the same tick rate within the rated accuracies of the watches. If the tick rate of the world atomic clock decreases with time and the quartz watches freeze the original tick rates, the older quartz watches will run faster than the newer ones. For example, if a quartz watch was made in August 1980, the tick rate of the quartz clock should be the same as that of the world atomic clock in August 1980 within the accuracy of the watch. If these watches still run correctly at present, then comparing the present tick rate of the world atomic clock with those of the quartz watches of different ages can tell us whether the tick rate of the world atomic clock has changed over time or not.

Experiment

Seiko Holdings Corporation has produced the most accurate quartz clocks in the world by using very high-quality quartz crystals. Developed in 1993, the Grand Seiko 9F family of quartz movements utilize the most advanced quartz movement to achieve supreme accuracy. The less accurate 9F's are rated for 10 seconds per year. Many 9F movements are rated for 5 seconds per year. Today, the most accurate Grand Seiko line has a movement rated as +5/-3 seconds per year, and some of those movements are even certified to +4/-2 seconds per year.

We purchased a total of 4 Seiko quartz watches, which were made in 1980, 1991, 2007, and 2013, and have accuracies rated as ±5, ±10, ±10, and ±5 seconds per year, respectively. The model numbers, serial numbers, the dates of their manufacture, the rated accuracies of the watches, and their purchase dates are summarized in Table BI. (The serial numbers convey their manufacture dates.)

Table BI: The specifications of four Seiko quartz watches and their purchased dates

	Model number	Serial number	Manufacture date	Rated accuracy	Purchased date
1	Seiko Quartz 9481-5000	080793	08/1980	±5 s	04/30/2018
2	Grand Seiko 9587-8000	1D0431	12/1991	±10 s	04/21/2018
3	Grand Seiko 9F62-0A10	760040	06/2007	±10 s	04/13/2017
4	Grand Seiko 20th Anniversary	1133/2000	01/2013	±5 s	11/03/2017

In order to simultaneously read the times of the world atomic clock and the quartz watch, we take several photos of the quartz watch together with the screen of our computer, which shows the date and the reading of the world atomic clock (UTC). Since the rotation speed of the earth slows down over time, the UTC follows the earth's rotation by inserting a leap second approximately every 19 months while keeping the same tick rate as the atomic clock.

We have stored all the watches in the same room with a temperature of about 23 °C and an altitude of about 600 feet above the sea level. In order to prevent any unnecessary damage to the purchased watches, we did not reset the times of the watches even though their readings were completely off from that of the world atomic clock. This offset does not influence our measurement of the tick rates of the two clocks because we only compare the differences in the readings of the clocks at different dates. If the differences in their readings at different dates are time independent, the two clocks have the same tick rate. If not, we can determine the tick-rate difference of the two clocks.

Results

 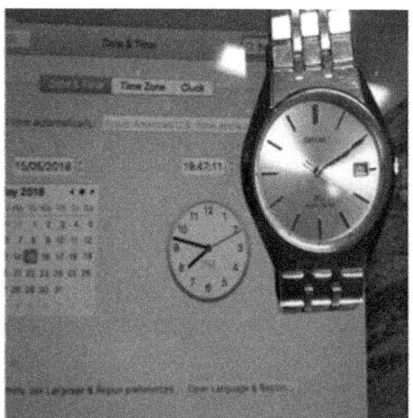

Figure B1: The photos of the 1991 quartz watch together with the screen of our computer, which shows the date and the reading of the world atomic clock. The left panel of Figure B1 shows a photo taken on 21 April 2018 while the photo in the right-panel was taken on 15 May 2018.

Two of the photos are shown in Figure B1. The left panel of Figure B1 shows a photo of the 1991 watch taken on 21 April 2018. Since the tick rates of the two clocks cannot differ by more than 1 minute within several months, we need only focus on reading the seconds. At a moment on 21 April 2018, the world atomic clock read 18 seconds while the quartz watch read 23 seconds. Thus, the quartz watch was offset by a 5 second advance. The right panel of Figure B1 shows a photo taken on 15 May 2018. At a moment on 15 May 2018, the world atomic clock read 11 seconds while the quartz watch read 21 seconds, so the quartz watch was then offset by a 10 second advance. Therefore, within 22 days the world atomic clock slowed by 5 seconds. This result corresponds to the fourth data point in Figure B2b below.

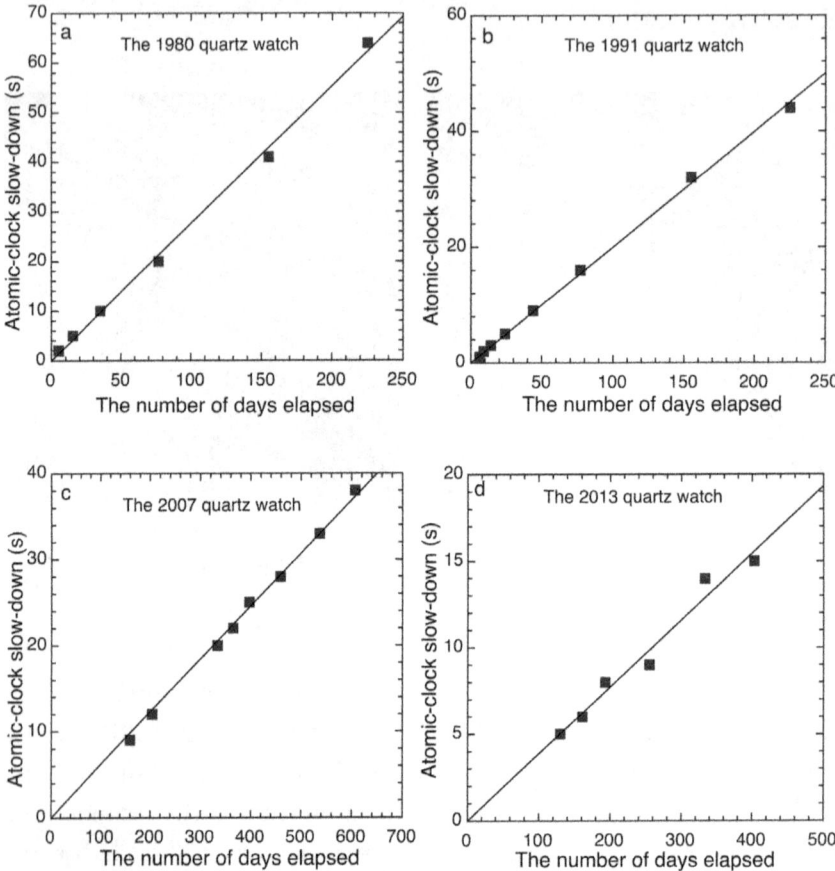

Figure B2: The slow-down times (in seconds) of the world atomic clock compared with the 1980, 1991, 2007, and 2013 quartz watches, respectively. The zero day corresponds to the purchased date of a quartz watch. It is apparent that the slow-down time of the world clock is linearly proportional to the number of days elapsed from the first comparison between the world clock and one of the quartz watches. The maximum deviation from the linear line is less than 2 seconds.

In Figure B2, we plot the slow-down times (in seconds) of the world atomic clock compared with the 1980, 1991, 2007, and 2013 quartz watches, respectively. It is apparent that the slow-down time of the world atomic clock is linearly proportional to the number of days elapsed from the first comparison between the world atomic clock and one of the quartz watches. A linear fit to one set of data points with zero intercept yields the slow-down rate in seconds per day. Multiplying this rate by

365.242 days per year, we obtain the slow-down rate in seconds per year. The fitting parameters and related errors are summarized in Table BII.

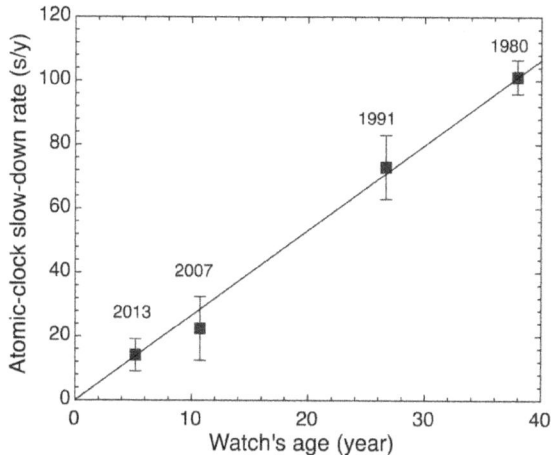

Figure B3: The present slow-down rate (seconds/year) of the world atomic clock compared with the quartz watches of different ages. The age of the watch is the time difference between the present date (corresponding to the middle of the data points in Figure B2) and the manufacture date of the watch. The older the watch is, the faster it runs. Over a period of about 40 years, it follows a linear relationship between the slow-down rate and the age of the watch.

In Figure B3, we plot the present slow-down rate (seconds per year) of the world atomic clock compared with the quartz watches of different ages. The age of the watch is the time difference between the present date (corresponding to the middle of the data points in Figure B2) and the manufacture date of the watch. As discussed above, we expect the tick rate of a quartz watch to freeze in time the tick rate of the world atomic clock at the manufacture date of the quartz watch.

Figure B3 shows that the present tick rate of the world atomic clock slows down by about 100 seconds per year compared with that of the 1980 quartz watch. The older the quartz watch is, the faster it runs. This is the opposite of what one expects from thermodynamics. Over a period of about 40 years, it follows a linear relationship between the slow-down rate and the age of the watch. A linear fit to the data with zero intercept yields a slope of 2.66±0.08 seconds/year². This means that compared with the quartz watches, the world atomic clock is slowing down by 2.66±0.08 seconds every year or by 84.3±2.5 ppb every year. The fact that all the data points fall on the straight line within the error bars implies that all the quartz watches we have purchased keep the time correctly.

Table BII: The linearly fitted slopes in Figure 2B and other parameters.

The age of the watch is calculated from the watch's manufacture date to the present (the middle of the data points in Figure B2). The statistical error σ_{st} is obtained from the linear fitting in Figure B2 and the systematic error σ_{sy} is the rated accuracy of the watch. The total error σ_t is calculated according to the formula: $\sigma_t = \sqrt{\sigma_{st}^2 + \sigma_{sy}^2}$. Here, leap second correction is not considered because it is smaller than the reading uncertainty of each data point in Figure B2 (±2 seconds).

	Watch's age (y)	Slow-down rate (s/y)	σ_{st} (s/y)	σ_{sy} (s/y)	σ_t (s/y)
1	37.96	101.17	1.75	5	5.30
2	26.66	73.01	0.76	10	10.03
3	10.71	22.44	0.18	10	10.00
4	5.18	14.11	0.41	5	5.02

Discussion

It is interesting that the most accurate Grand Seiko movement is rated as +4/–2 seconds per year. On the basis of the quadrature error analysis, the asymmetric accuracy specification (+4 vs –2 seconds) suggests a systematic error of +2 seconds per year and random error of ±2 seconds per year. This asymmetric accuracy specification indicates that the world atomic clock should systematically run slower than the quartz watches by about 2 seconds per year, in agreement with our time-keeping result.

After we theoretically proved that the frequency of the Ce-atomic clock is linearly proportional to the speed of light, we decided to compare it with accurate quartz clocks. So we first purchased the 2007 Grand Seiko quartz watch and compared its tick rate with that of the world atomic clock. After we found that the quartz watch ran faster than the world atomic clock, we decided to purchase a newer (2013) and more accurate watch with a rated accuracy of ±5 seconds per year. If our previous conclusion is relevant, the newer quartz watch should also run faster than the world atomic clock, but with a smaller difference. The result indeed came with our expectation. Then we decided to purchase two older watches to further verify our conclusion. But there is a risk that the older watches might not keep the time correctly. Surprisingly, both watches ran faster than the world atomic clock with much larger differences in the tick rates. The linear relation between the slow-down rates and the ages of the watches shown in Figure B3 rules out the possibility that the older watches may not keep the time correctly. The linear relationship also demonstrates the reliability of our time-keeping result.

There are three possible explanations to the current data. The first one is that the atomic clock ticks with a constant rate while the quartz watch runs faster with time. There appears to be no mechanism that could cause Young's modulus and the quartz vibration frequency to increase with time [10,11]. If the frequency of the quartz vibration would keep increasing with time, then phonon energies in a crystal, which are proportional to the vibration frequencies, would keep increasing with time. This violates the law of energy conservation. The aging and radiation effects cause the quartz's frequency to decrease over time [10,11]. We thus discount this interpretation. The second one is that the quartz watch ticks with a constant rate while the atomic clock slows down with time. This is possible if the speed of light is slowing down over time, as predicted from the general theory of relativity and Maxwell's equations (see Introduction above). In this case, the slow-down of the atomic clock implies that the light speed should also slow down by the same rate. The third one is that both the atomic and quartz clocks tick slower over time and the atomic clock slows down with a higher rate than the quartz clock. As discussed above, the aging and radiation effects can cause the quartz's frequency to decrease over time.

Since $I = dq/dt$ and $1/\Delta t \propto c$, $I = V/R \propto c$ according to the Ohm's law. If c decreases with time, the current expressed in as-maintained ampere is K times smaller than the current expressed in the absolute ampere defined originally. This means that as-maintained ampere is K times larger than the absolute ampere. In the 1960's, several groups underwent different measurements to check a possible shift in as-maintained ampere relative to the absolute ampere A_{ABS}, which was set in 1908 at National Physical Laboratory (NPL) of Great Britain by Ayrton, Mather, and Smith (see page 401-428 of Ref. [12]). The apparatus for such an experiment is called a current balance and usually consists of two concentric and coaxial coils with the outer one fixed and the inner one suspended from one arm of a balance beam. Using the NPL current balance, Vigoureux [12] found in 1968 that A_{NPL}/A_{ABS} = 1.000 008 6±6.0 ppm, where A_{NPL} is the ampere maintained by NPL. Because the uncertainty is so large, the result is not conclusive.

More accurate measurements of the proton's low-field gyromagnetic ratio γ_p(low) and the high-field gyromagnetic ratio γ_p(high) were carried out in Bureau International des Poids et Mesures (BIPM) and also in National Bureau of Standards (NBS). The γ_p(low) value was determined using γ_p(low) = $\omega_p^{low}/(\mu_0 n I_{low})$, where n is the number of turns per unit length of a coil and I_{low} is the applied current in terms of as-maintained ampere. The γ_p(high) value was determined using γ_p(high) = $\omega_p^{high}/(F/I_{high}L)$, where F is the force on a conductor carrying the current I_{high} in a field B normal to the conductor's length L (in this case $F = I_{high}LB$). F was determined by balancing with the gravitational force, and its reading was assumed to be time independent. Then γ_p(low)/γ_p(high) = $(\omega_p^{low}/\omega_p^{high})F/(\mu_0 n L I_{low} I_{high})$ = K^2 (since the ratio $\omega_p^{low}/\omega_p^{high}$ is independent of whether the tick rate of a clock is time-dependent or not). The measured values of γ_p(low)/γ_p(high) in BIPM and NBS led to $K_{BIPM} = A_{BIPM}/A_{ABS}$ = 1.000 011 4±2.7 ppm and $K_{NBS} = A_{NBS}/A_{ABS}$ = 1.000 009 0±2.7 ppm, respectively (see page 442 of Ref. [12]). Since $I \propto c$, the BIPM result implies that c decreases by 11.4±2.7 ppm over the 60-year period between 1908 and 1968. Similarly, the NBS result implies that c decreases by 9.0±2.7 ppm. The average of the two measurements is 10.2±1.5 ppm. Thus, the speed of light should have decreased with a rate of 170±25 ppb per year within the 60-year period between 1908 and 1968.

Because of these results, BIPM and NBS decided that after 1 January 1969, as-maintained ampere and volt were reduced by 11.0 ppm and 8.4 ppm, respectively (see page 442 of Ref. [12]). In 1988, the volt standard was re-examined using a liquid electrometer [13]. On the assumption that g and ϵ_0 were constants, the determined volt standard was the same as the absolute volt, which discounted the previous reduction of the volt standard in 1969.

If the quartz clock would be time-independent, the tick rate of the atomic clock and thus the speed of light would slow down by 84.3±2.5 ppb per year between 1980 and 2018, which is significantly smaller than 170±25 ppb per year inferred from the experiments on as-maintained electrical units in BIPM and NBS (see above). This difference implies that both atomic and quartz clocks should slow down while the atomic clock slows down with a higher rate than the quartz clock.

The intrinsic slow-down of a quartz clock can be understood by the law of refraction. The quartz's vibration frequency should be proportional to c/n_{av}, where n_{av} is the index of refraction averaged over the whole spectrum of the electromagnetic wave. Since dn/df is always positive and f is proportional to c (see Introduction), we have $dn/dc > 0$ and $dn_{av}/dc > 0$. The relationship: $dn_{av}/dc > 0$ implies that a quartz clock should slow down with a rate smaller than that of an atomic clock, in agreement with the conclusion drawn above from the present and previous experimental results.

Because the measured gravitational wave travels at the same speed as the electromagnetic wave [14] in vacuum and the gravitational force has exactly the same form as the electromagnetic force within the framework of the general theory of relativity, the gravitational constant G should be proportional to $1/\epsilon_0 \propto c^2$. This idea is similar to that proposed earlier by Dirac [15]. Since the tick rates of celestial clocks (by the Kepler third law of planetary motion) and pendulum clocks are both proportional to $\sqrt{G}$, they are also linearly proportional to c. When g, Mg, ϵ_0, and c are measured using these linearly c-dependent clocks, their measured values are apparently constants. Thus, the physical laws like the theory of general relativity should be still valid when the physical quantities are measured with the linearly c-dependent clocks.

The current cosmological model is based on the theory of general relativity and on the assumption of the constancy of the speed of light. Based on the earth-centered cosmological model we have proposed in Appendix C, we find that the age of the universe is 13.84 billion years, as measured from a moving clock at the boundary of the universe, which is moving away from us with a speed (v) close to the speed of light.

Due to the time dilation of the moving clock, the age of the universe measured from an observer on the earth (t_0) is much older than that measured from an observer at the boundary of the universe (t'_0), that is, $t_0 = t'_0/(1-(v/c)^2)^{1/2}$.

From the relation: $a(t) \propto a'(t') \propto 1/c^2$, we can easily show that $\frac{da'}{dt'}/a' = \frac{-2dc}{dt'}/c = 1/t'_0$. Using $\frac{-dc}{dt'}/c = 170\pm25$ ppb per year and $t_0 =13.84$ billion years, we obtain $t'_0 = 2.94\pm0.43$ million years and $v = 0.999\,999\,98c$. Therefore, according to the proper clock our universe is about 3 million years old, and the boundary of the universe is moving with a speed very close to the speed of light.

Conclusion

In summary, we report our time-keeping results for four extremely precise quartz watches of different ages against the world atomic clock. We found that the tick rate of the world atomic clock is slowing down by 84.3±2.5 ppb every year compared with that of the quartz watches. Our data suggest that both the atomic clock and the speed of light should slow down over time, in agreement with the independent experiments on as-maintained electrical units and with the theoretical prediction of both the general theory of relativity and Maxwell's equations. The symmetry of the matter (positive mass) and antimatter (negative mass) [16] ensures energy conservation of the universe independent of whether c is a constant or not.

Acknowledgments:

I would like to thank Dr. Pieder Beeli and Mr. Joshua Zhao for discussion and comment.

References

[1] E. R. Cohen and B. N. Taylor, Rev. Mod. Phys. **59**, 1121 (1987).
[2] P. J. Mohr and B. N. Taylor, Rev. Mod. Phys. **72**, 351 (2000).
[3] P. J. Mohr, B. N. Taylor, and D. B. Newell, Rev. Mod. Phys. **80**, 633 (2008).
[4] P. J. Mohr, D. B. Newell, and B. N. Taylor, Rev. Mod. Phys. **88**, 035009 (2016).
[5] C. Møller, *The Theory of Relativity* (Oxford, Clarendon, 1952).
[6] L. D. Landau and E. M. Lifshitz, *The Classical Theory of the Fields*, 4th revised English ed. (Oxford: Peramon, 1975).
[7] W. O. Sumner, Astrophys. J. **429**, 491 (1994).
[8] https://en.wikipedia.org/wiki/Planck_constant
[9] G. K. Woodgate, Elementary Atomic Structure. Oxford University Press (1999).
[10] J. R. Vig, *Introduction to Quartz Frequency Standard*, Research and Development Technical Support (SLCET-TR-921), 1992.
[11] C. Frondel, *"Effect of Radiation on the elasticity of quartz"*, (This article is available at the website: http://www.minsocam.org/ammin/AM30/AM30_432.pdf)
[12] B. N. Taylor, W. H. Parker, and D. N. Langenberg, Rev. Mod. Phys. **41**, 375 (1969).
[13] W. K. Clothier, G. J. Sloggett, H. Bairnsfather, M. F. Currey, and D. J. Benjamin, Metrologia **26**, 9 (1989).
[14] B. P. Abbott *et al.*, Astrophys. J. Lett. **848**, L13 (2017).
[15] P. A. M. Dirac, Nature **139**, 323 (1937).
[16] J. S. Farnes, Astronomy & Astrophysics, **620**, A92 (2018).

APPENDIX C
PAPER ON ZHAO'S MODIFIED COSMOLOGICAL MODEL

Negative Mass of Cold Dark Matter in Zhao's Cosmological Model

Peter Zhao

Taizhou Research Institute, Zhejiang University, China

Abstract

The inflation-based Lambda Cold Dark Matter cosmological model has been accepted as the standard model of big bang cosmology. The success of the model lies with its ability of explaining the clear structure in the power spectra of the cosmic microwave background. The parameters inferred from the power spectra can predict light-element abundances based on big bang nucleosynthesis, and the observed abundances are in good agreement with the predicted values except for the ^7Li abundance. More seriously, the inferred Hubble constant $H_0 = 67.4\pm0.5$ kms^{-1}Mpc^{-1} is significantly lower than the value (74.03$\pm$1.42 kms^{-1}Mpc^{-1}) measured locally from 70 long-period Cepheids in the Large Magellanic Cloud (LMC). Here, we show that all the discrepancies can be naturally resolved if we assume that the cold dark matter is the antimatter with negative mass, and that the universe has a fixed center close to the earth. The earth-center universe agrees with consistent observations of the quantized red shift.

Introduction

The inflation-based Lambda Cold Dark Matter (ΛCDM) cosmological model assumes that the universe contains three major components: dark energy, cold dark matter, and ordinary matter. The model contains seven adjustable parameters and can well explain the clear structure in the power spectra of the cosmic microwave background (CMB). Based on the inferred parameters from the CMB spectra, the cosmologists can quantitatively explain the observed primordial abundances of light-elements such as ^{4}He, deuterium, and ^{3}He. Because of its simplicity and reasonable success in explaining the most cosmic properties, it has been called the standard model of big bang cosmology.

On the other hand, there are some important drawbacks in the model. First, the observed primordial ^{7}Li abundance is about a factor of 2-3 smaller than the predicted value [1]. Second, the Hubble constant $H_0 = 67.4\pm0.5$ kms^{-1}Mpc^{-1} inferred from the CBM power spectra [2] is much lower than that (74.03$\pm$1.42 kms^{-1}Mpc^{-1}) measured locally from 70 long-period Cepheids in the Large Magellanic Cloud (LMC) [3]. Third, the model assumes asymmetry of matter and antimatter, which is inconsistent with the standard model of particle physics.

Here, we show that these discrepancies can be naturally resolved if we assume that the cold dark matter has negative mass, and the universe has a fixed center close to the earth. The negative mass of the cold dark matter (the cold antimatter) provides a gravitational red shift, which is also proportional to the distance r from us if the total matter density $\rho_m(r)$ at present is proportional to $1/r$ at sufficiently large r. Then, the locally measured Hubble constant H_{loc} is the sum of H_0 due to the expansion of the universe and H_g due to the gravitational red shift. The assumption of the earth-center universe agrees with frequent observations of the quantized red shift [4].

Model

We are quite familiar with positive mass, but the concept of negative mass is quite exotic. We know that a positive mass gravitationally attracts all surrounding positive masses. However, a negative mass gravitationally repels all surrounding positive masses. The situation here is just opposite to the electrostatic interaction between charged particles: like charges repel each other while unlike charges attract each other. For a positive-negative mass particle pair, the net mass of the pair is equal to zero if both masses have the same magnitude. They will repel each other and undergo a runaway motion.

In our current model, the matter density $\rho_m(r)$ at present is assumed to be ρ_0 for $r < a$ and $\rho_m(r) = a\rho_0/r$ for $r \geq a$ (where a is a finite radius). The boundary of the current universe comprises the cold matter and anti-baryons to keep the symmetry of matter and antimatter. The matter and antimatter in the boundary do not produce any gravity in the interior of the universe according to the gravitational Gauss' law (by analogy to the electric Gauss' law), so the ΛCDM cosmological model is still valid for the interior of the universe. The boundary of the universe should expand with a speed close to the speed of light c. Then the radius R_0 of the present universe is approximately equal to ct_0, where t_0 is the age of the universe.

We now use the gravitational Gauss' law to determine the gravitational field in the interior of the universe. When the negatively massed cold dark matter dominates over the positively massed baryons, the gravitational field $\vec{g}(r)$ points radially outward. The light traveling towards the center will undergo a red shift in such a gravitational field according to the Einstein theory of general relativity:

$$-\frac{\Delta v}{v} c = \frac{g(r)r}{c}. \qquad (1)$$

Applying the Gauss' law in the region of $r > a$ yields,

$$4\pi r^2 g(r) = 4\pi G M_{<r}, \qquad (2)$$

where

$$M_{<r} = \frac{4}{3}\pi a^3 \rho_0 + \int_a^r 4\pi x^2 \frac{a\rho_0}{x} dx$$

$$= \frac{4}{3}\pi a^3 \rho_0 + 2\pi a \rho_0 r^2 - 2\pi a^3 \rho_0$$

$$= 2\pi a \rho_0 r^2 - \frac{2\pi}{3} a^3 \rho_0.$$

Then

$$g(r) = 2\pi G a \rho_0 - \frac{2\pi G a^3 \rho_0}{3r^2} = 2\pi G a \rho_0 \left(1 - \frac{a^2}{3r^2}\right). \tag{3}$$

The total mass in the interior of the universe can be expressed as $\frac{4}{3}\pi R_0^3 \rho_m$, where ρ_m is the average matter density. The total mass is also given by

$$\frac{4}{3}\pi a^3 \rho_0 + \int_a^{R_0} 4\pi x^2 \frac{a\rho_0}{x} dx = 2\pi a \rho_0 R_0^2 - \frac{2\pi}{3} a^3 \rho_0.$$

Then

$$2\pi a \rho_0 R_0^2 - \frac{2\pi}{3} a^3 \rho_0 = \frac{4}{3}\pi R_0^3 \rho_m. \tag{4}$$

Using the fact that $R_0 \gg a$, we obtain

$$\rho_0 = \frac{2R_0}{3a} \rho_m.$$

Finally, we obtain the magnitude of the gravitational field for $r > a$:

$$g(r) = \frac{4\pi G \rho_m R_0}{3}\left(1 - \frac{a^2}{3r^2}\right). \tag{5}$$

Substituting Eq. 5 into Eq. 1, we have

$$-\frac{\Delta v}{v}c = \frac{4\pi G \rho_m R_0}{3c}\left(1 - \frac{a^2}{3r^2}\right)r = H_g r,$$

where

$$H_g = \frac{4\pi G \rho_m R_0}{3c}\left(1 - \frac{a^2}{3r^2}\right).$$

Then

$$H_{loc} = H_0 + H_g$$
$$= H_0 + \frac{4\pi G \rho_m R_0}{3c}\left(1 - \frac{a^2}{3r^2}\right) \cong H_0 + \frac{4\pi G \rho_m t_0}{3}\left(1 - \frac{a^2}{3r^2}\right). \qquad (6)$$

For $r \gg a$,

$$H_g = \frac{4\pi G \rho_m R_0}{3c}.$$

Therefore

$$H_{loc} = H_0 + H_g = H_0 + \frac{4\pi G \rho_m R_0}{3c} \cong H_0 + \frac{4\pi G \rho_m t_0}{3}. \qquad (7)$$

Now we apply the Gauss' law to the region of $r < a$:

$$g(r) = \frac{4\pi G r}{3}\rho_0 = \frac{8\pi G \rho_m c t_0}{9a}r,$$

then

$$-\frac{\Delta v}{v}c = \frac{8\pi G \rho_m t_0}{9a}r^2 = Br^2, \qquad (8)$$

where $B = 8\pi G \rho_m t_0/9a$.

In the ΛCDM cosmological model, the expansion of the universe is parametrized by a dimensionless scale factor $a = a(t)$ with t counted from the birth of the universe. At present, $a_0 = a(t_0) = 1$. The expansion rate is described by the time-dependent Hubble parameter $H(t)$, defined as $H(t) = da/(adt)$. The first Friedmann equation is used to describe the expansion of the universe, and this equation can be conveniently written in terms of various density parameters as:

$$H(a) = H_0\sqrt{(\Omega_b + \Omega_c)a^{-3} + \Omega_{rad}a^{-4} + \Omega_k a^{-2} + \Omega_{DE}a^{-3(1+w)}},$$

where the present-day density parameter Ω_x for various species is defined as the dimensionless ratio:

$$\Omega_x = \frac{8\pi G \rho_x}{3H_0^2},$$

where the subscript x is: b for baryons, c for cold dark matter, *rad* for radiation, and *DE* for dark energy. In the minimal six-parameter model with $w = -1$, $\Omega_x = 0$, and $\Omega_{rad} \sim 0$ Friedmann equation is simplified as

$$H(a) = H_0\sqrt{(\Omega_b + \Omega_c)a^{-3} + \Omega_{DE}} \qquad (9)$$

with $\Omega_m + \Omega_{DE} = 1$ and $\Omega_m = \Omega_b + \Omega_c$. The equation has an analytic solution

$$a(t_0) = 1 = \left(\frac{\Omega_m}{1-\Omega_m}\right)^{\frac{1}{3}} \sin^{\frac{2}{3}}\left(\frac{3t_0 H_0 \sqrt{1-\Omega_m}}{2}\right). \qquad (10)$$

In the above equations, Ω_b, Ω_c, and Ω_{DE} are all positive numbers because only matter with positive mass is considered in the Friedmann equation. However, when the cold dark matter with negative mass is considered, the space is filled with both matter and antimatter, we need to consider the sign of each component. If the matter dominates over the antimatter, the net matter density is still positive and the net gravitational interaction is attractive. This naturally ensures that the first term $8\pi G\rho/3$ of the Friedmann equation is a positive number. On the other hand, if the antimatter dominates over the matter, the net matter density is negative, but the net gravitational interaction is still attractive. To agree with the Friedmann equation, we still keep the positive signs of Ω_c, Ω_b and Ω_{DE} (absolute values) but replace $\Omega_m = \Omega_c + \Omega_b$ in the matter-dominated case with $\Omega_m = \Omega_c - \Omega_b$ in the antimatter-dominated case.

Now we consider the CMB experiments that reveal sound waves in the fine angular structure of the temperature anisotropies. The power spectrum of the temperature maps exhibits clear peaks, which are closely related to the acoustic phenomena of the universe. A simple way to understand this phenomenon is to consider that the universe was a photon-baryon plasma (fluid) when its temperature was above 3,000 K. The photon-baryon fluid is sitting in the gravitational potential wells that are the seeds of structure in the universe. As gravity tries to compress the fluid, the radiation pressure resists, which leads to acoustic oscillations. The system is equivalent to a baryon mass on a spring falling under gravity. Compression occurs in the gravitational potential wells while rarefaction in the hills. Sound waves stop oscillating at recombination when the baryons release the photons. The acoustic modes at extrema of their oscillations become the peaks in the CMB power spectrum by recombination. The first peak represents the mode that the compressed one inside potential well before recombination, the second peak corresponds to the mode that compressed and then rarefied, and so on. Amplitudes of the odd-number peaks are higher than those of even-number peaks because the mass loading of baryons makes the oscillation asymmetric: the extrema that represent compressions inside the wells are enhanced over those that represent rarefactions in the hills.

At the early universe, quantum fluctuations may generate both density enhancements and deficits. When the matter dominates over the antimatter in the space (the net matter density is positive), the gravitational potential hills appear in regions of deficits and the potential wells in regions of enhancements. This is because a baryon gravitationally attracts the surrounding matter with a net mass of the positive sign. In contrast, when the antimatter dominates over the matter in the space (the net matter density is negative), the gravitational potential hills appear in regions of enhancements and the potential wells in regions of deficits. This is because a baryon gravitationally repels the surrounding matter with a net mass of the negative sign.

Solving three equations with three unknown variables

The above simple picture tells us that the gravitational potential landscapes (containing plane waves of various wavelengths) in both cases are the same. This implies that the CMB spectra in both cases are identical if Ω_b, Ω_m, Ω_{DE}, and H_0 are identical. Therefore, the parameters inferred from the CMB spectra are equally applicable to the current case where the antimatter dominates over the matter.

In two equations (Eq. 7 and Eq. 10), there are three unknown variables: H_0, Ω_m, and t_0. In order to find the solutions of H_0, Ω_m, and t_0, we need a third equation related to these variables. Fortunately, W. J. Percival et al. found an important constraint on the flat cosmologies from CMB power spectra [5]. They showed that $\Omega_m h^{3.4}$ = constant independent of other parameters, where $h = H_0/(100 \text{ kms}^{-1}\text{Mpc}^{-1})$. From the CMB spectra before 2002, they obtained $\Omega_m h^{3.4} = 0.081 \pm 0.012$. From more accurate CMB spectra of 2018 Planck final mission [2], we find that

$$\Omega_m h^{3.4} = 0.08241 \pm 0.00046 \qquad (11)$$

It is apparent that the values of $\Omega_m h^{3.4}$ inferred from the previous and current CMR spectra are the same within the uncertainties. With $H_{loc} = 74.03 \pm 1.42 \text{ kms}^{-1}\text{Mpc}^{-1}$, we can solve Eq. 7, Eq. 10, and the equation: $\Omega_m h^{3.4} = 0.08241$ to find the solutions of H_0, Ω_m, and t_0. Our solutions are the following: $t_0 = 13.8157 \pm 0.0021$ Gyr, $\Omega_m = 0.400^{+0.043}_{-0.039}$, and $H_0 = 62.838^{+1.922}_{-1.858} \text{ kms}^{-1}\text{Mpc}^{-1}$.

W. J. Percival et al. also showed that $\Omega_b h^2$ depends on h. The contour of $\Omega_b h^2$ vs h corresponding to the maximum likelihood of 2.3 is replotted in Figure C1. From Figure C1 and the inferred H_0, we obtain $\Omega_b h^2 = 0.0198 \pm 0.0005$ and the ratio of the baryon density to the photon density $\eta_{10} = 5.55 \pm 0.13$. From the calculated light element abundances based on the big-bang nucleosynthesis (BBN) model [6] and $\Omega_b h^2 = 0.0198 \pm 0.0005$, we find the following primordial abundances: ^{7}Li/H = $(3.90 \pm 1.50) \times 10^{-10}$, D/H = $(3.17 \pm 0.77) \times 10^{-5}$, ^{4}He/H = 0.2474 ± 0.0002, and ^{3}He/H = $(1.10 \pm 0.19) \times 10^{-5}$.

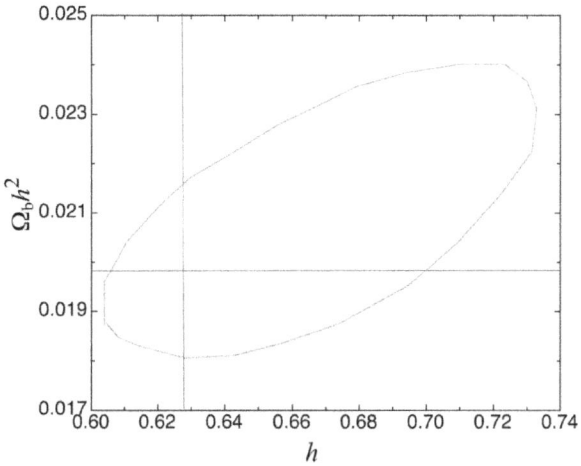

Figure C1: The contour of $\Omega_b h^2$ vs h, which corresponds to the maximum likelihood of 2.3. The figure is replotted from figure 2 of Ref. 5.

Compared with the observed results

Different groups have measured Li/H abundances and the results are summarized in Figure C2. The predicted ^{7}Li/H abundance is in the range of $(2.61\text{-}4.49) \times 10^{-10}$ while the measured abundance is in the range of $(1.34\text{-}3.23) \times 10^{-10}$. A simple averaging for the five data points yields ^{7}Li/H $= (2.18 \pm 0.07) \times 10^{-10}$. The predicted lower limit of 2.40×10^{-10} is close to the average value within the standard deviation. Therefore, the lower limit of the $\Omega_b h^2$ parameter is in reasonable agreement with the measured Li/H abundance.

There are two consistent data [12,13] for the primordial ^{4}He/H abundance: 0.2449 ± 0.0040 and 0.2446 ± 0.0029. Both data agree with the predicted value of 0.2474 ± 0.0002 within the experimental uncertainties.

The measured deuterium abundance D/H is $2.50 \pm 0.5 \times 10^{-5}$ (Ref. 14), which is within the predicted range: $(3.17 \pm 0.77) \times 10^{-5}$. The measured ^{3}He/H $= 1.5 \pm 0.2 \times 10^{-5}$ (Ref. 15). The lower limit of the measured value is very close to the predicted upper limit of 1.29×10^{-5}. Therefore, the lower limit of the $\Omega_b h^2$ parameter is in good agreement with the measured value of the ^{3}He abundance.

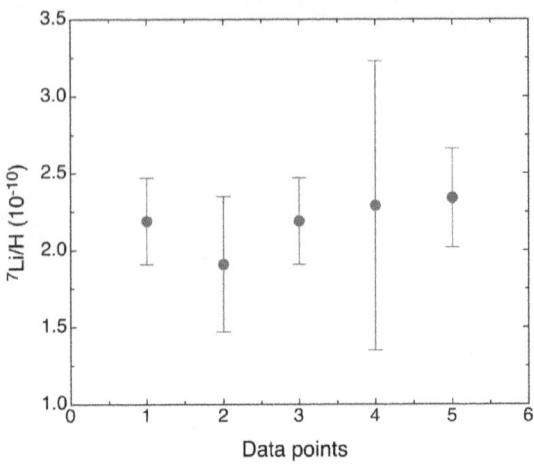

Figure C2: The measured ^{7}Li/H abundances from different groups. The data points are taken from Refs. [7-11].

If we use the lower limit of $H_{loc} = 72.6$ kms^{-1}Mpc^{-1} and the lower limit of $\Omega_m h^{3.4} = 0.08195$, we find $t_0 = 13.8398$ billion years, $\Omega_m = 0.440$, and $H_0 = 61.0$ kms^{-1}Mpc^{-1}. These parameters lead to the lowest value of $\Omega_b h^2 = 0.0193$. This value predicts the lowest deuterium abundance of 2.40×10^{-5}, the highest ^{3}He abundance of 1.29×10^{-5}, and the lowest ^{7}Li abundance of 2.61×10^{-10}. All these predicted values are consistent with the observed ones within the experimental uncertainties. Therefore, the CMB spectra and the observed light-element abundances narrow down the parameters: $H_{loc} = 72.6$ kms^{-1}Mpc^{-1}, $H_0 = 61.0$ kms^{-1}Mpc^{-1}, $\Omega_b h^2 = 0.0193$, $\Omega_m = 0.440$, and $t_0 = 13.8398$ billion years. It is remarkable that $t_0 = 13.8398$ billion years, which is very close to 7^{12} years. The difference between 13.8398 billion years and 7^{12} years is only 0.011%.

We now turn to the red shift data at distances below Virgo Cluster (Figure C3), which are taken from Figure 1.3 of Ref. 16 and Figure 1 of Ref. [17]. The best linear fit to the data yields $H_{loc} = 67.48 \pm 2.70$ kms^{-1}Mpc^{-1}. This number is consistent with $H_0 = 67.4 \pm 0.5$ kms^{-1}Mpc^{-1} inferred from the CMB data but disagrees with the value (74.03 ± 1.42 kms^{-1}Mpc^{-1}) measured locally from 70 long-period Cepheids in the Large Magellanic Cloud. The solid black line in Figure C3 is the best fitted curve by Eq. 8 with the fixed parameters inferred from $H_{loc} = 72.6$ kms^{-1}Mpc^{-1} and $\Omega_m h^{3.4} = 0.08195$ and a fitting parameter

a. The fitting parameter a is found to be 12.31 ± 3.87 Mpc. Therefore, our model can naturally resolve the discrepancy.

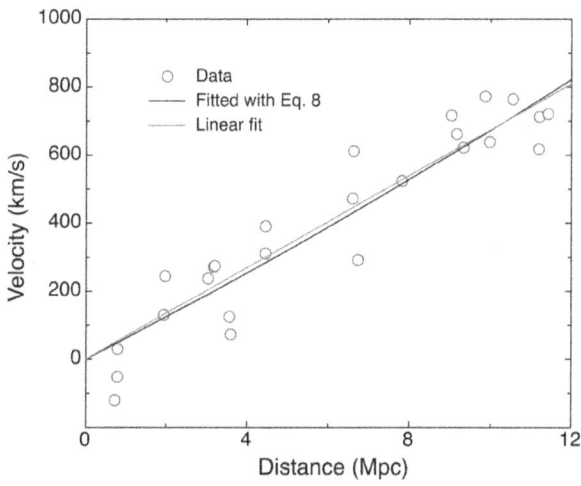

Figure C3: Red shift velocities at the distances below Virgo Cluster. The data are taken from Figure 1.3 of Ref. 16 and Figure 1 of Ref. [17].

For $r > a$, our model agrees with the red shift data at larger distances (>15 Mpc) compilated by the Hubble Space Telescope Key Project that finalized in 2001 (see Ref. 17). In Figure C4, we plot the data at the distances between 15-392 Mpc. The open squares represent the calculated values of Eq. 6 with the fixed parameters inferred from H_{loc} = 72.6 kms^{-1}Mpc^{-1} and $\Omega_m h^{3.4}$ = 0.08195 and the fixed parameter a = 12.31 Mpc. The calculated points have no adjustable parameter.

We can also fit the data by a linear equation: red-shift velocity = $H_{loc} d$, where d is the distance from us. The best liner fit to the data yields H_{loc} = 72.71 ± 0.79 kms^{-1}Mpc^{-1} (see solid black line). The differences between the calculated values of Eq. 6 and the best linearly fitted curve are negligibly small. If we fit the data by Eq. 6 with one free parameter H_0, we obtain H_0 = 61.14 ± 0.79 kms^{-1}Mpc^{-1}, which is very close to the value of 61.0 kms^{-1}Mpc^{-1} inferred from H_{loc} = 72.6 kms^{-1}Mpc^{-1} and $\Omega_m h^{3.4}$ = 0.08195.

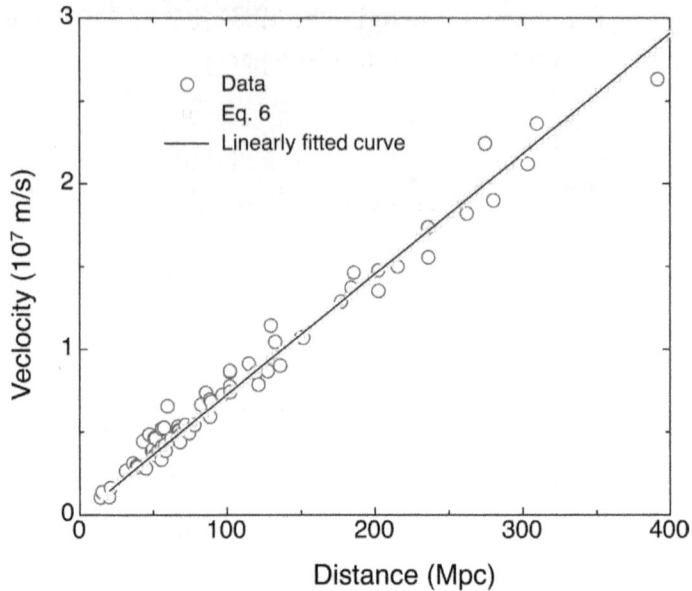

Figure C4: Red-shift velocities at large distances. These data were compilated by the Hubble Space Telescope Key Project that finalized in 2001 [17]. The open squares represent the calculated values of Eq. 6 with the fixed parameters inferred from H_{loc} = 72.6 kms^{-1}Mpc^{-1} and $\Omega_m b^{3.4}$ = 0.08195 and the fixed parameter a = 12.31 Mpc. The best linear fit to the data yields H_{loc} = 72.71 ± 0.79 kms^{-1}Mpc^{-1} (solid line).

Conclusion

In conclusion, our modified ΛCDM cosmological model almost perfectly resolves all the discrepancies between the model and the observed cosmic properties. The negative mass of the cold dark matter and the earth-centered universe are the essential components in the modified model. The age of our universe is almost exactly equal to 7^{12} years if we assume that the speed of light is a constant and the theory of general relativity is valid.

References

[1] R. H. Cyburt, B. D. Fields, and K. A. Olive, JCAP **11**, 012 (2008).
[2] Planck 2018 results. VI. Cosmological parameters, arXiv:1807.06209v1 [astro-ph.CO], 17 June 2018.
[3] A. G. Riess et al., APJ **876**, 85 (2019).
[4] D. R. Humphreys, TJ **16**, 95 (2002); and references therein.
[5] W. J. Percival et al., MNRAS **337**, 1068; arXiv:astro-ph/0206256v2, 22 Aug 2002.
[6] C. J. Copi, D. M. Schramm, and M. S. Turner, Science **267**, 192 (1994).
[7] P. Bonifacio et al., Astron. Astrophys. **390**, 91 (2002)
[8] L. Pasquini and P. Molaro, 1996 Astron. Astrophys. **307**, 761 (1996).
[9] F. Thevenin et al., Astron. Astrophys. **373**, 905 (2001).
[10] P. Bonifacio, Astron. Astrophys. **395**, 515 (2002)
[11] J. Melendez and I. Ramirez, Astrophys. J. **615**, L33 (2004).
[12] E. Aver, K. A. Olive, and E. D. Skillman, JCAP **2015**, 011 (2015).
[13] A. Peimbert, M. Peimbert, and V. Luridiana, Rev. Mex. Astron. Astrofis. **52**, 419, (2016).
[14] F. Hersant, D. Gautier, and J. M. Hure, APJ **554**, 391 (2001).
[15] J. Geiss and G. Gloeckler, Space Science Review **84**, 239 (1998).
[16] W. C. Keel, The Road to Galaxy Formation (2nd ed. Springer, 2007), pp 7.
[17] W. Freeman et al., Astrophys. J **553**, 47 (2001).

APPENDIX D
HEBREW LUNISOLAR CALENDARS OF IMPORTANT YEARS

In the following pages, we selectively present the Hebrew lunisolar calendars of some important years, which may be used in the main texts of the book. A lunisolar calendar is superimposed on a Julian solar calendar to save space. The first day of each lunar month is indicated with **bold face** and the 15th day of the month with ***italic bold face***. The name of a lunar month is on the left side in alignment with the first day of the month. The name of a Julian solar month is on the right side aligned with the first day of the month. Sunday is the first day of a week which is in the second column, and Saturday is the 7th day of a week which is in the 8th column. The calendars before 1417 BC listed in Appendix D are the true calendars, which have been corrected by the one-day shift due to the doubling of a day-length in the time of Joshua (see Chapter 10).

Julian year 3971 BC

						1	2	January
	3	4	5	6	7	8	9	
	10	11	*12*	13	14	15	16	
	17	18	19	20	21	22	23	
(11) Shebet	24	25	26	*27*	28	29	30	
	31	1	2	3	4	5	6	February
	7	8	9	*10*	11	12	13	
	14	15	16	17	18	19	20	
(12a) Adar I	21	22	23	24	25	*26*	27	
	28	1	2	3	4	5	6	March
	7	8	9	10	11	*12*	13	
	14	15	16	17	18	19	20	
	21	22	23	24	25	26	27	
(12b) Adar II	*28*	29	30	31	1	2	3	April
	4	5	6	7	8	9	10	
	11	12	13	14	15	16	17	
	18	19	20	21	22	23	24	
(1) Nisan	25	*26*	27	28	29	30	1	May
	2	3	4	5	6	7	8	
	9	*10*	11	12	13	14	15	
	16	17	18	19	20	21	22	
(2) Iyar	23	24	25	*26*	27	28	29	
	30	31	1	2	3	4	5	June
	6	7	8	*9*	10	11	12	
	13	14	15	16	17	18	19	
(3) Sivan	20	21	22	23	*24*	25	26	
	27	28	29	30	1	2	3	July
	4	5	6	7	*8*	9	10	
	11	12	13	14	15	16	17	
(4) Tammuz	18	19	20	21	22	23	*24*	
	25	26	27	28	29	30	31	
	1	2	3	4	5	6	*7*	August
	8	9	10	11	12	13	14	
	15	16	17	18	19	20	21	

(5) Av	**22**	23	24	25	26	27	28	
	29	30	31	1	2	3	4	September
	5	6	7	8	9	10	11	
	12	13	14	15	16	17	18	
(6) Elul	19	20	**21**	22	23	24	25	
	26	27	28	29	30	1	2	October
	3	4	*5*	6	7	8	9	
	10	11	12	13	14	15	16	
(7) Tishri	17	18	19	**20**	21	22	23	
	24	25	26	27	28	29	30	
	31	1	2	*3*	4	5	6	November
	7	8	9	10	11	12	13	
(8) Heshvan	14	15	16	17	18	**19**	20	
	21	22	23	24	25	26	27	
	28	29	30	1	2	*3*	4	December
	5	6	7	8	9	10	11	
(9) Kislev	12	13	14	15	16	17	**18**	
	19	20	21	22	23	24	25	
	26	27	28	29	30	31		

Julian year 3970 BC

							1	January
	2	3	4	5	6	7	8	
(10) Tebet	9	**10**	11	12	13	14	15	
	16	17	18	19	20	21	22	
	23	*24*	25	26	27	28	29	
	30	31	1	2	3	4	5	February
	6	7	8	9	10	11	12	
(11) Shebet	13	14	**15**	16	17	18	19	
	20	21	22	23	24	25	26	
	27	28	*1*	2	3	4	5	March
	6	7	8	9	10	11	12	
(12) Adar	13	14	15	16	**17**	18	19	
	20	21	22	23	24	25	26	
	27	28	29	30	*31*	1	2	April
	3	4	5	6	7	8	9	
(1) Nisan	10	11	12	13	14	**15**	16	
	17	18	19	20	21	22	23	
	24	25	26	27	28	*29*	30	
	1	2	3	4	5	6	7	May
	8	9	10	11	12	13	14	
(2) Iyar	**15**	16	17	18	19	20	21	
	22	23	24	25	26	27	28	
	29	30	31	1	2	3	4	June
	5	6	7	8	9	10	11	
(3) Sivan	12	**13**	14	15	16	17	18	
	19	20	21	22	23	24	25	
	26	*27*	28	29	30	1	2	July
	3	4	5	6	7	8	9	
(4) Tammuz	10	11	12	**13**	14	15	16	
	17	18	19	20	21	22	23	
	24	25	26	*27*	28	29	30	
	31	1	2	3	4	5	6	August
(5) Av	7	8	9	10	**11**	12	13	
	14	15	16	17	18	19	20	
	21	22	23	24	*25*	26	27	
	28	29	30	31	1	2	3	September

(6) Elul	4	5	6	7	8	9	**10**	
	11	12	13	14	15	16	17	
	18	19	20	21	22	23	***24***	
	25	26	27	28	29	30	1	October
	2	3	4	5	6	7	8	
(7) Tishri	**9**	10	11	12	13	14	15	
	16	17	18	19	20	21	22	
	23	24	25	26	27	28	29	
	30	31	1	2	3	4	5	November
(8) Heshvan	6	7	**8**	9	10	11	12	
	13	14	15	16	17	18	19	
	20	21	***22***	23	24	25	26	
	27	28	29	30	1	2	3	December
(9) Kislev	4	5	6	7	**8**	9	10	
	11	12	13	14	15	16	17	
	18	19	20	21	***22***	23	24	
	25	26	27	28	29	30	31	

Julian year 2315 BC

				1	2	*3*	4	January
	5	6	7	8	9	10	11	
(11) Shebet	12	13	14	15	16	17	**18**	
	19	20	21	22	23	24	25	
	26	27	28	29	30	31	*1*	February
	2	3	4	5	6	7	8	
	9	10	11	12	13	14	15	
(12a) Adar I	16	**17**	18	19	20	21	22	
	23	24	25	26	27	28	1	March
	2	*3*	4	5	6	7	8	
	9	10	11	12	13	14	15	
(12b) Adar II	16	17	18	**19**	20	21	22	
	23	24	25	26	27	28	29	
	30	31	1	*2*	3	4	5	April
	6	7	8	I 9	10	11	12	
(1) Nisan	13	14	15	16	**17**	18	19	
	20	21	22	23	24	25	26	
	27	28	29	30	*1*	2	3	May
	4	5	6	7	8	II 9	10	
(2) Iyar	11	12	13	14	15	16	**17**	
	18	19	20	21	22	23	24	
	25	26	27	28	29	30	*31*	
		1	2	3	4	5	6	7	June
	III 8	9	10	11	12	13	14	
(3) Sivan	**15**	16	17	18	19	20	21	
	22	23	24	25	26	27	28	
	29	30	1	2	3	4	5	July
	6	7	8	IV 9	10	11	12	
(4) Tammuz	13	14	**15**	16	17	18	19	
	20	21	22	23	24	25	26	
	27	28	*29*	30	31	1	2	August
	3	4	5	6	7	V 8	9	
(5) Av	10	11	12	**13**	14	15	16	
	17	18	19	20	21	22	23	
	24	25	26	*27*	28	29	30	
	31	1	2	3	4	5	6	September

(6) Elul	**VI** 7	8	9	10	11	**12**	13	
	14	15	16	17	18	19	20	
	21	22	23	24	25	**26**	27	
	28	29	30	1	2	3	4	October
(7) Tishri	5	6	7	**VII** 8	9	10	**11**	
	12	13	14	15	16	17	18	
	19	20	21	22	23	24	**25**	
	26	27	28	29	30	31	1	November
	2	3	4	5	6	7	8	
(8) Heshvan	9	**10**	11	12	13	14	15	
	16	17	18	19	20	21	22	
	23	**24**	25	26	27	28	29	
	30	1	2	3	4	5	6	December
(9) Kislev	7	8	9	**10**	11	12	13	
	14	15	16	17	18	19	20	
	21	22	23	**24**	25	26	27	
	28	29	30	31				

I, II, III, IV, V, VI, and VII mark the beginning of the 1st, 2nd, 3rd, 4th, 5th, 6th, and 7th month in Enoch's solar calendar.

Julian year 2314 BC

					1	2	3	January
(10) Tebet	4	5	6	7	8	*9*	10	
	11	12	13	14	15	16	17	
	18	19	20	21	22	*23*	24	
	25	26	27	28	29	30	31	
(11) Shebet	1	2	3	4	5	6	7	February
	8	9	10	11	12	13	14	
	15	16	17	18	19	20	*21*	
	22	23	24	25	26	27	28	
	1	2	3	4	5	6	7	March
(12) Adar	8	*9*	10	11	12	13	14	
	15	16	17	18	19	20	21	
	22	*23*	24	25	26	27	28	
	29	30	31	1	2	3	4	April
(1) Nisan	5	6	*7*	I 8	9	10	11	
	12	13	14	15	16	17	18	
	19	20	*21*	22	23	24	25	
	26	27	28	29	30	1	2	May
(2) Iyar	3	4	5	6	*7*	II 8	9	
	10	11	12	13	14	15	16	
	17	18	19	20	*21*	22	23	
	24	25	26	27	28	29	30	
(3) Sivan	31	1	2	3	4	*5*	6	June
	III 7	8	9	10	11	12	13	
	14	15	16	17	18	*19*	20	
	21	22	23	24	25	26	27	
	28	29	30	1	2	3	4	July
(4) Tammuz	*5*	6	7	8	9	10	11	
	12	13	14	15	16	17	18	
	19	20	21	22	23	24	25	
	26	27	28	29	30	31	1	August
(5) Av	2	*3*	4	5	6	7	8	
	9	10	11	12	13	14	15	
	16	*17*	18	19	20	21	22	
	23	24	25	26	27	28	29	

(6) Elul	30	31	1	**2**	3	4	5	September
	6	7	8	9	10	11	12	
	13	14	15	*16*	17	18	19	
	20	21	22	23	24	25	26	
(7) Tishri	27	28	29	30	1	2	3	October
	4	5	6	7	8	9	10	
	11	12	13	14	*15*	16	17	
	18	19	20	21	22	23	24	
(8) Heshvan	25	26	27	28	29	30	**31**	
	1	2	3	4	5	6	7	November
	8	9	10	11	12	13	*14*	
	15	16	17	18	19	20	21	
	22	23	24	25	26	27	28	
(9) Kislev	29	**30**	1	2	3	4	5	December
	6	7	8	9	10	11	12	
	13	*14*	15	16	17	18	19	
	20	21	22	23	24	25	26	
(10) Tebet	27	28	**29**	30	31			

I, II, and III mark the beginning of the 1st, 2nd, and 3rd month in Enoch's solar calendar.

Julian year 1550 BC

	1	2	3	4	5	6	7	January
	8	9	10	11	12	13	14	
(11) Shebet	15	16	17	18	19	20	21	
	22	23	24	25	26	27	28	
	29	30	31	1	2	3	*4*	
		5	6	7	8	9	10	11	February
	12	13	14	15	16	17	18	
(12a) Adar I	19	**20**	21	22	23	24	25	
	26	27	28	1	2	3	4	
	5	*6*	7	8	9	10	11	March
	12	13	14	15	16	17	18	
(12b) Adar II	19	20	21	**22**	23	24	25	
	26	27	28	29	30	31	1	
	2	3	4	*5*	6	7	8	April
	9	10	11	12	13	14	15	
(1) Nisan	16	17	18	19	**20**	21	22	
	23	24	25	26	27	28	29	
	30	1	2	3	*4*	5	6	
	7	8	9	10	11	12	13	May
(2) Iyar	14	15	16	17	18	19	**20**	
	21	22	23	24	25	26	27	
	28	29	30	31	1	2	*3*	
	4	5	6	7	8	9	10	June
	11	12	13	14	15	16	17	
(3) Sivan	**18**	19	20	21	22	23	24	
	25	26	27	28	29	30	1	
	2	3	4	5	6	7	8	July
	9	10	11	12	13	14	15	
(4) Tammuz	16	17	**18**	19	20	21	22	
	23	24	25	26	27	28	29	
	30	31	*1*	2	3	4	5	
	6	7	8	9	10	11	12	August
(5) Av	13	14	15	**16**	17	18	19	
	20	21	22	23	24	25	26	
	27	28	29	*30*	31	1	2	
	3	4	5	6	7	8	9	September

(6) Elul	10	11	12	13	14	**15**	16	
	17	18	19	20	21	22	23	
	24	25	26	27	28	*29*	30	
	1	2	3	4	5	6	7	October
(7) Tishri	8	9	10	11	12	13	**14**	
	15	16	17	18	19	20	21	
	22	23	24	25	26	27	*28*	
	29	30	31	1	2	3	4	
	5	6	7	8	9	10	11	November
(8) Heshvan	12	**13**	14	15	16	17	18	
	19	20	21	22	23	24	25	
	26	*27*	28	29	30	1	2	
	3	4	5	6	7	8	9	December
(9) Kislev	10	11	**12**	13	14	15	16	
	17	18	19	20	21	22	23	
	24	25	*26*	27	28	29	30	
	31							

Julian year 1542 BC

				1	2	3	4	January
	5	6	7	8	9	10	11	
	12	13	14	15	16	17	18	
(11) Shebet	19	20	21	22	23	24	25	
	26	27	28	29	30	31	1	
	2	3	4	5	6	7	8	February
	9	10	11	12	13	14	15	
(12) Adar	16	17	18	19	20	21	22	
	23	24	25	26	27	28	1	
	2	3	4	5	6	7	8	March
	9	10	11	12	13	14	15	
(1) Nisan	16	17	18	19	20	21	22	
	23	24	25	26	27	28	29	
	30	31	1	2	3	4	5	April
	6	7	8	9	10	11	12	
	13	14	15	16	17	18	19	
(2) Iyar	20	21	22	23	24	25	26	
	27	28	29	30	1	2	3	May
	4	5	6	7	8	9	10	
	11	12	13	14	15	16	17	
(3) Sivan	18	19	20	21	22	23	24	
	25	26	27	28	29	30	31	
	1	2	3	4	5	6	7	June
	8	9	10	11	12	13	14	
(4) Tammuz	15	16	17	18	19	20	21	
	22	23	24	25	26	27	28	
	29	30	1	2	3	4	5	July
	6	7	8	9	10	11	12	
(5) Av	13	14	15	16	17	18	19	
	20	21	22	23	24	25	26	
	27	28	29	30	31	1	2	
	3	4	5	6	7	8	9	August
	10	11	12	13	14	15	16	

(6) Elul	**17**	18	19	20	21	22	23	
	24	25	26	27	28	29	30	
	31	1	2	3	4	5	6	September
	7	8	9	10	11	12	13	
(7) Tishri	14	**15**	16	17	18	19	20	
	21	22	23	24	25	26	27	
	28	*29*	30	1	2	3	4	October
	5	6	7	8	9	10	11	
(8) Heshvan	12	13	14	**15**	16	17	18	
	19	20	21	22	23	24	25	
	26	27	28	*29*	30	31	1	
	2	3	4	5	6	7	8	November
(9) Kislev	9	10	11	12	**13**	14	15	
	16	17	18	19	20	21	22	
	23	24	25	26	*27*	28	29	
	30	1	2	3	4	5	6	December
(10) Tebet	7	8	9	10	11	12	**13**	
	14	15	16	17	18	19	20	
	21	22	23	24	25	26	*27*	
	28	29	30	31				

Julian year 1534 BC

								1	January
	2	3	4	5	6	7	8	
	9	10	11	12	13	14	15	
	16	17	18	19	20	21	22	
(11) Shebet	23	**24**	25	26	27	28	29	
	30	31	1	2	3	4	5	February
	6	*7*	8	9	10	11	12	
	13	14	15	16	17	18	19	
(12) Adar	20	21	22	**23**	24	25	26	
	27	28	1	2	3	4	5	March
	6	7	8	*9*	10	11	12	
	13	14	15	16	17	18	19	
(1) Nisan	20	21	22	23	**24**	25	26	
	27	28	29	30	31	1	2	April
	3	4	5	6	*7*	8	9	
	10	11	12	13	14	15	16	
(2) Iyar	17	18	19	20	21	22	**23**	
	24	25	26	27	28	29	30	
	1	2	3	4	5	6	*7*	May
	8	9	10	11	12	13	14	
	15	16	17	18	19	20	21	
(3) Sivan	**22**	23	24	25	26	27	28	
	29	30	31	1	2	3	4	June
	5	6	7	8	9	10	11	
	12	13	14	15	16	17	18	
(4) Tammuz	19	20	**21**	22	23	24	25	
	26	27	28	29	30	1	2	July
	3	4	*5*	6	7	8	9	
	10	11	12	13	14	15	16	
(5) Av	17	18	19	**20**	21	22	23	
	24	25	26	27	28	29	30	
	31	1	2	*3*	4	5	6	August
	7	8	9	10	11	12	13	

(6) Elul	14	15	16	17	18	**19**	20	
	21	22	23	24	25	26	27	
	28	29	30	31	1	*2*	3	September
	4	5	6	7	8	9	10	
(7) Tishri	11	12	13	14	15	16	**17**	
	18	19	20	21	22	23	24	
	25	26	27	28	29	30	*1*	October
	2	3	4	5	6	7	8	
	9	10	11	12	13	14	15	
(8) Heshvan	16	**17**	18	19	20	21	22	
	23	24	25	26	27	28	29	
	30	*31*	1	2	3	4	5	November
	6	7	8	9	10	11	12	
(9) Kislev	13	14	**15**	16	17	18	19	
	20	21	22	23	24	25	26	
	27	28	*29*	30	1	2	3	December
	4	5	6	7	8	9	10	
(10) Tebet	11	12	13	14	**15**	16	17	
	18	19	20	21	22	23	24	
	25	26	27	28	*29*	30	31	

Julian year 1457 BC

					1	2	3	January
	4	5	6	7	8	9	10	
(11) Shebet	11	12	**13**	14	15	16	17	
	18	19	20	21	22	23	24	
	25	26	**27**	28	29	30	31	
	1	2	3	4	5	6	7	February
(12a) Adar I	8	9	10	11	**12**	13	14	
	15	16	17	18	19	20	21	
	22	23	24	25	**26**	27	28	
	29	1	2	3	4	5	6	March
(12b) Adar II	7	8	9	10	11	**12**	13	
	14	15	16	17	18	19	20	
	21	22	23	24	25	**26**	27	
	28	29	30	31	1	2	3	April
	4	5	6	7	8	9	10	
(1) Nisan	**11**	12	13	14	15	16	17	
	18	19	20	21	22	23	24	
	25	26	27	28	29	30	1	May
	2	3	4	5	6	7	8	
(2) Iyar	9	10	**11**	12	13	14	15	
	16	17	18	19	20	21	22	
	23	24	**25**	26	27	28	29	
	30	31	1	2	3	4	5	June
(3) Sivan	6	7	8	**9**	10	11	12	
	13	14	15	16	17	18	19	
	20	21	22	**23**	24	25	26	
	27	28	29	30	1	2	3	July
(4) Tammuz	4	5	6	7	8	**9**	10	
	11	12	13	14	15	16	17	
	18	19	20	21	22	**23**	24	
	25	26	27	28	29	30	31	
(5) Av	1	2	3	4	5	6	**7**	August
	8	9	10	11	12	13	14	
	15	16	17	18	19	20	**21**	
	22	23	24	25	26	27	28	
	29	30	31	1	2	3	4	September

(6) Elul	5	**6**	7	8	9	10	11	
	12	13	14	15	16	17	18	
	19	***20***	21	22	23	24	25	
	26	27	28	29	30	1	2	October
(7) Tishri	3	4	**5**	6	7	8	9	
	10	11	12	13	14	15	16	
	17	18	***19***	20	21	22	23	
	24	25	26	27	28	29	30	
(8) Heshvan	31	1	2	3	**4**	5	6	November
	7	8	9	10	11	12	13	
	14	15	16	17	***18***	19	20	
	21	22	23	24	25	26	27	
(9) Kislev	28	29	30	1	2	**3**	4	December
	5	6	7	8	9	10	11	
	12	13	14	15	16	***17***	18	
	19	20	21	22	23	24	25	
	26	27	28	29	30	31		

Julian year 977 BC

			1	*2*	3	4	5	January
	6	7	8	9	10	11	12	
(11) Shebet	13	14	15	16	**17**	18	19	
	20	21	22	23	24	25	26	
	27	28	29	30	*31*	1	2	February
	3	4	5	6	7	8	9	
(12) Adar	10	11	12	13	14	15	**16**	
	17	18	19	20	21	22	23	
	24	25	26	27	28	29	*1*	March
	2	3	4	5	6	7	8	
	9	10	11	12	13	14	15	
(1) Nisan	**16**	17	18	19	20	21	22	
	23	24	25	26	27	28	29	
	30	31	1	2	3	4	5	April
	6	7	8	9	10	11	12	
(2) Iyar	13	14	**15**	16	17	18	19	
	20	21	22	23	24	25	26	
	27	28	*29*	30	1	2	3	May
	4	5	6	7	8	9	10	
(3) Sivan	11	12	13	**14**	15	16	17	
	18	19	20	21	22	23	24	
	25	26	27	*28*	29	30	31	
	1	2	3	4	5	6	7	June
(4) Tammuz	8	9	10	11	12	**13**	14	
	15	16	17	18	19	20	21	
	22	23	24	25	26	*27*	28	
	29	30	1	2	3	4	5	July
(5) Av	6	7	8	9	10	11	**12**	
	13	14	15	16	17	18	19	
	20	21	22	23	24	25	*26*	
	27	28	29	30	31	1	2	August
	3	4	5	6	7	8	9	
(6) Elul	10	**11**	12	13	14	15	16	
	17	18	19	20	21	22	23	
	24	*25*	26	27	28	29	30	
	31	1	2	3	4	5	6	September

(7) Tishri	7	8	**9**	10	11	12	13	
	14	15	16	17	18	19	20	
	21	22	**23**	24	25	26	27	
	28	29	30	1	2	3	4	October
(8) Heshvan	5	6	7	8	**9**	10	11	
	12	13	14	15	16	17	18	
	19	20	21	22	**23**	24	25	
	26	27	28	29	30	31	1	November
(9) Kislev	2	3	4	5	6	**7**	8	
	9	10	11	12	13	14	15	
	16	17	18	19	20	**21**	22	
	23	24	25	26	27	28	29	
	30	1	2	3	4	5	6	December
(10) Tebet	**7**	8	9	10	11	12	13	
	14	15	16	17	18	19	20	
	21	22	23	24	25	26	27	
	28	29	30	31				

Julian year 976 BC

					1	2	3	January
(11) Shebet	4	*5*	6	7	8	9	10	
	11	12	13	14	15	16	17	
	18	*19*	20	21	22	23	24	
	25	26	27	28	29	30	31	
(12a) Adar I	1	2	3	4	5	6	7	February
	8	9	10	11	12	13	14	
	15	16	17	*18*	19	20	21	
	22	23	24	25	26	27	28	
(12b) Adar II	1	2	3	4	5	*6*	7	March
	8	9	10	11	12	13	14	
	15	16	17	18	19	*20*	21	
	22	23	24	25	26	27	28	
(1) Nisan	29	30	31	1	2	3	4	April
	5	6	7	8	9	10	11	
	12	13	14	15	16	17	*18*	
	19	20	21	22	23	24	25	
	26	27	28	29	30	1	2	May
(2) Iyar	3	*4*	5	6	7	8	9	
	10	11	12	13	14	15	16	
	17	*18*	19	20	21	22	23	
	24	25	26	27	28	29	30	
(3) Sivan	31	1	*2*	3	4	5	6	June
	7	8	9	10	11	12	13	
	14	15	*16*	17	18	19	20	
	21	22	23	24	25	26	27	
(4) Tammuz	28	29	30	1	*2*	3	4	July
	5	6	7	8	9	10	11	
	12	13	14	15	*16*	17	18	
	19	20	21	22	23	24	25	
(5) Av	26	27	28	29	30	*31*	1	August
	2	3	4	5	6	7	8	
	9	10	11	12	13	*14*	15	
	16	17	18	19	20	21	22	
	23	24	25	26	27	28	29	

(6) Elul	**30**	31	1	2	3	4	5	September
	6	7	8	9	10	11	12	
	13	14	15	16	17	18	19	
	20	21	22	23	24	25	26	
(7) Tishri	27	**28**	29	30	1	2	3	October
	4	5	6	7	8	9	10	
	11	*12*	13	14	15	16	17	
	18	19	20	21	22	23	24	
(8) Heshvan	25	26	27	**28**	29	30	31	
	1	2	3	4	5	6	7	November
	8	9	10	*11*	12	13	14	
	15	16	17	18	19	20	21	
(9) Kislev	22	23	24	25	**26**	27	28	
	29	30	1	2	3	4	5	December
	6	7	8	9	*10*	11	12	
	13	14	15	16	17	18	19	
(10) Tebet	20	21	22	23	24	25	**26**	
	27	28	29	30	31			

Julian year 969 BC

						1	2	January
	3	4	5	6	7	8	9	
	10	11	12	13	14	15	16	
(11) Shebet	17	**18**	19	20	21	22	23	
	24	25	26	27	28	29	30	
	31	*1*	2	3	4	5	6	February
	7	8	9	10	11	12	13	
(12) Adar	14	15	16	**17**	18	19	20	
	21	22	23	24	25	26	27	
	28	29	1	*2*	3	4	5	March
	6	7	8	9	10	11	12	
(1) Nisan	13	14	15	16	**17**	18	19	
	20	21	22	23	24	25	26	
	27	28	29	30	*31*	1	2	April
	3	4	5	6	7	8	9	
(2) Iyar	10	11	12	13	14	15	**16**	
	17	18	19	20	21	22	23	
	24	25	26	27	28	29	*30*	
	1	2	3	4	5	6	7	May
	8	9	10	11	12	13	14	
(3) Sivan	**15**	16	17	18	19	20	21	
	22	23	24	25	26	27	28	
	29	30	31	1	2	3	4	June
	5	6	7	8	9	10	11	
(4) Tammuz	12	13	**14**	15	16	17	18	
	19	20	21	22	23	24	25	
	26	27	*28*	29	30	1	2	July
	3	4	5	6	7	8	9	
(5) Av	10	11	12	**13**	14	15	16	
	17	18	19	20	21	22	23	
	24	25	26	*27*	28	29	30	
	31	1	2	3	4	5	6	August
(6) Elul	7	8	9	10	11	**12**	13	
	14	15	16	17	18	19	20	
	21	22	23	24	25	*26*	27	
	28	29	30	31	1	2	3	September

(7) Tishri	4	5	6	7	8	9	**10**	
	11	12	13	14	15	16	17	
	18	19	20	21	22	23	*24*	
	25	26	27	28	29	30	1	October
	2	3	4	5	6	7	8	
(8) Heshvan	9	**10**	11	12	13	14	15	
	16	17	18	19	20	21	22	
	23	*24*	25	26	27	28	29	
	30	31	1	2	3	4	5	November
(9) Kislev	6	7	**8**	9	10	11	12	
	13	14	15	16	17	18	19	
	20	21	*22*	23	24	25	26	
	27	28	29	30	1	2	3	December
(10) Tebet	4	5	6	**7**	8	9	10	
	11	12	13	14	15	16	17	
	18	19	20	*21*	22	23	24	
	25	26	27	28	29	30	31	

Julian year 605 BC

						1	2	January
	3	4	5	6	7	8	9	
(11) Shebet	10	11	**12**	13	14	15	16	
	17	18	19	20	21	22	23	
	24	25	***26***	27	28	29	30	
	31	1	2	3	4	5	6	February
(12a) Adar I	7	8	9	10	**11**	12	13	
	14	15	16	17	18	19	20	
	21	22	23	24	***25***	26	27	
	28	29	1	2	3	4	5	March
(12b) Adar II	6	7	8	9	10	11	**12**	
	13	14	15	16	17	18	19	
	20	21	22	23	24	25	***26***	
	27	28	29	30	31	1	2	April
	3	4	5	6	7	8	9	
(1) Nisan	**10**	11	12	13	14	15	16	
	17	18	19	20	21	22	23	
	24	25	26	27	28	29	30	
	1	2	3	4	5	6	7	May
(2) Iyar	8	9	**10**	11	12	13	14	
	15	16	17	18	19	20	21	
	22	23	***24***	25	26	27	28	
	29	30	31	1	2	3	4	June
(3) Sivan	5	6	7	**8**	9	10	11	
	12	13	14	15	16	17	18	
	19	20	21	***22***	23	24	25	
	26	27	28	29	30	1	2	July
(4) Tammuz	3	4	5	6	7	**8**	9	
	10	11	12	13	14	15	16	
	17	18	19	20	21	***22***	23	
	24	25	26	27	28	29	30	
(5) Av	31	1	2	3	4	5	**6**	August
	7	8	9	10	11	12	13	
	14	15	16	17	18	19	***20***	
	21	22	23	24	25	26	27	
	28	29	30	31	1	2	3	September

(6) Elul	4	**5**	6	7	8	9	10	
	11	12	13	14	15	16	17	
	18	*19*	20	21	22	23	24	
	25	26	27	28	29	30	1	October
(7) Tishri	2	3	**4**	5	6	7	8	
	9	10	11	12	13	14	15	
	16	17	*18*	19	20	21	22	
	23	24	25	26	27	28	29	
(8) Heshvan	30	31	1	2	**3**	4	5	November
	6	7	8	9	10	11	12	
	13	14	15	16	*17*	18	19	
	20	21	22	23	24	25	26	
(9) Kislev	27	28	29	30	1	2	**3**	December
	4	5	6	7	8	9	10	
	11	12	13	14	15	16	*17*	
	18	19	20	21	22	23	24	
	25	26	27	28	29	30	31	

Julian year 599 BC

							1	January
(10) Tebet	2	3	4	5	**6**	7	8	
	9	10	11	12	13	14	15	
	16	17	18	19	**20**	21	22	
	23	24	25	26	27	28	29	
(11) Shebet	30	31	1	2	3	**4**	5	February
	6	7	8	9	10	11	12	
	13	14	15	16	17	**18**	19	
	20	21	22	23	24	25	26	
	27	28	1	2	3	4	5	March
(12) Adar	6	**7**	8	9	10	11	12	
	13	14	15	16	17	18	19	
	20	**21**	22	23	24	25	26	
	27	28	29	30	31	1	2	April
(1) Nisan	3	4	**5**	6	7	8	9	
	10	11	12	13	14	15	16	
	17	18	**19**	20	21	22	23	
	24	25	26	27	28	29	30	
(2) Iyar	1	2	3	4	**5**	6	7	May
	8	9	10	11	12	13	14	
	15	16	17	18	**19**	20	21	
	22	23	24	25	26	27	28	
(3) Sivan	29	30	31	1	2	**3**	4	June
	5	6	7	8	9	10	11	
	12	13	14	15	16	**17**	18	
	19	20	21	22	23	24	25	
	26	27	28	29	30	1	2	July
(4) Tammuz	3	4	5	6	7	8	9	
	10	11	12	13	14	15	16	
	17	18	19	20	21	22	23	
	24	25	26	27	28	29	30	
(5) Av	31	**1**	2	3	4	5	6	August
	7	8	9	10	11	12	13	
	14	**15**	16	17	18	19	20	
	21	22	23	24	25	26	27	

(6) Elul	28	29	30	**31**	1	2	3	September
	4	5	6	7	8	9	10	
	11	12	13	*14*	15	16	17	
	18	19	20	21	22	23	24	
(7) Tishri	25	26	27	28	**29**	30	1	October
	2	3	4	5	6	7	8	
	9	10	11	12	*13*	14	15	
	16	17	18	19	20	21	22	
(8) Heshvan	23	24	25	26	27	28	**29**	
	30	31	1	2	3	4	5	November
	6	7	8	9	10	11	*12*	
	13	14	15	16	17	18	19	
	20	21	22	23	24	25	26	
(9) Kislev	**27**	28	29	30	1	2	3	December
	4	5	6	7	8	9	10	
	11	12	13	14	15	16	17	
	18	19	20	21	22	23	24	
(10) Tebet	25	26	**27**	28	29	30	31	

Julian year 598 BC

		1	2	3	4	5	6	7	January
		8	9	*10*	11	12	13	14	
		15	16	17	18	19	20	21	
(11) Shebet		22	23	24	*25*	26	27	28	
		29	30	31	1	2	3	4	February
		5	6	7	*8*	9	10	11	
		12	13	14	15	16	17	18	
(12) Adar		19	20	21	22	23	*24*	25	
		26	27	28	1	2	3	4	March
		5	6	7	8	9	*10*	11	
		12	13	14	15	16	17	18	
(1) Nisan		19	20	21	22	23	24	*25*	
		26	27	28	29	30	31	1	April
		2	3	4	5	6	7	*8*	
		9	10	11	12	13	14	15	
		16	17	18	19	20	21	22	
(2) Iyar		23	*24*	25	26	27	28	29	
		30	1	2	3	4	5	6	May
		7	*8*	9	10	11	12	13	
		14	15	16	17	18	19	20	
(3) Sivan		21	22	*23*	24	25	26	27	
		28	29	30	31	1	2	3	June
		4	5	*6*	7	8	9	10	
		11	12	13	14	15	16	17	
(4) Tammuz		18	19	20	21	*22*	23	24	
		25	26	27	28	29	30	1	July
		2	3	4	5	*6*	7	8	
		9	10	11	12	13	14	15	
(5) Av		16	17	18	19	20	*21*	22	
		23	24	25	26	27	28	29	
		30	31	1	2	3	*4*	5	August
		6	7	8	9	10	11	12	
		13	14	15	16	17	18	19	

(6) Elul	**20**	21	22	23	24	25	26	
	27	28	29	30	31	1	2	September
	3	4	5	6	7	8	9	
	10	11	12	13	14	15	16	
(7) Tishri	17	**18**	19	20	21	22	23	
	24	25	26	27	28	29	30	
	1	*2*	3	4	5	6	7	October
	8	9	10	11	12	13	14	
(8) Heshvan	15	16	17	**18**	19	20	21	
	22	23	24	25	26	27	28	
	29	30	31	*1*	2	3	4	November
	5	6	7	8	9	10	11	
(9) Kislev	12	13	14	15	16	**17**	18	
	19	20	21	22	23	24	25	
	26	27	28	29	30	*1*	2	December
	3	4	5	6	7	8	9	
	10	11	12	13	14	15	16	
(10) Tebet	**17**	18	19	20	21	22	23	
	24	25	26	27	28	29	30	
	31							

Julian year 597 BC

		1	2	3	4	5	6	January
	7	8	9	10	11	12	13	
(11) Shebet	14	**15**	16	17	18	19	20	
	21	22	23	24	25	26	27	
	28	*29*	30	31	1	2	3	February
	4	5	6	7	8	9	10	
(12) Adar	11	12	13	**14**	15	16	17	
	18	19	20	21	22	23	24	
	25	26	27	**28**	29	1	2	March
	3	4	5	6	7	8	9	
(1) Nisan	10	11	12	13	**14**	15	16	
	17	18	19	20	21	22	23	
	24	25	26	27	**28**	29	30	
	31	1	2	3	4	5	6	April
(2) Iyar	7	8	9	10	11	12	**13**	
	14	15	16	17	18	19	20	
	21	22	23	24	25	26	**27**	
	28	29	30	1	2	3	4	May
	5	6	7	8	9	10	11	
(3) Sivan	**12**	13	14	15	16	17	18	
	19	20	21	22	23	24	25	
	26	27	28	29	30	31	1	June
	2	3	4	5	6	7	8	
(4) Tammuz	9	10	**11**	12	13	14	15	
	16	17	18	19	20	21	22	
	23	24	**25**	26	27	28	29	
	30	1	2	3	4	5	6	July
(5) Av	7	8	9	**10**	11	12	13	
	14	15	16	17	18	19	20	
	21	22	23	**24**	25	26	27	
	28	29	30	31	1	2	3	August
(6) Elul	4	5	6	7	8	**9**	10	
	11	12	13	14	15	16	17	
	18	19	20	21	22	*23*	24	
	25	26	27	28	29	30	31	

(7) Tishri	1	2	3	4	5	6	7	September
	8	9	10	11	12	13	14	
	15	16	17	18	19	20	*21*	
	22	23	24	25	26	27	28	
	29	30	1	2	3	4	5	October
(8) Heshvan	6	*7*	8	9	10	11	12	
	13	14	15	16	17	18	19	
	20	*21*	22	23	24	25	26	
	27	28	29	30	31	1	2	November
(9) Kislev	3	4	*5*	6	7	8	9	
	10	11	12	13	14	15	16	
	17	18	*19*	20	21	22	23	
	24	25	26	27	28	29	30	
(10) Tebet	1	2	3	4	*5*	6	7	December
	8	9	10	11	12	13	14	
	15	16	17	18	*19*	20	21	
	22	23	24	25	26	27	28	
	29	30	31					

Julian year 587 BC

	1	2	3	4	5	6	7	
	1	2	3	4	5	6	7	January
	8	9	10	11	12	13	14	
	15	16	17	18	19	20	21	
(11) Shebet	22	**23**	24	25	26	27	28	
	29	30	31	1	2	3	4	February
	5	*6*	7	8	9	10	11	
	12	13	14	15	16	17	18	
(12) Adar	19	20	21	**22**	23	24	25	
	26	27	28	1	2	3	4	March
	5	6	7	*8*	9	10	11	
	12	13	14	15	16	17	18	
(1) Nisan	19	20	21	22	**23**	24	25	
	26	27	28	29	30	31	1	April
	2	3	4	5	*6*	7	8	
	9	10	11	12	13	14	15	
(2) Iyar	16	17	18	19	20	21	**22**	
	23	24	25	26	27	28	29	
	30	1	2	3	4	5	*6*	May
	7	8	9	10	11	12	13	
	14	15	16	17	18	19	20	
(3) Sivan	**21**	22	23	24	25	26	27	
	28	29	30	31	1	2	3	June
	4	5	6	7	8	9	10	
	11	12	13	14	15	16	17	
(4) Tammuz	18	19	**20**	21	22	23	24	
	25	26	27	28	29	30	1	July
	2	3	*4*	5	6	7	8	
	9	10	11	12	13	14	15	
(5) Av	16	17	18	**19**	20	21	22	
	23	24	25	26	27	28	29	
	30	31	1	*2*	3	4	5	August
	6	7	8	9	10	11	12	
(6) Elul	13	14	15	16	17	**18**	19	
	20	21	22	23	24	25	26	
	27	28	29	30	31	*1*	2	September
	3	4	5	6	7	8	9	

(7) Tishri	10	11	12	13	14	15	**16**	
	17	18	19	20	21	22	23	
	24	25	26	27	28	29	*30*	
	1	2	3	4	5	6	7	October
	8	9	10	11	12	13	14	
(8) Heshvan	15	**16**	17	18	19	20	21	
	22	23	24	25	26	27	28	
	29	*30*	31	1	2	3	4	November
	5	6	7	8	9	10	11	
(9) Kislev	12	13	**14**	15	16	17	18	
	19	20	21	22	23	24	25	
	26	27	*28*	29	30	1	2	December
	3	4	5	6	7	8	9	
(10) Tebet	10	11	12	13	**14**	15	16	
	17	18	19	20	21	22	23	
	24	25	26	27	*28*	29	30	
	31							

Julian year 586 BC

		1	2	3	4	5	6	January
(11) Shebet	7	8	9	10	11	12	**13**	
	14	15	16	17	18	19	20	
	21	22	23	24	25	26	*27*	
	28	29	30	31	1	2	3	February
	4	5	6	7	8	9	10	
(12a) Adar I	11	**12**	13	14	15	16	17	
	18	19	20	21	22	23	24	
	25	*26*	27	28	1	2	3	March
	4	5	6	7	8	9	10	
(12b) Adar II	11	12	13	**14**	15	16	17	
	18	19	20	21	22	23	24	
	25	26	27	*28*	29	30	31	
	1	2	3	4	5	6	7	April
(1) Nisan	8	9	10	11	**12**	13	14	
	15	16	17	18	19	20	21	
	22	23	24	25	*26*	27	28	
	29	30	1	2	3	4	5	May
(2) Iyar	6	7	8	9	10	11	**12**	
	13	14	15	16	17	18	19	
	20	21	22	23	24	25	*26*	
	27	28	29	30	31	1	2	June
	3	4	5	6	7	8	9	
(3) Sivan	**10**	11	12	13	14	15	16	
	17	18	19	20	21	22	23	
	24	25	26	27	28	29	30	
	1	2	3	4	5	6	7	July
(4) Tammuz	8	9	**10**	11	12	13	14	
	15	16	17	18	19	20	21	
	22	23	*24*	25	26	27	28	
	29	30	31	1	2	3	4	August
(5) Av	5	6	7	**8**	9	10	11	
	12	13	14	15	16	17	18	
	19	20	21	*22*	23	24	25	
	26	27	28	29	30	31	1	September

(6) Elul	2	3	4	5	6	**7**	8	
	9	10	11	12	13	14	15	
	16	17	18	19	20	**21**	22	
	23	24	25	26	27	28	29	
(7) Tishri	30	1	2	3	4	5	**6**	October
	7	8	9	10	11	12	13	
	14	15	16	17	18	19	**20**	
	21	22	23	24	25	26	27	
	28	29	30	31	1	2	3	November
(8) Heshvan	4	**5**	6	7	8	9	10	
	11	12	13	14	15	16	17	
	18	**19**	20	21	22	23	24	
	25	26	27	28	29	30	1	December
(9) Kislev	2	3	**4**	5	6	7	8	
	9	10	11	12	13	14	15	
	16	17	**18**	19	20	21	22	
	23	24	25	26	27	28	29	
	30	31						

Julian year 573 BC

					1	2	3	4	January
		5	6	7	8	9	10	11	
		12	13	14	15	16	17	18	
(11) Shebet		19	**20**	21	22	23	24	25	
		26	27	28	29	30	31	1	February
		2	*3*	4	5	6	7	8	
		9	10	11	12	13	14	15	
(12) Adar		16	17	18	**19**	20	21	22	
		23	24	25	26	27	28	29	
		1	2	3	*4*	5	6	7	March
		8	9	10	11	12	13	14	
(1) Nisan		15	16	17	18	**19**	20	21	
		22	23	24	25	26	27	28	
		29	30	31	1	*2*	3	4	April
		5	6	7	8	9	10	11	
(2) Iyar		12	13	14	15	16	17	**18**	
		19	20	21	22	23	24	25	
		26	27	28	29	30	1	*2*	May
		3	4	5	6	7	8	9	
		10	11	12	13	14	15	16	
(3) Sivan		**17**	18	19	20	21	22	23	
		24	25	26	27	28	29	30	
		31	1	2	3	4	5	6	June
		7	8	9	10	11	12	13	
(4) Tammuz		14	15	**16**	17	18	19	20	
		21	22	23	24	25	26	27	
		28	29	*30*	1	2	3	4	July
		5	6	7	8	9	10	11	
(5) Av		12	13	14	**15**	16	17	18	
		19	20	21	22	23	24	25	
		26	27	28	*29*	30	31	1	August
		2	3	4	5	6	7	8	
(6) Elul		9	10	11	12	13	**14**	15	
		16	17	18	19	20	21	22	
		23	24	25	26	27	**28**	29	
		30	31	1	2	3	4	5	September

(7) Tishri	6	7	8	9	10	11	**12**	
	13	14	15	16	17	18	19	
	20	21	22	23	24	25	*26*	
	27	28	29	30	1	2	3	October
	4	5	6	7	8	9	10	
(8) Heshvan	11	**12**	13	14	15	16	17	
	18	19	20	21	22	23	24	
	25	*26*	27	28	29	30	31	
	1	2	3	4	5	6	7	November
(9) Kislev	8	9	**10**	11	12	13	14	
	15	16	17	18	19	20	21	
	22	23	*24*	25	26	27	28	
	29	30	1	2	3	4	5	December
(10) Tebet	6	7	8	**9**	10	11	12	
	13	14	15	16	17	18	19	
	20	21	22	*23*	24	25	26	
	27	28	29	30	31			

Julian year 572 BC

							1	2	January
(11) Shebet	3	4	5	6	**7**	8	9	
	10	11	12	13	14	15	16	
	17	18	19	20	**21**	22	23	
	24	25	26	27	28	29	30	
(12a) Adar I	31	1	2	3	4	5	**6**	February
	7	8	9	10	11	12	13	
	14	15	16	17	18	19	**20**	
	21	22	23	24	25	26	27	
	28	1	2	3	4	5	6	March
(12b) Adar II	7	**8**	9	10	11	12	13	
	14	15	16	17	18	19	20	
	21	**22**	23	24	25	26	27	
	28	29	30	31	1	2	3	April
(1) Nisan	4	5	**6**	7	8	9	10	
	11	12	13	14	15	16	17	
	18	19	**20**	21	22	23	24	
	25	26	27	28	29	30	1	May
(2) Iyar	2	3	4	5	**6**	7	8	
	9	10	11	12	13	14	15	
	16	17	18	19	**20**	21	22	
	23	24	25	26	27	28	29	
(3) Sivan	30	31	1	2	3	**4**	5	June
	6	7	8	9	10	11	12	
	13	14	15	16	17	**18**	19	
	20	21	22	23	24	25	26	
	27	28	29	30	1	2	3	July
(4) Tammuz	**4**	5	6	7	8	9	10	
	11	12	13	14	15	16	17	
	18	19	20	21	22	23	24	
	25	26	27	28	29	30	31	
(5) Av	1	**2**	3	4	5	6	7	August
	8	9	10	11	12	13	14	
	15	**16**	17	18	19	20	21	
	22	23	24	25	26	27	28	

(6) Elul	29	30	31	**1**	2	3	4	September
	5	6	7	8	9	10	11	
	12	13	14	*15*	16	17	18	
	19	20	21	22	23	24	25	
(7) Tishri	26	27	28	29	**30**	1	2	October
	3	4	5	6	7	8	9	
	10	11	12	13	*14*	15	16	
	17	18	19	20	21	22	23	
(8) Heshvan	24	25	26	27	28	29	**30**	
	31	1	2	3	4	5	6	November
	7	8	9	10	11	12	*13*	
	14	15	16	17	18	19	20	
	21	22	23	24	25	26	27	
(9) Kislev	**28**	29	30	1	2	3	4	December
	5	6	7	8	9	10	11	
	12	13	14	15	16	17	18	
	19	20	21	22	23	24	25	
(10) Tebet	26	27	**28**	29	30	31		

Julian year 561 BC

					1	2	3	January
(10) Tebet	4	5	6	*7*	8	9	10	
	11	12	13	14	15	16	17	
	18	19	20	*21*	22	23	24	
	25	26	27	28	29	30	31	
(11) Shebet	1	2	3	4	*5*	6	7	February
	8	9	10	11	12	13	14	
	15	16	17	18	*19*	20	21	
	22	23	24	25	26	27	28	
(12) Adar	29	1	2	3	4	5	*6*	March
	7	8	9	10	11	12	13	
	14	15	16	17	18	19	*20*	
	21	22	23	24	25	26	27	
	28	29	30	31	1	2	3	April
(1) Nisan	4	5	6	7	8	9	10	
	11	12	13	14	15	16	17	
	18	19	20	21	22	23	24	
	25	26	27	28	29	30	1	May
(2) Iyar	2	3	4	5	6	7	8	
	9	10	11	12	13	14	15	
	16	17	*18*	19	20	21	22	
	23	24	25	26	27	28	29	
(3) Sivan	30	31	1	*2*	3	4	5	June
	6	7	8	9	10	11	12	
	13	14	15	*16*	17	18	19	
	20	21	22	23	24	25	26	
(4) Tammuz	27	28	29	30	1	*2*	3	July
	4	5	6	7	8	9	10	
	11	12	13	14	15	*16*	17	
	18	19	20	21	22	23	24	
(5) Av	25	26	27	28	29	30	*31*	
	1	2	3	4	5	6	7	August
	8	9	10	11	12	13	*14*	
	15	16	17	18	19	20	21	
	22	23	24	25	26	27	28	

(6) Elul	29	**30**	31	1	2	3	4	September
	5	6	7	8	9	10	11	
	12	*13*	14	15	16	17	18	
	19	20	21	22	23	24	25	
(7) Tishri	26	27	**28**	29	30	1	2	October
	3	4	5	6	7	8	9	
	10	11	*12*	13	14	15	16	
	17	18	19	20	21	22	23	
(8) Heshvan	24	25	26	27	**28**	29	30	
	31	1	2	3	4	5	6	November
	7	8	9	10	*11*	12	13	
	14	15	16	17	18	19	20	
(9) Kislev	21	22	23	24	25	26	**27**	
	28	29	30	1	2	3	4	December
	5	6	7	8	9	10	*11*	
	12	13	14	15	16	17	18	
	19	20	21	22	23	24	25	
(10) Tebet	26	**27**	28	29	30	31		

Julian year 457 BC

			1	2	3	4	5	6	January
	7	8	9	10	11	*12*	13	
		14	15	16	17	18	19	20	
(11) Shebet	21	22	23	24	25	26	27	
	28	29	30	31	1	2	3	February
	4	5	6	7	8	9	*10*	
	11	12	13	14	15	16	17	
	18	19	20	21	22	23	24	
(12) Adar	25	*26*	27	28	29	1	2	March
	3	4	5	6	7	8	9	
	10	*11*	12	13	14	15	16	
	17	18	19	20	21	22	23	
(1) Nisan	24	25	*26*	27	28	29	30	
	31	1	2	3	4	5	6	April
	7	8	*9*	10	11	12	13	
	14	15	16	17	18	19	20	
(2) Iyar	21	22	23	24	*25*	26	27	
	28	29	30	1	2	3	4	May
	5	6	7	8	*9*	10	11	
	12	13	14	15	16	17	18	
(3) Sivan	19	20	21	22	23	*24*	25	
	26	27	28	29	30	31	1	June
	2	3	4	5	6	*7*	8	
	9	10	11	12	13	14	15	
	16	17	18	19	20	21	22	
(4) Tammuz	*23*	24	25	26	27	28	29	
	30	1	2	3	4	5	6	July
	7	8	9	10	11	12	13	
	14	15	16	17	18	19	20	
(5) Av	21	*22*	23	24	25	26	27	
	28	29	30	31	1	2	3	August
	4	*5*	6	7	8	9	10	
	11	12	13	14	15	16	17	

(6) Elul	18	19	20	**21**	22	23	24	
	25	26	27	28	29	30	31	
	1	2	3	*4*	5	6	7	September
	8	9	10	11	12	13	14	
(7) Tishri	15	16	17	18	**19**	20	21	
	22	23	24	25	26	27	28	
	29	30	1	2	*3*	4	5	October
	6	7	8	9	10	11	12	
(8) Heshvan	13	14	15	16	17	**18**	19	
	20	21	22	23	24	25	26	
	27	28	29	30	31	*1*	2	November
	3	4	5	6	7	8	9	
	10	11	12	13	14	15	16	
(9) Kislev	**17**	18	19	20	21	22	23	
	24	25	26	27	28	29	30	
	1	2	3	4	5	6	7	December
	8	9	10	11	12	13	14	
(10) Tebet	15	**16**	17	18	19	20	21	
	22	23	24	25	26	27	28	
	29	*30*	31					

Julian year 168 BC

							1	January
	2	3	4	5	6	7	8	
(11) Shebet	9	10	11	**12**	13	14	15	
	16	17	18	19	20	21	22	
	23	24	25	**26**	27	28	29	
	30	31	1	2	3	4	5	February
(12) Adar	6	7	8	9	10	**11**	12	
	13	14	15	16	17	18	19	
	20	21	22	23	24	**25**	26	
	27	28	1	2	3	4	5	March
(1) Nisan	6	7	8	9	10	11	**12**	
	13	14	15	16	17	18	19	
	20	21	22	23	24	25	**26**	
	27	28	29	30	31	1	2	April
	3	4	5	6	7	8	9	
(2) Iyar	10	**11**	12	13	14	15	16	
	17	18	19	20	21	22	23	
	24	**25**	26	27	28	29	30	
	1	2	3	4	5	6	7	May
(3) Sivan	8	9	**10**	11	12	13	14	
	15	16	17	18	19	20	21	
	22	23	**24**	25	26	27	28	
	29	30	31	1	2	3	4	June
(4) Tammuz	5	6	7	8	**9**	10	11	
	12	13	14	15	16	17	18	
	19	20	21	22	**23**	24	25	
	26	27	28	29	30	1	2	July
(5) Av	3	4	5	6	7	**8**	9	
	10	11	12	13	14	15	16	
	17	18	19	20	21	**22**	23	
	24	25	26	27	28	29	30	
	31	1	2	3	4	5	6	August
6) Elul	**7**	8	9	10	11	12	13	
	14	15	16	17	18	19	20	
	21	22	23	24	25	26	27	
	28	29	30	31	1	2	3	September

(7) Tishri	4	**5**	6	7	8	9	10	
	11	12	13	14	15	16	17	
	18	*19*	20	21	22	23	24	
	25	26	27	28	29	30	1	October
(8) Heshvan	2	3	4	**5**	6	7	8	
	9	10	11	12	13	14	15	
	16	17	18	*19*	20	21	22	
	23	24	25	26	27	28	29	
(9) Kislev	30	31	1	2	**3**	4	5	November
	6	7	8	9	10	11	12	
	13	14	15	16	*17*	18	19	
	20	21	22	23	24	25	26	
(10) Tebet	27	28	29	30	1	2	**3**	December
	4	5	6	7	8	9	10	
	11	12	13	14	15	16	*17*	
	18	19	20	21	22	23	24	
	25	26	27	28	29	30	31	

Julian year 165 BC

				1	2	3	4	5	January
(11) Shebet	6	7	**8**	9	10	11	12		
	13	14	15	16	17	18	19		
	20	21	**22**	23	24	25	26		
	27	28	29	30	31	1	2	February	
(12a) Adar I	3	4	5	6	**7**	8	9		
	10	11	12	13	14	15	16		
	17	18	19	20	**21**	22	23		
	24	25	26	27	28	29	1	March	
(12b) Adar II	2	3	4	5	6	7	**8**		
	9	10	11	12	13	14	15		
	16	17	18	19	20	21	**22**		
	23	24	25	26	27	28	29		
	30	31	1	2	3	4	5	April	
(1) Nisan	**6**	7	8	9	10	11	12		
	13	14	15	16	17	18	19		
	20	21	22	23	24	25	26		
	27	28	29	30	1	2	3	May	
(2) Iyar	4	5	**6**	7	8	9	10		
	11	12	13	14	15	16	17		
	18	19	**20**	21	22	23	24		
	25	26	27	28	29	30	31		
(3) Sivan	1	2	3	**4**	5	6	7	June	
	8	9	10	11	12	13	14		
	15	16	17	**18**	19	20	21		
	22	23	24	25	26	27	28		
(4) Tammuz	29	30	1	2	3	**4**	5	July	
	6	7	8	9	10	11	12		
	13	14	15	16	17	**18**	19		
	20	21	22	23	24	25	26		
(5) Av	27	28	29	30	31	1	**2**	August	
	3	4	5	6	7	8	9		
	10	11	12	13	14	15	**16**		
	17	18	19	20	21	22	23		
	24	25	26	27	28	29	30		

(6) Elul	31	**1**	2	3	4	5	6	September
	7	8	9	10	11	12	13	
	14	*15*	16	17	18	19	20	
	21	22	23	24	25	26	27	
(7) Tishri	28	29	**30**	1	2	3	4	October
	5	6	7	8	9	10	11	
	12	13	*14*	15	16	17	18	
	19	20	21	22	23	24	25	
(8) Heshvan	26	27	28	29	**30**	31	1	November
	2	3	4	5	6	7	8	
	9	10	11	12	*13*	14	15	
	16	17	18	19	20	21	22	
(9) Kislev	23	24	25	26	27	**28**	29	
	30	1	2	3	4	5	6	December
	7	8	9	10	11	*12*	13	
	14	15	16	17	18	19	20	
	21	22	23	24	25	26	27	
(10) Tebet	**28**	29	30	31				

Julian year 38 BC

	1	2	3	4	5	6	7	
	1	2	3	4	5	6	7	January
(11) Shebet	8	9	10	11	12	13	**14**	
	15	16	17	18	19	20	21	
	22	23	24	25	26	27	**28**	
	29	30	31	1	2	3	4	February
	5	6	7	8	9	10	11	
(12) Adar	12	**13**	14	15	16	17	18	
	19	20	21	22	23	24	25	
	26	**27**	28	1	2	3	4	March
	5	6	7	8	9	10	11	
(1) Nisan	12	13	**14**	15	16	17	18	
	19	20	21	22	23	24	25	
	26	27	**28**	29	30	31	1	April
	2	3	4	5	6	7	8	
(2) Iyar	9	10	11	12	**13**	14	15	
	16	17	18	19	20	21	22	
	23	24	25	26	**27**	28	29	
	30	1	2	3	4	5	6	May
(3) Sivan	7	8	9	10	11	**12**	13	
	14	15	16	17	18	19	20	
	21	22	23	24	25	**26**	27	
	28	29	30	31	1	2	3	June
	4	5	6	7	8	9	10	
(4) Tammuz	**11**	12	13	14	15	16	17	
	18	19	20	21	22	23	24	
	25	26	27	28	29	30	1	July
	2	3	4	5	6	7	8	
(5) Av	9	**10**	11	12	13	14	15	
	16	17	18	19	20	21	22	
	23	**24**	25	26	27	28	29	
	30	31	1	2	3	4	5	August
(6) Elul	6	7	8	**9**	10	11	12	
	13	14	15	16	17	18	19	
	20	21	22	**23**	24	25	26	
	27	28	29	30	31	1	2	September

(7) Tishri	3	4	5	6	*7*	8	9	
	10	11	12	13	14	15	16	
	17	18	19	20	*21*	22	23	
	24	25	26	27	28	29	30	
(8) Heshvan	1	2	3	4	5	*6*	7	October
	8	9	10	11	12	13	14	
	15	16	17	18	19	*20*	21	
	22	23	24	25	26	27	28	
	29	30	31	1	2	3	4	November
(9) Kislev	*5*	6	7	8	9	10	11	
	12	13	14	15	16	17	18	
	19	20	21	22	23	24	25	
	26	27	28	29	30	1	2	December
(10) Tebet	3	4	*5*	6	7	8	9	
	10	11	12	13	14	15	16	
	17	18	*19*	20	21	22	23	
	24	25	26	27	28	29	30	
	31							

Julian year 37 BC

(10) Tebet		1	2	3	4	**5**	6	January
	7	8	9	10	11	12	13	
	14	15	16	17	18	*19*	20	
	21	22	23	24	25	26	27	
(11) Shebet	28	29	30	31	1	2	**3**	February
	4	5	6	7	8	9	10	
	11	12	13	14	15	16	*17*	
	18	19	20	21	22	23	24	
	25	26	27	28	29	1	2	March
(12) Adar	3	**4**	5	6	7	8	9	
	10	11	12	13	14	15	16	
	17	*18*	19	20	21	22	23	
	24	25	26	27	28	29	30	
(1) Nisan	31	1	**2**	3	4	5	6	April
	7	8	9	10	11	12	13	
	14	15	*16*	17	18	19	20	
	21	22	23	24	25	26	27	
(2) Iyar	28	29	30	1	**2**	3	4	May
	5	6	7	8	9	10	11	
	12	13	14	15	*16*	17	18	
	19	20	21	22	23	24	25	
(3) Sivan	26	27	28	29	30	**31**	1	June
	2	3	4	5	6	7	8	
	9	10	11	12	13	*14*	15	
	16	17	18	19	20	21	22	
	23	24	25	26	27	28	29	
(4) Tammuz	**30**	1	2	3	4	5	6	July
	7	8	9	10	11	12	13	
	14	15	16	17	18	19	20	
	21	22	23	24	25	26	27	
(5) Av	28	**29**	30	31	1	2	3	August
	4	5	6	7	8	9	10	
	11	*12*	13	14	15	16	17	
	18	19	20	21	22	23	24	

(6) Elul	25	26	27	**28**	29	30	31	
	1	2	3	4	5	6	7	September
	8	9	10	*11*	12	13	14	
	15	16	17	18	19	20	21	
(7) Tishri	22	23	24	25	**26**	27	28	
	29	30	1	2	3	4	5	October
	6	7	8	9	*10*	11	12	
	13	14	15	16	17	18	19	
(8) Heshvan	20	21	22	23	24	25	**26**	
	27	28	29	30	31	1	2	November
	3	4	5	6	7	8	*9*	
	10	11	12	13	14	15	16	
	17	18	19	20	21	22	23	
(9) Kislev	**24**	25	26	27	28	29	30	
	1	2	3	4	5	6	7	December
	8	9	10	11	12	13	14	
	15	16	17	18	19	20	21	
(10) Tebet	22	23	**24**	25	26	27	28	
	29	30	31					

Julian year 31 BC

			1	2	3	4	5	January
	6	7	8	9	10	*11*	12	
	13	14	15	16	17	18	19	
(11) Shebet	20	21	22	23	24	25	**26**	
	27	28	29	30	31	1	2	February
	3	4	5	6	7	8	*9*	
	10	11	12	13	14	15	16	
	17	18	19	20	21	22	23	
(12) Adar	24	**25**	26	27	28	1	2	March
	3	4	5	6	7	8	9	
	10	*11*	12	13	14	15	16	
	17	18	19	20	21	22	23	
(1) Nisan	24	25	**26**	27	28	29	30	
	31	1	2	3	4	5	6	April
	7	8	*9*	10	11	12	13	
	14	15	16	17	18	19	20	
(2) Iyar	21	22	23	24	**25**	26	27	
	28	29	30	1	2	3	4	May
	5	6	7	8	*9*	10	11	
	12	13	14	15	16	17	18	
(3) Sivan	19	20	21	22	23	**24**	25	
	26	27	28	29	30	31	1	June
	2	3	4	5	6	*7*	8	
	9	10	11	12	13	14	15	
	16	17	18	19	20	21	22	
(4) Tammuz	**23**	24	25	26	27	28	29	
	30	1	2	3	4	5	6	July
	7	8	9	10	11	12	13	
	14	15	16	17	18	19	20	
(5) Av	21	**22**	23	24	25	26	27	
	28	29	30	31	1	2	3	August
	4	*5*	6	7	8	9	10	
	11	12	13	14	15	16	17	

(6) Elul	18	19	20	**21**	22	23	24	
	25	26	27	28	29	30	31	
	1	2	3	*4*	5	6	7	September
	8	9	10	11	12	13	14	
(7) Tishri	15	16	17	18	**19**	20	21	
	22	23	24	25	26	27	28	
	29	30	1	2	*3*	4	5	October
	6	7	8	9	10	11	12	
(8) Heshvan	13	14	15	16	17	18	**19**	
	20	21	22	23	24	25	26	
	27	28	29	30	31	1	*2*	November
	3	4	5	6	7	8	9	
	10	11	12	13	14	15	16	
(9) Kislev	17	**18**	19	20	21	22	23	
	24	25	26	27	28	29	30	
	1	*2*	3	4	5	6	7	December
	8	9	10	11	12	13	14	
(10) Tebet	15	16	**17**	18	19	20	21	
	22	23	24	25	26	27	28	
	29	30	*31*					

Julian year 6 BC

						1	2	January
	3	4	*5*	6	7	8	9	
	10	11	12	13	14	15	16	
(11) Shebet	17	18	19	**20**	21	22	23	
	24	25	26	27	28	29	30	
	31	1	2	*3*	4	5	6	February
	7	8	9	10	11	12	13	
(12) Adar	14	15	16	17	18	**19**	20	
	21	22	23	24	25	26	27	
	28	1	2	3	4	*5*	6	March
	7	8	9	10	11	12	13	
(1) Nisan	14	15	16	17	18	19	**20**	
	21	22	23	24	25	26	27	
	28	29	30	31	1	2	*3*	April
	4	5	6	7	8	9	10	
	11	12	13	14	15	16	17	
(2) Iyar	18	**19**	20	21	22	23	24	
	25	26	27	28	29	30	1	May
	2	*3*	4	5	6	7	8	
	9	10	11	12	13	14	15	
(3) Sivan	16	17	**18**	19	20	21	22	
	23	24	25	26	27	28	29	
	30	31	*1*	2	3	4	5	June
	6	7	8	9	10	11	12	
(4) Tammuz	13	14	15	16	**17**	18	19	
	20	21	22	23	24	25	26	
	27	28	29	30	*1*	2	3	July
	4	5	6	7	8	9	10	
(5) Av	11	12	13	14	15	**16**	17	
	18	19	20	21	22	23	24	
	25	26	27	28	29	**30**	31	
	1	2	3	4	5	6	7	August
	8	9	10	11	12	13	14	

(6) Elul	**15**	16	17	18	19	20	21	
	22	23	24	25	26	27	28	
	29	30	31	1	2	3	4	September
	5	6	7	8	9	10	11	
(7) Tishri	12	**13**	14	15	16	17	18	
	19	20	21	22	23	24	25	
	26	*27*	28	29	30	1	2	October
	3	4	5	6	7	8	9	
(8) Heshvan	10	11	12	**13**	14	15	16	
	17	18	19	20	21	22	23	
	24	25	26	*27*	28	29	30	
	31	1	2	3	4	5	6	November
(9) Kislev	7	8	9	10	**11**	12	13	
	14	15	16	17	18	19	20	
	21	22	23	24	*25*	26	27	
	28	29	30	1	2	3	4	December
(10) Tebet	5	6	7	8	9	10	**11**	
	12	13	14	15	16	17	18	
	19	20	21	22	23	24	*25*	
	26	27	28	29	30	31		

Julian year 5 BC

							1	January
	2	3	4	5	6	7	8	
(11) Shebet	9	**10**	11	12	13	14	15	
	16	17	18	19	20	21	22	
	23	*24*	25	26	27	28	29	
	30	31	1	2	3	4	5	February
(12) Adar	6	7	8	**9**	10	11	12	
	13	14	15	16	17	18	19	
	20	21	22	*23*	24	25	26	
	27	28	29	1	2	3	4	March
(1) Nisan	5	6	7	8	**9**	10	11	
	12	13	14	15	16	17	18	
	19	20	21	22	*23*	24	25	
	26	27	28	29	30	31	1	April
(2) Iyar	2	3	4	5	6	7	**8**	
	9	10	11	12	13	14	15	
	16	17	18	19	20	21	*22*	
	23	24	25	26	27	28	29	
	30	1	2	3	4	5	6	May
(3) Sivan	**7**	8	9	10	11	12	13	
	14	15	16	17	18	19	20	
	21	22	23	24	25	26	27	
	28	29	30	31	1	2	3	June
(4) Tammuz	4	5	**6**	7	8	9	10	
	11	12	13	14	15	16	17	
	18	19	*20*	21	22	23	24	
	25	26	27	28	29	30	1	July
(5) Av	2	3	4	**5**	6	7	8	
	9	10	11	12	13	14	15	
	16	17	18	*19*	20	21	22	
	23	24	25	26	27	28	29	
(6) Elul	30	31	1	2	3	**4**	5	August
	6	7	8	9	10	11	12	
	13	14	15	16	17	*18*	19	
	20	21	22	23	24	25	26	

(7) Tishri	27	28	29	30	31	1	2	September
	3	4	5	6	7	8	9	
	10	11	12	13	14	15	*16*	
	17	18	19	20	21	22	23	
	24	25	26	27	28	29	30	
(8) Heshvan	1	*2*	3	4	5	6	7	October
	8	9	10	11	12	13	14	
	15	*16*	17	18	19	20	21	
	22	23	24	25	26	27	28	
(9) Kislev	29	30	**31**	1	2	3	4	November
	5	6	7	8	9	10	11	
	12	13	*14*	15	16	17	18	
	19	20	21	22	23	24	25	
(10) Tebet	26	27	28	29	**30**	1	2	December
	3	4	5	6	7	8	9	
	10	11	12	13	*14*	15	16	
	17	18	19	20	21	22	23	
(11) Shebet	24	25	26	27	28	**29**	30	

Julian year 4 BC

		1	2	3	4	5	6	January
	7	8	9	10	11	*12*	13	
		14	15	16	17	18	19	20	
		21	22	23	24	25	26	27	
(12a) Adar I	28	*29*	30	31	1	2	3	February
		4	5	6	7	8	9	10	
		11	*12*	13	14	15	16	17	
		18	19	20	21	22	23	24	
(12b) Adar II	25	26	27	*28*	1	2	3	March
		4	5	6	7	8	9	10	
		11	12	13	*14*	15	16	17	
		18	19	20	21	22	23	24	
(1) Nisan	25	26	27	28	*29*	30	31	
		1	2	3	4	5	6	7	April
		8	9	10	11	*12*	13	14	
		15	16	17	18	19	20	21	
(2) Iyar	22	23	24	25	26	27	*28*	
		29	30	1	2	3	4	5	May
		6	7	8	9	10	11	*12*	
		13	14	15	16	17	18	19	
		20	21	22	23	24	25	26	
(3) Sivan	*27*	28	29	30	31	1	2	June
		3	4	5	6	7	8	9	
		10	11	12	13	14	15	16	
		17	18	19	20	21	22	23	
(4) Tammuz	24	25	*26*	27	28	29	30	
		1	2	3	4	5	6	7	July
		8	9	*10*	11	12	13	14	
		15	16	17	18	19	20	21	
(5) Av	22	23	24	*25*	26	27	28	
		29	30	31	1	2	3	4	August
		5	6	7	*8*	9	10	11	
		12	13	14	15	16	17	18	

(6) Elul	19	20	21	22	23	**24**	25	
	26	27	28	29	30	31	1	September
	2	3	4	5	6	7	8	
	9	10	11	12	13	14	15	
(7) Tishri	16	17	18	19	20	21	**22**	
	23	24	25	26	27	28	29	
	30	1	2	3	4	5	*6*	October
	7	8	9	10	11	12	13	
	14	15	16	17	18	19	20	
(8) Heshvan	21	**22**	23	24	25	26	27	
	28	29	30	31	1	2	3	November
	4	*5*	6	7	8	9	10	
	11	12	13	14	15	16	17	
(9) Kislev	18	19	**20**	21	22	23	24	
	25	26	27	28	29	30	1	December
	2	3	*4*	5	6	7	8	
	9	10	11	12	13	14	15	
(10) Tebet	16	17	18	19	**20**	21	22	
	23	24	25	26	27	28	29	
	30	31						

Julian year 26 AD

			1	2	3	4	5	January
(11) Shebet	6	7	8	9	10	11	12	
	13	14	15	16	17	18	19	
	20	*21*	22	23	24	25	26	
	27	28	29	30	31	1	2	February
(12a) Adar I	3	4	5	*6*	7	8	9	
	10	11	12	13	14	15	16	
	17	18	19	*20*	21	22	23	
	24	25	26	27	28	1	2	March
(12b) Adar II	3	4	5	6	7	*8*	9	
	10	11	12	13	14	15	16	
	17	18	19	20	21	*22*	23	
	24	25	26	27	28	29	30	
(1) Nisan	31	1	2	3	4	5	*6*	April
	7	8	9	10	11	12	13	
	14	15	16	17	18	19	*20*	
	21	22	23	24	25	26	27	
	28	29	30	1	2	3	4	May
(2) Iyar	5	*6*	7	8	9	10	11	
	12	13	14	15	16	17	18	
	19	*20*	21	22	23	24	25	
	26	27	28	29	30	31	1	
(3) Sivan	2	3	*4*	5	6	7	8	June
	9	10	11	12	13	14	15	
	16	17	*18*	19	20	21	22	
	23	24	25	26	27	28	29	
(4) Tammuz	30	1	2	3	*4*	5	6	July
	7	8	9	10	11	12	13	
	14	15	16	17	*18*	19	20	
	21	22	23	24	25	26	27	
(5) Av	28	29	30	31	1	*2*	3	August
	4	5	6	7	8	9	10	
	11	12	13	14	15	*16*	17	
	18	19	20	21	22	23	24	
	25	26	27	28	29	30	31	

(6) Elul	**1**	2	3	4	5	6	7	September
	8	9	10	11	12	13	14	
	15	16	17	18	19	20	21	
	22	23	24	25	26	27	28	
(7) Tishri	29	**30**	1	2	3	4	5	October
	6	7	8	9	10	11	12	
	13	*14*	15	16	17	18	19	
	20	21	22	23	24	25	26	
(8) Heshvan	27	28	29	**30**	31	1	2	November
	3	4	5	6	7	8	9	
	10	11	12	*13*	14	15	16	
	17	18	19	20	21	22	23	
(9) Kislev	24	25	26	27	28	**29**	30	
	1	2	3	4	5	6	7	December
	8	9	10	11	12	*13*	14	
	15	16	17	18	19	20	21	
	22	23	24	25	26	27	28	
(10) Tebet	**29**	30	31					

Julian year 27 AD

				1	2	3	4	January
	5	6	7	8	9	10	11	
	12	13	14	15	16	17	18	
	19	20	21	22	23	24	25	
(11) Shebet	26	*27*	28	29	30	31	1	February
	2	3	4	5	6	7	8	
	9	*10*	11	12	13	14	15	
	16	17	18	19	20	21	22	
(12) Adar	23	24	25	*26*	27	28	1	March
	2	3	4	5	6	7	8	
	9	10	11	*12*	13	14	15	
	16	17	18	19	20	21	22	
(1) Nisan	23	24	25	26	*27*	28	29	
	30	31	1	2	3	4	5	April
	6	7	8	9	*10*	11	12	
	13	14	15	16	17	18	19	
(2) Iyar	20	21	22	23	24	25	*26*	
	27	28	29	30	1	2	3	May
	4	5	6	7	8	9	*10*	
	11	12	13	14	15	16	17	
	18	19	20	21	22	23	24	
(3) Sivan	*25*	26	27	28	29	30	31	
	1	2	3	4	5	6	7	June
	8	9	10	11	12	13	14	
	15	16	17	18	19	20	21	
(4) Tammuz	22	23	*24*	25	26	27	28	
	29	30	1	2	3	4	5	July
	6	7	*8*	9	10	11	12	
	13	14	15	16	17	18	19	
(5) Av	20	21	22	*23*	24	25	26	
	27	28	29	30	31	1	2	August
	3	4	5	*6*	7	8	9	
	10	11	12	13	14	15	16	

(6) Elul	17	18	19	20	21	**22**	23	
	24	25	26	27	28	29	30	
	31	1	2	3	4	5	6	September
	7	8	9	10	11	12	13	
(7) Tishri	14	15	16	17	18	19	**20**	
	21	22	23	24	25	26	27	
	28	29	30	1	2	3	*4*	October
	5	6	7	8	9	10	11	
	12	13	14	15	16	17	18	
(8) Heshvan	19	**20**	21	22	23	24	25	
	26	27	28	29	30	31	1	November
	2	*3*	4	5	6	7	8	
	9	10	11	12	13	14	15	
(9) Kislev	16	17	**18**	19	20	21	22	
	23	24	25	26	27	28	29	
	30	1	*2*	3	4	5	6	December
	7	8	9	10	11	12	13	
(10) Tebet	14	15	16	**17**	18	19	20	
	21	22	23	24	25	26	27	
	28	29	30	*31*				

Julian year 28 AD

					1	2	3	January
	4	5	6	7	8	9	10	
(11) Shebet	11	12	13	14	**15**	16	17	
	18	19	20	21	22	23	24	
	25	26	27	28	*29*	30	31	
	1	2	3	4	5	6	7	February
(12) Adar	8	9	10	11	12	13	**14**	
	15	16	17	18	19	20	21	
	22	23	24	25	26	27	*28*	
	29	1	2	3	4	5	6	March
	7	8	9	10	11	12	13	
(1) Nisan	**14**	15	16	17	18	19	20	
	21	22	23	24	25	26	27	
	28	29	30	31	1	2	3	April
	4	5	6	7	8	9	10	
(2) Iyar	11	12	**13**	14	15	16	17	
	18	19	20	21	22	23	24	
	25	26	*27*	28	29	30	1	May
	2	3	4	5	6	7	8	
(3) Sivan	9	10	11	**12**	13	14	15	
	16	17	18	19	20	21	22	
	23	24	25	*26*	27	28	29	
	30	31	1	2	3	4	5	June
(4) Tammuz	6	7	8	9	10	**11**	12	
	13	14	15	16	17	18	19	
	20	21	22	23	24	*25*	26	
	27	28	29	30	1	2	3	July
(5) Av	4	5	6	7	8	9	**10**	
	11	12	13	14	15	16	17	
	18	19	20	21	22	23	*24*	
	25	26	27	28	29	30	31	
	1	2	3	4	5	6	7	August
(6) Elul	8	**9**	10	11	12	13	14	
	15	16	17	18	19	20	21	
	22	*23*	24	25	26	27	28	
	29	30	31	1	2	3	4	September

(7) Tishri	5	6	**7**	8	9	10	11	
	12	13	14	15	16	17	18	
	19	20	**21**	22	23	24	25	
	26	27	28	29	30	1	2	October
(8) Heshvan	3	4	5	6	**7**	8	9	
	10	11	12	13	14	15	16	
	17	18	19	20	**21**	22	23	
	24	25	26	27	28	29	30	
(9) Kislev	31	1	2	3	4	5	**6**	November
	7	8	9	10	11	12	13	
	14	15	16	17	18	19	**20**	
	21	22	23	24	25	26	27	
	28	29	30	1	2	3	4	December
(10) Tebet	5	**6**	7	8	9	10	11	
	12	13	14	15	16	17	18	
	19	**20**	21	22	23	24	25	
	26	27	28	29	30	31		

Julian year 29 AD

								1	January
(11) Shebet	2	3	4	5	6	7	8		
	9	10	11	12	13	14	15		
	16	17	*18*	19	20	21	22		
	23	24	25	26	27	28	29		
(12a) Adar I	30	31	1	2	3	4	5	February
	6	7	8	9	10	11	12		
	13	14	15	16	*17*	18	19		
	20	21	22	23	24	25	26		
(12b) Adar II	27	28	1	2	3	4	5	March
	6	7	8	9	10	11	12		
	13	14	15	16	17	18	*19*		
	20	21	22	I 23	24	25	26		
	27	28	29	30	31	1	2	April
(1) Nisan	3	4	5	6	7	8	9		
	10	11	12	13	14	15	16		
	17	18	19	20	21	22	23		
	24	25	26	27	28	29	30		
(2) Iyar	1	2	3	4	5	6	7	May
	8	9	10	11	12	13	14		
	15	16	*17*	18	19	20	21		
	22	23	24	25	26	27	28		
(3) Sivan	29	30	31	1	2	3	4	June
	5	6	7	8	9	10	11		
	12	13	14	*15*	16	17	18		
	19	20	21	22	23	24	25		
(4) Tammuz	26	27	28	29	30	1	2	July
	3	4	5	6	7	8	9		
	10	11	12	13	14	*15*	16		
	17	18	19	20	21	22	23		
(5) Av	24	25	26	27	28	29	30		
	31	1	2	3	4	5	6	August
	7	8	9	10	11	12	*13*		
	14	15	16	17	18	19	20		
	21	22	23	24	25	26	27		

(6) Elul	28	**29**	30	31	1	2	3	September
	4	5	6	7	8	9	10	
	11	**12**	13	14	15	16	17	
	18	19	20	21	22	23	24	
(7) Tishri	25	26	**27**	28	29	30	1	October
	2	3	4	5	6	7	8	
	9	10	**11**	12	13	14	15	
	16	17	18	19	20	21	22	
(8) Heshvan	23	24	25	26	**27**	28	29	
	30	31	1	2	3	4	5	November
	6	7	8	9	**10**	11	12	
	13	14	15	16	17	18	19	
(9) Kislev	20	21	22	23	24	**25**	26	
	27	28	29	30	1	2	3	December
	4	5	6	7	8	**9**	10	
	11	12	13	14	15	16	17	
	18	19	20	21	22	23	24	
(10) Tebet	**25**	26	27	28	29	30	31	

I marks the beginning of the 1st month in Enoch's solar calendar.

Julian year 30 AD

		1	2	3	4	5	6	7	January
		8	9	10	11	12	13	14	
		15	16	17	18	19	20	21	
(11) Shebet		22	**23**	24	25	26	27	28	
		29	30	31	1	2	3	4	February
		5	*6*	7	8	9	10	11	
		12	13	14	15	16	17	18	
(12) Adar		19	20	21	**22**	23	24	25	
		26	27	28	1	2	3	4	March
		5	6	7	*8*	9	10	11	
		12	13	14	15	16	17	18	
(1) Nisan		19	20	21	I 22	**23**	24	25	
		26	27	28	29	30	31	1	April
		2	3	4	5	*6*	7	8	
		9	10	11	12	13	14	15	
(2) Iyar		16	17	18	19	20	21	**22**	
		23	24	25	26	27	28	29	
		30	1	2	3	4	5	*6*	May
		7	8	9	10	11	12	13	
		14	15	16	17	18	19	20	
(3) Sivan		**21**	22	23	24	25	26	27	
		28	29	30	31	1	2	3	June
		4	5	6	7	8	9	10	
		11	12	13	14	15	16	17	
(4) Tammuz		18	19	**20**	21	22	23	24	
		25	26	27	28	29	30	1	July
		2	3	*4*	5	6	7	8	
		9	10	11	12	13	14	15	
(5) Av		16	17	18	**19**	20	21	22	
		23	24	25	26	27	28	29	
		30	31	1	*2*	3	4	5	August
		6	7	8	9	10	11	12	
(6) Elul		13	14	15	16	17	**18**	19	
		20	21	22	23	24	25	26	
		27	28	29	30	31	*1*	2	September
		3	4	5	6	7	8	9	

(7) Tishri	10	11	12	13	14	15	**16**	
	17	18	19	20	21	22	23	
	24	25	26	27	28	29	*30*	
	1	2	3	4	5	6	7	October
	8	9	10	11	12	13	14	
(8) Heshvan	15	**16**	17	18	19	20	21	
	22	23	24	25	26	27	28	
	29	*30*	31	1	2	3	4	November
	5	6	7	8	9	10	11	
(9) Kislev	12	13	14	**15**	16	17	18	
	19	20	21	22	23	24	25	
	26	27	28	*29*	30	1	2	December
	3	4	5	6	7	8	9	
(10) Tebet	10	11	12	13	14	**15**	16	
	17	18	19	20	21	22	23	
	24	25	26	27	28	*29*	30	
	31							

I marks the beginning of the 1ˢᵗ month in Enoch's solar calendar.

Julian year 31 AD

		1	2	3	4	5	6	January
(11) Shebet	7	8	9	10	11	12	**13**	
	14	15	16	17	18	19	20	
	21	22	23	24	25	26	**27**	
	28	29	30	31	1	2	3	February
	4	5	6	7	8	9	10	
(12) Adar	11	**12**	13	14	15	16	17	
	18	19	20	21	22	23	24	
	25	**26**	27	28	1	2	3	March
	4	5	6	7	8	9	10	
(1) Nisan	11	12	**13**	14	15	16	17	
	18	19	20	I 21	22	23	24	
	25	26	**27**	28	29	30	31	
	1	2	3	4	5	6	7	April
(2) Iyar	8	9	10	11	**12**	13	14	
	15	16	17	18	19	20	21	
	22	23	24	25	**26**	27	28	
	29	30	1	2	3	4	5	May
(3) Sivan	6	7	8	9	10	**11**	12	
	13	14	15	16	17	18	19	
	20	21	22	23	24	**25**	26	
	27	28	29	30	31	1	2	June
	3	4	5	6	7	8	9	
(4) Tammuz	**10**	11	12	13	14	15	16	
	17	18	19	20	21	22	23	
	24	25	26	27	28	29	30	
	1	2	3	4	5	6	7	July
(5) Av	8	**9**	10	11	12	13	14	
	15	16	17	18	19	20	21	
	22	**23**	24	25	26	27	28	
	29	30	31	1	2	3	4	August
(6) Elul	5	6	7	**8**	9	10	11	
	12	13	14	15	16	17	18	
	19	20	21	**22**	23	24	25	
	26	27	28	29	30	31	1	September

(7) Tishri	2	3	4	5	**6**	7	8	
	9	10	11	12	13	14	15	
	16	17	18	19	*20*	21	22	
	23	24	25	26	27	28	29	
(8) Heshvan	30	1	2	3	4	5	**6**	October
	7	8	9	10	11	12	13	
	14	15	16	17	18	19	*20*	
	21	22	23	24	25	26	27	
	28	29	30	31	1	2	3	November
(9) Kislev	**4**	5	6	7	8	9	10	
	11	12	13	14	15	16	17	
	18	19	20	21	22	23	24	
	25	26	27	28	29	30	1	December
(10) Tebet	2	**3**	4	5	6	7	8	
	9	10	11	12	13	14	15	
	16	*17*	18	19	20	21	22	
	23	24	25	26	27	28	29	
	30	31						

I marks the beginning of the 1st month in Enoch's solar calendar.

Julian year 32 AD

(11) Shebet			1	2	3	4	5	January
	6	7	8	9	10	11	12	
	13	14	*15*	16	17	18	19	
	20	21	22	23	24	25	26	
(12a) Adar I	27	28	29	30	31	1	2	February
	3	4	5	6	7	8	9	
	10	11	12	13	*14*	15	16	
	17	18	19	20	21	22	23	
(12b) Adar II	24	25	26	27	28	29	1	March
	2	3	4	5	6	7	8	
	9	10	11	12	13	14	*15*	
	16	17	18	I 19	20	21	22	
	23	24	25	26	27	28	29	
(1) Nisan	**30**	31	1	2	3	4	5	April
	6	7	8	9	10	11	12	
	13	14	15	16	17	18	19	
	20	21	22	23	24	25	26	
(2) Iyar	27	28	**29**	30	1	2	3	May
	4	5	6	7	8	9	10	
	11	12	*13*	14	15	16	17	
	18	19	20	21	22	23	24	
(3) Sivan	25	26	27	**28**	29	30	31	
	1	2	3	4	5	6	7	June
	8	9	10	*11*	12	13	14	
	15	16	17	18	19	20	21	
(4) Tammuz	22	23	24	25	26	**27**	28	
	29	30	1	2	3	4	5	July
	6	7	8	9	10	*11*	12	
	13	14	15	16	17	18	19	
(5) Av	20	21	22	23	24	25	**26**	
	27	28	29	30	31	1	2	August
	3	4	5	6	7	8	*9*	
	10	11	12	13	14	15	16	
	17	18	19	20	21	22	23	

(6) Elul	24	**25**	26	27	28	29	30	
	31	1	2	3	4	5	6	September
	7	*8*	9	10	11	12	13	
	14	15	16	17	18	19	20	
(7) Tishri	21	22	**23**	24	25	26	27	
	28	29	30	1	2	3	4	October
	5	6	*7*	8	9	10	11	
	12	13	14	15	16	17	18	
(8) Heshvan	19	20	21	22	**23**	24	25	
	26	27	28	29	30	31	1	November
	2	3	4	5	*6*	7	8	
	9	10	11	12	13	14	15	
(9) Kislev	16	17	18	19	20	21	**22**	
	23	24	25	26	27	28	29	
	30	1	2	3	4	5	*6*	December
	7	8	9	10	11	12	13	
	14	15	16	17	18	19	20	
(10) Tebet	**21**	22	23	24	25	26	27	
	28	29	30	31				

1 marks the beginning of the 1ˢᵗ month in Enoch's solar calendar.

Julian year 33 AD

						1	2	3	January
	4	5	6	7	8	9	10		
	11	12	13	14	15	16	17		
(11) Shebet	18	**19**	20	21	22	23	24		
	25	26	27	28	29	30	31		
	1	*2*	3	4	5	6	7	February	
	8	9	10	11	12	13	14		
(12) Adar	15	16	17	**18**	19	20	21		
	22	23	24	25	26	27	28		
	1	2	3	*4*	5	6	7	March	
	8	9	10	11	12	13	14		
(1) Nisan	15	16	17	18	**19**	20	21		
	22	23	24	I 25	26	27	28		
	29	30	31	1	*2*	3	4	April	
	5	6	7	8	9	10	11		
(2) Iyar	12	13	14	15	16	17	**18**		
	19	20	21	22	23	24	25		
	26	27	28	29	30	1	*2*	May	
	3	4	5	6	7	8	9		
	10	11	12	13	14	15	16		
(3) Sivan	**17**	18	19	20	21	22	23		
	24	25	26	27	28	29	30		
	31	1	2	3	4	5	6	June	
	7	8	9	10	11	12	13		
(4) Tammuz	14	15	**16**	17	18	19	20		
	21	22	23	24	25	26	27		
	28	29	*30*	1	2	3	4	July	
	5	6	7	8	9	10	11		
(5) Av	12	13	14	**15**	16	17	18		
	19	20	21	22	23	24	25		
	26	27	28	*29*	30	31	1	August	
	2	3	4	5	6	7	8		
(6) Elul	9	10	11	12	13	**14**	15		
	16	17	18	19	20	21	22		
	23	24	25	26	27	*28*	29		
	30	31	1	2	3	4	5	September	

(7) Tishri	6	7	8	9	10	11	**12**	
	13	14	15	16	17	18	19	
	20	21	22	23	24	25	**26**	
	27	28	29	30	1	2	3	October
	4	5	6	7	8	9	10	
(8) Heshvan	11	**12**	13	14	15	16	17	
	18	19	20	21	22	23	24	
	25	**26**	27	28	29	30	31	
	1	2	3	4	5	6	7	November
(9) Kislev	8	9	10	**11**	12	13	14	
	15	16	17	18	19	20	21	
	22	23	24	**25**	26	27	28	
	29	30	1	2	3	4	5	December
(10) Tebet	6	7	8	9	**10**	11	12	
	13	14	15	16	17	18	19	
	20	21	22	23	**24**	25	26	
	27	28	29	30	31			

I marks the beginning of the 1st month in Enoch's solar calendar.

Julian year 67 AD

					1	2	3	January
(10) Tebet	4	5	**6**	7	8	9	10	
	11	12	13	14	15	16	17	
	18	19	***20***	21	22	23	24	
	25	26	27	28	29	30	31	
(11) Shebet	1	2	3	**4**	5	6	7	February
	8	9	10	11	12	13	14	
	15	16	17	***18***	19	20	21	
	22	23	24	25	26	27	28	
(12) Adar	1	2	3	4	5	**6**	7	March
	8	9	10	11	12	13	14	
	15	16	17	18	19	***20***	21	
	22	23	24	25	26	27	28	
(1) Nisan	29	30	31	1	2	3	**4**	April
	5	6	7	8	9	10	11	
	12	13	14	15	16	17	***18***	
	19	20	21	22	23	24	25	
	26	27	28	29	30	1	2	May
(2) Iyar	3	**4**	5	6	7	8	9	
	10	11	12	13	14	15	16	
	17	***18***	19	20	21	22	23	
	24	25	26	27	28	29	30	
(3) Sivan	31	1	**2**	3	4	5	6	June
	7	8	9	10	11	12	13	
	14	15	***16***	17	18	19	20	
	21	22	23	24	25	26	27	
(4) Tammuz	28	29	30	1	**2**	3	4	July
	5	6	7	8	9	10	11	
	12	13	14	15	***16***	17	18	
	19	20	21	22	23	24	25	
(5) Av	26	27	28	29	30	**31**	1	August
	2	3	4	5	6	7	8	
	9	10	11	12	13	***14***	15	
	16	17	18	19	20	21	22	
	23	24	25	26	27	28	29	

(6) Elul	**30**	31	1	2	3	4	5	September
	6	7	8	9	10	11	12	
	13	14	15	16	17	18	19	
	20	21	22	23	24	25	26	
(7) Tishri	27	**28**	29	30	1	2	3	October
	4	5	6	7	8	9	10	
	11	*12*	13	14	15	16	17	
	18	19	20	21	22	23	24	
(8) Heshvan	25	26	27	**28**	29	30	31	
	1	2	3	4	5	6	7	November
	8	9	10	*11*	12	13	14	
	15	16	17	18	19	20	21	
(9) Kislev	22	23	24	25	**26**	27	28	
	29	30	1	2	3	4	5	December
	6	7	8	9	*10*	11	12	
	13	14	15	16	17	18	19	
(10) Tebet	20	21	22	23	24	**25**	26	
	27	28	29	30	31			

Julian year 70 AD

(10) Tebet		1	**2**	3	4	5	6	January
	7	8	9	10	11	12	13	
	14	15	*16*	17	18	19	20	
	21	22	23	24	25	26	27	
(11) Shebet	28	29	30	**31**	1	2	3	February
	4	5	6	7	8	9	10	
	11	12	13	*14*	15	16	17	
	18	19	20	21	22	23	24	
(12) Adar	25	26	27	28	1	**2**	3	March
	4	5	6	7	8	9	10	
	11	12	13	14	15	*16*	17	
	18	19	20	21	22	23	24	
(1) Nisan	25	26	27	28	29	30	**31**	
	1	2	3	4	5	6	7	April
	8	9	10	11	12	13	*14*	
	15	16	17	18	19	20	21	
	22	23	24	25	26	27	28	
(2) Iyar	29	**30**	1	2	3	4	5	May
	6	7	8	9	10	11	12	
	13	*14*	15	16	17	18	19	
	20	21	22	23	24	25	26	
(3) Sivan	27	28	**29**	30	31	1	2	June
	3	4	5	6	7	8	9	
	10	11	*12*	13	14	15	16	
	17	18	19	20	21	22	23	
(4) Tammuz	24	25	26	27	**28**	29	30	
	1	2	3	4	5	6	7	July
	8	9	10	11	*12*	13	14	
	15	16	17	18	19	20	21	
(5) Av	22	23	24	25	26	**27**	28	
	29	30	31	1	2	3	4	August
	5	6	7	8	9	*10*	11	
	12	13	14	15	16	17	18	
	19	20	21	22	23	24	25	

(6) Elul	**26**	27	28	29	30	31	1	September
	2	3	4	5	6	7	8	
	9	10	11	12	13	14	15	
	16	17	18	19	20	21	22	
(7)Tishri	23	**24**	25	26	27	28	29	
	30	1	2	3	4	5	6	October
	7	*8*	9	10	11	12	13	
	14	15	16	17	18	19	20	
(8) Heshvan	21	22	23	**24**	25	26	27	
	28	29	30	31	1	2	3	November
	4	5	6	*7*	8	9	10	
	11	12	13	14	15	16	17	
(9) Kislev	18	19	20	21	**22**	23	24	
	25	26	27	28	29	30	1	December
	2	3	4	5	*6*	7	8	
	9	10	11	12	13	14	15	
(10) Tebet	16	17	18	19	20	21	**22**	
	23	24	25	26	27	28	29	
	30	31						

Julian year 269 AD

							1	2	January
		3	4	*5*	6	7	8	9	
		10	11	12	13	14	15	16	
(11) Shebet		17	18	19	**20**	21	22	23	
		24	25	26	27	28	29	30	
		31	1	2	*3*	4	5	6	February
		7	8	9	10	11	12	13	
(12) Adar		14	15	16	17	**18**	19	20	
		21	22	23	24	25	26	27	
		28	1	2	3	*4*	5	6	March
		7	8	9	10	11	12	13	
(1) Nisan		14	15	16	17	18	19	**20**	
		21	22	23	24	25	26	27	
		28	29	30	31	1	2	*3*	April
		4	5	6	7	8	9	10	
		11	12	13	14	15	16	17	
(2) Iyar		18	**19**	20	21	22	23	24	
		25	26	27	28	29	30	1	May
		2	*3*	4	5	6	7	8	
		9	10	11	12	13	14	15	
(3) Sivan		16	17	**18**	19	20	21	22	
		23	24	25	26	27	28	29	
		30	31	*1*	2	3	4	5	June
		6	7	8	9	10	11	12	
(4) Tammuz		13	14	15	16	**17**	18	19	
		20	21	22	23	24	25	26	
		27	28	29	30	*1*	2	3	July
		4	5	6	7	8	9	10	
(5) Av		11	12	13	14	15	**16**	17	
		18	19	20	21	22	23	24	
		25	26	27	28	29	***30***	31	
		1	2	3	4	5	6	7	August
		8	9	10	11	12	13	14	

(6) Elul	**15**	16	17	18	19	20	21	
	22	23	24	25	26	27	28	
	29	30	31	1	2	3	4	September
	5	6	7	8	9	10	11	
(7) Tishri	12	**13**	14	15	16	17	18	
	19	20	21	22	23	24	25	
	26	*27*	28	29	30	1	2	October
	3	4	5	6	7	8	9	
(8) Heshvan	10	11	12	**13**	14	15	16	
	17	18	19	20	21	22	23	
	24	25	26	*27*	28	29	30	
	31	1	2	3	4	5	6	November
(9) Kislev	7	8	9	10	**11**	12	13	
	14	15	16	17	18	19	20	
	21	22	23	24	*25*	26	27	
	28	29	30	1	2	3	4	December
(10) Tebet	5	6	7	8	9	10	**11**	
	12	13	14	15	16	17	18	
	19	20	21	22	23	24	*25*	
	26	27	28	29	30	31		

Julian year 277 AD

		1	2	3	4	5	6	January
	7	8	9	10	11	12	13	
		14	15	16	17	18	19	20	
(11) Shebet	21	22	23	24	25	26	27	
	28	29	30	31	1	2	3	February
	4	5	6	7	8	9	10	
	11	12	13	14	15	16	17	
(12) Adar	18	19	20	21	22	23	24	
	25	26	27	28	1	2	3	March
	4	5	6	7	8	9	10	
	11	12	13	14	15	16	17	
(1) Nisan	18	19	20	21	22	23	24	
	25	26	27	28	29	30	31	
	1	2	3	4	5	6	7	April
	8	9	10	11	12	13	14	
(2) Iyar	15	16	17	18	19	20	21	
	22	23	24	25	26	27	28	
	29	30	1	2	3	4	5	May
	6	7	8	9	10	11	12	
	13	14	15	16	17	18	19	
(3) Sivan	20	21	22	23	24	25	26	
	27	28	29	30	31	1	2	June
	3	4	5	6	7	8	9	
	10	11	12	13	14	15	16	
(4) Tammuz	17	18	19	20	21	22	23	
	24	25	26	27	28	29	30	
	1	2	3	4	5	6	7	July
	8	9	10	11	12	13	14	
(5) Av	15	16	17	18	19	20	21	
	22	23	24	25	26	27	28	
	29	30	31	1	2	3	4	August
	5	6	7	8	9	10	11	
(6) Elul	12	13	14	15	16	17	18	
	19	20	21	22	23	24	25	
	26	27	28	29	30	31	1	September
	2	3	4	5	6	7	8	

(7) Tishri	9	10	11	12	13	14	**15**	
	16	17	18	19	20	21	22	
	23	24	25	26	27	28	*29*	
	30	1	2	3	4	5	6	October
	7	8	9	10	11	12	13	
(8) Heshvan	14	**15**	16	17	18	19	20	
	21	22	23	24	25	26	27	
	28	*29*	30	31	1	2	3	November
	4	5	6	7	8	9	10	
(9) Kislev	11	12	**13**	14	15	16	17	
	18	19	20	21	22	23	24	
	25	26	*27*	28	29	30	1	December
	2	3	4	5	6	7	8	
(10) Tebet	9	10	11	**12**	13	14	15	
	16	17	18	19	20	21	22	
	23	24	25	**26**	27	28	29	
	30	31						

Julian year 688 AD

				1	2	3	4	January
(11) Shebet	5	6	7	8	*9*	10	11	
	12	13	14	15	16	17	18	
	19	20	21	22	*23*	24	25	
	26	27	28	29	30	31	1	February
(12) Adar	2	3	4	5	6	7	*8*	
	9	10	11	12	13	14	15	
	16	17	18	19	20	21	*22*	
	23	24	25	26	27	28	29	
	1	2	3	4	5	6	7	March
(1) Nisan	*8*	9	10	11	12	13	14	
	15	16	17	18	19	20	21	
	22	23	24	25	26	27	28	
	29	30	31	1	2	3	4	April
(2) Iyar	5	6	*7*	8	9	10	11	
	12	13	14	15	16	17	18	
	19	20	*21*	22	23	24	25	
	26	27	28	29	30	1	2	May
(3) Sivan	3	4	5	*6*	7	8	9	
	10	11	12	13	14	15	16	
	17	18	19	*20*	21	22	23	
	24	25	26	27	28	29	30	
(4) Tammuz	31	1	2	3	4	*5*	6	June
	7	8	9	10	11	12	13	
	14	15	16	17	18	*19*	20	
	21	22	23	24	25	26	27	
(5) Av	28	29	30	1	2	3	*4*	July
	5	6	7	8	9	10	11	
	12	13	14	15	16	17	*18*	
	19	20	21	22	23	24	25	
	26	27	28	29	30	31	1	August
(6) Elul	2	*3*	4	5	6	7	8	
	9	10	11	12	13	14	15	
	16	*17*	18	19	20	21	22	
	23	24	25	26	27	28	29	

(7) Tishri	30	31	**1**	2	3	4	5	September
	6	7	8	9	10	11	12	
	13	14	*15*	16	17	18	19	
	20	21	22	23	24	25	26	
(8) Heshvan	27	28	29	30	1	2	3	October
	4	5	6	7	8	9	10	
	11	12	13	14	*15*	16	17	
	18	19	20	21	22	23	24	
(9) Kislev	25	26	27	28	29	**30**	31	
	1	2	3	4	5	6	7	November
	8	9	10	11	12	*13*	14	
	15	16	17	18	19	20	21	
	22	23	24	25	26	27	28	
(10) Tebet	**29**	30	1	2	3	4	5	December
	6	7	8	9	10	11	12	
	13	14	15	16	17	18	19	
	20	21	22	23	24	25	26	
(11) Shebet	27	**28**	29	30	31			

The first day of the first month of 69 AH was on July 5.

Julian year 692 AD

		1	2	3	4	5	6	January
	7	8	9	*10*	11	12	13	
	14	15	16	17	18	19	20	
(11) Shebet	21	22	23	24	**25**	26	27	
	28	29	30	31	1	2	3	February
	4	5	6	7	*8*	9	10	
	11	12	13	14	15	16	17	
(12) Adar	18	19	20	21	22	23	**24**	
	25	26	27	28	29	1	2	March
	3	4	5	6	7	8	*9*	
	10	11	12	13	14	15	16	
	17	18	19	20	21	22	23	
(1) Nisan	**24**	25	26	27	28	29	30	
	31	1	2	3	4	5	6	April
	7	8	9	10	11	12	13	
	14	15	16	17	18	19	20	
(2) Iyar	21	22	**23**	24	25	26	27	
	28	29	30	1	2	3	4	May
	5	6	*7*	8	9	10	11	
	12	13	14	15	16	17	18	
(3) Sivan	19	20	21	**22**	23	24	25	
	26	27	28	29	30	31	1	June
	2	3	4	*5*	6	7	8	
	9	10	11	12	13	14	15	
(4) Tammuz	16	17	18	19	20	**21**	22	
	23	24	25	26	27	28	29	
	30	1	2	3	4	*5*	6	July
	7	8	9	10	11	12	13	
(5) Av	14	15	16	17	18	19	**20**	
	21	22	23	24	25	26	27	
	28	29	30	31	1	2	*3*	August
	4	5	6	7	8	9	10	
	11	12	13	14	15	16	17	
(6) Elul	18	**19**	20	21	22	23	24	
	25	26	27	28	29	30	31	
	1	*2*	3	4	5	6	7	September

	8	9	10	11	12	13	14	
(7) Tishri	15	16	**17**	18	19	20	21	
	22	23	24	25	26	27	28	
	29	30	***1***	2	3	4	5	October
	6	7	8	9	10	11	12	
(8) Heshvan	13	14	15	16	**17**	18	19	
	20	21	22	23	24	25	26	
	27	28	29	30	***31***	1	2	November
	3	4	5	6	7	8	9	
(9) Kislev	10	11	12	13	14	**15**	16	
	17	18	19	20	21	22	23	
	24	25	26	27	28	***29***	30	
	1	2	3	4	5	6	7	December
	8	9	10	11	12	13	14	
(10) Tebet	**15**	16	17	18	19	20	21	
	22	23	24	25	26	27	28	
	29	30	31					

April 24 is the first day of the last month (Dhual-Hijjah) of 72 AH. The 10th day of Dhual-Hijjah was on May 3.

Julian year 771 AD

			1	2	3	4	5	January
		6	7	8	9	10	11	12	
		13	14	15	16	17	18	19	
(11) Shebet		20	21	22	23	24	25	26	
		27	28	29	30	31	1	2	February
		3	4	5	6	7	8	9	
		10	11	12	13	14	15	16	
(12) Adar		17	18	19	20	21	22	23	
		24	25	26	27	28	1	2	March
		3	4	5	6	7	8	9	
		10	11	12	13	14	15	16	
(1) Nisan		17	18	19	20	21	22	23	
		24	25	26	27	28	29	30	
		31	1	2	3	4	5	6	April
		7	8	9	10	11	12	13	
(2) Iyar		14	15	16	17	18	19	20	
		21	22	23	24	25	26	27	
		28	29	30	1	2	3	4	May
		5	6	7	8	9	10	11	
		12	13	14	15	16	17	18	
(3) Sivan		19	20	21	22	23	24	25	
		26	27	28	29	30	31	1	June
		2	3	4	5	6	7	8	
		9	10	11	12	13	14	15	
(4) Tammuz		16	17	18	19	20	21	22	
		23	24	25	26	27	28	29	
		30	1	2	3	4	5	6	July
		7	8	9	10	11	12	13	
(5) Av		14	15	16	17	18	19	20	
		21	22	23	24	25	26	27	
		28	29	30	31	1	2	3	August
		4	5	6	7	8	9	10	
		11	12	13	14	15	16	17	
(6) Elul		18	19	20	21	22	23	24	
		25	26	27	28	29	30	31	
		1	2	3	4	5	6	7	September

(7) Tishri	8	9	10	11	12	13	**14**	
	15	16	17	18	19	20	21	
	22	23	24	25	26	27	**28**	
	29	30	1	2	3	4	5	October
	6	7	8	9	10	11	12	
(8) Heshvan	13	**14**	15	16	17	18	19	
	20	21	22	23	24	25	26	
	27	**28**	29	30	31	1	2	November
	3	4	5	6	7	8	9	
(9) Kislev	10	11	12	**13**	14	15	16	
	17	18	19	20	21	22	23	
	24	25	26	**27**	28	29	30	
	1	2	3	4	5	6	7	December
(10) Tebet	8	9	10	11	**12**	13	14	
	15	16	17	18	19	20	21	
	22	23	24	25	**26**	27	28	
	29	30	31					

Julian year 1948

					1	2	3	January
	4	5	6	7	8	9	10	
(11) Shebet	11	**12**	13	14	15	16	17	
	18	19	20	21	22	23	24	
	25	*26*	27	28	29	30	31	
	1	2	3	4	5	6	7	February
(12) Adar	8	9	10	**11**	12	13	14	
	15	16	17	18	19	20	21	
	22	23	24	*25*	26	27	28	
	29	1	2	3	4	5	6	March
(1) Nisan	7	8	9	10	**11**	12	13	
	14	15	16	17	18	19	20	
	21	22	23	24	*25*	26	27	
	28	29	30	31	1	2	3	April
(2) Iyar	4	5	6	7	8	9	**10**	
	11	12	13	14	15	16	17	
	18	19	20	21	22	23	*24*	
	25	26	27	28	29	30	1	May
	2	3	4	5	6	7	8	
(3) Sivan	**9**	10	11	12	13	14	15	
	16	17	18	19	20	21	22	
	23	24	25	26	27	28	29	
	30	31	1	2	3	4	5	June
(4) Tammuz	6	7	**8**	9	10	11	12	
	13	14	15	16	17	18	19	
	20	21	*22*	23	24	25	26	
	27	28	29	30	1	2	3	July
(5) Av	4	5	6	**7**	8	9	10	
	11	12	13	14	15	16	17	
	18	19	20	*21*	22	23	24	
	25	26	27	28	29	30	31	
(6) Elul	1	2	3	4	5	**6**	7	August
	8	9	10	11	12	13	14	
	15	16	17	18	19	*20*	21	
	22	23	24	25	26	27	28	

(7) Tishri	29	30	31	1	2	3	4	September
	5	6	7	8	9	10	11	
	12	13	14	15	16	17	*18*	
	19	20	21	22	23	24	25	
	26	27	28	29	30	1	2	October
(8) Heshvan	3	4	5	6	7	8	9	
	10	11	12	13	14	15	16	
	17	*18*	19	20	21	22	23	
	24	25	26	27	28	29	30	
(9) Kislev	31	1	*2*	3	4	5	6	November
	7	8	9	10	11	12	13	
	14	15	*16*	17	18	19	20	
	21	22	23	24	25	26	27	
(10) Tebet	28	29	30	1	2	3	4	December
	5	6	7	8	9	10	11	
	12	13	14	*15*	16	17	18	
	19	20	21	22	23	24	25	
(11) Shebet	26	27	28	29	**30**	31		

May 14 is the feast day of Pentecost.

Julian year 2019

				1	2	3	4	5	January
(11) Shebet		6	*7*	8	9	10	11	12	
		13	14	15	16	17	18	19	
		20	*21*	22	23	24	25	26	
		27	28	29	30	31	1	2	February
(12a) Adar I		3	4	5	*6*	7	8	9	
		10	11	12	13	14	15	16	
		17	18	19	*20*	21	22	23	
		24	25	26	27	28	1	2	March
(12b) Adar II		3	4	5	6	7	*8*	9	
		10	11	12	13	14	15	16	
		17	18	19	20	21	*22*	23	
		24	25	26	27	28	29	30	
(1) Nisan		31	1	2	3	4	5	*6*	April
		7	8	9	10	11	12	13	
		14	15	16	17	18	19	*20*	
		21	22	23	24	25	26	27	
		28	29	30	1	2	3	4	May
(2) Iyar		5	*6*	7	8	9	10	11	
		12	13	14	15	16	17	18	
		19	*20*	21	22	23	24	25	
		26	27	28	29	30	31	1	June
(3) Sivan		2	3	4	5	6	7	8	
		9	10	11	12	13	14	15	
		16	17	*18*	19	20	21	22	
		23	24	25	26	27	28	29	
(4) Tammuz		30	1	2	3	*4*	5	6	July
		7	8	9	10	11	12	13	
		14	15	16	17	*18*	19	20	
		21	22	23	24	25	26	27	
(5) Av		28	29	30	31	1	*2*	3	August
		4	5	6	7	8	9	10	
		11	12	13	14	15	*16*	17	
		18	19	20	21	22	23	24	
		25	26	27	28	29	30	31	

(6)Elul	1	2	3	4	5	6	7	September
	8	9	10	11	12	13	14	
	15	16	17	18	19	20	21	
	22	23	24	25	26	27	28	
(7) Tishri	29	30	1	2	3	4	5	October
	6	7	8	9	10	11	12	
	13	*14*	15	16	17	18	19	
	20	21	22	23	24	25	26	
(8) Heshvan	27	28	29	30	31	1	2	November
	3	4	5	6	7	8	9	
	10	11	12	*13*	14	15	16	
	17	18	19	20	21	22	23	
(9) Kislev	24	25	26	27	**28**	29	30	
	1	2	3	4	5	6	7	December
	8	9	10	11	*12*	13	14	
	15	16	17	18	19	20	21	
(11) Tebet	22	23	24	25	26	**27**	28	
	29	30	31					

Julian year 2020

					1	2	3	4	January
		5	6	7	8	9	*10*	11	
		12	13	14	15	16	17	18	
(11) Shebet		19	20	21	22	23	24	**25**	
		26	27	28	29	30	31	1	February
		2	3	4	5	6	7	*8*	
		9	10	11	12	13	14	15	
		16	17	18	19	20	21	22	
(12) Adar		23	**24**	25	26	27	28	29	
		1	2	3	4	5	6	7	March
		8	*9*	10	11	12	13	14	
		15	16	17	18	19	20	21	
(1) Nisan		22	23	**24**	25	26	27	28	
		29	30	31	1	2	3	4	April
		5	6	*7*	8	9	10	11	
		12	13	14	15	16	17	18	
(2) Iyar		19	20	21	22	**23**	24	25	
		26	27	28	29	30	1	2	May
		3	4	5	6	*7*	8	9	
		10	11	12	13	14	15	16	
(3) Sivan		17	18	19	20	21	**22**	23	
		24	25	26	27	28	29	30	
		31	1	2	3	4	*5*	6	June
		7	8	9	10	11	12	13	
		14	15	16	17	18	19	20	
(4) Tammuz		**21**	22	23	24	25	26	27	
		28	29	30	1	2	3	4	July
		5	6	7	8	9	10	11	
		12	13	14	15	16	17	18	
(5) Av		19	**20**	21	22	23	24	25	
		26	27	28	29	30	31	1	August
		2	*3*	4	5	6	7	8	
		9	10	11	12	13	14	15	

(6) Elul	16	17	18	**19**	20	21	22	
	23	24	25	26	27	28	29	
	30	31	1	*2*	3	4	5	September
	6	7	8	9	10	11	12	
(7) Tishri	13	14	15	16	**17**	18	19	
	20	21	22	23	24	25	26	
	27	28	29	30	*1*	2	3	October
	4	5	6	7	8	9	10	
(8) Heshvan	11	12	13	14	15	16	**17**	
	18	19	20	21	22	23	24	
	25	26	27	28	29	30	*31*	
	1	2	3	4	5	6	7	November
	8	9	10	11	12	13	14	
(9) Kislev	15	**16**	17	18	19	20	21	
	22	23	24	25	26	27	28	
	29	*30*	1	2	3	4	5	December
	6	7	8	9	10	11	12	
(10) Tebet	13	14	15	**16**	17	18	19	
	20	21	22	23	24	25	26	
	27	28	29	*30*	31			

Julian year 2021

						1	2	January
	3	4	5	6	7	8	9	
(11) Shebet	10	11	12	13	**14**	15	16	
	17	18	19	20	21	22	23	
	24	25	26	27	*28*	29	30	
	31	1	2	3	4	5	6	February
(12) Adar	7	8	9	10	11	12	**13**	
	14	15	16	17	18	19	20	
	21	22	23	24	25	26	*27*	
	28	1	2	3	4	5	6	March
	7	8	9	10	11	12	13	
(1) Nisan	**14**	15	16	17	18	19	20	
	21	22	23	24	25	26	27	
	28	29	30	31	1	2	3	April
	4	5	6	7	8	9	10	
(2) Iyar	11	12	**13**	14	15	16	17	
	18	19	20	21	22	23	24	
	25	26	*27*	28	29	30	1	May
	2	3	4	5	6	7	8	
(3) Sivan	9	10	11	**12**	13	14	15	
	16	17	18	19	20	21	22	
	23	24	25	*26*	27	28	29	
	30	31	1	2	3	4	5	June
(4) Tammuz	6	7	8	9	10	**11**	12	
	13	14	15	16	17	18	19	
	20	21	22	23	24	*25*	26	
	27	28	29	30	1	2	3	July
(5) Av	4	5	6	7	8	9	**10**	
	11	12	13	14	15	16	17	
	18	19	20	21	22	23	*24*	
	25	26	27	28	29	30	31	
	1	2	3	4	5	6	7	August
(6) Elul	8	**9**	10	11	12	13	14	
	15	16	17	18	19	20	21	
	22	*23*	24	25	26	27	28	
	29	30	31	1	2	3	4	September

(7) Tishri	5	6	*7*	8	9	10	11	
	12	13	14	15	16	17	18	
	19	20	*21*	22	23	24	25	
	26	27	28	29	30	1	2	October
(8) Heshvan	3	4	5	6	*7*	8	9	
	10	11	12	13	14	15	16	
	17	18	19	20	*21*	22	23	
	24	25	26	27	28	29	30	
(9) Kislev	31	1	2	3	4	*5*	6	November
	7	8	9	10	11	12	13	
	14	15	16	17	18	*19*	20	
	21	22	23	24	25	26	27	
	28	29	30	1	2	3	4	December
(10) Tebet	*5*	6	7	8	9	10	11	
	12	13	14	15	16	17	18	
	19	20	21	22	23	24	25	
	26	27	28	29	30	31		

Julian year 2022

							1	January
(11) Shebet	2	**3**	4	5	6	7	8	
	9	10	11	12	13	14	15	
	16	*17*	18	19	20	21	22	
	23	24	25	26	27	28	29	
(12a) Adar I	30	31	1	**2**	3	4	5	February
	6	7	8	9	10	11	12	
	13	14	15	*16*	17	18	19	
	20	21	22	23	24	25	26	
(12b) Adar II	27	28	1	2	3	**4**	5	March
	6	7	8	9	10	11	12	
	13	14	15	16	17	*18*	19	
	20	21	22	23	24	25	26	
(1) Nisan	27	28	29	30	31	1	**2**	April
	3	4	5	6	7	8	9	
	10	11	12	13	14	15	*16*	
	17	18	19	20	21	22	23	
	24	25	26	27	28	29	30	
(2) Iyar	1	**2**	3	4	5	6	7	May
	8	9	10	11	12	13	14	
	15	*16*	17	18	19	20	21	
	22	23	24	25	26	27	28	
(3) Sivan	29	30	**31**	1	2	3	4	June
	5	6	7	8	9	10	11	
	12	13	*14*	15	16	17	18	
	19	20	21	22	23	24	25	
(4) Tammuz	26	27	28	29	**30**	1	2	July
	3	4	5	6	7	8	9	
	10	11	12	13	*14*	15	16	
	17	18	19	20	21	22	23	
(5) Av	24	25	26	27	28	**29**	30	
	31	1	2	3	4	5	6	August
	7	8	9	10	11	*12*	13	
	14	15	16	17	18	19	20	
	21	22	23	24	25	26	27	

(6) Elul	**28**	29	30	31	1	2	3	September
	4	5	6	7	8	9	10	
	11	12	13	14	15	16	17	
	18	19	20	21	22	23	24	
(7) Tishri	25	**26**	27	28	29	30	1	October
	2	3	4	5	6	7	8	
	9	*10*	11	12	13	14	15	
	16	17	18	19	20	21	22	
(8) Heshvan	23	24	25	**26**	27	28	29	
	30	31	1	2	3	4	5	November
	6	7	8	*9*	10	11	12	
	13	14	15	16	17	18	19	
(9) Kislev	20	21	22	23	24	**25**	26	
	27	28	29	30	1	2	3	December
	4	5	6	7	8	*9*	10	
	11	12	13	14	15	16	17	
	18	19	20	21	22	23	24	
(10) Tebet	**25**	26	27	28	29	30	31	

Julian year 2023

		1	2	3	4	5	6	7	January
		8	9	10	11	12	13	14	
		15	16	17	18	19	20	21	
(11) Shebet		22	**23**	24	25	26	27	28	
		29	30	31	1	2	3	4	February
		5	*6*	7	8	9	10	11	
		12	13	14	15	16	17	18	
(12) Adar		19	20	21	**22**	23	24	25	
		26	27	28	1	2	3	4	March
		5	6	7	*8*	9	10	11	
		12	13	14	15	16	17	18	
(1) Nisan		19	20	21	22	**23**	24	25	
		26	27	28	29	30	31	1	April
		2	3	4	5	*6*	7	8	
		9	10	11	12	13	14	15	
(2) Iyar		16	17	18	19	20	21	**22**	
		23	24	25	26	27	28	29	
		30	1	2	3	4	5	*6*	May
		7	8	9	10	11	12	13	
		14	15	16	17	18	19	20	
(3) Sivan		**21**	22	23	24	25	26	27	
		28	29	30	31	1	2	3	June
		4	5	6	7	8	9	10	
		11	12	13	14	15	16	17	
(4) Tammuz		18	19	**20**	21	22	23	24	
		25	26	27	28	29	30	1	July
		2	3	*4*	5	6	7	8	
		9	10	11	12	13	14	15	
(5) Av		16	17	18	**19**	20	21	22	
		23	24	25	26	27	28	29	
		30	31	1	*2*	3	4	5	August
		6	7	8	9	10	11	12	
(6) Elul		13	14	15	16	17	**18**	19	
		20	21	22	23	24	25	26	
		27	28	29	30	31	*1*	2	September
		3	4	5	6	7	8	9	

(7) Tishri	10	11	12	13	14	15	**16**	
	17	18	19	20	21	22	23	
	24	25	26	27	28	29	*30*	
	1	2	3	4	5	6	7	October
	8	9	10	11	12	13	14	
(8) Heshvan	15	**16**	17	18	19	20	21	
	22	23	24	25	26	27	28	
	29	*30*	31	1	2	3	4	November
	5	6	7	8	9	10	11	
(9) Kislev	12	13	**14**	15	16	17	18	
	19	20	21	22	23	24	25	
	26	27	*28*	29	30	1	2	December
	3	4	5	6	7	8	9	
(10) Tebet	10	11	12	**13**	14	15	16	
	17	18	19	20	21	22	23	
	24	25	26	*27*	28	29	30	
	31							

Julian year 2024

		1	2	3	4	5	6	January
(11) Shebet	7	8	9	10	**11**	12	13	
	14	15	16	17	18	19	20	
	21	22	23	24	*25*	26	27	
	28	29	30	31	1	2	3	February
(12) Adar	4	5	6	7	8	9	**10**	
	11	12	13	14	15	16	17	
	18	19	20	21	22	23	*24*	
	25	26	27	28	29	1	2	March
	3	4	5	6	7	8	9	
(1) Nisan	**10**	11	12	13	14	15	16	
	17	18	19	20	21	22	23	
	24	25	26	27	28	29	30	
	31	1	2	3	4	5	6	April
(2) Iyar	7	8	**9**	10	11	12	13	
	14	15	16	17	18	19	20	
	21	22	*23*	24	25	26	27	
	28	29	30	1	2	3	4	May
(3) Sivan	5	6	7	**8**	9	10	11	
	12	13	14	15	16	17	18	
	19	20	21	*22*	23	24	25	
	26	27	28	29	30	31	1	June
(4) Tammuz	2	3	4	5	6	**7**	8	
	9	10	11	12	13	14	15	
	16	17	18	19	20	*21*	22	
	23	24	25	26	27	28	29	
(5) Av	30	1	2	3	4	5	**6**	July
	7	8	9	10	11	12	13	
	14	15	16	17	18	19	*20*	
	21	22	23	24	25	26	27	
	28	29	30	31	1	2	3	August
(6) Elul	4	**5**	6	7	8	9	10	
	11	12	13	14	15	16	17	
	18	*19*	20	21	22	23	24	
	25	26	27	28	29	30	31	

(7) Tishri	1	2	3	4	5	6	7	September
	8	9	10	11	12	13	14	
	15	16	*17*	18	19	20	21	
	22	23	24	25	26	27	28	
(8) Heshvan	29	30	1	2	3	4	5	October
	6	7	8	9	10	11	12	
	13	14	15	16	*17*	18	19	
	20	21	22	23	24	25	26	
(9) Kislev	27	28	29	30	31	1	2	November
	3	4	5	6	7	8	9	
	10	11	12	13	14	*15*	16	
	17	18	19	20	21	22	23	
	24	25	26	27	28	29	30	
(10) Tebet	**1**	2	3	4	5	6	7	December
	8	9	10	11	12	13	14	
	15	16	17	18	19	20	21	
	22	23	24	25	26	27	28	
(11) Shebet	29	**30**	31					

Julian year 2025

				1	2	3	4	January
	5	6	7	8	9	10	11	
	12	*13*	14	15	16	17	18	
	19	20	21	22	23	24	25	
(12a) Adar I	26	27	28	*29*	30	31	1	February
	2	3	4	5	6	7	8	
	9	10	11	*12*	13	14	15	
	16	17	18	19	20	21	22	
(12b) Adar II	23	24	25	26	27	*28*	1	March
	2	3	4	5	6	7	8	
	9	10	11	12	13	*14*	15	
	16	17	18	19	20	21	22	
(1) Nisan	23	24	25	26	27	28	*29*	
	30	31	1	2	3	4	5	April
	6	7	8	9	10	11	*12*	
	13	14	15	16	17	18	19	
	20	21	22	23	24	25	26	
(2) Iyar	27	*28*	29	30	1	2	3	May
	4	5	6	7	8	9	10	
	11	*12*	13	14	15	16	17	
	18	19	20	21	22	23	24	
(3) Sivan	25	26	*27*	28	29	30	31	
	1	2	3	4	5	6	7	June
	8	9	*10*	11	12	13	14	
	15	16	17	18	19	20	21	
(4) Tammuz	22	23	24	25	*26*	27	28	
	29	30	1	2	3	4	5	July
	6	7	8	9	*10*	11	12	
	13	14	15	16	17	18	19	
(5) Av	20	21	22	23	24	*25*	26	
	27	28	29	30	31	1	2	August
	3	4	5	6	7	*8*	9	
	10	11	12	13	14	15	16	
	17	18	19	20	21	22	23	

(6) Elul	**24**	25	26	27	28	29	30	
	31	1	2	3	4	5	6	September
	7	8	9	10	11	12	13	
	14	15	16	17	18	19	20	
(7) Tishri	21	**22**	23	24	25	26	27	
	28	29	30	1	2	3	4	October
	5	*6*	7	8	9	10	11	
	12	13	14	15	16	17	18	
(8) Heshvan	19	20	21	**22**	23	24	25	
	26	27	28	29	30	31	1	November
	2	3	4	*5*	6	7	8	
	9	10	11	12	13	14	15	
(9) Kislev	16	17	18	19	20	**21**	22	
	23	24	25	26	27	28	29	
	30	1	2	3	4	*5*	6	December
	7	8	9	10	11	12	13	
	14	15	16	17	18	19	20	
(10) Tebet	**21**	22	23	24	25	26	27	
	28	29	30	31				

Julian year 2026

						1	2	3	January
		4	5	6	7	8	9	10	
		11	12	13	14	15	16	17	
(11) Shebet		18	**19**	20	21	22	23	24	
		25	26	27	28	29	30	31	
		1	*2*	3	4	5	6	7	February
		8	9	10	11	12	13	14	
(12) Adar		15	16	17	**18**	19	20	21	
		22	23	24	25	26	27	28	
		1	2	3	*4*	5	6	7	March
		8	9	10	11	12	13	14	
(1) Nisan		15	16	17	18	**19**	20	21	
		22	23	24	25	26	27	28	
		29	30	31	1	*2*	3	4	April
		5	6	7	8	9	10	11	
(2) Iyar		12	13	14	15	16	17	**18**	
		19	20	21	22	23	24	25	
		26	27	28	29	30	1	*2*	May
		3	4	5	6	7	8	9	
		10	11	12	13	14	15	16	
(3) Sivan		**17**	18	19	20	21	22	23	
		24	25	26	27	28	29	30	
		31	1	2	3	4	5	6	June
		7	8	9	10	11	12	13	
(4) Tammuz		14	15	**16**	17	18	19	20	
		21	22	23	24	25	26	27	
		28	29	*30*	1	2	3	4	July
		5	6	7	8	9	10	11	
(5) Av		12	13	14	**15**	16	17	18	
		19	20	21	22	23	24	25	
		26	27	28	*29*	30	31	1	August
		2	3	4	5	6	7	8	
(6) Elul		9	10	11	12	13	**14**	15	
		16	17	18	19	20	21	22	
		23	24	25	26	27	*28*	29	
		30	31	1	2	3	4	5	September

(7) Tishri	6	7	8	9	10	11	**12**	
	13	14	15	16	17	18	19	
	20	21	22	23	24	25	**26**	
	27	28	29	30	1	2	3	October
	4	5	6	7	8	9	10	
(8) Heshvan	11	**12**	13	14	15	16	17	
	18	19	20	21	22	23	24	
	25	**26**	27	28	29	30	31	
	1	2	3	4	5	6	7	November
(9) Kislev	8	9	10	**11**	12	13	14	
	15	16	17	18	19	20	21	
	22	23	24	**25**	26	27	28	
	29	30	1	2	3	4	5	December
(10) Tebet	6	7	8	9	10	**11**	12	
	13	14	15	16	17	18	19	
	20	21	22	23	24	**25**	26	
	27	28	29	30	31			

Julian year 2027

						1	2	January
(11) Shebet	3	4	5	6	7	8	**9**	
	10	11	12	13	14	15	16	
	17	18	19	20	21	22	**23**	
	24	25	26	27	28	29	30	
	31	1	2	3	4	5	6	February
(12) Adar	7	**8**	9	10	11	12	13	
	14	15	16	17	18	19	20	
	21	**22**	23	24	25	26	27	
	28	1	2	3	4	5	6	March
(1) Nisan	7	8	**9**	10	11	12	13	
	14	15	16	17	18	19	20	
	21	22	**23**	24	25	26	27	
	28	29	30	31	1	2	3	April
(2) Iyar	4	5	6	7	**8**	9	10	
	11	12	13	14	15	16	17	
	18	19	20	21	**22**	23	24	
	25	26	27	28	29	30	1	May
(3) Sivan	2	3	4	5	6	**7**	8	
	9	10	11	12	13	14	15	
	16	17	18	19	20	**21**	22	
	23	24	25	26	27	28	29	
	30	31	1	2	3	4	5	June
(4) Tammuz	**6**	7	8	9	10	11	12	
	13	14	15	16	17	18	19	
	20	21	22	23	24	25	26	
	27	28	29	30	1	2	3	July
(5) Av	4	**5**	6	7	8	9	10	
	11	12	13	14	15	16	17	
	18	**19**	20	21	22	23	24	
	25	26	27	28	29	30	31	
(6) Elul	1	2	3	4	5	6	7	August
	8	9	10	11	12	13	14	
	15	16	17	**18**	19	20	21	
	22	23	24	25	26	27	28	

(7) Tishri	29	30	31	1	2	3	4	September
	5	6	7	8	9	10	11	
	12	13	14	15	*16*	17	18	
	19	20	21	22	23	24	25	
(8) Heshvan	26	27	28	29	30	1	2	October
	3	4	5	6	7	8	9	
	10	11	12	13	14	15	*16*	
	17	18	19	20	21	22	23	
	24	25	26	27	28	29	30	
(9) Kislev	**31**	1	2	3	4	5	6	November
	7	8	9	10	11	12	13	
	14	15	16	17	18	19	20	
	21	22	23	24	25	26	27	
(10) Tebet	28	**29**	30	1	2	3	4	December
	5	6	7	8	9	10	11	
	12	*13*	14	15	16	17	18	
	19	20	21	22	23	24	25	
(11) Shebet	26	27	**28**	29	30	31		

Julian year 2028

							1	January
	2	3	4	5	6	7	8	
	9	10	*11*	12	13	14	15	
	16	17	18	19	20	21	22	
(12a) Adar I	23	24	25	26	**27**	28	29	
	30	31	1	2	3	4	5	February
	6	7	8	9	*10*	11	12	
	13	14	15	16	17	18	19	
(12b) Adar II	20	21	22	23	24	25	**26**	
	27	28	29	1	2	3	4	March
	5	6	7	8	9	10	*11*	
	12	13	14	15	16	17	18	
	19	20	21	22	23	24	25	
(1) Nisan	**26**	27	28	29	30	31	1	April
	2	3	4	5	6	7	8	
	9	10	11	12	13	14	15	
	16	17	18	19	20	21	22	
(2) Iyar	23	24	**25**	26	27	28	29	
	30	1	2	3	4	5	6	May
	7	8	*9*	10	11	12	13	
	14	15	16	17	18	19	20	
(3) Sivan	21	22	23	**24**	25	26	27	
	28	29	30	31	1	2	3	June
	4	5	6	*7*	8	9	10	
	11	12	13	14	15	16	17	
(4) Tammuz	18	19	20	21	22	**23**	24	
	25	26	27	28	29	30	1	July
	2	3	4	5	6	*7*	8	
	9	10	11	12	13	14	15	
(5) Av	16	17	18	19	20	21	**22**	
	23	24	25	26	27	28	29	
	30	31	1	2	3	4	5	August
	6	7	8	9	10	11	12	
	13	14	15	16	17	18	19	

(6) Elul	20	**21**	22	23	24	25	26	
	27	28	29	30	31	1	2	September
	3	*4*	5	6	7	8	9	
	10	11	12	13	14	15	16	
(7) Tishri	17	18	**19**	20	21	22	23	
	24	25	26	27	28	29	30	
	1	2	*3*	4	5	6	7	October
	8	9	10	11	12	13	14	
(8) Heshvan	15	16	17	18	**19**	20	21	
	22	23	24	25	26	27	28	
	29	30	31	1	*2*	3	4	November
	5	6	7	8	9	10	11	
(9) Kislev	12	13	14	15	16	**17**	18	
	19	20	21	22	23	24	25	
	26	27	28	29	30	*1*	2	December
	3	4	5	6	7	8	9	
	10	11	12	13	14	15	16	
(10) Tebet	**17**	18	19	20	21	22	23	
	24	25	26	27	28	29	30	
	31							

Julian year 2029

		1	2	3	4	5	6	January
	7	8	9	10	11	12	13	
(11) Shebet	14	**15**	16	17	18	19	20	
	21	22	23	24	25	26	27	
	28	*29*	30	31	1	2	3	February
	4	5	6	7	8	9	10	
(12) Adar	11	12	13	**14**	15	16	17	
	18	19	20	21	22	23	24	
	25	26	27	**28**	1	2	3	March
	4	5	6	7	8	9	10	
(1) Nisan	11	12	13	14	**15**	16	17	
	18	19	20	21	22	23	24	
	25	26	27	28	*29*	30	31	
	1	2	3	4	5	6	7	April
(2) Iyar	8	9	10	11	12	13	**14**	
	15	16	17	18	19	20	21	
	22	23	24	25	26	27	**28**	
	29	30	1	2	3	4	5	May
	6	7	8	9	10	11	12	
(3) Sivan	**13**	14	15	16	17	18	19	
	20	21	22	23	24	25	26	
	27	28	29	30	31	1	2	June
	3	4	5	6	7	8	9	
(4) Tammuz	10	11	**12**	13	14	15	16	
	17	18	19	20	21	22	23	
	24	25	**26**	27	28	29	30	
	1	2	3	4	5	6	7	July
(5) Av	8	9	10	**11**	12	13	14	
	15	16	17	18	19	20	21	
	22	23	24	**25**	26	27	28	
	29	30	31	1	2	3	4	August
(6) Elul	5	6	7	8	9	**10**	11	
	12	13	14	15	16	17	18	
	19	20	21	22	23	**24**	25	
	26	27	28	29	30	31	1	September
(7) Tishri	2	3	4	5	6	7	**8**	

		9	10	11	12	13	14	15	
		16	17	18	19	20	21	*22*	
		23	24	25	26	27	28	29	
		30	1	2	3	4	5	6	October
	(8) Heshvan	7	**8**	9	10	11	12	13	
		14	15	16	17	18	19	20	
		21	*22*	23	24	25	26	27	
		28	29	30	31	1	2	3	November
	(9) Kislev	4	5	6	**7**	8	9	10	
		11	12	13	14	15	16	17	
		18	19	20	*21*	22	23	24	
		25	26	27	28	29	30	1	December
	(10) Tebet	2	3	4	5	6	**7**	8	
		9	10	11	12	13	14	15	
		16	17	18	19	20	*21*	22	
		23	24	25	26	27	28	29	
		30	31						

Julian year 2030

(11) Shebet			1	2	3	4	**5**	January
	6	7	8	9	10	11	12	
	13	14	15	16	17	18	**19**	
	20	21	22	23	24	25	26	
	27	28	29	30	31	1	2	February
(12a) Adar I	3	**4**	5	6	7	8	9	
	10	11	12	13	14	15	16	
	17	**18**	19	20	21	22	23	
	24	25	26	27	28	1	2	March
(12b) Adar II	3	4	5	**6**	7	8	9	
	10	11	12	13	14	15	16	
	17	18	19	**20**	21	22	23	
	24	25	26	27	28	29	30	
(1) Nisan	31	1	2	3	**4**	5	6	April
	7	8	9	10	11	12	13	
	14	15	16	17	**18**	19	20	
	21	22	23	24	25	26	27	
(2) Iyar	28	29	30	1	2	3	**4**	May
	5	6	7	8	9	10	11	
	12	13	14	15	16	17	**18**	
	19	20	21	22	23	24	25	
	26	27	28	29	30	31	1	June
(3) Sivan	**2**	3	4	5	6	7	8	
	9	10	11	12	13	14	15	
	16	17	18	19	20	21	22	
	23	24	25	26	27	28	29	
(4) Tammuz	30	1	**2**	3	4	5	6	July
	7	8	9	10	11	12	13	
	14	15	**16**	17	18	19	20	
	21	22	23	24	25	26	27	
(5) Av	28	29	30	**31**	1	2	3	August
	4	5	6	7	8	9	10	
	11	12	13	**14**	15	16	17	
	18	19	20	21	22	23	24	
(6) Elul	25	26	27	28	29	**30**	31	
	1	2	3	4	5	6	7	September

		8	9	10	11	12	_13_	14	
		15	16	17	18	19	20	21	
(7) Tishri		22	23	24	25	26	27	**28**	
		29	30	1	2	3	4	5	October
		6	7	8	9	10	11	_12_	
		13	14	15	16	17	18	19	
		20	21	22	23	24	25	26	
(8) Heshvan		27	**28**	29	30	31	1	2	November
		3	4	5	6	7	8	9	
		10	_11_	12	13	14	15	16	
		17	18	19	20	21	22	23	
(9) Kislev		24	25	26	**27**	28	29	30	
		1	2	3	4	5	6	7	December
		8	9	10	_11_	12	13	14	
		15	16	17	18	19	20	21	
(10) Tebet		22	23	24	25	26	**27**	28	
		29	30	31					

Julian year 2031

					1	2	3	4	January
		5	6	7	8	9	*10*	11	
		12	13	14	15	16	17	18	
(11) Shebet		19	20	21	22	23	24	**25**	
		26	27	28	29	30	31	1	February
		2	3	4	5	6	7	*8*	
		9	10	11	12	13	14	15	
		16	17	18	19	20	21	22	
(12) Adar		23	**24**	25	26	27	28	1	March
		2	3	4	5	6	7	8	
		9	*10*	11	12	13	14	15	
		16	17	18	19	20	21	22	
(1) Nisan		23	24	**25**	26	27	28	29	
		30	31	1	2	3	4	5	April
		6	7	*8*	9	10	11	12	
		13	14	15	16	17	18	19	
(2) Iyar		20	21	22	23	**24**	25	26	
		27	28	29	30	1	2	3	May
		4	5	6	7	*8*	9	10	
		11	12	13	14	15	16	17	
(3) Sivan		18	19	20	21	22	**23**	24	
		25	26	27	28	29	30	31	
		1	2	3	4	5	*6*	7	June
		8	9	10	11	12	13	14	
		15	16	17	18	19	20	21	
(4) Tammuz		**22**	23	24	25	26	27	28	
		29	30	1	2	3	4	5	July
		6	7	8	9	10	11	12	
		13	14	15	16	17	18	19	
(5) Av		20	**21**	22	23	24	25	26	
		27	28	29	30	31	1	2	August
		3	*4*	5	6	7	8	9	
		10	11	12	13	14	15	16	
(6) Elul		17	18	19	**20**	21	22	23	
		24	25	26	27	28	29	30	
		31	1	2	*3*	4	5	6	September

	7	8	9	10	11	12	13	
(7) Tishri	14	15	16	17	**18**	19	20	
	21	22	23	24	25	26	27	
	28	29	30	1	*2*	3	4	October
	5	6	7	8	9	10	11	
(8) Heshvan	12	13	14	15	16	17	**18**	
	19	20	21	22	23	24	25	
	26	27	28	29	30	31	*1*	November
	2	3	4	5	6	7	8	
	9	10	11	12	13	14	15	
(9) Kislev	**16**	17	18	19	20	21	22	
	23	24	25	26	27	28	29	
	30	1	2	3	4	5	6	December
	7	8	9	10	11	12	13	
(10) Tebet	14	**15**	16	17	18	19	20	
	21	22	23	24	25	26	27	
	28	*29*	30	31				

Julian year 3030

						1	2	January
	3	4	5	6	7	8	9	
	10	11	*12*	13	14	15	16	
	17	18	19	20	21	22	23	
(11) Shebet	24	25	26	**27**	28	29	30	
	31	1	2	3	4	5	6	February
	7	8	9	*10*	11	12	13	
	14	15	16	17	18	19	20	
(12) Adar	21	22	23	24	25	**26**	27	
	28	1	2	3	4	5	6	March
	7	8	9	10	11	*12*	13	
	14	15	16	17	18	19	20	
(1) Nisan	21	22	23	24	25	26	**27**	
	28	29	30	31	1	2	3	April
	4	5	6	7	8	9	*10*	
	11	12	13	14	15	16	17	
	18	19	20	21	22	23	24	
(2) Iyar	25	**26**	27	28	29	30	1	May
	2	3	4	5	6	7	8	
	9	*10*	11	12	13	14	15	
	16	17	18	19	20	21	22	
(3) Sivan	23	24	**25**	26	27	28	29	
	30	31	1	2	3	4	5	June
	6	7	*8*	9	10	11	12	
	13	14	15	16	17	18	19	
(4) Tammuz	20	21	22	23	**24**	25	26	
	27	28	29	30	1	2	3	July
	4	5	6	7	*8*	9	10	
	11	12	13	14	15	16	17	
(5) Av	18	19	20	21	22	**23**	24	
	25	26	27	28	29	30	31	
	1	2	3	4	5	**6**	7	August
	8	9	10	11	12	13	14	
	15	16	17	18	19	20	21	
(6) Elul	**22**	23	24	25	26	27	28	
	29	30	31	1	2	3	4	September

		5	6	7	8	9	10	11	
		12	13	14	15	16	17	18	
(7) Tishri		19	20	21	22	23	24	25	
		26	27	28	29	30	1	2	October
		3	4	5	6	7	8	9	
		10	11	12	13	14	15	16	
(8) Heshvan		17	18	19	20	21	22	23	
		24	25	26	27	28	29	30	
		31	1	2	3	4	5	6	November
		7	8	9	10	11	12	13	
(9) Kislev		14	15	16	17	18	19	20	
		21	22	23	24	25	26	27	
		28	29	30	1	2	3	4	December
		5	6	7	8	9	10	11	
(10) Tebet		12	13	14	15	16	17	18	
		19	20	21	22	23	24	25	
		26	27	28	29	30	31		

Julian year 3031

							1	January
	2	3	4	5	6	7	8	
	9	10	11	12	13	14	15	
(11) Shebet	16	**17**	18	19	20	21	22	
	23	24	25	26	27	28	29	
	30	*31*	1	2	3	4	5	February
	6	7	8	9	10	11	12	
(12) Adar	13	14	15	**16**	17	18	19	
	20	21	22	23	24	25	26	
	27	28	1	*2*	3	4	5	March
	6	7	8	9	10	11	12	
(1) Nisan	13	14	15	16	**17**	18	19	
	20	21	22	23	24	25	26	
	27	28	29	30	*31*	1	2	April
	3	4	5	6	7	8	9	
(2) Iyar	10	11	12	13	14	15	**16**	
	17	18	19	20	21	22	23	
	24	25	26	27	28	29	*30*	
	1	2	3	4	5	6	7	May
	8	9	10	11	12	13	14	
(3) Sivan	**15**	16	17	18	19	20	21	
	22	23	24	25	26	27	28	
	29	30	31	1	2	3	4	June
	5	6	7	8	9	10	11	
(4) Tammuz	12	13	**14**	15	16	17	18	
	19	20	21	22	23	24	25	
	26	27	*28*	29	30	1	2	July
	3	4	5	6	7	8	9	
(5) Av	10	11	12	**13**	14	15	16	
	17	18	19	20	21	22	23	
	24	25	26	*27*	28	29	30	
	31	1	2	3	4	5	6	August
(6) Elul	7	8	9	10	11	**12**	13	
	14	15	16	17	18	19	20	
	21	22	23	24	25	*26*	27	
	28	29	30	31	1	2	3	September

(7) Tishri	4	5	6	7	8	9	**10**	
	11	12	13	14	15	16	17	
	18	19	20	21	22	23	*24*	
	25	26	27	28	29	30	1	October
	2	3	4	5	6	7	8	
(8) Heshvan	9	**10**	11	12	13	14	15	
	16	17	18	19	20	21	22	
	23	*24*	25	26	27	28	29	
	30	31	1	2	3	4	5	November
(9) Kislev	6	7	**8**	9	10	11	12	
	13	14	15	16	17	18	19	
	20	21	*22*	23	24	25	26	
	27	28	29	30	1	2	3	December
(10) Tebet	4	5	6	7	**8**	9	10	
	11	12	13	14	15	16	17	
	18	19	20	21	*22*	23	24	
	25	26	27	28	29	30	31	

INDEX OF SCRIPTURES

Symbols

1 Esdras 1:
  45 147
1 John 2:
  22-2 150
1 John 5:
  19 120
1 Kings 6:
  1 67, 78, 93
  37 93
  38 93
1 Kings 8:
  1-2 93
1 Kings 14:
  20 89, 91
  21 89, 91
1 Kings 15:
  1 89, 91
  9 89, 91
  25 89, 91
  33 89, 91
1 Kings 16:
  8 89, 91
  23 89, 91
  29 89, 91
1 Kings 20:
  1-34 99
1 Kings 22 99
1 Kings 22:
  41-42 89, 91
  51 89, 91
1 Maccabees 16:
  14 118

2 Chronicles 3:
  2 67, 78, 93
2 Chronicles 5:
  26 178
2 Chronicles 28:
  19-20 97
  24-25 146
2 Chronicles 29:
  3 90, 93
2 Chronicles 32:
  1 95
  2-8 96
  26 96
  31 96, 97
2 Chronicles 35:
  20-24 179
2 Chronicles 36:
  1-4 180
  6 148
  6-9 146
2 Kings 1:
  17 89, 92
2 Kings 3:
  1 89, 92
2 Kings 6:
  8-23 99
2 Kings 8:
  16 89, 92
  25 89, 92
2 Kings 9:
  29 89, 92
2 Kings 9-10 89, 92
2 Kings 11:
  1-4 89, 92

2 Kings 12:
   1 89, 92
2 Kings 13:
   1 89, 92
   10 89, 92
2 Kings 14:
   1-2 89, 92
   23 90, 92
2 Kings 15:
   1 89, 90, 92
   8 90, 92
   17 90, 92
   19,29 178
   23 90, 92
   27 90, 92
   30 90, 92
   32-33 90, 92
2 Kings 16:
   1 90, 92, 183
   3 183
   9 214
   19 96
2 Kings 17:
   1 90, 92
   1-2 214
   3 214
   6 90, 93, 183
   24 183
   25 183
   25-26 183
   27 183
   28 183
   33,41 184
   34 184
2 Kings 18:
   1 97
   1-2 90, 93
   2 97
   9-10 100
   10 90, 93
   13 94, 95

   14 97
   14-16 98
2 Kings 19:
   9 96
   36-37 97
2 Kings 20:
   1 97
   6 97
2 Kings 21:
   1 90, 93
   19 90, 93
2 Kings 22:
   1 90, 93
2 Kings 23:
   29 179
   31 180
   36 90, 93
2 Kings 24:
   14 126, 146, 148
   18 90, 93
2 Kings 25:
   1 85
   8 90, 93
   11 126

A

Acts 1:
   3 108
Acts 7:
   4 74
Amos 1:
   1 101
Amos 8:
   1-3 101, 102
   2 101
   8 101
   9-10 101

D

Daniel 1:
   1,3,6 180

1-4 126, 179
5,18 181
Daniel 2:
  1 181
  24-45 181
Daniel 4:
  10-17 xxiii, 153
  12-13 155
  28-33 159
  28-36 154
  29-31 156
Daniel 5:
  31 177
Daniel 7:
  1-14 266
  11 268
  13-14 155, 203, 212
  23 142
  23-28 265
  25 268
Daniel 8 142
Daniel 8:
  9 142
  13-14 xxiii, 141, 144
  23 142
Daniel 9:
  1 177, 179
  24 139
  24-25 130
  24-27 xxii, 259
  25 68, 136
  26 68, 139
  26-27 69, 205, 231, 243
  27 68, 136, 138, 140, 148, 274
Daniel 11:
  1 177
  31 148, 149
Daniel 12 128
Daniel 12:
  4 258
  5-7 xxv, 162, 271

  7 127, 164
  9-10 258
  9-11 145
  9-13 xxv
  11 149, 151, 152
  11-13 262
  12 151
Deuteronomy 16:
  16 166
Deuteronomy 18:
  17-22 244
  18 247
Deuteronomy 31:
  9 116
  9-13 116, 117
  10 115

E

Enoch 72:
  26 198
Enoch 73:
  4 6
  6-8 5
Exodus 3:
  15 77
Exodus 12:
  1-2 5, 114
  2 12
  3 104, 160
  40-41 67, 77
Exodus 13:
  8 115
  21 235
Exodus 14:
  19-20 235
Exodus 19:
  1 246
  3 246
  4 254
  7-8 246
Exodus 23:

20-23 235, 246
26 115
Exodus 24:
  16-18 247
Exodus 25:
  8 69, 246
Exodus 34:
  22 115
Exodus 40:
  1 69
  2-3 246
  17 246
Ezekiel 1:
  1 247
  5 254
  10 254
Ezekiel 4:
  1-3 79, 169
  1-6 168
  1-8 xxvii
  4-5 68, 79, 169
  5-6 127
  6 69, 80
Ezekiel 8:
  3 233
Ezekiel 21:
  25-27 155
Ezekiel 24:
  1 84
Ezekiel 29:
  17 157
  18 157
  19-20 157, 158
  21 157
Ezekiel 33:
  21 146, 148
Ezekiel 36:
  37-38 xxvi, 166
Ezekiel 37:
  10 188
  12-14 188

25-27 188
Ezekiel 38:
  8 187
Ezekiel 38-39 278
Ezekiel 39:
  17-20 278
  23-24 187, 271
  26 188
  28-29 187
Ezekiel 40:
  1 146, 160
Ezra 1:
  1 176
  1-4 131
Ezra 3:
  1 176
  2 235
  10-11 132
Ezra 4 132
Ezra 4:
  1-2,10 184
  6 132
  6-23 132
  11-12 132
  21 132
  23 133
  24 132
Ezra 6:
  15 132, 181
Ezra 7:
  6 133
  6-26 131
  7-9 85
  8 134
  9 135, 176, 181
  14 133
  18 133
Ezra 9:
  9 133

G

Genesis 1:
  1 196
  1-39 194
Genesis 2:
  1-3 196
Genesis 3:
  15 120, 207
Genesis 5:
  3 65
  6 65
  9 65
  12 65
  15 65
  18 65
  21 65
  25 65
  28 65
  32 74
Genesis 7:
  4 73
  6 75
  11 65, 72, 128
Genesis 8:
  3-4 128
  13 72, 75
  13-15 66
  22 8, 127
Genesis 9:
  24 75
Genesis 10:
  8-12 80
  21 75
Genesis 11:
  10 66, 75
  12 66
  16 66
  20 66
  22 66
  24 66
  26 74
  32 67, 74
Genesis 12:
  1-3 77
  1-4 67
  4 67, 74
  4-5 76
  10 67, 76
Genesis 13:
  16 207
Genesis 16:
  16 76
Genesis 17:
  17 74, 75
Genesis 18:
  11 76
Genesis 21:
  12 77
Genesis 23:
  1-2 76
Genesis 25:
  1-6 76
Genesis 26:
  3-4 77
Genesis 28:
  14–15 77
Genesis 37:
  6-9 269
Genesis 50:
  24 77

H

Hosea 10:
  15 209
Hosea 11:
  1 209

I

Isaiah 7:
  3-8 xxix
  4-8 182, 213
  14-16 213

16 214
17 185
Isaiah 8:
   3 214
   4 214
Isaiah 9:
   6 209, 210, 211, 212
Isaiah 41:
   21-24 xxxiv
Isaiah 43:
   10 207
Isaiah 49:
   2 208, 210
   3 208
   5 208
   6 208, 210
Isaiah 53:
   4-6 138
   8 138
   9 207
   10 138, 139
   11 139
   12 139
Isaiah 54:
   5-6 270

J

Jeremiah 1:
   3 83
Jeremiah 4:
   31 270
Jeremiah 11:
   16-17 155
Jeremiah 12:
   12 151
Jeremiah 22:
   18-19 148
Jeremiah 25:
   1 180
   11 176

Jeremiah 29:
   1-2 146
   10 xxix, 125, 176
Jeremiah 32:
   6-15 xxviii, 171
Jeremiah 36:
   30 148
Jeremiah 41:
   27 159
   30 159
Jeremiah 44:
   11-12 156
Jeremiah 52:
   1 84
   1-14 84
   4 84
   12 83
   12-14 84
   15-30 84
   28 146, 147
   29 83, 151
John 1:
   1 246
   14 245
   17 205
   18 209, 235, 246
   28 219
   28-51 219
   29 219
   29-34 104
   29-36 104
   35 160
   35-42 106
   43 219
John 2:
   1 219
   1-2 219
   1-11 104
   13 104
   19-21 105
   20 233, 234

John 3:
  19 220
John 4:
  31-38 109
  35 110
John 6:
  4-14 106
John 10:
  22-23 144
John 11:
  55 107
John 12:
  12 160
John 14:
  28 212
  30 120
John 15:
  27 108
John 17:
  20-21 108
John 19:
  14 220
  31 220, 221
  40 220
John 20:
  1 222
  1-2 224
  14-17 108
  19 108
John 21:
  21-23 243
Jonah 1:
  17 216
Jonah 2:
  1-10 216
Joshua 10:
  12-13 70
  13 70

L

Leviticus 12:
  1-4 250
Leviticus 23:
  4-44 10
  24-25 114
Leviticus 25:
  8-10 118
  20-22 116, 117
Luke 23:
  54 223

M

Malachi 4:
  5 237, 277
Matthew 1:
  21 235
  23 245
Matthew 2:
  1 247
  1-12 248
  2 249, 252
  9 249, 253
  13-14 270
  15 210
  16 270
Matthew 3:
  1 139
Matthew 4:
  1-2 105
Matthew 10:
  16-23 232
  16-23 xxxii
  23 243
Matthew 11:
  14 237
  27 235
Matthew 12:
  38-40 xiv, xxxi, 216, 217
  38-41 169

40 126, 220
Matthew 13:
   41 230, 231
Matthew 14:
   1-12 107
   13-21 107
Matthew 16:
   27 243
   28 243
Matthew 17:
   2 234
Matthew 18:
   21-22 15
Matthew 20:
   1-16 218
   18-19 217
Matthew 23:
   8 205
   9 212
   37-39 169
Matthew 24:
   1-2 169
   1-3 xxxii, 226
   3 257
   4-5 227, 229
   6-14 227
   15-16 149, 272
   15-20 227
   21-22 228
   23-28 228
   26-31 233
   29 221
   29-31 229, 276
   32-34 229
   34 226, 230
   36 257
   40-41. 276
Matthew 26:
   29 278
   31 186
   32 108

Matthew 27:
   9-10 171, 174
   45 220, 221
   45-50 220
   57 217, 220
   62-66 221
   63 217
Matthew 28:
   1 223
   2 223
   2-3 225
   5 223
   9 108
   10 108, 210
   16 108
   18 210, 237
   19 260
   19-20 108
Micah 4:
   9-10 270

N

Nehemiah 1:
   1 85
   1-3 133
   3 133
Nehemiah 2 133
Nehemiah 2:
   1 85, 117
   1-6 131
   7-8 131
Nehemiah 6:
   15 117, 134
Nehemiah 8:
   18 117
Numbers 13:
   16 235
Numbers 14:
   34 127
Numbers 24:
   15-19 250

Numbers 28:
16-31 166
Numbers 29:
1-40 166

P

Proverb 15:
8 138
Psalm 2 204
Psalm 2:
9 210
Psalm 40:
6-8 138
Psalm 44:
1-3 154
Psalm 74:
17 8, 127
Psalm 80:
8-11 155
Psalm 81:
3 6
Psalm 90:
4 xxxi, 193, 194

R

Revelation 1:
4,8 212
9 237
10-11 242
Revelation 3:
3 257, 258
Revelation 9:
12 276
Revelation 10:
1-2 233
1-3 234
3 234
Revelation 11 237
Revelation 11:
2 233, 234, 241
2-3 128

3 236
5-6 237
6 277
17-18 277
Revelation 12 127
Revelation 12:
1 269
4 270
5 270
6 127, 164, 271
7-8 271
7-16 272
13-16 271
14 128
15 270
Revelation 13:
1 273
5 128, 273
6 150
11 273
13-14 273
16 273
17 273
18 273
Revelation 14:
1-4 264
Revelation 16:
15 277
Revelation 17:
8-11 275
12 142
12-14 275
16 275
18 275
Revelation 18:
20 275
Revelation 19:
11-21 278
15 210
Revelation 20:
6 69

Revelation 21:
  1 69
  3 69, 246
  7 279
  8 279
  9 236
  22 80, 169
Revelation 22:
  6-7 236
  9 210
  9-16 236
  14 279
  15 279

Z

Zechariah 8:
  19 111
Zechariah 11:
  12-13 174
  13 174
Zechariah 13:
  7-9 xxx, 186
Zechariah 14 278

www.ingramcontent.com/pod-product-compliance
Lightning Source LLC
Chambersburg PA
CBHW03202815042
43194CB00006B/191